SOCIAL STAR

General Interaction Skills
(Book 1)

Nancy Gajewski

Polly Hirn

Patty Mayo

Thinking Publications
Eau Claire, Wisconsin

09 08 07 06 05 04 10 9 8 7

Library of Congress Cataloging-in-Publication Data

Gajewski, Nancy.
General interaction skills / Nancy Gajewski, Polly Hirn, Patty Mayo.
p. cm. — (Social Star ; bk. 1)
ISBN 0-930599-79-9
1. Social skills—Study and teaching (Elementary) 2. Social interaction—Study and teaching (Elementary) I. Hirn, Polly. II. Mayo, Patty. III. Title. IV. Series: Gajewski, Nancy.
Social star ; bk. 1.
HQ783.G33 1993
372.83—dc20 92-39097
CIP

Illustrations by Kris Madsen

Printed in the United States of America

THINKING PUBLICATIONS®
A Division of McKinley Companies, Inc.

424 Galloway Street • Eau Claire, WI 54703
715-832-2488 • Fax 715-832-9082
Email: custserv@ThinkingPublications.com

COMMUNICATION SOLUTIONS THAT CHANGE LIVES®

DEDICATION

To Luke, Anna, Jenny, and Katie

NG

To Tom, Rebecca, and Matthew

PH

To Mike, Emily, and Jessica

PM

Table of Contents

Preface

We are excited to present *Social Star: General Interaction Skills (Book 1)*, an elementary curriculum for teaching social communication skills. We developed *Social Star* to fill a need for a comprehensive, experiential curriculum that teaches students appropriate social skills.

We believe that an effective social skills program must provide numerous structured opportunities for students to apply and practice newly acquired skills. Teaching social skills in a traditional teacher-directed format, where students are rarely given an opportunity to interact, would be like teaching students how to use a computer but never allowing them to actually use one. *Social Star* incorporates frequent opportunities for students to interact cooperatively.

We believe that an effective educator asks, "What are my students' social skill strengths and how can those strengths be used to expand their social skill repertoire?" rather than asking, "What are my students' social skill weaknesses and how can I fix them?" In addition, the effective educator encourages students to be unique, to express their feelings, and to make their own choices rather than attempting to stifle expression of feelings to force compliance.

The social skills in *Social Star* reflect the conventions of mainstream America, which have been traditionally accepted and expected in educational and employment settings. It is critical to remember that there are marked cultural differences in social skill conventions. The intent of *Social Star* is not to strip students of their cultural beliefs or to make them feel that their beliefs are bad. Rather, the intent is to provide students with the flexibility to move between their cultures and that of mainstream America.

In a world with ever-increasing violence, it is critical that our students learn how to communicate and solve problems with one another in a non-violent manner. *Social Star* is not just intended for those children with severe social skill deficits. All children can benefit and grow from direct instruction of social skills.

We hope you enjoy using *Social Star*. Remember, you may be planting seeds that will ultimately change your students' destinies!

Acknowledgments

The authors would like to express their appreciation to all those people who have helped in the completion of this curriculum. We thank Jan Burns, Bonnie Goertz, Ann Gorton, Paula Guhlke, Steve Heer, Paul Kennedy, Barbara Koeckley, Christine McFarlane, Lee Murphy, Fran Neilitz, Linda Parise, Patty Shirer, Candace Sobotta, Suzanne Steege, and Judy Wheeler for generously devoting their time in field-testing units from *Social Star*. A very special thank you to Dr. Lynda Miller and Pattii Waldo for their many hours in reviewing *Social Star* in its entirety. An additional thank you to Pattii Waldo, who shared many creative ideas which were included in *Social Star*. We are grateful to Nancy McKinley and Linda Schreiber for their technical and editorial advice, to Kris Madsen for her artistic contributions, and to the rest of the Thinking Publications staff for making it possible for this curriculum to be shared with you.

As always, we thank our husbands, Luke Gajewski, Tom Hirn, and Mike Mayo, for their encouragement, support, and patience.

Chapter 1

Getting Started

SOCIAL SKILL INSTRUCTION—A NECESSITY!

Every educator has experienced the frustration of seeing children isolated or teased by other students. "Mandy" sits by herself at recess. No one wants to work with "Jason." "Peter" makes irrelevant comments. "Ashley" asks a question every sixty seconds. These children are in all classrooms.

Research clearly indicates that children who are unaccepted by their peers will have learning and adjustment problems both in and out of school and later in life (Hartup, 1978; Putallaz and Gottman, 1981; Roff and Sells, 1978). Unpopular students often associate with other unpopular students or with younger children. This makes it difficult for them to gain the skills necessary to interact with more socially skilled children (Bullock, 1988). Children's reputations are often established early in elementary grades and become more and more stable each year (Meichenbaum, 1991).

Therefore, it is crucial that elementary educators address social skills. Time is of the essence for some students. Children who are rejected by their peers or who stand out negatively in some social skills, need to have the opportunity to learn acceptable social behavior. Social skills may well be the single most important subject educators teach their students! By teaching appropriate social skills, educators will have a positive impact on the lives of their students.

SOCIAL STAR: A NEW APPROACH

Instruction of social skills has increased rapidly over the past 10 years. While many strides have been made in the area of social skill instruction (e.g., awareness of the need for instruction, development of curriculum, program research), three major areas of concern remain.

One area of concern is that of teaching social competence as isolated skills when, in fact, any given situation requires that social skills be used in combination with each other. In addition to addressing individual social skills, *Social Star* provides numerous opportunities for students to use a combination of social skills in real-life situations through cooperative experiences.

A second concern (Neel, 1988) is over social skill instruction occurring in isolated environments, thus limiting opportunities for students to interact. *Social Star* is a unique program that provides many opportunities for students to use social skills while they are learning. As stated in the Preface, it is critical that students continually be given opportunities to interact in a positive manner with peers. *Social Star* offers numerous activities structured to encourage cooperative interaction among students. The *Social Star* program is an ideal match for a collaborative regular education program.

A third concern (Lovitt, 1987) is that social skills are taught during a specified time period and then tend to be forgotten during the remainder of the day. *Social Star* advocates teaching a social skills class but, in addition, the program provides numerous strategies to encourage incidental teaching and reinforcement of social skills throughout the school day.

SOCIAL STAR: CULTURAL CONSIDERATIONS

Marked differences in social behavior exist among cultures. *Social Star* teaches social skills that reflect the conventions of mainstream America, which have been traditionally accepted and expected in educational and employment settings. These social skills will not match the norms and expectations within some children's home settings. This awareness of diversity is critical to the success of the program, and educators are encouraged in each unit to invite adults from various cultures to speak with children about differences in cultural conventions.

Never should students be stripped of social skills appropriate for their cultures or be made to feel that their beliefs are bad or wrong. Rather, the intent of *Social Star* is to provide children with the flexibility to move between their cultures and that of mainstream America when they choose to do so.

SOCIAL STAR: GENERAL DESCRIPTION

The *Social Star* program is a series of books that emphasizes general interaction skills, peer interaction, problem solving/dealing with conflict, emotions, and classroom work habits. Each book includes basically the same beginning two chapters and appendices; however, the books contain different social skill units.

Social Star is a curriculum intended for use with elementary-age students (approximately grades 2–5). It is appropriate for students in regular education, special education, and at-risk programs. Professionals (e.g., regular educators, special educators, speech-language clinicians, counselors, psychologists, principals) involved with students will find this resource valuable for providing social skill instruction.

Each unit within *Social Star* includes a goal statement, educator information (information unique to the social skill being addressed), a series of lessons for teaching the social skill, a list of related activities, a list of related literature, and suggested ways to integrate social skill instruction throughout the school day. The length of each unit varies depending on the complexity of the specific social skill.

The units incorporate a wide variety of instructional techniques (e.g., guided practice pages, scripts, cooperative teamwork, games, role plays, puppet shows, cartoons, visualizations, drill and practice). Units do not have to be taught in their entirety. Strategies for adapting units when appropriate are given on page 37. Educators are urged to choose units appropriate for specific students' needs. Each unit contains lessons titled Lesson A, B, C, etc. and Lessons X, Y, and Z. Lessons X, Y, and Z follow basically the same format in every unit; therefore, a skeleton lesson for each is provided in *Appendix A*.

Each unit lesson provides an objective or objectives, a list of materials needed, a preparatory set, and a specific plan for completion of the lesson. Each unit incorporates six components. (See Figure 1.1.) These six components are described in detail in Chapter 2 and are referred to in the lesson plans within each unit.

Figure 1.1

UNIT COMPONENTS

- **Introduction/Instruction**
- **Modeling**
- **Rehearsal**
- **Feedback**
- **Cognitive Planning**
- **Transfer/Generalization**

TYPES OF SOCIAL SKILL DEFICITS

Elliott and Gresham (1991) have conceptualized social skill deficits along five dimensions as summarized in Table 1.1:

Table 1.1

Reasons for Social Skill Deficits
(Elliott and Gresham, 1991)

1. A lack of knowledge
2. A lack of practice or feedback
3. A lack of cues or opportunities
4. A lack of reinforcement
5. The presence of interfering problems

A lack of knowledge indicates that (1) a student has not learned the appropriate goals for social interaction (e.g., "Victor" may believe that the goal of playing a card game is merely to win rather than to get along and have fun with the other players); (2) the student has not learned the specific social skills necessary to reach appropriate social goals (e.g., "Ann" may want to talk more with other kids at school, but doesn't know conversational skills such as listening, asking questions, or staying on topic/switching topics appropriately); or, (3) the student has not learned how to match social skills with appropriate situational contexts. The student may not recognize or understand cues within the environment that prompt use of specific social skills (e.g., when interrupting, "Jolisa" may not recognize reactions indicating that it's the wrong time to do so).

A lack of practice or feedback describes the person who has the knowledge but does not perform the skill. Elliott and Gresham (1991) note that some social skill programs do not provide enough practice for newly learned skills. This can result in the student's appearing awkward or performing the skill in a rote manner (e.g., "Maria" knows how to introduce people, but when she does, her introduction sounds artificial).

A third deficit area involves *a lack of cues or opportunities* (Elliott and Gresham, 1991). Some people can only perform social skills when specific cues are present (e.g., "Victor" may be able to initiate a conversation with someone new only when seeing his mother's reassuring look). Stokes and Baer's (1977) "multiple exemplar strategy" of having students train with more than one person when providing social skills instruction is important to implement.

A lack of reinforcement is the fourth area for social skill deficiencies (Elliott and Gresham, 1991). Some people do not exhibit appropriate social skills because they receive no reinforcement for doing so. For example, "Mike" may not be encouraged by his parents to use self-control. He may even be reinforced for negative behaviors such as fighting (e.g., "What's wrong, aren't you tough enough?").

According to Elliott and Gresham (1991), a final reason for social skill deficiencies is *the presence of interfering problems*. Some behaviors (e.g., word-retrieval problems, hyperactivity, impulsiveness, anxiety) may prevent students from learning or performing social skills.

Social Star includes materials and ideas that will be effective for teaching social skills to students with any type or combination of social skill deficits. In addition, the reader is referred to Elliott and Gresham's (1991) *Social Skills Intervention Guide: Practical Strategies for Social Skill Training* for further information regarding specific strategies to use for each type of deficit.

IDENTIFYING A STUDENT'S SOCIAL SKILL NEEDS

A common concern of educators is determining which social skills are problematic for students. Social competence is a complex and synergistic system. In many respects, social competence and standardized tests are not a natural fit. Few, if any, well-standardized instruments have been developed to assess social competence. A comprehensive system of assessment has yet to be developed. Educators need to be aware of the problems associated with the exclusive use of standardized instruments when assessing social behaviors. The trend appears to be moving away from the use of standardized tests. Close attention should be paid to new research about the assessment of social skills.

Six alternatives for assessing social competence have proven valuable to date (Gresham, 1981; McGinnis and Goldstein, 1990; Schumaker and Hazel, 1984). These alternatives are listed in Table 1.2:

Table 1.2 **Types of Social Skill Assessment**

1. Naturalistic behavioral observation
2. Analogue observation
3. Behavioral rating scales
4. Behavioral checklists
5. Sociometric devices
6. Hypothetical situations

Naturalistic behavioral observation involves observing a person socialize in real-life situations. Information obtained from naturalistic observations can be documented on the Social Communication Skills Rating Scale or the Student Social Skill Summary Form included in *Social Star* (see a description of these forms on pages 6–8; blank forms can be found in *Appendices B* and *C)*.

Analogue observation involves observing a person socialize in contrived rather than naturalistic settings. The educator can purposely do something which will result in the student's having to demonstrate use of a specific social skill (e.g., give the student a compliment and observe the response). Information obtained from analogue observations can also be documented on the Social Communication Skills Rating Scale or the Student Social Skill Summary Form.

Behavioral rating scales require an adult to rate on a scale a child's use of various social skills. Again, the Social Communication Skills Rating Scale could be used.

Behavioral checklists require an adult to look at a list of various social skills and check which ones a specific student needs to improve. The Student Social Skill Summary Form could be used for this purpose.

Sociometric devices involve children identifying which of their peers are most accepted and most rejected in their class or group. Reliable (albeit intrusive) data are collected about children's social impact on their peer group, but little information is gained about specific social skills or behaviors. *Social Star* skill assessment forms do not address this type of assessment.

Assessment using *hypothetical situations* involves asking a child to explain what a person should do in various social situations. Each unit in *Social Star* includes hypothetical home, school, and community situations. These situations could be used to assess a child's knowledge of various social skills.

The authors believe that a combination of several approaches will be effective for identifying the social skills to be included for instruction. An educator who has worked with a group of students for a given period of time can usually identify a student's social skill strengths and weaknesses by using observation techniques and checklists.

SOCIAL COMMUNICATION SKILLS RATING SCALE

Social Star provides a Social Communication Skills Rating Scale which can be used for several types of skill assessment as summarized in the last section. The scale could be completed by an educator and/or a parent or another adult who has observed the student's use of social skills in a natural setting. When used as a behavioral rating scale, more than one person might complete the Social Communication Skills Rating Scale because people's perceptions vary. The scale is partially shown in Figure 1.2 and is provided in *Appendix B*.

Figure 1.2

	SOCIAL COMMUNICATION SKILL	RATING		
		SELDOM	SOMETIMES	ALMOST ALWAYS
2.	VOLUME—Uses a speaking volume appropriate for the situation. Comments:	1	2	3
3.	TONE OF VOICE—Avoids using inappropriate voice tones (braggy, whiney, bossy, sarcastic). Comments:	1	2	3
4.	FACIAL EXPRESSION—Avoids using inappropriate	1	2	3

The Social Communication Skills Rating Scale asks the adult to rate the student on each of the social skills contained in *Social Star: General Interaction Skills (Book 1)* based on past experience with the student. Each social skill is described on the rating scale to make it as explicit as possible. The adult rates the student on a scale of 1–3: 1 if the skill is seldom used correctly, 2 if the skill is sometimes used correctly, or 3 if the skill is almost always used correctly. The educator may view a rating of 1 and possibly 2 as being problematic. The estimated readability for this rating scale is an 8.5 grade level, according to the Flesch-Kincaid Readability Scale (Readability Plus, 1988), and it is evaluated as "easy" reading using the "general purpose" scale for adults.

STUDENT SOCIAL SKILL SUMMARY FORM: DETERMINING INDIVIDUAL NEEDS

When the Social Communication Skills Rating Scale has been completed, the scores may be compiled on the Student Social Skill Summary Form, which is partially shown in Figure 1.3 and is provided in *Appendix* C.

Figure 1.3

STUDENT SOCIAL SKILL SUMMARY FORM

STUDENT'S NAME: MARiA	Identified as a strength	Identified as problematic	Skill has been taught in class		
1. Eye Contact	✓	✓	✓	✓	✓
2. Volume	✓	✓	✓	✓	✓
3. Tone of Voice	✓	✓	✓	✓	✓
4. Facial Expression	✓	✓	✓	✓	✓
5. Posture	✓	✓	✓	✓	✓
6. Personal Space	✓	✓	✓	✓	✓
7. Hygiene	✓	✓	✓	✓	✓
8. Body Talk	✓	✓	✓	✓	✓
9. Manners	✓	✓	✓	✓	✓
10. Listening Basics	✓	✓	✓	✓	✓

The summary form lists all 15 social skills, with a place to mark skills identified as strengths and those identified as weaknesses. It also includes a place to mark the social skills for which the student has received instruction. Two additional blank columns have been provided for the educator to document additional information (e.g., results from naturalistic behavioral observation, analogue observation, or hypothetical situations).

There are several uses for the Student Social Skill Summary Form after its completion. A copy of the summary form may be placed in the student's file and may be attached to a student's report card. For a student in special education, a copy can be included with a specialist's report about the student or in the student's Individualized Education Plan (IEP).

CLASS SUMMARY FORM: DETERMINING WHICH UNITS TO TEACH

The educator may wish to compile each student's data on the Class Summary Form, shown in Figure 1.4, to analyze common needs. The Class Summary Form is provided in *Appendix D*.

Figure 1.4

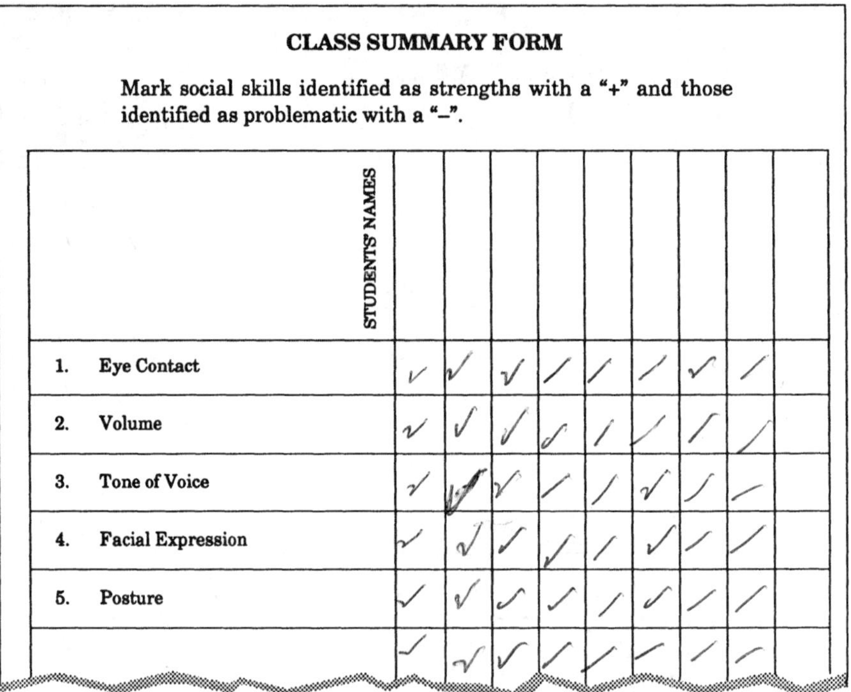

CLASS SUMMARY FORM

Mark social skills identified as strengths with a "+" and those identified as problematic with a "–".

STUDENTS' NAMES									
1. Eye Contact	✓	✓	✓	✓	✓	✓	✓	✓	
2. Volume	✓	✓	✓	✓	✓	✓	✓	✓	
3. Tone of Voice	✓	✓	✓	✓	✓	✓	✓	✓	
4. Facial Expression	✓	✓	✓	✓	✓	✓	✓	✓	
5. Posture	✓	✓	✓	✓	✓	✓	✓	✓	
	✓	✓	✓	✓	✓	✓	✓	✓	

To complete the form, write the name of each student across the top. For each student, mark the social skills found to be strengths and those found to be problematic areas. Thus, a profile of each student's needs will be established. The Class Summary Form will identify the priority social skills and generate a sequence in which the skills may be taught. If a certain social skill is not problematic for any of the students, instruction may not be necessary for that skill. However, the educator may wish to provide a mini-lesson to promote maintenance of the skill. Suppose, conversely, a social skill is found to be a problem for several students, but not for all. When teaching that social skill, the students who are not deficient in that area can be asked to be "special assistants" (e.g., helping the educator model the social skill).

Although some skills are prerequisites for others (e.g., the *Eye Contact* unit should be taught before the *Conversations* unit, if eye contact is identified as an problem for students), there is no clear-cut hierarchy of skills. Therefore, the educator should teach the skills in order of need or interest and not necessarily in the order presented in *Social Star.* However, the *Cognitive Planning* unit must be taught before teaching other units, because it introduces students to key strategies used throughout the program. Depending on students' needs, the educator might teach all or some of the first seven units of *Eye Contact, Volume, Tone of Voice, Facial Expression, Posture, Personal Space,* and *Hygiene*. The *Body Talk* unit (an important and more global unit, which incorporates concepts from units 1–7) should not be eliminated, because it becomes incorporated into the skill steps for the social skills in units 9–15.

SOCIAL STAR CHARACTERS

The *Social Star* program revolves around six main characters, named Mike Olson, Ann Olson, Maria Parra, Victor Parra, Lee Vue, and Jolisa Walker (see Figure 1.5). They are elementary-age children going to McKinley School and living in a community called Socialville. (Major buildings in Socialville are illustrated in *Appendix E* and may be duplicated. Educators are encouraged to build a Socialville community using the building designs provided. Construction of Socialville is further explained in the *Cognitive Planning* unit.)

Figure 1.5

These six characters are also incorporated in *Communicate Junior* (Mayo, Hirn, Gajewski, and Kafka, 1991), which is an educational game board activity (see pages 36–37) to reinforce social skills taught with *Social Star.* The children, along with their parents and teachers, are referred to frequently throughout *Social Star.* The

Socialville characters (17 in all and printed in *Appendix F*) provide a common theme and continuity between units. The characters are portrayed as realistic people with social skill strengths and weaknesses. The characters interact in various home, school, and community situations and come from varied ethnic, socio-economic, and family backgrounds as described in the next sections.

The Jackson (Olson) Family

Mike Olson, Ann Olson, Mary Jackson, and Joe Jackson

Ann and Mike live with their mother and stepfather. Their stepfather (Joe) works in a toy factory (Get Along Toy Factory) and their mother (Mary) works at a restaurant (Good Meals–Good Manners Restaurant).

The Parra Family

Maria Parra, Victor Parra, Juanita Parra, and Ricardo Parra

Maria and Victor live with their mother and father. Their mother (Juanita) is a physician at a clinic (Helping Hands Clinic) and their father (Ricardo) is an executive at the Get Along Toy Factory.

The Vue Family

Lee Vue, Ho Vue, Mika Vue

Lee lives with his father and his grandmother. His father (Ho) is a construction worker for Happy Homes and his grandmother (Mika) is a cook at McKinley School.

The Walker Family

Jolisa Walker, Corin Walker, Jesse Walker

Jolisa lives with her mother and father. Her father (Jesse) works for the Socialville Parks Department and her mother (Corin) is a teacher's aide at McKinley School.

McKinley School Classroom Teachers

Ms. Paula Hess, Mr. Marcus Aaron, and Mrs. Cora Marrero

SOCIAL STAR WALL CHART CONSTRUCTION

Three types of wall charts are utilized during each *Social Star* unit. They include (1) the *Cognitive Planning Formula* chart; (2) classroom posters; and (3) the *Social Super Stars* display. Directions for making these wall charts are provided in the next three sections (or preprinted color wall charts can be purchased through the publisher; see page 485).

Cognitive Planning Formula Chart

During the *Cognitive Planning* unit and in the final lesson (Lesson Z) of each social skill unit, students are taken through the four cognitive planning steps (STOP, PLOT, GO, SO). Cognitive planning, one of the six components to teaching a social skill, is explained in Chapter 2. The educator should construct a large *Cognitive Planning Formula* chart according to the pattern in Figure 1.6. The chart is used to remind students of the four steps of cognitive planning (described in the *Cognitive Planning* unit).

Figure 1.6

Classroom Posters

Lessons from each unit in the *Social Star* program call for a classroom poster. Each poster includes the skill step(s) for a specific social skill and the symbol for each step. This information is described in Lesson A within each unit and should be reproduced large enough for the whole group of students to see. An example is shown in Figure 1.7. The educator could also construct a second poster that has the Socialville characters saying "catchy" phrases reminding students to use each skill appropriately (e.g., "Be polite! Use manners day and night"). The posters provide an excellent resource for promoting social skills on a schoolwide basis (see pages 29–30).

Figure 1.7

(During the *Interrupting* unit, students learn that the acronym *GAG* means (1) Get the person's attention, (2) Apologize for interrupting, and (3) Give the reason for interrupting.)

Social Super Stars Display

Lesson Z (the final lesson in each unit) calls for the use of the *Social Super Stars* display. It is used to display social skill badges that students bring back to school after their parents have signed them (see pages 23–24). The *Social Super Stars* display should be constructed as a large chart with the heading "Social Super Stars." An example is provided in Figure 1.8.

The poster should be laminated for easy removal of the "old" badges when badges from a new unit are brought to school.

Figure 1.8

Chapter 2

Social Star: A Closer Look

Social Star provides interesting and creative ways to teach each social skill unit to students, and the variety of activities makes each social skill unit unique. As discussed in Chapter 1, however, all units have six critical components in common:

1. Social Skill Introduction/Instruction
2. Modeling
3. Rehearsal
4. Feedback
5. Cognitive Planning
6. Transfer/Generalization

This chapter describes each of these components in detail.

SOCIAL SKILL INTRODUCTION/INSTRUCTION

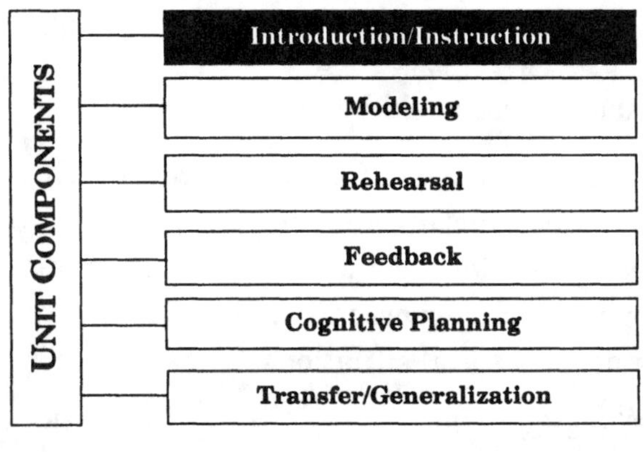

Each unit in *Social Star* includes introductory material that is critical for effective instruction and consists of these sections:

- Unit Goal
- Educator Information
- Related Activities
- Related Literature
- Social Skills All Day Long

The Unit Goal summarizes the overall focus within the chosen social skill area. Most units focus on demonstrating comprehension and use of the social skill.

Educator Information includes background information relevant to each unit that provides data or insights essential for teaching the social skill. This information may influence the way an educator teaches a unit.

Next, Related Activities are suggested that may be completed before, during, or after the lessons in the unit. They may also be used for homework (see pages 23–24).

Similarly, Related Literature may be used at any point in the unit. Related Literature has been included so that children can hear or read stories (or excerpts) that naturally incorporate the social skills being taught. Most units have both picture book and text examples of Related Literature that incorporate the target social skill.

The Related Literature books do not directly teach or discuss the target social skill. Rather, they show characters using a given social skill in context. When text examples are used, the page numbers are included. When the social skill is self-evident on the pages cited, no explanation is provided. When the text example is more subtle, an explanatory comment accompanies the page number(s).

An attempt was made to include award-winning children's literature whenever possible. Consideration was also given to accessibility; books that are commonly found in school and public libraries were chosen over alternative press titles. In general, only stories that depict realistic characters are included (e.g., folk tales were avoided because they tend to have animal or mythical characters).

The Social Skills All Day Long section provides the means for addressing social skills throughout the day. It is the last section in the introductory pages to each unit and is discussed on pages 26–29.

The lesson plans for each unit include a motivating Preparatory Set that can be used at the beginning of each class. After catching students' interest, instruction of the social skill begins. Lesson A within each unit provides students with the following:

1. A definition of the social skill
2. The skill step(s) used to execute the skill
3. A rationale for why it's important to use the social skill correctly

Other lessons within each unit involve students in hands-on, fun, experiential activities (e.g., reading scripts, performing skits, conducting interviews, producing tapes). Students are asked to complete these activities with a partner or in small groups. Partner and small group interactions provide opportunities for students to integrate the skills they are learning within natural social situations.

Printed materials are often included in lessons for students' use. Many times, the educator is also instructed to prepare an overhead transparency and read the material along with the student. On the Flesch-Kincaid Readability Scale (Readability Plus, 1988), the student pages are at a 2.2 grade level. The pages are evaluated as "very easy" using the "children's book" scale.

The number of social skill introduction/instruction lessons within each unit varies depending on the complexity of the social skill. The lessons during the introduction and instruction component are labeled A, B, C, etc. depending on the number of lessons. The final three lessons within each unit (during which modeling, rehearsal, feedback, and cognitive planning take place) are labeled X, Y, and Z.

The length of each lesson within a unit varies. Educators should allow a minimum of 30 minutes per lesson and plan on spending several time periods for longer lessons. The average lesson length is approximately 45 minutes.

MODELING

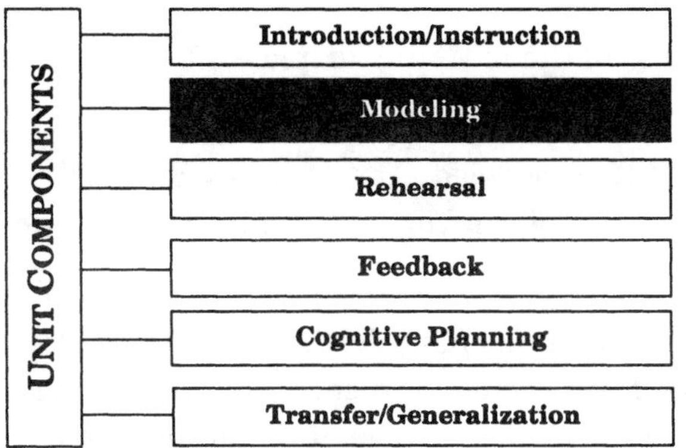

The use of modeling has been documented as an effective strategy for teaching new behaviors (Bandura, 1977; Gresham, 1981). Modeling involves having the educator demonstrate how to use a social skill appropriately. Several opportunities to model correct use of a social skill are built into each unit in *Social Star*.

When modeling, the educator should first demonstrate a social skill while verbalizing thoughts (self-talk) aloud, and then demonstrate the same social skill without verbalizing thoughts aloud. Modeling the use of self-talk for various social skills increases the likelihood that transfer/generalization will occur (Meichenbaum, 1977). Modeling scripts are provided for the educator throughout each unit. Here is an example of modeling with self-talk from the *Tone of Voice* unit:

Modeling Example

Model use of the tone of voice skill steps while thinking aloud. A scripted example follows:

Introduction

I am going to pretend that I'm one of you and my mom says I have to stay home because we are having company. I really want to go to my friend's house instead. I will use an appropriate tone of voice and tell you the thoughts I'm having. When I hold up this Thought Bubble, *you'll know the words I'm saying are actually what I'm thinking.*

Actual Model

While holding up the *Thought Bubble* say, *Oh boy, I'm really angry! How does my voice sound? I'd better not sound sarcastic or Mom will scold me. I'll let her know I'm a little disappointed, though.* Put the *Thought Bubble* down and say disappointedly, *OK Mom, I'll stay home.*

In Lesson X of each unit, the educator models the social skill in three different situations (i.e., home, school, and community). Several other tips the educator should keep in mind when modeling social skills are these:

1. Modeling is more effective when a "coping model" (Bandura, 1977) is used. For instance, when modeling the social skill of *tone of voice* as in the example above, the person modeling should look and sound as though he or she is disappointed

about accepting the no response. Not accepting the no too calmly and too politely is important, or the model will be unrealistic.

2. Careful thinking and planning beforehand of the modeling display is important (McGinnis, Goldstein, Sprafkin, and Gershaw, 1984).
3. At least two examples of the skill should be modeled (McGinnis et al., 1984). For example, situations from the home, school, and/or community should be modeled.
4. Situations modeled should be realistic for the students (McGinnis et al., 1984). The educator may need to alter the role plays included in each unit depending on the age, socio-economic background, and ethnic heritage of the group of students being taught.
5. Students must pay attention to the modeling display being done. Cuing students that they will be asked to identify or discuss various parts of the social skill when the modeling is completed might increase the students' level of interest while observing the modeling display.
6. Negative modeling involves showing how the social skill should NOT be done (e.g., when modeling the social skill of *having a conversation,* one might talk incessantly and not give the other person a chance to talk). Research on the use of negative modeling examples is unclear. McGinnis et al. (1984) advocate that all modeling displays depict positive outcomes. However, Ladd and Mize (1983) state that modeling negative examples may be helpful in making the parameters of the social skill more explicit. Elliott and Gresham (1991) include examples of negative modeling for each social skill in their program. *Social Star* sometimes uses negative modeling in an exaggerated, humorous manner (e.g., for one of the Preparatory Sets in the *Volume* unit, the educator talks too loudly and then too softly).

REHEARSAL

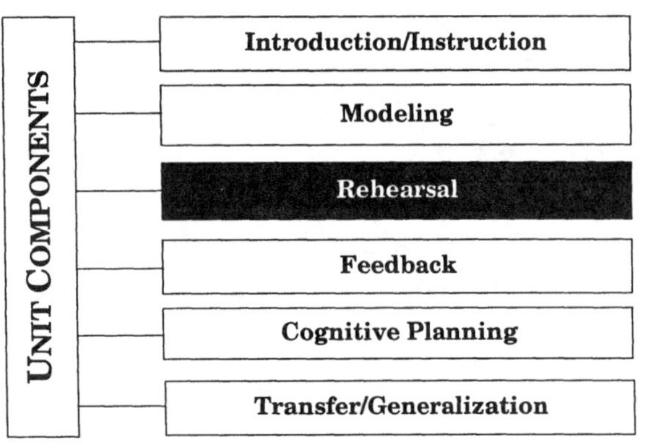

Behavioral rehearsal is an essential component when teaching children social skills. Elliott and Gresham (1991) state that repeated practice of a social skill increases retention of the skill concept and improves performance of the skill. They identify three types of rehearsal:

Covert rehearsal—thinking about and visualizing how to perform a social skill

Verbal rehearsal—reciting the components (skill steps) of a social skill

Overt rehearsal—performing (role playing) a social skill

Covert rehearsal is incorporated in the Preparatory Set of every social skill unit in *Social Star*. A script is provided which the educator reads to guide students through a visualization of the correct use of the social skill.

Social Star emphasizes *verbal rehearsal* by having students work in pairs to tell each other the skill step(s) for the unit several times.

Each *Social Star* unit includes several opportunities for students to engage in role playing, thereby providing *overt rehearsal* of the social skill. Many units also provide opportunities for students to drill and practice individual skill steps (e.g., to practice the first skill step in having a conversation, which involves greeting a person). In Lesson X of every unit (after students have watched the educator model correct use of the social skill in a home, school, or community situation), a student volunteer is asked to demonstrate the social skill using the following two-step approach:

1. The student demonstrates the social skill *while* verbalizing thoughts (self-talk) aloud.

2. The student demonstrates the social skill *without* verbalizing thoughts (self-talk) aloud.

In the Lesson Y *Show Time* of every unit in *Social Star*, each student is provided the opportunity to role play (overtly rehearse) a home, school, and/or community situation. Situations to role play are provided. These examples are from the *Interrupting* unit:

Home—Pretend your parents are having a conversation during breakfast. Show how you could politely interrupt to tell your dad that you need a permission slip signed for school today.

School—Pretend the school secretary is working on the computer. Show how you could politely interrupt to give the secretary an important note from your teacher.

Community—Pretend that you are at a grocery store and can't find an item on your parent's list. Show how you could politely interrupt a clerk to ask for help.

Additional role-play situations can be found in other commercially prepared programs such as *Skillstreaming the Elementary School Child* (McGinnis et al., 1984); *Skillstreaming in Early Childhood* (McGinnis and Goldstein, 1990); *Communicate Junior* (Mayo, Hirn, Gajewski, and Kafka, 1991); *Scripting* (Mayo and Waldo, 1987); and *Social Skills Intervention Guide* (Elliott and Gresham, 1991).

The role plays in *Social Star* have been provided to decrease teacher preparation time. However, it is critical that the role-play situations be realistic and relevant for the students. The educator is encouraged to substitute relevant role plays if the ones provided in *Social Star* are not realistic for a specific child or a group of children. The educator may wish to elicit role-play situations from the students themselves.

Other tips the educator should keep in mind when asking students to role play are these:

1. Give students the choice of whether or not they wish to participate in the role play (McGinnis et al., 1984); this will enhance the role play.
2. Determine the role play to be done, then elicit more specific information from the main actor as to the physical setting and events which might precede the role-play situation (McGinnis et al., 1984).
3. Use a multiple exemplar strategy (Stokes and Baer, 1977), which involves students role playing with several different people instead of just one person.
4. Intervene if the student begins to do the role play incorrectly or is not taking role playing seriously (McGinnis et al., 1984).
5. Use role reversal by having students switch roles (Goldstein, Sprafkin, Gershaw, and Klein, 1986).
6. Focus on how the student will use the new role-play behaviors in the future rather than how the behaviors could have been used in past situations (McGinnis et al., 1984).
7. Include a variety of opportunities for the students to drill individual skill steps for a social skill as opposed to performing the entire social skill only once or twice. Georges (1988) recommends drilling each skill step to the mastery level before moving on to the next skill step. For example, for the social skill of *interrupting,* the students would drill on the first skill step of asking themselves whether they needed to interrupt. They would not move on to the second step (interrupting politely) until they could accurately identify when it is OK to interrupt.
8. Use the word "pretend" with younger children rather than "role play" when explaining what to do.
9. Provide a box of props that can be used during role playing. Various hats, shirts, and artifacts (e.g., eyeglasses, purses, clipboards and pens, etc.) can be available for students' use.

FEEDBACK

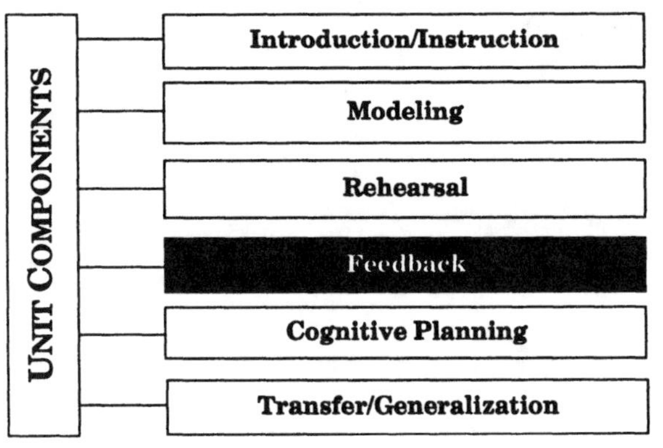

Master educators recognize the importance of providing feedback to students. Thus, it is important that students receive feedback immediately after they perform a social skill so they can make improvements. The feedback can occur formally (during class while the students are role playing) or informally (throughout the day as appropriate or inappropriate social skill use is observed [see pages 26–29]).

When giving feedback on a student's role play of a particular social skill, be sure to:

1. Give specific feedback on the skill steps of the social skill. Students sometimes forget skill steps or may do them inappropriately. Those students should be asked to redo the role play (possibly with educator assistance) to ensure success.

2. Begin by pointing out the positive aspects of the role play before giving any constructive criticism.

3. Give feedback immediately, particularly to young children. The educator should always provide oral feedback. Additional written feedback is also recommended. For example, the educator could put a smile face next to each of the skill steps the student has successfully performed.

4. Provide feedback to parents on how their children are doing on specific targeted social skills.

COGNITIVE PLANNING

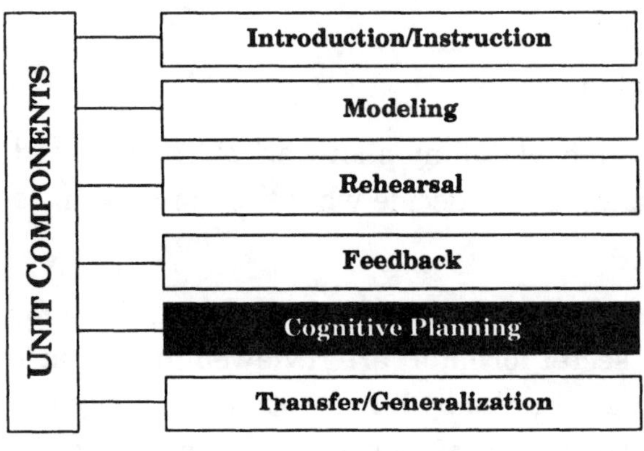

Along with learning comprehension of social skills, students need to learn and use cognitive planning. The phrase "cognitive planning strategies" refers to the independent thinking that students do about social skills.

Students need to be able to do the following:

- Keep themselves calm and in control
- Maintain a positive focus and be open-minded
- Perceive social situations accurately
- Brainstorm social skill options
- Consider consequences for each option
- Choose an option
- Develop a plan
- Carry out their plan
- Evaluate the outcomes
- Reward themselves for their successes and/or decide what to do differently the next time

Social Star has incorporated these cognitive planning strategies into a four-step "secret formula" called STOP, PLOT, GO, SO. Social skill interventions that incorporate cognitive planning strategies are described as being more effective in promoting the acquisition, transfer, and generalization of social skills than programs that do not incorporate these strategies (Hughes, 1988; Kendall and Braswell, 1982).

The first unit in *Social Star* is the *Cognitive Planning* unit. In addition to introducing students to the Socialville characters, this five-lesson unit describes the "secret formula" (the cognitive planning strategies) used by Socialville characters to solve problems and set goals. The secret formula consists of the following steps:

STOP: Students think "stop" in their minds to stay calm by using self-control strategies.

PLOT: Students decide what their problem is, brainstorm options, consider possible consequences for each option, and then choose the best option to use in the situation. They also think about the social skills needed to carry out their plan.

GO: Students implement their plan.

SO: Students ask themselves, "So, how did my plan work?" They reward themselves for their successes, and/or decide what they may want to do differently next time.

The *Cognitive Planning* unit should be taught first because it is a prerequisite for the remaining units. The four steps of the "secret formula" are reviewed in Lesson Z (Lesson Z Plot Situation) of all other social skill units by having students apply the steps to a hypothetical situation. The hypothetical situation describes a typical problem that a child might encounter and may not be specific to the particular social skill unit. For example, in the *Facial Expression* unit, students are asked to pretend they are walking through the park and then to hypothesize what they would do if some older kids start following and calling them names. Students are encouraged to use the "secret formula" in all areas of their lives.

TRANSFER/GENERALIZATION

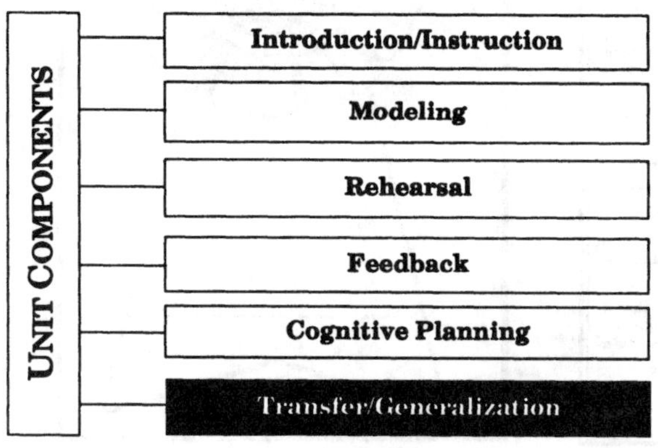

One of the major problems with any social skills training is that the skills often do not transfer/generalize to other settings. Students perform the social skill accurately while in class, yet fail to use the social skill in real-life situations. Each unit of *Social Star* has activities which increase the likelihood that transfer will occur. Some transfer ideas previously discussed are these:

- Use of cognitive planning strategies, which includes using self-control statements, developing a plan, evaluating oneself, and rewarding oneself
- Use of self-talk during modeling and role plays
- Use of relevant role-play situations from the home, school, and community
- Use of verbal rehearsal and visualization

In addition, *Social Star* provides and/or encourages use of the transfer and generalization activities described in the remainder of this chapter.

Homework

A homework assignment is included in Lesson Z of every unit. The assignment asks students to take a *Home-A-Gram* and a social skill badge home to their parents or other significant adults. Figure 2.1 on the next page provides an example of a *Home-A-Gram* and a badge.

The *Home-A-Gram* is a note written from a child's perspective. The note should be signed by each child during Lesson Z. The *Home-A-Gram* gives information about the social skill and provides an opportunity for the student to practice the social skill with a parent or other significant adult. The parent is asked to sign the social skill badge verifying that the activity was successfully completed. The student returns the badge to be displayed on the *Social Super Stars* display (see page 13).

Before sending home the first *Home-A-Gram* and social skill badge, supply each student's family with information about the rationale for the activity. A letter is provided in *Appendix G*.

Jackson, Jackson, and Monroe (1983) stress that homework should not be limited due to a lack of skills, time, or interest on the part of parents. Therefore, if a parent

Figure 2.1

HOME-A-GRAM

Dear Family,

At school, we have been talking about the social skill called

VOLUME

I learned that *voice volume* means how quiet or loud I talk.

I know that whenever I want to talk, I need to ask myself, "What volume should I use (quiet, normal, or loud)?"

I learned that people will enjoy talking to me more when I use a volume that is right for the situation (quiet, normal, or loud). It brings a good feeling inside.

Below, I have written a situation appropriate for each voice volume.

QUIET VOLUME: ______________________

NORMAL VOLUME: ______________________

LOUD VOLUME: ______________________

I'll show you the difference between a quiet, normal, and loud volume at home. After I do, please sign my "Volume" badge so I can return it to school and become a SOCIAL SUPER STAR this week.

From: ______________________

is unable or unwilling to complete the *Home-A-Gram*, it should be completed with another predetermined adult.

Related Activities

In addition to using the *Home-A-Gram*, the authors advocate that the educator provide motivating homework throughout each unit. The Related Activities listed at the beginning of each unit may also be utilized as homework assignments. These activities help integrate social skills into other content areas and into community settings.

Self-Management Strategies for Social Skills

The use of self-monitoring to learn self-management strategies (e.g., the SO step in the *Cognitive Planning* unit) appears to be a highly promising method for increasing the transfer and generalization of skills (Turkewitz, O'Leary, and Ironsmith, 1975). Dunlap, Dunlap, Koegel, and Koegel (1991) provide a five-step approach for designing and implementing a self-monitoring program. The approach is summarized in Table 2.1 and described in sections 1–5 that follow:

Table 2.1

Self-Monitoring Program
(Dunlap, Dunlap, Koegel, and Koegel, 1991)

1. Define the behavior to be monitored.
2. Develop a method for self-monitoring.
3. Teach the student how to use a self-monitoring device.
4. Allow the student to select reinforcement.
5. Fade the use of a self-monitoring device.

1. Define the behavior to be monitored. Students must understand and accurately assess themselves. For example, if children are to assess the amount of time they are "on task," they will need to understand exactly what "on task" means. In the *Social Star* program, students are asked to self-monitor in Lesson Z of every unit.

2. Develop a method for each student to monitor social skills. It is important that the educator include the student in this decision-making process. *Social Star* includes 10 *Self-Management* sheets (see *Appendix H*) which can be used with various social skill units. The educator must be careful to choose (or encourage students to choose) the type of self-management sheet that would work best for the given social skill (e.g., use a tally-sheet type shown on page 456 with a skill, such as *eye contact*, that happens frequently).

3. Teach the student to use the self-management sheets accurately. Students need to understand how to recognize the appropriate behavior and how to record when the behavior occurs. The educator should model how to use the chosen self-management device. Younger students should be asked to self-monitor relatively short, simple tasks. For example, a young child might be asked to self-monitor eye contact for a five-minute period.

4. Allow the student to assist in selecting a predetermined reinforcement for accurately performing the social skill. Students should be rewarded for accurately monitoring themselves in addition to accurately performing the social skill. At first, the educator may provide the reinforcement after the student has completed the self-management sheet. However, students should eventually learn to reward themselves, and extrinsic rewards (e.g., stickers, candy) should be replaced by intrinsic rewards (e.g., self-praise). The educator may wish to ask questions such as "When you learn to use this skill appropriately, what special feelings do you think you'll have? What can you say to praise yourself?" to assist students in moving toward being intrinsically motivated.

5. Fade the use of self-monitoring devices gradually, once the student has demonstrated mastery and generalization of the skill.

Self-Monitoring of Classroom Discussion Skills

In addition to the self-management activity during Lesson Z, students are also asked to self-monitor a classroom discussion skill once within each unit by completing a page called *Checking Myself* (see *Appendix I*). Development of appropriate classroom discussion skills along with social skills will facilitate a positive learning environment.

The educator is provided with a script to model how the *Checking Myself* sheet should be completed. An example follows:

Introduction

I am going to pretend to be one of you completing this sheet during the discussion we will be having. I will tell you the thoughts I'm having while I'm completing the sheet. When I hold up this Thought Bubble, *you'll know the words I'm saying are actually what I'm thinking.*

Actual Model

While holding up the *Thought Bubble* say, *OK, the teacher just called on Bill. I'd better give him eye contact so he knows I'm listening to his answer. I'll put an "X" on my sheet because I gave him eye contact.* Put the *Thought Bubble* down and mark an "X" on the *Checking Myself* transparency.

These classroom discussion skills are emphasized in the *Checking Myself* model scripts:

- Listen to others
- Think about an answer to each question asked
- Use interested body talk
- Use appropriate eye contact
- Use a straight sitting posture
- Raise my hand

Educators may substitute other classroom discussion goals more appropriate for their students. For example, not all educators teach children to raise their hands during class discussion. The purpose of completing the *Checking Myself* activity in each unit is to reinforce the classroom discussion skills relevant to the children being taught. The specific selected content for these skills is up to the individual educator.

If the educator is concerned that a specific student may have difficulty monitoring the selected classroom discussion goal accurately, the educator can monitor the individual and compare the results with those of the student.

Social Skills All Day Long

Social skills should be addressed continually throughout the day. Each unit in *Social Star* provides suggestions in the form of encouraging, sharing a personal example, prompting students, and giving corrective feedback that educators can use to reinforce specific social skills. The authors strongly advocate that social skills be addressed throughout the day in a positive, nonthreatening manner.

Encouraging and giving corrective feedback were inspired by *The Dubuque Management System* (Keystone Area Education Agency, 1990), a highly successful social skill program that focuses on appropriate and inappropriate social skills as they occur throughout the day. The procedures for encouraging and giving corrective feedback are further explained in the next sections.

Encouraging

Educators need to reinforce students as frequently as possible when social skills are correctly used. This reinforcement is called "specific effective encouragement" in *The Dubuque Management System* (Keystone Area Education Agency, 1990). The steps involved in this encouragement are summarized in Table 2.2 and described in the next six points:

Table 2.2

Specific Effective Encouragement
(Keystone Area Education Agency, 1990)

1. Approach student positively.
2. Describe appropriate behavior.
3. Provide a rationale for appropriate behavior.
4. Ask for acknowledgment.
5. Tell the consequence.
6. Provide a transition.

1. Approach the student positively—the educator gives an initial positive greeting (e.g., smile at the student).
2. Describe the appropriate behavior—the educator describes the appropriate behavior the student used (e.g., "You offered help to Lee in such a polite way").
3. Provide a rationale for the appropriate behavior—the educator gives the reason for using the appropriate behavior (e.g., "When you offer help in such a nice way, people will want you to help them").
4. Ask for acknowledgment from the student—the educator asks the student to acknowledge (verbally or nonverbally) that there is understanding of what is said (e.g., "Do you understand?").
5. Tell the student the consequence—the educator tells the consequence the student has earned by the appropriate behavior (e.g., "When it's lunch time, you can go a minute early for offering help to Lee").
6. Provide a transition statement—the educator provides a statement that helps the student get back on task (e.g., "Why don't you spend the last five minutes reading quietly?").

Encouraging is also included at the end of each lesson in *Social Star* in the form of positive statements that are made by teachers. Children either listen to the positive statement or read it aloud in unison. The positive statements reinforce appropriate social skills and provide closure for each lesson.

Giving Corrective Feedback

The Dubuque Management System (Keystone Area Education Agency, 1990) uses a 10-step "teaching interaction" similar to that of Northrup, Wood, and Clark (1979), when inappropriate behavior occurs. "Giving corrective feedback" as modeled in *Social Star* encompasses only the first four steps of the 10-step teaching interaction process. The teaching interaction steps are summarized in Table 2.3 and are described in sections 1–10 that follow:

Table 2.3

Teaching Interaction
(Northrup, Wood, and Clark, 1979)

1. Approach student positively.
2. Describe inappropriate behavior.
3. Describe appropriate behavior.
4. Provide a rationale for appropriate behavior.
5. Model appropriate behavior.
6. Have student practice.
7. Give feedback to student.
8. Provide additional practice.
9. Give praise for accomplishments.
10. Give a homework assignment.

1. Approach the student positively—the educator gives an initial positive greeting (e.g., "Hi, Maria").

2. Describe the inappropriate behavior—the educator describes the inappropriate behavior to the student in specific terms (e.g., "Just now you were turned around in your desk making faces at Victor while I was talking").

3. Describe the appropriate behavior—the educator describes the appropriate behavior to be used by the student (e.g., "Maria, you could have been using your listening skills. Your body could have been facing the front and you could have been looking at me").

4. Provide a rationale for the appropriate behavior—the educator gives the reason for using the appropriate behavior (e.g., "When you face the front and look at me, you let me know you are listening. You won't miss the important things I'm saying") and/or the consequences of not behaving appropriately (e.g., "If you are

turned around in your chair, not giving eye contact, your teacher or parent may become upset because you are not listening").

5. Model the appropriate behavior—the educator demonstrates the appropriate behavior (e.g., the educator sits in a desk and models body language appropriate for listening).

6. Have the student practice—the educator asks the student to practice the appropriate behavior (e.g., "Maria, show me how to sit so that I'll know you are listening").

7. Give feedback to the student—the educator comments on the student's practice of the appropriate behavior. This feedback may include positive and/or negative feedback (e.g., "You're facing the front with your body. That's great! You still need to look at me when I'm talking, though").

8. Provide additional practice—the educator may request additional practice by the student (e.g., "Try that again, Maria. This time, make sure you are looking at me").

9. Give praise for accomplishments—the educator gives praise to the student for performing and participating.

10. Give a homework assignment—the educator directs the student to practice the appropriate behavior in another setting, or at a later time, or with a different person.

This model provides a positive method for changing inappropriate student behavior. While it may appear to be a time-consuming process, a teaching interaction can often be completed in a few minutes, particularly if the social skill has been previously taught. The use of teaching interactions throughout the day greatly increases the chances for skill transfer and generalization. The authors want to caution that the teaching interaction is but one small component of *The Dubuque Management System* model. Those wishing further information about this comprehensive program should contact Keystone Area Education Agency, 1473 Central Avenue, Dubuque, Iowa 52001.

Schoolwide Promotion of Social Skills

Transfer and generalization of social skills will occur more readily if the use of appropriate social skills is promoted on a schoolwide basis. The school staff can jointly decide on a social skill to emphasize each week ("Social Skill of the Week"). The skill could be introduced and defined during the morning announcements. A rationale for using the skill can be given.

Educators could prepare a bulletin board which identifies a specific social skill to emphasize schoolwide. This skill could be changed periodically (weekly or monthly). For example, the elementary school cited in Figure 2.2 chose a theme and goal for each month; October's theme was football. The football was moved 10 yards each time a classroom teacher observed 10 incidents of students in his or her class "giving a compliment." The football field board could be cooperative (i.e., once a class reaches the goal, they give their additional yards to the class farthest behind; when all classes arrive at the goal line, there is an all-school reward) or competitive (i.e., the first class to get to the goal line receives a reward).

Figure 2.2

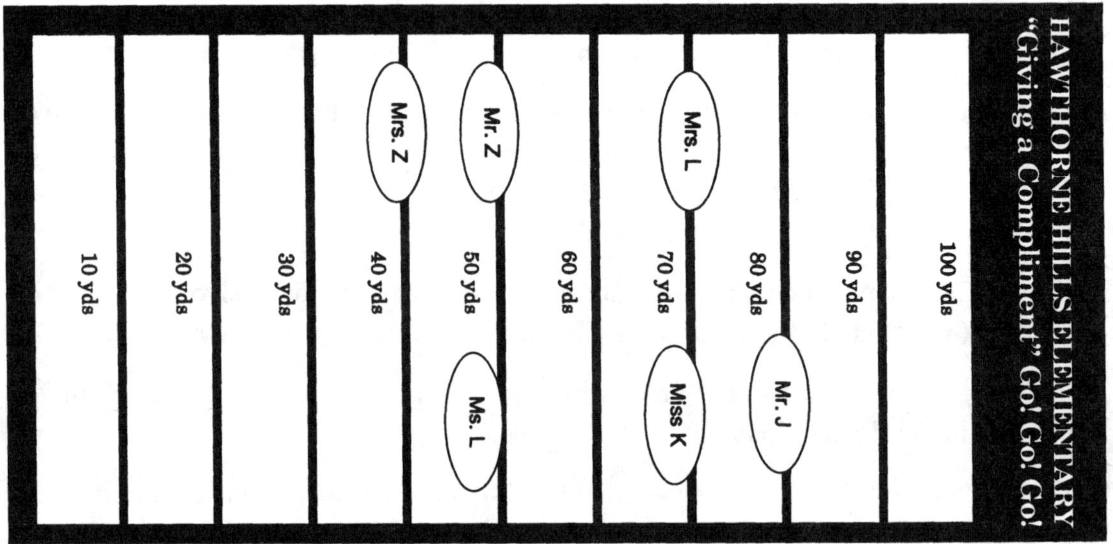

Example of schoolwide promotion of social skills, compliments of Hawthorne Hills Elementary School, Wausau, WI

Individual educators can further teach the skill using materials from *Social Star*. The "Social Skill of the Month" can be described in a school newsletter. Posters (see page 13) explaining social skills can be hung throughout the school. Students displaying appropriate social skills may be awarded coupons (see page 31), which can be turned in for a drawing. Emphasis on social skill excellence should be recognized at award presentations.

Red Flag

McGinnis, Sauerbry, and Nichols (1985) describe a "Red Flag" strategy in which the educator tells students that they will be "set up" later in the day (or the next day). *Being set up* means that the educator will purposely do something which will cause a child to demonstrate use of a particular social skill. For example, a student might be told that sometime later in the day, the educator will give (the student) some constructive criticism. The student is encouraged to demonstrate the proper way to handle criticism during the setup. After the "Red Flag" situation has taken place, the educator and student should discuss how the social skill situation was handled.

Parental Involvement/Training

In addition to involving parents through the *Home-A-Gram*, training should also be available for parents. Two or three parent meetings would be a start at instructing parents on how to identify and praise specific appropriate behaviors in their children. Parents can be taught to view inappropriate behavior as a skill deficit that needs to be taught rather than as "naughty behavior." Parents could learn a shortened version of a teaching interaction (such as steps 1–4) to use with their children.

Often it is difficult to get parents to attend parent-training sessions. One method of getting the message to parents is to ask the PTO/PTA organization to devote one meeting to the topic of "Communitywide Social Skills." Have the PTO/PTA brainstorm ways for their organization to get involved in this worthwhile goal.

Keep cultural diversity in mind as parent meetings are being planned and implemented. Emphasize that children are being taught flexibility in their use of social skills (see page 2).

Reward/Behavioral Programs

Many students have not reached the level at which they can self-reinforce and may need external controls to help themselves use appropriate behavior. Some ways to reinforce appropriate social behavior follow:

1. *Social Gram*

   A *Social Gram* (see *Appendix J*) can be used to reinforce the student's use of social skills. The educator fills in the student's name and appropriate information, then signs and delivers the *Social Gram* to the student. The educator may wish to describe the student's specific behavior in the blank space.

2. *Sunshine Call*

   The *Sunshine Call* is another method for reinforcing social skills. The educator keeps the names/addresses/phone numbers of all students on note cards in a card file box. Each day, the educator takes the first card from the box and either calls or writes a note to that student's family. It is important that the educator discuss only positive behaviors the child has exhibited when writing to or speaking with the family.

3. *The Great Coupon Caper*

   Each member of the class is given one coupon (see *Appendix K*) at the beginning of the day. At random, the name of a specific student is targeted. When other class members observe that student using appropriate social skills (e.g., using manners, showing appropriate facial expressions), they write down why they are awarding the coupon to the target student, and sign their own name. They then give it to the student. At the end of the day, the student turns the coupons in to the teacher. The next day, a different student is targeted to receive the social coupons. When the class earns a specified number of coupons, the students can earn a reward they cooperatively choose. All students should have an opportunity to be the target student.

4. *Student of the Week Graffiti Poster*

Display a large paper with the title "Student of the Week" written on it. Choose a class member to be the "Student of the Week" and write that student's name on the graffiti poster. Class members are instructed to write times when the student has used appropriate social skills (e.g., "Lee was listening during reading today. Great job, Lee!"). At the end of the week, send the poster home with the student. Give each student the opportunity to be "Student of the Week."

5. *Bell-Ringer*

At the beginning of the school day, identify a "Social Skill of the Day" (e.g., helping others). This skill may be chosen by the teacher or the class. When the teacher observes the social skill, the teacher rings a bell in celebration!

6. *We're Hot!*

Display a large paper thermometer with increments marked. Each time students use appropriate social skills (e.g., interrupting appropriately), one increment on the thermometer is colored. When the entire thermometer is filled, the class receives a special reward.

7. *Cooperative Treat*

The educator may wish to use cooperative reward activities. These include cooperative root beer floats, tacos, cookies and cookie decorating, and pizzas. For example, when making cooperative root beer floats, one person is responsible for glasses, one for the root beer, one for the ice cream, one for the spoons, and one for the straws. The students put the floats together cooperatively. Students are allowed to consume their floats when all of the floats are ready.

Peer Reminders

Students should be encouraged to remind fellow students about using social skills (e.g., "Come on, Ann. Tell yourself to calm down. You can do it"). The educator may need to instruct students on how to give reminders in a positive manner. The *Cognitive Planning* unit uses the analogy of a stoplight to remind students to stay in control of their emotions. Students can use the word "stoplight" to remind each other to stay calm. In addition, students should encourage each other for using appropriate social skills (e.g., "Great ignoring. You didn't let Bud get you angry").

Student Mediators

"Mediated Dispute Resolution" involves student conflicts being resolved by the students themselves with the help of a trained peer mediator (Koch and Miller,

1987). When a conflict arises, the students are asked if they would like to "get mediated." Students then put the disagreement "on hold" until a peer mediator is found. In a mediation session, the peer mediator first explains the ground rules. Then each student takes turns telling "his side of the story." The students then come up with a list of solutions, decide upon a solution, and sign a written agreement. This strategy, which can be used anytime throughout the school day, teaches students to compromise and negotiate. Transfer of social skills occurs when students learn to solve problems on their own rather than needing adults to intervene. This process may be appropriate for slightly older children, since it requires perspective taking and negotiating skills.

Use of Cooperative Learning

The use of cooperative learning techniques during academic classes reinforces social skills taught to students and promotes transfer and generalization of social skills. A list of Cooperative Learning Resources is provided on page 40.

The major differences between cooperative learning and traditional learning are depicted in Table 2.4.

Table 2.4

Differences in Learning Groups
(Johnson, Johnson, and Johnson Holubec, 1990)

Cooperative Learning Groups	*Traditional Learning Groups*
Positive interdependence	No interdependence
Individual accountability	No individual accountability
Heterogeneous groups	Homogeneous groups
Leadership is shared	One leader is appointed
Responsible for self and to others	Responsible for self
Task and maintenance emphasized	Only task emphasized
Social skills are directly taught	Social skills are assumed or ignored
Educator observes and intervenes	Educator ignores the groups
Group processing	No group processing

Johnson, Johnson, and Johnson Holubec (1990) describe five components necessary for cooperative learning. They are listed in Table 2.5 and elaborated upon in sections 1–5 that follow:

Table 2.5

Cooperative Learning Components
(Johnson et al., 1990)

1. Positive interdependence
2. Individual accountability
3. Face-to-face interaction
4. Social skills
5. Group processing

1. *Positive Interdependence*

Johnson et al. (1990) state that one necessary component of a cooperative group is that students believe they "sink or swim together." Students have two responsibilities: learn the assigned material, and make sure that all members of their group learn the assigned material. This dual responsibility is "positive interdependence." Positive interdependence occurs when students feel they are linked with group members in a way that they cannot succeed unless their group members succeed. Positive interdependence promotes a situation in which students recognize that their work benefits group members and vice versa. When positive interdependence is clearly understood, students are aware of the following:

- Each group member's efforts are required and indispensable for group success (i.e., there can be no "free-riders").
- Each group member has a unique contribution to make to the joint effort because of his or her resources and/or role and task responsibilities.

Positive interdependence can be structured in a cooperative group in several ways. Group members can work toward a "group goal" (e.g., learn the material, and make sure all group members learn the material). A "group reward" can be offered (e.g., if all group members score 85 percent on the quiz, they will receive 10 bonus points). "Dividing resources" gives each group member a necessary part of the total information to be learned so that the member must teach that part to others. Additionally, the use of "group roles" (e.g., reader, checker, timer, encourager) is yet another way to structure positive interdependence.

2. *Individual Accountability*

According to Johnson et al. (1990), *individual accountability* means that each student's efforts are assessed and the results are given to all group members. This helps group members understand that they cannot "hitchhike" on the work of others. To structure individual accountability:

- Assess how much effort each group member is contributing to the group's work.

- Provide feedback to groups and individual students.
- Help groups avoid redundant efforts by members.
- Ensure that every member is responsible for the final outcome.

3. *Face-to-Face Interaction*

Cooperative learning requires that face-to-face interaction takes place among students. Johnson et al. (1990) explain that this verbal and nonverbal interaction among group members promotes helping, assisting, supporting, encouraging, and praising. It allows students to pressure unmotivated group members to achieve. Students get to know each other as people.

4. *Social Skills*

Johnson et al. (1990) warn that, oftentimes, simply placing students into a group and telling them to cooperate does not ensure that they will do so. Students need to be taught the social skills needed for positive group interaction (e.g., taking turns listening and talking, giving encouragement, having appropriate body language). These social skills are necessary if the group is to function productively. Social skills are taught by Johnson et al. (1990) through the use of *T-Charts. Appendix L* contains a blank *T-Chart* that can be used for any unit in *Social Star*; a completed *T-Chart* is also included in Lesson X of every unit. Use of *T-Charts* is further explained in *Appendix A*.

5. *Group Processing*

Group processing, as described by Johnson et al. (1990), means that students discuss how well they did at achieving their goal and working together. This helps to provide for generalization of the concepts presented. During group processing, students:

- Describe what member actions were helpful and not helpful.
- Make decisions about what actions to continue or change.

The purpose of group processing is to improve each member's effectiveness in achieving the group's goals.

Kagan (1992) describes a cooperative learning structure called "Numbered Heads Together" that is useful in checking for understanding and reviewing key concepts. This structure is incorporated into some of the lessons within *Social Star* and consists of four steps: (1) team members number off; (2) educator announces a question and a time limit; (3) students put their heads together; and (4) educator calls a number.

Step 1. Team members number off.

Each student on the team numbers off. (Teams may not all have the same number of members. For example, some of the teams may have three members and some of the teams may have four members. When this happens, Person 3 from a team of three may answer when either number 3 or number 4 is called.)

Step 2. Educator announces a question and a time limit.

During this step, the educator should pose a question in the form of a directive. Instead of asking, "Why didn't Jolisa use eye contact?" it's better to say, "Make sure everyone on the team can explain why Jolisa didn't use eye contact." To keep the activity moving, the teacher may specify the amount of time teams will be given to put their heads together (e.g., "Why didn't Jolisa use eye contact? You have 45 seconds to make sure everyone on your team knows").

Step 3. Students put their heads together.

Students actually put their heads together to discuss the answer to the proposed question and to make certain everyone knows and can say the answer.

Step 4. Educator calls a number.

The educator calls a number at random and students with that number answer the question. An overhead spinner can be used to truly randomize the numbers being called. The educator then calls on one student to answer the question.

If only one or two students raise their hands (and there are many more than two teams), the educator can say, "Not enough two's have their hands up; I'll give you one more minute to make sure your team's number two knows the answer. Then I want to see all two's hands up." (Or use another system to identify who's ready to answer if raising hands is contrary to your philosophy and/or to the students' cultures.)

If the answer has several parts, then the educator should ask a number one to answer part one, a number two to answer part two, and so on. If a student gives a partially correct response, the educator might ask, "Is there a number three who can add to that response?"

Real-Life Outings

Some students require that social skills be isolated so that direct instruction can be provided. However, in real life, students must identify which social skills to use when and must use a combination of social skills at all times. It is important to provide real-life outings so that students can practice their social skills. Each unit in *Social Star* provides a suggestion for a real-life outing in the Related Activities section. The educator should have students develop a list of social skills they feel will be necessary before going on the outing. After the outing, the educator and students should discuss the students' use of social skills.

Communicate Junior

One means of reinforcing social skill concepts previously learned is the use of educational board games, which can be effective, fun, and motivating (Cartledge and

Milburn, 1986). *Communicate Junior* (Mayo et al., 1991) is a game board activity for elementary students that focuses on 12 social skills. Each player earns an invitation to a party by responding appropriately to question or demonstration items. One by one, players earn their invitation, but the party doesn't begin until everyone is invited. Players are encouraged to help each other get to the party so they can have fun together. The original *Communicate* game (Mayo and Waldo, 1986) is appropriate for upper elementary students.

Social Skill Unit Adaptations

Educators may wish to integrate social skill instruction into content area curriculum. For example, an educator may wish to teach the social skill of *eye contact* as a part of a cooperative learning lesson during social studies by using the page called *Eye Contact* from Lesson A (the page which provides students with the definition, skill step, and reasons for using eye contact), or the educator may wish to address the social skill of *posture* during music class by using the *T-Chart* and modeling the skill.

The units in *Social Star* can also be adapted for use in English-as-a-second-language classrooms. For example, educators may focus on how students can cross between their home cultures and common American cultural norms with regard to social skills when they choose to do so in response to a given situation.

Special attention was given to deleting "should" whenever possible in *Social Star*. Rather than dictating what educators *should* teach children about social skills, the focus is on what *could* be selected. When teaching from *Social Star*, educators are encouraged to honor the "could" terminology rather than lapsing into "shoulds" with children. Likewise, use of "appropriate" is recommended whenever feasible, rather than the more judgmental word "good."

SOCIAL STAR: SUMMARY OF A COMPREHENSIVE RESOURCE

The unit that follows this chapter provides the foundation for other social skills to be taught. *Cognitive Planning* teaches essential thinking strategies and should not be skipped over. The teaching sequence of the remaining 15 social skill units should be determined based upon assessment results. In general, any deficit skills in units 1–8 should be taught before those in units 9–15.

Each unit contains specific information and materials for teaching a given social skill. Many times, the appendices are cited as containing necessary material to teach the unit. Any materials shared among a number of units are reproduced in an appendix section for easier accessibility.

As units are being taught, respect the diversity among your students. *Social Star* is not intended to produce carbon copies of the teacher's perception of "good" social communicators. Rather, the intent is to teach students the richness and flexibility of social communication rules and their impact on school, home, and community situations.

References

Althen, G. (1988). *American ways: A guide for foreigners in the United States.* Yarmouth, ME: Intercultural Press.

Bandura, A. (1977). *Social learning theory.* Englewood Cliffs, NJ: Prentice-Hall.

Bullock, J. (1988). Encouraging the development of social competence in young children. *Early Child Development and Care, 37,* 47–54.

Cartledge, G., and Milburn, J. (Eds.). (1986). *Teaching social skills to children: Innovative approaches (2nd ed.).* Elmsford, NY: Pergamon Press.

Cheng, L. (1987). Cross-cultural and linguistic considerations in working with Asian populations. *ASHA, 29*(6), 33–37.

Dunlap, L., Dunlap, G., Koegel, L., and Koegel, R. (1991). Using self-monitoring to increase independence. *Teaching Exceptional Children, 23*(3), 17–22.

Elliot, S., and Gresham, F. (1991). *Social skills intervention guide: Practical strategies for social skill training.* Circle Pines, MN: American Guidance Service.

Georges, J. (1988, April). Why soft-skill training doesn't take. *Training,* pp. 42–47.

Goldstein, A., Sprafkin, R., Gershaw, N., and Klein, P. (1986). The adolescent: Social skills training through structured learning. In G. Cartledge and J. Milburn (Eds.), *Teaching social skills to children: Innovative approaches (2nd ed.).* Elmsford, NY: Pergamon Press.

Gresham, F. (1981). Social skills training with handicapped children: A review. *Review of Educational Research, 51,* 139–176.

Hartup, W. (1978). Children and their friends. In H. McGurk (Ed.), *Issues in childhood social development* (pp. 130–170). London: Methuen.

Hirsch, E. (1989). *A first dictionary of cultural literacy: What our children need to know.* Boston, MA: Houghton Mifflin.

Hughes, J. (1988). *Cognitive behavior therapy with children in school.* New York: Pergamon.

Jackson, N., Jackson, D., and Monroe, C. (1983). *Getting along with others: Teaching social effectiveness to children.* Champaign, IL: Research Press.

Johnson, D., Johnson, R., and Johnson Holubec, E. (1990). *Circles of learning (3rd ed.).* Edina, MN: Interaction Book Company.

Kagan, S. (1992). *Cooperative learning.* San Juan Capistrano, CA: Resources for Teachers.

Kendall, P., and Braswell, L. (1982). Cognitive-behavioral self-control therapy for children: A component analysis. *Journal of Consulting and Clinical Psychology, 50,* 672–689.

Keystone Area Education Agency. (1990). *The Dubuque management system.* Dubuque, IA: Dubuque Community Schools.

Koch, M., and Miller, S. (1987). Resolving student conflicts with student mediators. *Principal, 66,* 59–62.

Ladd, G., and Mize, J. (1983). A cognitive-social learning model of social skill training. *Psychological Review, 10*(2), 127–157.

Lang, D., and Stinson, B. (1988). *Lazy dogs and sleeping frogs.* LaCrosse, WI: Coulee Press.

Lovitt, C. (1987). Social skills training: Which ones and where to do it? *Journal of Reading, Writing and Learning Disabilities International, 3*(3), 213–221.

Mayo, P., Hirn, P., Gajewski, N., and Kafka, J. (1991). *Communicate junior.* Eau Claire, WI: Thinking Publications.

Mayo, P., and Waldo, P. (1987). *Scripting.* Eau Claire, WI: Thinking Publications.

Mayo, P., and Waldo, P. (1986). *Communicate.* Eau Claire, WI: Thinking Publications.

McGinnis, E., and Goldstein, A. (1990). *Skillstreaming in early childhood: Teaching prosocial skills to the preschool and kindergarten child.* Champaign, IL: Research Press.

McGinnis, E., Goldstein, A., Sprafkin, R., and Gershaw, N. (1984). *Skillstreaming the elementary school child: A guide for teaching prosocial skills.* Champaign, IL: Research Press.

McGinnis, E., Sauerbry, L., and Nichols, P. (1985). Skill-streaming: Teaching social skills to children with behavioral disorders. *Teaching Exceptional Children, 17,* 160–167.

Meichenbaum, D. (1977). *Cognitive-behavior modification: An integrative approach.* New York: Plenum Press.

Meichenbaum, D. (1991, July). *Cognitive behavior therapy with adults, adolescents, and children.* Workshop presented to educators. Egg Harbor, WI.

Neel, R. (1988). Classroom conversion kit: A teacher's guide to teaching social competency. *Severe Behavior Disorders Monograph, 11,* 25–31.

Northrup, J., Wood, R., and Clark, H. (1979). *Social skill development in children: Application of individual and group training.* Invited workshop, Association for Behavior Analysis, Presented at the Fifth Annual Convention, Dearborn, MI.

Putallaz, M., and Gottman, J. (1981). Social skills and group acceptance. In S. Asher and J. Gottman (Eds.), *The development of children's friendship.* New York: Cambridge University Press.

Readability Plus (1988). Rockville, MD: Scandinavian PC Systems.

Roff, M., and Sells, S. (1978). Juvenile delinquency in relation to peer acceptance, rejection, and socioeconomic status. *Psychology in the Schools, 3,* 3–18.

Schumaker, J., and Hazel, J. (1984). Social skills assessment and training for the learning disabled: Who's on first and what's on second? Part I. *Journal of Learning Disabilities, 17*(7), 422–431.

Stokes, T., and Baer, D. (1977). An implicit technology of generalization. *Journal of Applied Behavior Analysis, 10,* 349–369.

Taylor, O. (1993). *Clinical practice as a social occasion: An ethnographic model.* Manuscript submitted for publication, Howard University, Washington, DC.

Turkewitz, H., O'Leary, K., and Ironsmith, M. (1975). Generalization and maintenance of appropriate behavior through self-control. *Journal of Consulting and Clinical Psychology, 43,* 577–583.

COOPERATIVE LEARNING RESOURCES

Blueprints for Thinking in the Cooperative Classroom (1990) by J. Bellanca and R. Fogarty. (Skylight Publishing, Inc., 200 E. Wood Street, Palatine, IL 60067; 1-800-922-4474)

Circles of Learning: Cooperation in the Classroom (3rd ed.) (1990) by D. Johnson, R. Johnson., and E. Johnson Holubec. (Interaction Book Company, 7208 Cornelia Drive, Edina, MN 55435; 1-612-831-9500)

Our Cooperative Classroom (1988) by D. Johnson, R. Johnson, L. Johnson, and J. Bartlett. (Interaction Book Company, 7208 Cornelia Drive, Edina, MN 55435; 1-612-831-9500)

Cooperative Learning (1992) by S. Kagan. (Resources for Teachers, 27128 Paseo Espada, Suite 622, San Juan Capistrano, CA 92675; 1-800-933-2667)

Cooperative Learning, Cooperative Lives: A Sourcebook of Learning Activities for Building a Peaceful World (1987) by N. Schniedewind and E. Davidson. (Brown Publishing ROA Media, 2460 Kerper Blvd., Dubuque, IA 52001; 1-800-922-7696)

Cooperative Learning Lessons for Little Ones: Literature Based Lessons (1990) by L. Curran and S. Kagan. (Resources for Teachers, 27128 Paseo Espada, Suite 622, San Juan Capistrano, CA 92675; 1-800-933-2667)

The Cooperative Sports and Games Book (1978) by T. Orlick. (Pantheon Books, 400 Hahn Road, Westminster, MD 21157; 1-800-733-3000)

The Cooperative Think Tank: Practical Techniques to Teach Thinking in the Cooperative Classroom (1990) by J. Bellanca. (Skylight Publishing, Inc., 200 E. Wood Street, Palatine, IL 60067; 1-800-922-4474)

The Cooperative Think Tank II: More Graphic Organizers to Teach Thinking in the Cooperative Classroom (1992) by J. Bellanca. (Skylight Publishing, Inc., 200 E. Wood Street, Palatine, IL 60067; 1-800-922-4474)

A Guidebook for Cooperative Learning: A Technique for Creating More Effective Schools (1984) by D. Dishon and P. Wilson-O'Leary. (Learning Publications, Inc., P.O. Box 1338, Holmes Beach, FL 34218; 1-800-222-1525)

Kids Can Cooperate: A Practical Guide to Teaching Problem Solving (1984) by E. Crary. (Parenting Press, Inc., 11065 5th Avenue, N.E. Suite F, Seattle, WA 98125; 1-800-922-6657)

Learning to Cooperate, Cooperating to Learn (1985) by R. Slavin, S. Sharan, S. Kagan, R. Hertz-Lazarowitz, and C. Webb, (Eds.). (Plenum Press, 233 Spring Street, New York, NY 10013; 1-800-221-9369)

The Nurturing Classroom (1989) by M. McCabe and J. Rhoades. (ITA Publications, 1500 W. El Camino, Suite 350, Sacramento, CA 95833; 1-916-922-1615)

Tools for the Cooperative Classroom (1990) by M. Archibald Marcus and P. McDonald. (Skylight Publishing, Inc., 200 East Wood Street, Palatine, IL 60067; 1-800-922-4474)

Tribes: A Process for Social Development and Cooperative Learning (1987) by J. Gibbs. (Center Source Publications, 305 Tesconi Circle, Santa Rosa, CA 954011; 707-577-8233)

Cognitive Planning

UNIT GOAL:

To demonstrate comprehension and use of a cognitive planning strategy called STOP, PLOT, GO, SO (a strategy that enables students to think about their behavior and its consequences before, during, and after initiating it)

EDUCATOR INFORMATION:

Cognitive planning is one of the six components involved in the instruction of social skills (see pages 21–23). These cognitive planning lessons have been provided to assist the educator in teaching the four steps of cognitive planning: STOP, PLOT, GO, SO. Within this unit, the class is instructed to construct the town of Socialville so that the *Social Star* characters might seem more realistic for students.

RELATED ACTIVITIES:

1. Ask students to run for a short time so they can practice one of the self-control strategies from the STOP step while their bodies experience the physical symptoms associated with anger (e.g., increased heart rate, heavy breathing, sweaty skin). Teach students that these are body cues that warn them of angry feelings.
2. Teach students how to do progressive relaxation (see *Appendix M*).
3. Discuss additional strategies for reducing stress (e.g., exercising, eating properly). Explain that having a high stress level can make self-control difficult to maintain.
4. Use the *Secret Formula Pages* (see *Appendix N*) to transfer use of STOP, PLOT, GO, SO to other areas of the students' lives (e.g., at home, with friends). Model the use of these pages. The page with four stars at the top is written in the present tense (e.g., "I can stay calm by..."), while the page with eight stars is written in the past tense (e.g., "I stayed calm by..."). Encourage students to use these pages to think about problems they may be facing or goals they may wish to set.
5. Inform parents of the secret formula strategy. Encourage parents to use the *Secret Formula Pages* with their children at home.
6. Discuss how the STOP, PLOT, GO, SO steps can work for academic subjects (e.g., to solve a math problem). Also, discuss how the STOP, PLOT, GO, SO steps can work for goal setting (e.g., a student could accomplish the goal of earning money to buy something special).
7. Have students work in pairs to write a story about someone using the problem-solving strategy of STOP, PLOT, GO, SO.

Lesson A

OBJECTIVE:

To be introduced to the characters in Socialville

MATERIALS:

1. Characters from Socialville (See *Appendix F*; enlarge, color, glue on tagboard, and laminate each character for use within this and other units from *Social Star.*)
2. *Socialville and the Social Star Club* (See pages 59–64; enlarge, color, and laminate, if desired, one copy of the story for educator use; as an alternative, duplicate one copy per student and let each one color the illustrations.)
3. Buildings from Socialville (See *Appendix E*; enlarge one copy of each building.)
4. Markers or crayons for each student

PREPARATORY SET:

Have students sit in a circle. Tell them to close their eyes and put their hands behind their backs. Give each student a Socialville character. (There are 17 characters. Depending on the group size, students may need to have more than one character or students may need to share a character.) Have students open their eyes and look at their Socialville character(s). Tell students they will be showing their character(s) during a story. For older students, the educator may wish to pass out characters and have students tell if the characters remind them of someone they know and/or guess what each character's personality is like.

PLAN:

1. Read *Socialville and the Social Star Club* to students. Stop to interact directly with students when a star appears in the story. As individual characters are introduced, have the student holding that character stand and show the character.
2. After reading the story, discuss the word "social." Webster defines *social* as:

   a. Marked by or passed in pleasant companionship with one's friends or associates b. Relating to human society, the interaction of the individual and the group, or the welfare of human beings as members of society c. Tending to form cooperative and interdependent relationships with one's fellows.

A definition of *social* for students might be "getting along with other people." Explain that a large amount of our time is spent in social situations.

3. Process this information by asking students the following questions:

   - Did any of the families in Socialville remind you of your family?
   - Are there any people from Socialville that you want to get to know better?
   - What thoughts do you have about their Social Star Club?

4. Tell students that they will be creating a town in which the Socialville characters will live. Distribute the markers or crayons and an enlarged building to each student. (There are nine buildings. Depending on group size, students may need to have more than one building, or students may need to share a building.) Ask students to help construct Socialville by coloring their building(s). After the buildings have been colored, they could be displayed on a bulletin board or propped up in a three-dimensional manner on a table. Roads, trees, etc. can be added as desired. Socialville can be the setting when putting on skits with the characters. Socialville characters can be stored in Socialville and students can be asked to get various characters when needed. The use of Socialville will help make the characters more realistic to students.

Lesson B

OBJECTIVE:

To practice the STOP step of the cognitive planning strategy called STOP, PLOT, GO, SO (The STOP step involves staying calm and using self-control.)

MATERIALS:

1. *STOP: Secret Formula Part 1* (See pages 65–71; enlarge, color, and laminate, if desired, one copy of the story for educator use; as an alternative, duplicate one copy per student and let each one color the illustrations.)
2. Bubble solution, a bubble blower, a soup spoon, and a bowl of water (To be used while reading the story during step 2 below.)
3. *Cognitive Planning Formula* chart (See page 12.)
4. Paper and color markers, pencils, or crayons
5. *Thought Bubble* (See *Appendix O;* one cut out for educator use.)

PREPARATORY SET:

Tell students, "I'm going to pretend to be a student in class. The teacher is handing back my corrected spelling test. Watch how I react when I get my test back and find out I got a low grade." During your role play, become upset and respond in an out-of-control manner (e.g., pouting, ripping up the test, saying, "I hate school"). Afterwards, discuss with the class how you looked when you were out of control. Review some of the problems associated with losing control (e.g., you can hurt other people's feelings; you feel embarrassed afterwards).

PLAN:

1. Remind students of the "Social Star Club" to which the Socialville students belong. Tell students you will be reading a story about a secret formula that will help them find a solution to the problem of losing control discussed previously.
2. Read *STOP: Secret Formula Part 1* to the class. Stop to interact directly with students when a star appears in the story. (When the story asks students to practice breathing as if they are blowing bubbles or blowing on a hot spoon of soup, model first for the students using the props listed in the Materials section.)

3. Show the *Cognitive Planning Formula* chart and tell students it will be displayed in the classroom to remind them of the importance of the four steps.

4. Process this information by asking students the following questions:

- Think about a time recently when you were angry. What did you do?
- Which "STOP" strategy for calming down do you like best?
- Have you ever seen your mom, dad, brother, or sister using any of these strategies? Which ones?
- Why is it important to calm down when you're upset?

5. Point to the first stoplight symbol on the *Cognitive Planning Formula* chart. For younger students, tell them they will hear a story about the stoplight called "Sammy Stoplight." Give them paper and color markers (or pencils or crayons) and tell them to draw a picture of "Sammy Stoplight." Explain how the stoplight on the *Cognitive Planning Formula* chart might be envisioned to grow arms and legs.

For older students, tell them they will hear a story called "Sam and the Stoplight." Give them paper and color markers (or pencils or crayons) and tell them to draw a picture of Sam, who is a boy their age. They could also include a *Thought Bubble* with a stoplight drawn inside since the story will have Sam thinking about the stoplight.

6. Read one of the stories below, depending on the age of the students.

Sammy Stoplight
(For Younger Children)

Point to the first stoplight symbol on the *Cognitive Planning Formula* chart. Tell students you will be reading a story about Sammy Stoplight. Have them look at their pictures of Sammy Stoplight while you are reading. The story follows:

Sammy Stoplight is going to Traffic School. Sammy really wants to graduate and become a stoplight at one of the intersections in town. One day, Sammy was having trouble learning a few of the traffic rules. Some of the other stoplights teased Sammy about it. Sammy lost control and broke their lights. Afterwards, Sammy felt embarrassed about losing control and sorry about hurting the others. On his way home, Sammy stopped at a very busy intersection to talk with a wise old stoplight named Sir Sidney. After hearing about Sammy's problem, Sir Sidney Stoplight said, "You already have the solution to your problem. You're just not using it." "I do? What is it?" Sammy asked. Sir Sidney said, "At traffic school, you're learning how and when to flash your red light on the outside so traffic knows when to stop. Well, you can also flash your red light on the inside, so only you can see it. When you have a problem and feel upset, flash your red light on the inside and think 'Stop—stay calm!' You're a smart stoplight, Sammy. If you stay calm, you can think of a good way to solve any problem." Sammy was eager to try the inside red light idea. The next day in school when Sammy was feeling frustrated, Sir Sidney's idea came to mind. Sammy tried it and it worked! Sammy started using the inside red light idea more each day. It helped Sammy use self-control and stay calm. Sammy Stoplight felt very proud!

Tell students that Sammy Stoplight can be either a girl or a boy because both girls and boys need to use self-control. Tell students that whenever they feel upset or frustrated, they can think of Sammy Stoplight. They can picture a stoplight in their minds. This will help them to stop so they can use one or more of the self-control strategies mentioned in the story about the Social Star Club.

Sam and the Stoplight
(For Older Children)

Point to the first stoplight symbol on the *Cognitive Planning Formula* chart. Tell students that you will be telling them a story about a boy named "Sam." The story follows:

One day when Sam was at school, he was having problems in gym class. He felt really frustrated. Some of the other kids teased Sam. Sam lost control and got into a fight with the kids. Afterwards, Sam felt embarrassed about losing control and sorry about hurting the others. On his way home from school, Sam stopped at his grandfather's house. After hearing about Sam's problem, his grandfather said, "Sam, when I'm driving in my car and I come to a signal with a red light, I know that I'm coming to a dangerous intersection. I need to STOP my car. If I don't stop, bad things could happen." Sam couldn't figure out why his grandpa was talking about driving his car. "Grandpa, what does that have to do with my problem at school?" Sam asked. Sam's grandpa said, "Well, Sam, you can use a stoplight in your head. When the red light flashes, it means, 'Stop, dangerous situation.' When you feel angry, picture a stoplight and say to yourself, 'I need to get calm. If I don't stop, something bad might happen.' " Sam's grandpa continued, "You're a smart kid, Sam. If you stop, you can stay calm and you can think of ways to solve any problem." Sam thanked his grandpa. He was eager to try the stoplight idea. The next day in school when Sam was feeling frustrated, the stoplight idea came to mind. Sam tried it and it worked. Sam started using the stoplight idea more each day. It helped Sam use self-control and stay calm. Sam felt very proud.

Tell students that all people need to use self-control. Tell students that whenever they feel upset or frustrated, they can picture a stoplight in their minds. This will help them to stop so they can use one or more of the self-control strategies mentioned in the story about the Social Star Club.

7. Model use of the cue word "stoplight" while thinking aloud. A scripted example follows:

Introduction

I am going to pretend that someone took my favorite pencil off my desk without asking. I will show you how I stop to stay calm and tell you the thoughts I'm having. When I hold up this Thought Bubble, *you'll know the words I'm saying are actually what I'm thinking.*

Actual Model

Where is my pencil? Oh, no, it's gone. I can't believe this. I am so angry! While holding up the *Thought Bubble* say, *Stoplight! OK, stay calm. Just calm down. I'll take a deep breath. I have to think of a good way to get my pencil back.*

8. Tell students that if they see someone else from their class getting frustrated or angry, they can remind the student to stay calm by quietly saying "Stoplight" to that person. When they see a classmate successfully staying calm in a difficult situation, they can also give a compliment by saying, "Good job using stoplight!"

9. Conclude the lesson by asking students to write a letter to Sammy Stoplight (or to Sam for older children). In the letter, students could say they are proud that Sammy (Sam) is using the inside red light (or stoplight) idea so successfully.

Lesson C

OBJECTIVE:

To practice the PLOT step of the cognitive planning strategy called STOP, PLOT, GO, SO (The PLOT step involves deciding what the problem is, brainstorming choices, thinking about consequences, deciding upon the best choice to use, and thinking about social skills to use.)

MATERIALS:

1. *Cognitive Planning Formula* chart (See page 12.)
2. *PLOT: Secret Formula Part 2* (See pages 72–76; enlarge, color, and laminate, if desired, one copy of the story for educator use; as an alternative, duplicate one copy per student and let each one color the illustrations.)

PREPARATORY SET:

Direct students' attention to the STOP step on the *Cognitive Planning Formula* chart and remind them about "Sammy Stoplight" (or "Sam and the Stoplight" for older children) and the inside red light idea. Read one of the following self-control scripts to students. Some students may have a difficult time seeing "pictures" in their heads. It may be helpful to provide them with a picture of the object to be visualized (e.g., a stoplight, the number "10") before they close their eyes so that they can visualize it more easily. (There will be additional opportunities during Lesson Z of each social skill unit to choose from and to use the scripts that follow.)

Self-Control Strategies

Script #1

When you have a problem, you need to stay in control so you can solve it. One way to stay calm is by using positive self-talk. That means you actually tell yourself to stay calm. Let's try it now. Pretend that you are being teased on the playground. First, tell yourself "stoplight" and picture a stoplight in your mind. Then tell yourself "Stay in control. Be calm. Think of a good way to solve this problem."

Script #2

When you are angry or upset, you need to be in control so you can think about how to solve your problem. When you are angry, you breathe faster. You need to slow your breathing down to stay calm. It helps to take a deep breath. Let's try it now. Pretend you are upset because something that's important to you got broken. First, tell yourself "stoplight" and picture a stoplight in your mind. Then breathe deeply and tell yourself to calm down. When you let the air out, pretend you are blowing bubbles or blowing on a spoon of hot soup.

Script #3

Have you ever been really angry at someone? When you feel yourself getting angry, you need to stay in control so that you don't do or say anything you'll feel bad about later. It might be helpful to put your hand over your mouth to stop yourself from saying something mean. Let's try that now. Pretend you are angry because a friend didn't keep a secret. First, tell yourself "stoplight" and picture a stoplight in your mind. Put your hand over your mouth before you say something mean.

Script #4

When you are frustrated about a problem, you need to help yourself stay in control. One way to give yourself time to stay in control is to count to 10. When you count to 10 you help your body relax so you can think clearly. Let's try that now. Pretend that you are frustrated with a homework assignment. First, tell yourself "stoplight" and picture a stoplight in your mind. Picture the number "10" in your head and count to 10. One, two, three, four, five, six, seven, eight, nine, ten. Take a deep breath.

Script #5

If you are disagreeing with a friend, you might help yourself calm down if you walk away. Let's try it now. First, tell yourself "stoplight" and picture a stoplight in your mind. Picture yourself walking away so you don't say or do something mean. It might be easier to calm down if you are away from the situation. After you have calmed down, you can go back and talk with your friend. Be careful, though. You might get in trouble if you walk away from a parent, teacher, or other adult.

Script #6

When you feel yourself getting upset, stay calm so you can think clearly. First, tell yourself "stoplight" and picture a stoplight in your mind. Now, think of a time when something funny happened to you and you couldn't stop laughing. When you do this, you should immediately feel less angry. This will help you stay calm so that you can solve your problem.

PLAN:

1. Tell students that they will be listening to a story about Mike and how he uses PLOT to solve a problem.

2. Read *PLOT: Secret Formula Part 2* to the class. Stop to interact directly with students when a star appears in the book.

3. After reading the story, direct students' attention to the *Cognitive Planning Formula* chart and review the five steps to PLOT. (PLOT is the most complex component of the cognitive planning strategy because it involves five steps.)

4. Lead students to understand they have more than one choice in most situations. Some students tend to view themselves as having only one choice and, unfortunately, their choice may be a negative one (e.g., when Billy is teased, he may feel that his only choice is to be physically aggressive).

   Ask students to work in pairs to brainstorm at least three choices they could make in each of the following problem situations:

   - You are told to bring a sack lunch for a field trip and you forget to bring one.
   - You spill your milk all over your pants during lunch at school.
   - Your neighbor compliments you on your bike safety and you're not sure what to say or do.
   - You are walking on the sidewalk and an older kid purposely bumps into you.

   Ask each pair to share one of their choices for each situation and record ideas where everyone can see them. Discuss possible consequences for a few of the choices listed.

5. Process the information provided in the story by asking the following questions:

   - Why is it important to know what your problem is?
   - Why is it helpful to brainstorm choices?
   - Why would you want to think ahead about what might happen after each of your choices?
   - How can you tell what your best choice is?
   - Why should you think about social skills when you go ahead and use your best choice?
   - Have you ever had a problem that you had to think about? What strategies did you use to solve your problem?
   - How do you think PLOT could help with a problem you might have?

Lesson D

OBJECTIVE:

To practice the GO step of the cognitive planning strategy called STOP, PLOT, GO, SO (The GO step means putting a plan into action.)

MATERIALS:

1. *Cognitive Planning Formula* chart (See page 12.)
2. *GO: Secret Formula Part 3* (See pages 77–79; enlarge, color, and laminate, if desired, one copy of the story for educator use; as an alternative, duplicate one copy per student and let each one color the illustrations.)
3. *Thought Bubble* (See *Appendix O;* one per pair of students.)

PREPARATORY SET:

Direct students' attention to the *Cognitive Planning Formula* chart and quickly review the STOP and PLOT steps. (Mention "Sammy Stoplight" or "Sam and the Stoplight" and the inside red light idea.) Remind students that they have a variety of choices for any given situation.

PLAN:

1. Tell students that they will be listening to a story about Mike and how he uses the GO step.
2. Read *GO: Secret Formula Part 3* to students.
3. Discuss why it is sometimes difficult to carry out the GO step (e.g., too scared, too embarrassed, it feels strange) even when one has decided on the best choice.
4. Process the information provided in the story by asking students the following questions:
   - Have you ever thought of a good idea, but had a difficult time actually doing it?
   - What are some things you can say to yourself so that you carry out your plan?
5. Read the following situation:

   One day after school, Mike saw a student throw a rock and break a school window. Mike thought "stoplight" and pictured a stoplight in his head. He stayed calm and thought about the choices he had. He decided that his best choice was to tell his teacher about what he saw. The next day, Mike got stuck on the GO step from the secret formula. When it was time to carry out his plan, he was having a difficult time actually telling his teacher.

6. Discuss why Mike might have had a difficult time with the GO step (e.g., he's afraid the other student might find out he told; he's afraid people will call him a tattletale).

7. Pair students (see *Appendix P*). Distribute a *Thought Bubble* to each pair. Ask students to work with their partners to write self-talk in their *Thought Bubbles* that Mike could have used to put his plan into action.

Lesson E

OBJECTIVES:

1. To practice the SO step of the cognitive planning strategy called STOP, PLOT, GO, SO (The SO step means asking yourself, "So, how did my plan work?")
2. To review the four steps of cognitive planning during a game activity

MATERIALS:

1. *Cognitive Planning Formula* chart (See page 12.)
2. *SO: Secret Formula Part 4* (See pages 80–87; enlarge, color, and laminate, if desired, one copy of the story for educator use; as an alternative, duplicate one copy per student and let each one color the illustrations.)
3. *Cue Cards* (See page 56; one set cut apart.)
4. *Problem Situations* (See page 57; one set cut apart.)
5. *Score Card* (See page 58; one per student.)

PREPARATORY SET:

Students need to internalize the phrase STOP, PLOT, GO, SO so when they are actually in a problem situation, they can recall the steps. The "Beat the Clock" activities that follow review the phrase. Choose one or more to try. (There will be additional opportunities to use these activities during Lesson Z of each social skill unit.)

Beat the Clock Activities

- Have students stay seated. Go around the room in round robin fashion and have each person say in order one of the words STOP, PLOT, GO, SO. See how many times they can go around the room in one minute.
- Have students say STOP, PLOT, GO, SO quietly to themselves. Each time students finish saying the phrase, they should put a tally mark on a piece of paper. Students could see how many times they can say the words in 30 seconds.
- Have students form small groups and stand in lines facing the front of the room. When the educator says "begin," the first student from each group writes STOP on the chalkboard, runs back, and stands at the back of the line. The next member of the small group then runs up and writes PLOT on the chalkboard, and so on in relay fashion. See how many complete phrases each group can write in two minutes.

- Have students form a circle and then pass a ball around the circle. The first person starts out saying STOP and then passes the ball to the next person who says PLOT, etc. The group tries to pass the ball around the entire circle as many times as they can in one minute.

PLAN:

1. Read *SO: Secret Formula Part 4* to students. Stop to interact directly with students when a star appears in the story.
2. After reading the story, process the information provided by asking students the following questions:
   - Do you ever think about things after you do them? Why might it be a good idea to do this?
   - Have you ever heard the saying "Learn from your mistakes"? What does this have to do with the SO step?
   - Why is it important to tell yourself you've done a good job when you do something right?
3. Present students with the following list of reasons a person's plan may not work. Encourage students to add to the list.
   - Didn't stay calm and in control
   - Didn't use an appropriate tone of voice during GO
   - Didn't choose an appropriate time and place for GO
   - Didn't think about the possible consequences of a choice

   The list can be displayed and added to as new reasons come to mind.
4. Model phrases the students can use to praise themselves when things have gone well. Make the model exciting and somewhat exaggerated (e.g., "Hey, way to go. I did an absolutely fantastic job talking with Mr. Bill! Marvelous!").
5. Ask students to participate in several activities at which they can be successful (e.g., jumping rope, skipping around the room, drawing 10 circles). After each activity, invite students to praise themselves. Tell them that for now you'd like them to praise themselves aloud but that normally they would do it quietly inside of their heads.
6. Tell students they will be playing a game of "Problem-Solving Softball" to practice using the STOP, PLOT, GO, SO steps.
7. Ask for six volunteers to fill the following positions: batter, pitcher, first base player, second base player, third base player, and catcher. Have the volunteers stand in an actual softball formation. All volunteers, except for the batter, will be asked to read from *Cue Cards*. The educator may need to assist with the reading.

- Give the stack of *Problem Situations* to the pitcher.
- Give Cue Card #1 to the first base player.
- Give Cue Card #2 to the second base player.
- Give Cue Card #3 to the third base player.
- Give Cue Card #4 to the catcher.

Explain that to score a run for the class, the batter must correctly follow the secret formula to solve a problem which will be described by the pitcher.

8. Distribute *Score Cards* to the remaining students. Explain that they are the fans.

9. The pitcher draws one of the *Problem Situations* and reads it aloud to the batter. The batter waits to advance to first base.

10. The first base player reads the "STOP means..." statement and any one of the four instructions printed on Cue Card #1 to the batter. If the batter is unable to follow the instruction, other members from the class may offer help or suggestions. The batter must, however, answer in his or her own words or actions after receiving help. After the batter has followed the instruction, the fans write a "1" on the first base of their *Score Cards* (indicating that batter #1 completed that step) while the batter advances to first base.

11. The second base player reads the "PLOT means..." statement and asks the batter all four questions (one at a time) printed on Cue Card #2. After the batter has answered all four questions, the fans write a "1" on the second base of their *Score Cards* while the batter advances to second base.

12. The third base player reads the "GO means..." statement and the instruction printed on Cue Card #3 to the batter. After the batter has followed the instruction, the fans write a "1" on the third base of their *Score Cards* while the batter advances to third base.

13. The catcher reads the "SO means..." statement and asks the batter both questions (one at a time) printed on Cue Card #4. After the batter has answered the questions, the fans write a "1" on the home plate of their *Score Cards* while the batter advances to home base.

14. Depending on class size, participants can be asked to rotate positions, or six new volunteers can take the positions described in step 7. For smaller groups, the educator can take the role of several positions.

15. The pitcher reads a new problem situation to the second batter, and play proceeds in the same manner as above, only fans write a "2" on their *Score Cards*.

16. Continue the activity until everyone in the group has had a chance to play one or more "parts" in the softball game. The educator may wish to continue this activity during the next class session. In addition, students may wish to develop their own problem situations for use in the game.

CUE CARDS

Cue Card #1

STOP: Secret Formula Part 1

STOP means stay calm and use self-control.

What can you say to tell yourself to stop and stay calm?

-or-

Show how to take slow deep breaths to stay calm.

-or-

Show how to count to 10 to stay calm.

-or-

Show how to put your hand over your mouth to stay calm.

Go to First Base.

Cue Card #2

PLOT: Secret Formula Part 2

PLOT means you plan how to solve your problem.

What is your problem?

-then-

What are at least two choices you have?

-then-

What might happen after each choice?

-then-

Which choice do you think will work best?

Go to Second Base.

Cue Card #3

GO: Secret Formula Part 3

GO means go ahead and do what you decided to do.

Tell what you can say to get yourself to go ahead and do what you decided to do.

Go to Third Base.

Cue Card #4

SO: Secret Formula Part 4

SO means you ask yourself, "So, how did my plan work?"

Pretend your plan worked well. What can you say to praise yourself?

-then-

Pretend your plan didn't work well. What should you do?

Good Job! Go to Home Plate. You scored 1 run.

PROBLEM SITUATIONS

Problem Situation #1

You are told to bring a sack lunch for a field trip and forget to bring one.

Start the secret formula now.

Problem Situation #2

You spill your milk all over your pants during lunch at school.

Start the secret formula now.

Problem Situation #3

Your neighbor compliments you on your bike safety and you're not sure what to say or do.

Start the secret formula now.

Problem Situation #4

You are walking on the sidewalk and an older kid purposely bumps into you.

Start the secret formula now.

Name ____________________

SCORE CARD

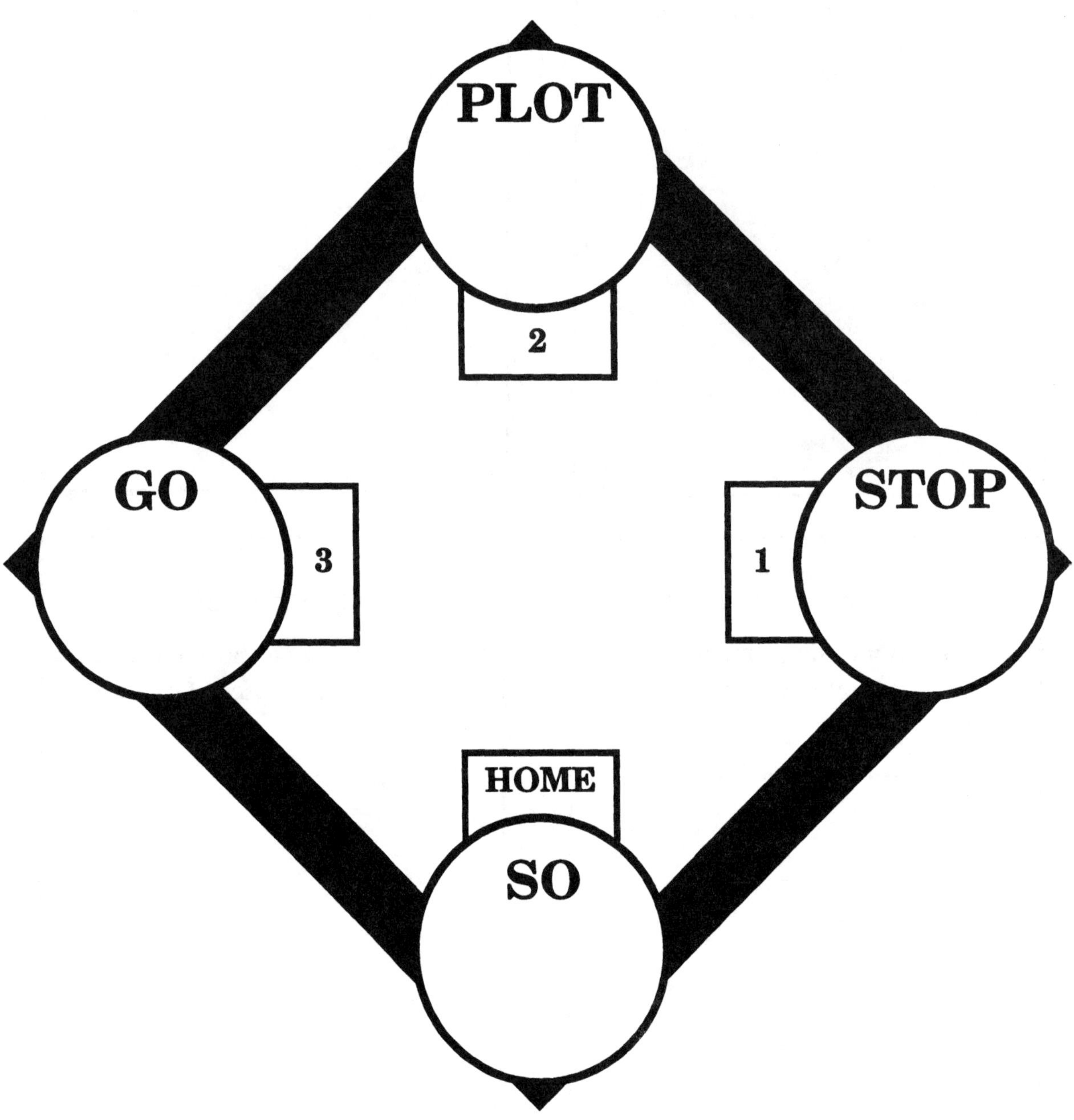

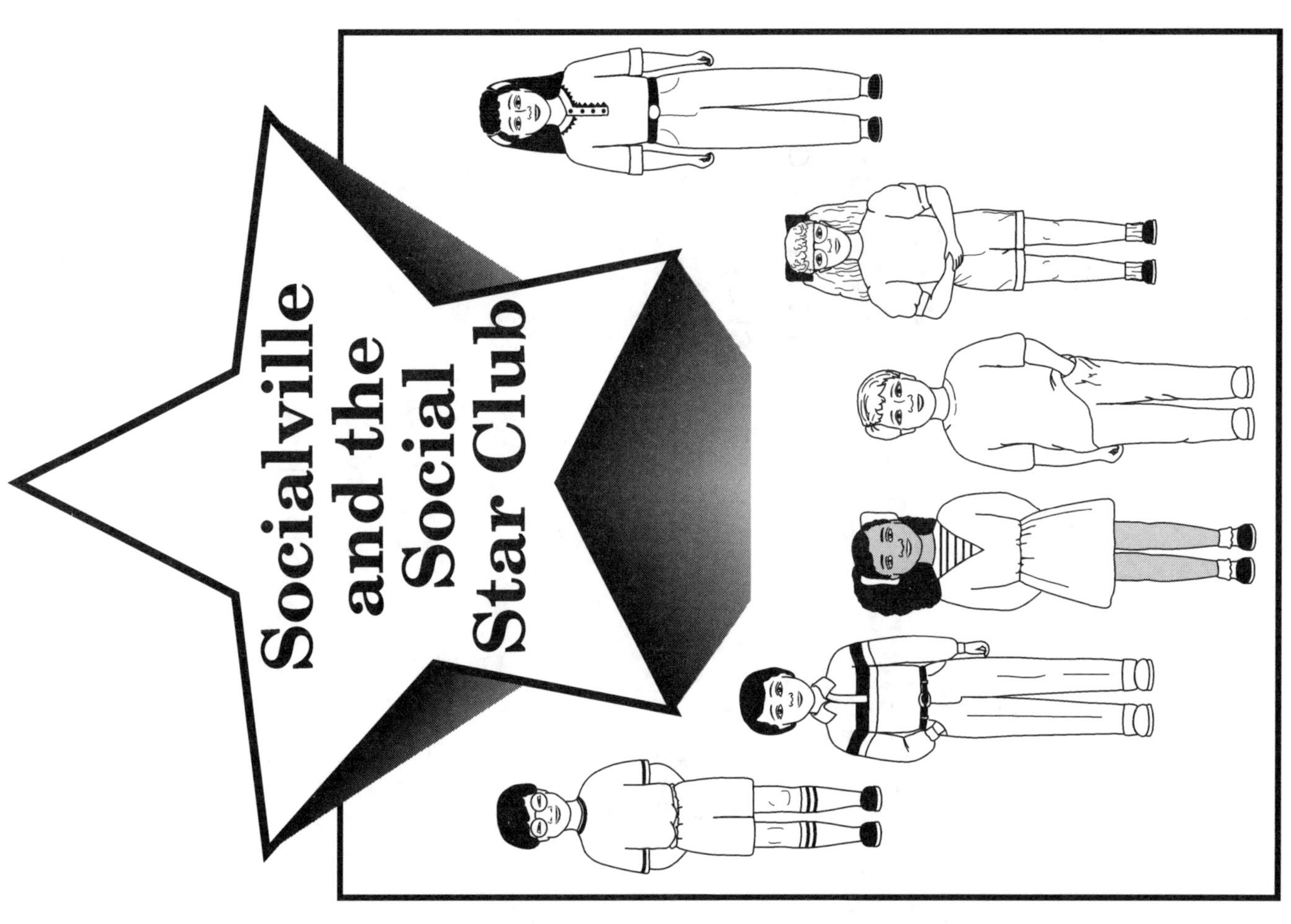
Socialville
and the
Social
Star Club

Hi!
I'm Lee Vue.
I live in Socialville
and I go to McKinley
School. I want you
to meet some friends
who go to school
with me.
2
Hi!
We're friends
of Lee. My name
is Ann Olson
and this is my
brother
Mike.
Hi!
Nice to
meet you.
We live
with our
mom and
stepdad.
3

Hello! I'm Mrs. Jackson. I'm Mike and Ann's mom.
And I'm Mr. Jackson. We're happy to meet you!
Our mom works at the Good Meals— Good Manners Restaurant. Our stepdad works at the Get Along Toy Factory. He works with Mr. Parra, Maria and Victor's dad. You'll meet them next.
4
Hello! Nice to meet you! I'm Mr. Parra. This is my wife, Mrs. Parra, and these are our children, Victor and Maria. We enjoy living in Socialville, because everyone always gets along.
5

Well,
Mr. Parra's not
totally right! We don't
always get along, but we do our
best! Mr. Parra is nice and so is
Mrs. Parra! Actually, I call her
Dr. Parra, because she's my doctor. She
works at the Helping Hands Clinic.
Next, I'd like you to meet
the Walkers.

6

7

I bet you've been wondering about my family! This is my dad. He builds great houses! And this is my grandmother. She lives with my dad and me. She is a cook at our school. The kids at school really like her!
8
The six of us have joined a club at school called the Social Star Club. Our teachers, Ms. Hess, Mr. Aaron, and Mrs. Marrero, are the club advisors. Can you guess what we talk about in our club?☆
9

Those were good guesses! In our club, we learn how to get along better with other people so our school, our town, and our whole world can be better! We talk about using appropriate manners and having appropriate behavior. Can you think of some ways to get along with other people?☆

OUR CLUB

10

11

STOP:
Secret
Formula
Part 1

Hi, everybody!
Welcome to our
Social Star Club!
We talk about how to get along with other people. It's a lot of fun! We have a secret formula we use to help us solve problems. It's our problem-solving strategy!

14

It's called:

SECRET FORMULA

STOP

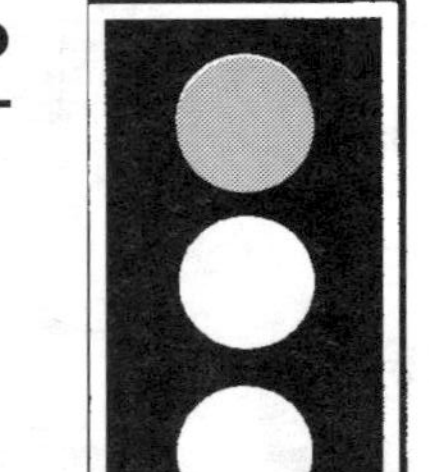

PLOT

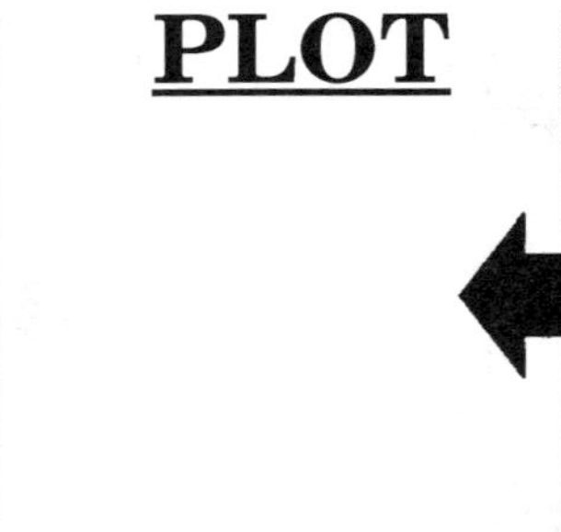

GO

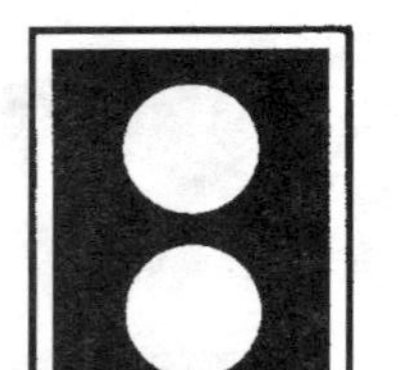

SO

Let's all say it:
STOP, PLOT, GO, SO....
STOP, PLOT, GO, SO....
It's kind of catchy!

15

STOP

means you STOP to stay calm and use self-control.

Do you know what *self-control* means?☆

Lots of things can happen if you don't STOP to stay calm and use self-control! It's not good to be out of control! It can be embarrassing and it can get you into trouble!

You could say something mean like...

I hate you!

Not a nice word to say

What other things might people do or say if they are out of control?☆

To stay calm, the first thing I do is tell myself to STOP and I think . . . Stay calm! That helps me stay in control so I don't do something crazy!
Hey! Why don't you try it now? Think, "STOP! Stay calm!"☆
18
My parents taught me how to take deep breaths to stay calm. It really works!
I breathe in deeply through my nose and I let the air out slowly through my mouth. I pretend I'm blowing bubbles or blowing on a spoon of hot soup. Try it a few times now.☆ Taking deep breaths helps me relax my whole body so I can stay in control and get along better with people—even my brother, Victor.
19

When I'm angry, I put my hand over my mouth to stop myself from saying something mean. It works great!
Pretend you're angry at your mom or dad. Quickly put your hand over your mouth so you don't say something mean. I'm so good at it now. I just picture myself putting my hand over my mouth and I stay calm.
20
Sometimes I feel angry if the teacher can't help me right away. To stay calm, I take a deep breath and think "10." Then I count up to 10 in my mind. By the time I get to 10, I've calmed down and I can wait for my turn with the teacher. Try it now! Think "10," then count.... ☆ Remember, you can take deep breaths while you count.
10
1 . . .
2 . . . 3 . . .
4 . . . 5 . . .
6 . . . 7 . . .
8 . . . 9 . . .
10
21

Sometimes, when I'm upset, I think "STOP." Then I walk away for awhile. If I'm angry at another kid and I feel like I'm going to lose control, I say, "I need to leave. I'm too mad to talk now." Then I walk away until I calm down. That way, I don't say or do something crazy.

Yes, it is also a good idea to tell the person that you're leaving or walking away to work on getting in control.

22

When I start to feel angry, I think of something funny and goofy, like a pig riding a bicycle. That makes me start to laugh!

I think of funny things, too. In the movie Mary Poppins, there's a part where these people keep laughing and laughing, and floating up in the air. It's so funny! As soon as I think of it, I get the giggles, even if I'm really angry.

When I get upset, I stick my finger in my ear and make a goofy face. I look kind of silly but it makes me and other people laugh and then we aren't angry with each other.

23

Hey,
those sound like
great ways to stay
calm when you're
angry. I'm going to
use those ideas
myself. Let's see . . .
you just gave me six
ideas. What were
some of those
ideas again?☆

24

To stay in control when you have a problem, you can:

1. Tell yourself to STOP and stay calm.
2. Take a deep breath and relax your body.
3. Put your hand over your mouth.
4. Think "10" and count to 10.
5. Walk away to calm down.
6. Think about something funny.

Can you think of other ways to STOP and stay calm?☆

Keep practicing these ideas and you'll get better at using them.

25

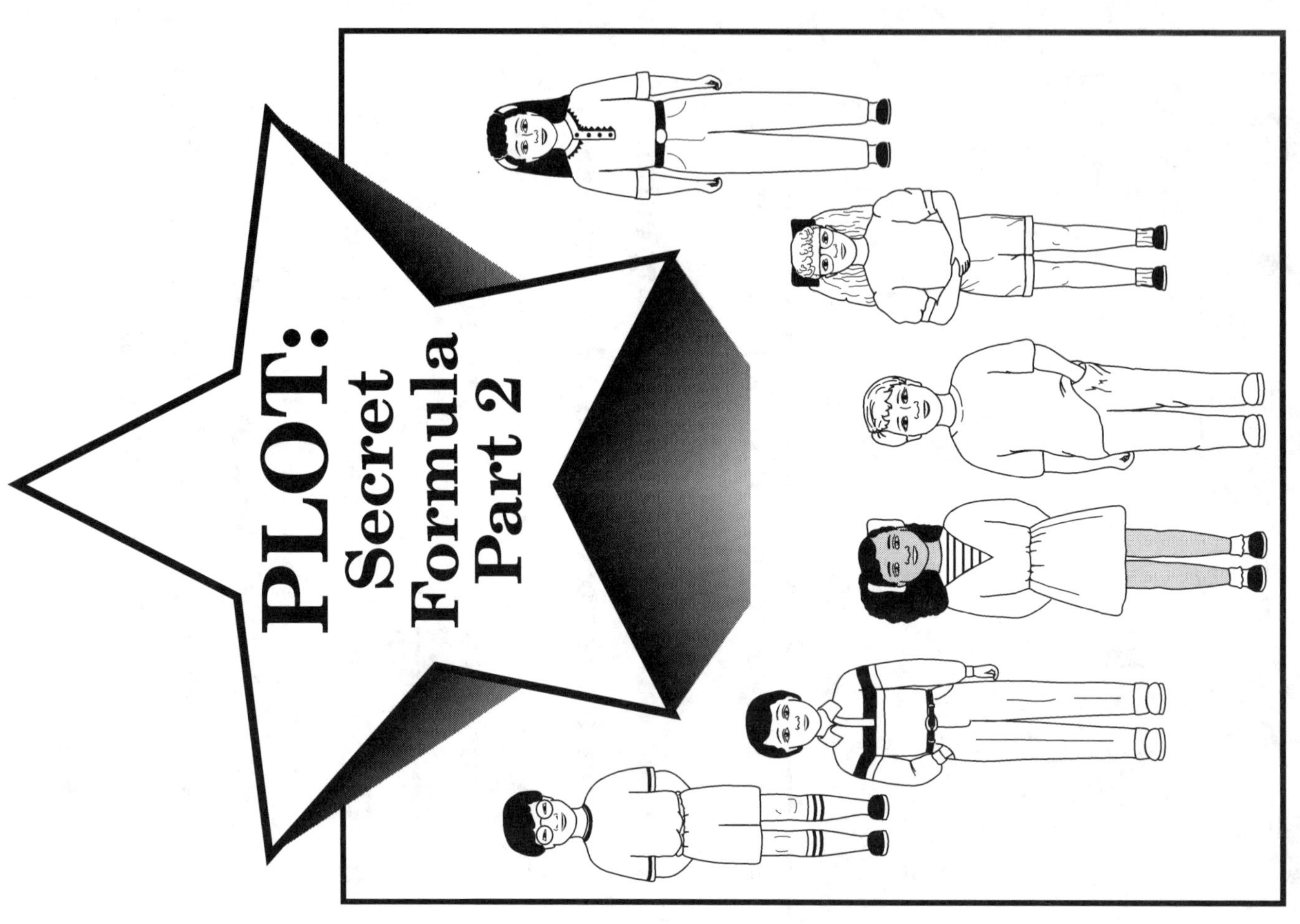
PLOT:
Secret
Formula
Part 2

Hi!
Our Social Star Club
has been busy practicing our
secret formula for solving problems.
We already told you about STOP.
(Remember, STOP means you should
tell yourself to stay calm.)
Now we're going to tell you
about PLOT!

STOP

PLOT

GO

SO

28

PLOT

means you plot a plan to solve your problem.

When you PLOT you:

1. **Decide exactly what your problem is.**
2. **Brainstorm the choices you have.**
3. **Think about what might happen after each of these choices (consequences).**
4. **Pick a choice you think will help solve the problem.**
5. **Think about the social skills you will need to use.**

This is the symbol for PLOT. It reminds me that when I have a problem, I can go in different directions. (I have different choices to solve the problem.)

29

To help you understand PLOT, I'd like to tell you about a problem Mike had.
Mike, you'll need to fix this paper before you can have free time!
Mike felt angry, but he reminded himself to STOP and stay calm.
STOP.... Stay calm.... I'll count to 10....
30
Mike knew he should use PLOT in this situation.
I used STOP to calm myself down. Now I have to PLOT.
PLOT
First, Mike decided exactly what his problem was.
What is my problem? I don't want to fix this paper, but I'd like to have free time.
31

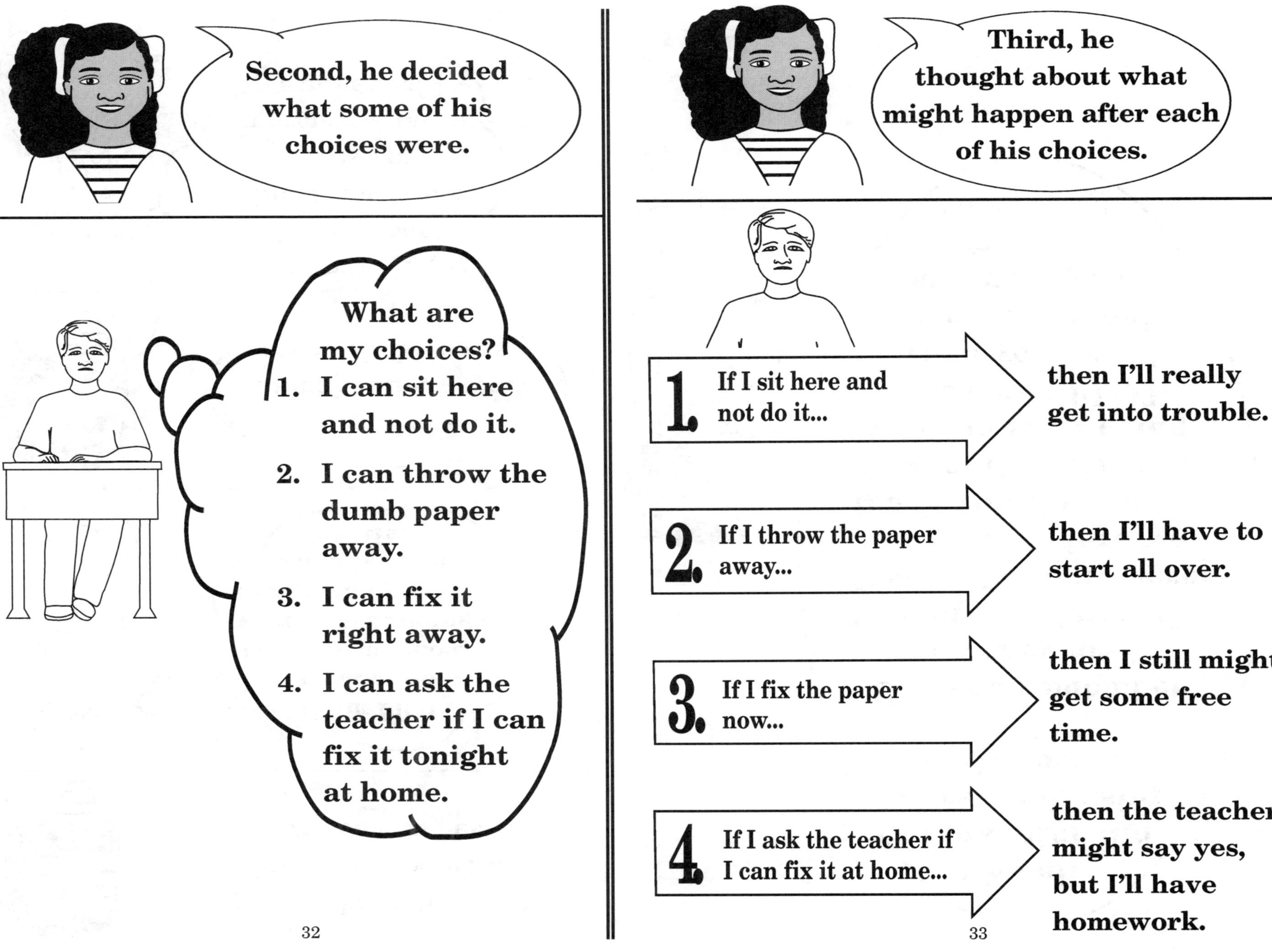
Second, he decided what some of his choices were.
What are my choices?
1. I can sit here and not do it.
2. I can throw the dumb paper away.
3. I can fix it right away.
4. I can ask the teacher if I can fix it tonight at home.
32
Third, he thought about what might happen after each of his choices.
1. If I sit here and not do it...
then I'll really get into trouble.
2. If I throw the paper away...
then I'll have to start all over.
3. If I fix the paper now...
then I still might get some free time.
4. If I ask the teacher if I can fix it at home...
then the teacher might say yes, but I'll have homework.
33

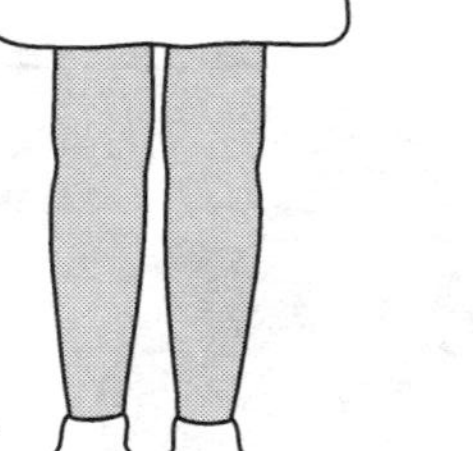
Fourth,
Mike decided which
choice was best.

I think I'll fix
the paper now.
Then I won't have to
worry about doing it
tonight. Maybe I can
still have some
free time.

Last, Mike
thought about what
social skills to use.

I won't pout
while I'm working.
I'll use an
appropriate facial
expression.

34

We all
think Mike did
a great job using
the five parts of
PLOT!
Can you remember
what they are?☆
You already know the
first half of our secret
formula. Before we
teach you the second
half of the formula,
you can start using
STOP and PLOT
when you are at
home, at school,
and with your
friends.
Good luck!

35

GO:
Secret
Formula
Part 3

Can you
remember our
secret formula? I can!
STOP, PLOT, GO, SO;
STOP, PLOT, GO, SO;
STOP, PLOT, GO!
I'm going to tell you about GO!
But first, let's review
STOP and PLOT.
STOP means you stay calm.
PLOT means you plan
what you will do.
38
GO
means you go ahead
and do what you
decided to do.
That's so
you don't just
think about it.
You actually
do it.
39

Remember when Ms. Hess asked me to fix my paper before I could have free time at school? I used STOP and told myself to calm down. I used PLOT and decided to fix my paper.
When I followed the GO step of the secret formula, I actually did what I decided to do. Here's a picture of me fixing my paper.
MATH
23 +16
+3
34 +7
14 +28
40
REMEMBER . . . GO means that you go ahead and carry out your plan. If you think it is going to be too hard, tell yourself, "I can do it!"
You only have one more part of the secret formula to learn. It's called SO. We'll talk about SO next time.
STOP
PLOT
GO
SO
41

SO:
Secret
Formula
Part 4

STOP PLOT GO SO

Hi! Let's all whisper our secret formula for solving problems five times....☆
Can you remember what STOP, PLOT, and GO mean?☆
Now we're going to tell you about the last step called SO.
Later you can come to an awards ceremony at our Social Star Club.

SO

means you ask yourself, "So, how did my plan work?"

A question mark is used for this step, because during SO, you ask yourself a question.

What question do you ask yourself?☆

46

Praising yourself means telling yourself you did a good job. You could say, "I did great solving my problem." What are some other things you could say to yourself when you make a plan that works well?☆

47

When I first learned about SO, I asked, "Why should I praise myself? Shouldn't I just wait for someone else to praise me for making a good plan?"
I like it when someone else praises me, but I found out I can't always count on other people to notice my good choice or to remember to praise me. I can count on myself though . . . and besides, it feels good when I say something nice to myself!
48
STOP, PLOT, GO, SO. SO is SO, SO, SO important!
It's time for the awards ceremony at our Social Star Club. Mike and Maria are receiving awards today, because they used the secret formula in a real-life situation. You'll find out how they used STOP, PLOT, GO, and SO.
49

Mike, you told us about using STOP, PLOT, and GO when Ms. Hess asked you to fix your paper before getting free time. Your plan was to fix your paper right away. Please tell us how you used SO in this situation.
When I asked myself, "So, how did my plan work?" I decided it worked great! I fixed my paper right away and still had a few minutes left for free time.
50
Excellent, Mike!
On behalf of the Social Star Club, we'd like to present you with this Social Super Star badge for successfully using the secret formula in your life.
Social Super Star
Mike
Olson
51

Maria,
can you tell us
how you used STOP,
PLOT, GO, and SO?
Sure!
Yesterday,
I was leaving to go
to Jolisa's house when my
mom told me to clean my
room first. During STOP, I
took three deep breaths.
When I PLOTTED, I decided
to ask if I could pick up my
room right away but wait
to dust and vacuum
until after I
got home.
52
During
GO, I went ahead
and asked my mom using
a nice tone of voice.
During SO, I decided my
choice worked well because
my mom said OK.
I told myself,
"Great job, Maria!"
Maria,
I'm glad you
praised yourself
during SO. Our Social
Star Club would like you
to keep this Social Super
Star badge as a
reminder of how well
you used STOP,
PLOT,
GO, and SO.
Social Super Star
53

That concludes our awards ceremony. Do you have anything you want to ask or talk about?

During the SO step, what if you decide your plan didn't work very well?

Good question, Jolisa! If you decide your plan didn't work very well, you may need to use STOP again so you don't get upset. When your choice doesn't work well, you need to decide what you'll do differently next time.

SO?

Plan went well → Praise

Plan didn't work well → What can I do differently next time?

54

One of my plans didn't work very well for me last week. I borrowed Lee's video game and accidentally broke it. I used the secret formula to solve the problem. During PLOT, I decided to keep telling Lee I left it at home. But then Lee said he would come over to my house to get it. My plan didn't work very well. I think I should have picked a different choice. I should have told the truth right away!

55

**STOP, PLOT, GO, SO
won't always work perfectly,
but don't give up using it. When your
choice doesn't work well, ask yourself
what you would do
differently next time.**

56

SECRET FORMULA

STOP

PLOT

GO

SO

STOP, PLOT, GO, SO....

**Use it when you're in a bind,
and hopefully you will find
that things are easier every day
when you pick the best to do and say!**

**Let's hear it for the
secret formula.**

***Hip, Hip,
Hooray!***

57

Eye Contact

UNIT GOAL:

To demonstrate comprehension and use of appropriate eye contact

EDUCATOR INFORMATION:

1. This unit teaches students that when they use eye contact (based on American common culture norms), they periodically look at the person they are talking with or listening to. This unit provides information about the possible consequences of using too much eye contact or not enough eye contact.

2. According to Althen (1988), there are significant cultural variations in norms for eye contact. He states that common culture Americans learn to distrust people who do not "look them in the eye" and that common culture Americans do not stare, unless sharing romantic feelings. They give eye contact when beginning to speak, then look away, and periodically look again while talking. When listening, however, common culture Americans look for longer periods of time, but still break eye contact occasionally. Asian Americans may avert direct eye contact and giggle when embarrassed, and Asian American children may stare at a stranger yet not maintain eye contact with their teachers (Cheng, 1987). Black Americans may have a preference for indirect eye contact during listening but direct eye contact during speaking as signs of attentiveness and respect (Taylor, 1993). Hispanic Americans may avoid direct eye contact as a sign of attentiveness and respect; sustained direct eye contact may be interpreted as a challenge to authority (Taylor, 1993). The educator should exert sensitivity and care in generalizing rules about eye contact into the children's home cultures.

RELATED ACTIVITIES:

1. Have students create interview questions about the use of eye contact. Students could then interview someone outside their class using the questions generated.

2. Have students write a story about "Never, Never Look Land" where people never look at each other. The story could address possible negative consequences of using inappropriate eye contact.

3. As a science extension, have students research the topic of "eyes."

4. Discuss situations when a student may not want to give eye contact to another person (e.g., ignoring someone who is doing something inappropriate).

5. Visit a home for the elderly, and practice using eye contact while meeting and visiting with the residents.

6. Have students write a poem, or compose lyrics about eye contact to a familiar melody. Examples follow:

   (Poem)

   Eye contact at home
   Eye contact at school
   Make this good choice
   You will look cool

   (Song—sung to the melody of "Row, Row, Row Your Boat")

   Look, look, look at me,
   Almost all the time.
   When you are listening
   When you are speaking
   Use your eye contact.

7. Invite adults from different cultures to talk to the students about how their cultures' conventions for eye contact compare with American common culture norms.

It is important for educators to provide opportunities for students to work in groups, so they can experience social skills in contexts where social communication is needed. Therefore, educators are encouraged to have students complete the Related Activities in small groups whenever possible. Educators trained in cooperative learning could incorporate the five components (see page 34) into the group activity.

RELATED LITERATURE:

Eat Up, Gemma (1988) by Sarah Hayes; Ill. by Jan Ormerod; Lothrop, Lee, and Shepard. (Picture book)

Gopher, Tanker and the Admiral (1984) by Shirley Climo, Crowell. (Text)
Christopher is forced to face terrible-tempered Admiral Clark when Tanker crashes a garbage can. (pages 3–7)

I Need a Lunch Box (1988) by Jeanette Caines, Ill. by Pat Cummings, Harper and Row. (Picture book)

One-Eyed Cat (1984) by Paula Fox, Bradbury. (Text)
Ned receives a gun and is afraid to look at his mother. (pages 47–49)

SOCIAL SKILLS ALL DAY LONG:

Look for opportunities to teach social skills throughout the day (incidental teaching). Four ways to reinforce good social skills and an example of each follow:

Encouragement

You are giving me excellent eye contact. That lets me know you are really listening. Great choice!

Personal Example

Yesterday we had parent-teacher conferences. I made sure I used appropriate eye contact with all the parents I spoke to.

Prompting

We've been invited to go to Mr. Wilson's classroom to watch his students put on a skit they wrote. Remember to give eye contact to the students performing the skit.

Corrective Feedback (must be positive, private, specific, and nonthreatening)

Jolisa, just now you were looking out the window while your other group members were talking about the group task. When you look at your other teammates and give them eye contact, they may feel more certain that you are a contributing member.

Lesson A

OBJECTIVES:

1. To state the meaning of *eye contact* and tell why it is important
2. To tell the self-talk associated with correct use of the skill

MATERIALS:

1. *Eye Contact* (See page 94; one per student and one transparency.)
2. *Thought Bubble* (See *Appendix O*; one for educator use.)
3. *Checking Myself* (See *Appendix I*; one per student and one transparency.)

PREPARATORY SET:

Pair students (see *Appendix P*). Ask the pairs to sit facing each other. Tell each pair to close their eyes and talk to one another about what they will do during recess. After students have talked briefly, ask them to respond to the question, "What thoughts did you have about not looking at each other while you talked?" These same pairs will work together during step 8 of this Plan.

PLAN:

1. Distribute and display *Eye Contact.* Discuss the definition. Explain the skill step and the symbol next to it. Remind students that the symbol is there to help them visualize and remember the skill step. Discuss the reasons for using eye contact.

2. Model use of the eye contact skill step while thinking aloud. A scripted example follows:

   Introduction

   I am going to pretend to be a student listening to a teacher. I will show you appropriate eye contact and tell you the thoughts I'm having. When I hold up this Thought Bubble, *you'll know the words I'm saying are actually what I'm thinking.*

   Actual Model

   While holding up the *Thought Bubble* say, *I want the teacher to know I'm paying attention. Am I looking at her? Yes, I'm using appropriate eye contact. The teacher will think I'm a good listener.*

3. Read the story at the bottom of *Eye Contact* aloud to students.

4. Distribute and display the discussion guideline sheet called *Checking Myself.* Ask students to complete the goal statement with the words "use eye contact," or use another classroom discussion goal more appropriate for your group (see page 26). Tell students that you will be having a discussion about the story they just heard. When a student is answering a question or making a comment during the discussion, it's important for everyone to give that student eye contact. Instruct them to put an "X" on their sheets each time they give eye contact to a student who is called on.

5. Model use of the *Checking Myself* sheet while thinking aloud. A scripted example follows:

Introduction

I am going to pretend to be one of you completing this sheet during the discussion we will be having. I will tell you the thoughts I'm having while I'm completing the sheet. When I hold up this Thought Bubble, *you'll know the words I'm saying are actually what I'm thinking.*

Actual Model

While holding up the *Thought Bubble* say, *OK, the teacher just called on Bill. I'd better give him eye contact so he knows I'm listening to his answer. I'll put an "X" on my sheet because I gave him eye contact.* Put the *Thought Bubble* down and mark an "X" on the overhead transparency.

During the discussion, periodically remind students to give eye contact to the student who is answering or commenting and to mark their discussion guideline sheets.

6. Proceed with the discussion by asking these questions: (The story may need to be reread first.)

- What did the girls do to have appropriate eye contact?
- How did Jolisa feel about Maria's eye contact?
- What might have happened if Maria had used inappropriate eye contact?

After the discussion, have students complete the bottom of *Checking Myself.*

7. Process use of the sheet by asking the following question or another one more appropriate for your group:

- Why do you think it's important to give eye contact to the person who is speaking during a discussion?

Process further by asking the students who volunteered to speak during the discussion to share their answers to the following question:

- You answered one of the questions during our discussion. How did you feel when the other students gave you eye contact while you were talking?

8. Ask student pairs to take turns telling each other the meaning of *eye contact* and why it's important to use the skill. Encourage students to use appropriate eye contact while completing this task. Students could be reminded that the information they are to say is printed on *Eye Contact.*

   As an option to add structure to this activity (see *Appendix Q*), ask partners to come to an agreement about which person will be called "John F. Kennedy" and which person will be called "Martin Luther King, Jr." After students have made their decisions, ask "Martin" to tell "John" the definition of *eye contact*. Next, ask "John" to tell "Martin" the definition. Ask the students to use the same procedure to tell each other the reasons for using appropriate eye contact.

9. Write the following where everyone can see it: I AM A SPECIAL PERSON! I CAN USE MY TALENTS TO GET ALONG WITH OTHERS. Have the students say this aloud, in unison, until they sound like they really mean it.

Name ____________________

Eye Contact

MEANING OF EYE CONTACT: Looking at others when you listen and talk

SKILL STEP:

1. Ask myself: Am I using appropriate eye contact?

REASONS FOR USING THIS SKILL:

Using eye contact helps you be a good listener and a good speaker. It helps you feel confident.

DIRECTIONS: Listen to the story below. Look at the picture of Jolisa and Maria while you are listening.

Jolisa felt sad because she lost a special ring. She told Maria about her problem. Both girls used appropriate eye contact during their conversation. Jolisa could tell Maria was listening. She felt Maria really cared.

Lesson B

OBJECTIVES:

1. To determine whether appropriate eye contact is used in given situations
2. To discuss the consequences of appropriate and inappropriate eye contact

MATERIALS:

1. *Animal Cards* (See *Appendix P.*)
2. *Eye Contact* classroom poster (See page 13.)
3. *Thought Bubble* (See *Appendix O*; one for educator use.)

PREPARATORY SET:

Pair students using the *Animal Cards*. These same pairs will work together during steps 2 and 8 of this Plan.

PLAN:

1. Review the definition and skill step for *eye contact* by referring the class to the *Eye Contact* classroom poster.
2. Ask student pairs to take turns telling each other the skill step for eye contact. Follow the procedure described in step 8 of Lesson A. (As an option, ask students to decide who will be "P.T. Barnum" and who will be "Walt Disney.") Next, ask students to work with their partners to think of a situation when the use of appropriate eye contact is important. Tell students that one or more pairs will be asked to share their situation. Have one or more pairs share their situation.
3. Model use of appropriate eye contact while thinking aloud. A scripted example follows:

   Introduction

   I am going to pretend to be speaking to a friend in the hallway. I will show appropriate eye contact and tell you the thoughts I'm having. When I hold up this Thought Bubble, *you'll know the words I'm saying are actually what I'm thinking.*

Actual Model

Hi Sue, how's it going? While holding up the *Thought Bubble* say, *I'm using appropriate eye contact while I'm talking.* Put the *Thought Bubble* down and ask, *What are you going to do after school today?*

4. Tell students, "Let's pretend we are going to hire someone to be our classroom helper. The classroom helper will be responsible for helping you with your work. Let's pretend we have three people applying for the job and we need to interview each person before deciding who we'll hire."

5. Brainstorm possible interview questions and then narrow the list to one or two questions. Decide which students will ask the interview questions.

6. Tell students, "I'm going to pretend to be the three people interviewing for the job. Each time I enter the room, I'll be pretending to be a different person. After I introduce myself, ask me the interview question(s)."

7. While pretending to be the first person, wear a nametag with "Ned Never Look" written on it. Introduce yourself and make it obvious that you are not giving the class any eye contact. While continuing your lack of eye contact, briefly answer the question(s) asked, and leave the room.

   While pretending to be the second person, wear a nametag with "Sam Starer" written on it. Introduce yourself and make it obvious that you are staring at the same person the entire time you are being interviewed. After briefly answering the question(s), leave the room.

   While pretending to be the third person, wear a nametag with "Eddie Eye Contact" written on it. Introduce yourself and use appropriate eye contact by looking at all class members while answering the question(s).

   If you are a female, use the names "Nellie Never Look," "Sally Starer," and "Ellen Eye Contact."

   Make your answers similar in quality so that the only striking difference between the three persons interviewed is use of eye contact.

8. Using the "Numbered Heads Together" structure (see pages 35–36), ask students to work with their partners to discuss the following ideas. (Two pairs could be asked to work together to form groups of four, if desired.)

   - Make sure everyone in your group can tell why the first person's name was "Ned (or Nellie) Never Look."

   - Make sure each member can share some thoughts about Ned's (Nellie's) eye contact.

- Be certain that every person in your group can tell why the second person's name was "Sam (Sally) Starer."
- Make sure all group members share their thoughts about Sam's (Sally's) eye contact.
- Be sure that each person has an opportunity to tell why the third person's name was "Eddie (Ellen) Eye Contact."
- Make sure each member can share some thoughts about Eddie's (Ellen's) eye contact.
- Be certain that, based on use of eye contact, each person tells who would likely be hired for the job.

9. Write the following where everyone can see it: USING GOOD SOCIAL SKILLS HELPS ME GET ALONG BETTER WITH OTHERS! Have the students say this aloud, in unison, with energy.

Lessons X, Y, and Z

Due to similarities in format, the final three lesson plans for each unit in *Social Star* are provided in *Appendix A*. Substitute the words "eye contact" whenever a "_____" appears in the lesson plans. Information specific to this unit follows.

LESSON X PREPARATORY SET:

Tell students you will be reading the following situations to them. They should put their thumbs up if the person in the situation used appropriate eye contact. They should put their thumbs down if the person in the situation did not use appropriate eye contact.

- Jolisa looked down when her teacher talked to her about some missing homework.
- When the lifeguard explained the pool rules, Victor looked at her most of the time.
- When Ann introduced herself to the new boy in a wheelchair, she looked away.

Discuss the idea that eye contact is used in all three situations when American common cultural rules apply.

LESSON Y PREPARATORY SET:

Darken the room, if you prefer, and ask students to visualize themselves correctly using this social skill by reading the following script:

> *Let's take a few moments to relax.... Make sure you are sitting in a comfortable position.... Close your eyes if you feel like it.... On the count of three, take a very slow, deep breath. One . . . two . . . three.... Breathe in deeply.... Now breathe out slowly.... Let your entire body relax.... Now imagine yourself talking to the principal. You remember to look at the principal during your conversation. Think about how happy you feel because you used appropriate eye contact.*

LESSON Z PLOT SITUATION:

Ask students to pretend that they are at home watching TV and that someone changes the channel without asking.

LESSON Z ROADBLOCK EXAMPLES:

- Using eye contact when experiencing feelings such as anger, boredom, embarrassment, nervousness
- Using eye contact with a person who is either not looking at you or is staring at you

Name MARIA E. CIA

Eye Contact T-Chart

LOOKS LIKE...	SOUNDS LIKE...
looking at the eyes of the person (people) you are talking to •••••• looking at the eyes of the person (people) you are listening to	no sound

HOME

Pretend your mother is talking with you about a new neighbor who has a son or daughter your age. Show eye contact while you talk and listen.

SCHOOL

Pretend you are talking with your teacher about what you did over the weekend. Show eye contact while you talk and listen.

COMMUNITY

Pretend you are talking with your friend at the park about your dog. Show eye contact while you talk and listen.

Use
Eye Contact
And Feel Confident

HOME-A-GRAM

Dear Family,

At school, we have been talking about the social skill called

EYE CONTACT

I learned that *eye contact* means looking at others when I listen and talk.

When I'm with other people, I should ask myself, "Am I using appropriate eye contact?"

I learned that using appropriate eye contact helps me be a good listener and a good speaker.

I completed the eyes below to show what appropriate eye contact looks like.

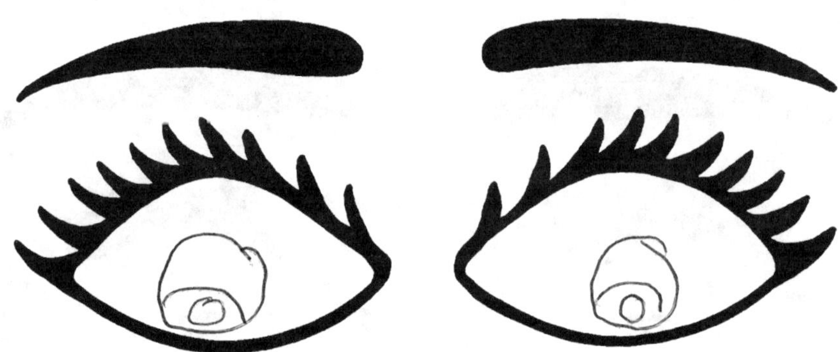

I will show you how I can use eye contact. After I do, please sign my "Eye Contact" badge so that I can return it to school and become a SOCIAL SUPER STAR this week.

From: ______________________

Volume

UNIT GOAL:

To demonstrate comprehension and use of appropriate voice volumes

EDUCATOR INFORMATION:

Many classrooms are moving from a traditional, teacher-centered environment to a more collaborative, student-centered environment. Students need to be directly taught voice volumes appropriate for various types of group work. This unit teaches students that they are capable of using quiet, normal, and loud volumes and that they need to know when each is appropriate. The unit provides activities for students to practice using quiet, normal, and loud volumes. The educator should exert sensitivity and care in generalizing rules about voice volume into the children's home cultures.

RELATED ACTIVITIES:

1. Have students prepare a video in which they demonstrate different voice volumes. The video could show situations in which various volumes might be used:

   Quiet volume—In the school library or when working in small groups

   Normal volume—When answering a question in class or when talking to the teacher before school

   Loud volume—At recess or during a sporting activity

2. Have students read chorally (e.g., during science or social studies). As they are reading together, periodically call out "quiet," "normal," or "loud," indicating which type of volume you would like them to use. Students may be asked to switch back and forth between the volumes.

3. Have students act as "consultants" and give advice to another teacher on dealing with a student who habitually speaks too softly or too loudly.

4. Ask a speech-language clinician to speak to the class about the effects on vocal cords of habitually using a loud voice.

5. Demonstrate how to adjust the volume on a computer in the classroom. Provide students with the opportunity to experiment with adjusting the volume.

6. Visit an audiologist to discuss the effects of loud rock music on hearing. Tour the audiologist's soundproof booth and experiment with the volume control of the audiometer.

7. Invite adults from different cultures to talk to the students about how their cultures' conventions for volume compare with American common culture norms.

It is important for educators to provide opportunities for students to work in groups, so they can experience social skills in contexts where social communication is needed. Therefore, educators are encouraged to have students complete the Related Activities in small groups whenever possible. Educators trained in cooperative learning could incorporate the five components (see page 34) into the group activity.

RELATED LITERATURE:

Meet the Austins (1960) by Madeleine L'Engle, Vanguard. (Text) (pages 13–14, 17–19)

Miss Nelson is Missing (1977) by Harry Allard, Ill. by James Marshall, Houghton Mifflin. (Picture book)

Shiloh (1991) by Phyllis Reynolds Naylor, Atheneum. (Text) (pages 109–112)

SOCIAL SKILLS ALL DAY LONG:

Look for opportunities to teach social skills throughout the day (incidental teaching). Four ways to reinforce good social skills and an example of each follow:

Encouragement

You are adjusting your volume nicely. Even though you are sitting in the back row, I can hear you clearly. Well done!

Personal Example

Yesterday after school, we had a faculty meeting. When I asked the principal a question, I spoke loud enough so everyone could hear me.

Prompting

In a few minutes, we'll be going into the library. Remember to use a quiet voice volume while we're there. When we leave, I'll ask the librarian how we all did at using a quiet volume.

Corrective Feedback (must be positive, private, specific, and nonthreatening)

Lee, just now when you came inside after recess, you were yelling. Think about talking at a normal or even quiet volume. When you enter the school using an appropriate volume, you won't disturb other people in the building.

Lesson A

OBJECTIVES:

1. To state the meaning of *volume* and tell why it is important
2. To tell the self-talk associated with correct use of the skill

MATERIALS:

1. Television
2. *Volume* (See page 108; one copy per student and one transparency.)
3. *Thought Bubble* (See *Appendix O*; one for educator use.)
4. *Volume Dial* (See page 109; one per pair of students.)
5. Scissors (One per pair of students)
6. Brass fasteners (One per pair of students)

PREPARATORY SET:

Ask students to watch and listen to a short segment of a television show. Turn the TV on, with the volume barely audible. When one of the students points out that the sound is too low, "accidentally" turn it up too loud for a few seconds. Quickly adjust the sound to a normal volume. Use this experience to introduce the topic of voice volume to the class.

PLAN:

1. Distribute and display *Volume.* Discuss the definition. Explain the skill step and the symbol next to it. Remind students that the symbol is there to help them visualize and remember the skill step. Read and explain the reasons for using an appropriate volume.
2. Model use of the volume skill step while thinking aloud. A scripted example for use of a quiet voice follows:

   Introduction

   I am going to pretend to be one of you at home. I need to phone my friend Chris. My dad is sleeping and I know that I need to talk with a soft voice volume. I will show you a quiet voice volume and tell you the thoughts I'm having. When I hold up this Thought Bubble, *you'll know the words that I'm saying are actually what I'm thinking.*

Actual Model

While holding up the *Thought Bubble* say, *Oh, Dad is sleeping. What volume should I use? Definitely quiet, so I don't wake him up....* Put the *Thought Bubble* down and quietly say, *Hi, Chris, how are you doing?* Put the *Thought Bubble* back up and say, *OK, I'm doing a good job talking quietly.*

3. Pair students (see *Appendix P*).

4. Complete the bottom of *Volume* by reading the story about Maria. Ask students to work with their partners to fill in the blanks as directed at the bottom of the page. Then, ask them to make sure that each person in the pair can tell the answer to the following questions:

   - When did Maria use a quiet volume? Why did Maria use a quiet volume?
   - Why did Maria use a normal volume on the bus? What might have happened to those who were shouting?
   - When did Maria use a loud volume? Why did Maria use a loud volume?

   Proceed by calling on students to answer the questions.

5. Distribute *Volume Dial* to each pair of students. Explain that a volume dial can be used to show how loud a noise is. Point out that it is divided into three sections: quiet volume, normal volume, and loud volume. Instruct the pairs to work together to think of situations when they could use quiet, normal, and loud voices, and then write their situations on the appropriate lines of their volume meters. Give students a specific amount of time in which to complete the activity. Encourage them to think of as many ideas as possible.

6. After time is up, distribute a pair of scissors and a brass fastener to each pair of students. Instruct the pairs to cut out and then fasten the dials using the brass fasteners.

7. Ask one pair of students to pick any one of the situations they wrote on their dial and read it orally. After the situation is read, the remaining student pairs move their volume dials to the appropriate level for that situation and hold their dials up. Choose another group to read a situation from their dial. Follow the procedure above until all pairs have had a chance to read one or more of their situations. Collect the dials for use in Lesson B.

8. Ask student pairs to take turns telling each other the meaning of *volume* and why it's important to use the skill. Encourage students to use quiet voices while completing this task. Students could be reminded that the information they are to say is printed on *Volume*.

As an option to add structure to this activity (see *Appendix Q*), ask partners to come to an agreement about which person will be called "Alexander Graham Bell" and which person will be called "Thomas Edison." After students have made their decisions, ask "Alexander" to tell "Thomas" the definition of *volume*. Next, ask "Thomas" to tell "Alexander" the definition. Ask the students to use the same procedure to tell each other the reasons for using appropriate volumes.

9. Write the following where everyone can see it: IT'S FUN LEARNING ABOUT SOCIAL SKILLS! IT'S TOTALLY DYNAMITE! Have the students say this aloud, in unison, enthusiastically.

Name ____________________

Volume

MEANING OF VOLUME: How quietly or loudly you talk

SKILL STEP:

1. Ask myself: What volume should I use?

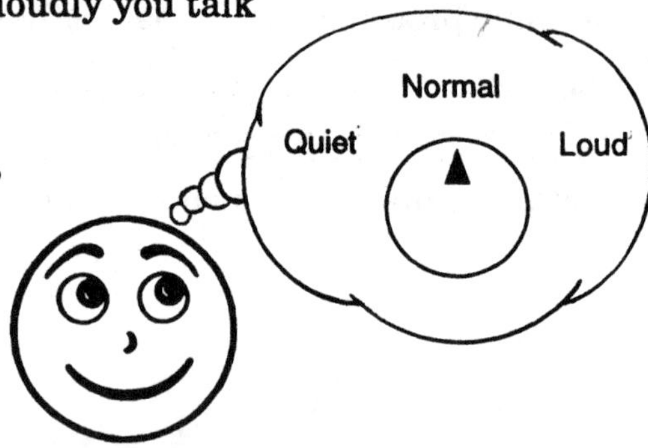

REASONS FOR USING THIS SKILL:

People may enjoy talking to you more when you use a volume that is right for the situation (quiet, normal, or loud). It brings a good feeling inside.

DIRECTIONS: Listen to the story below. Write the word **Quiet, Normal,** or **Loud** under the correct picture that shows Maria's volume.

Maria knows all about voice volume. On Saturday, she used different volumes at the right times. She was very excited because it was the day of her soccer team's big game. She was the first one up in the morning. She peeked into her parents' room and saw that her mother was awake. Her father was still sleeping, so she quietly asked her mother where her soccer uniform was. On the bus to the game, Maria and Jolisa talked in a normal volume. (The kids who were shouting bothered the bus driver.) At the soccer game, Maria cheered loudly for her teammates.

____________________ ____________________ ____________________

Names MARiA

Volume Dial

NORMAL

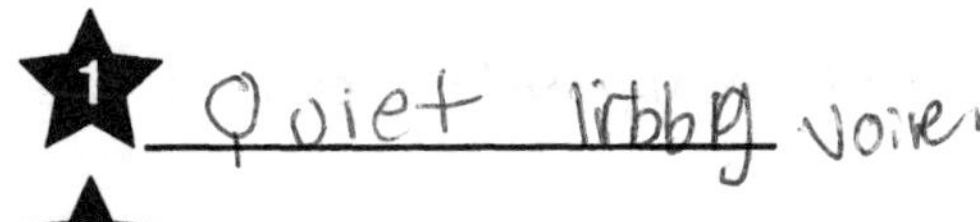

QUIET

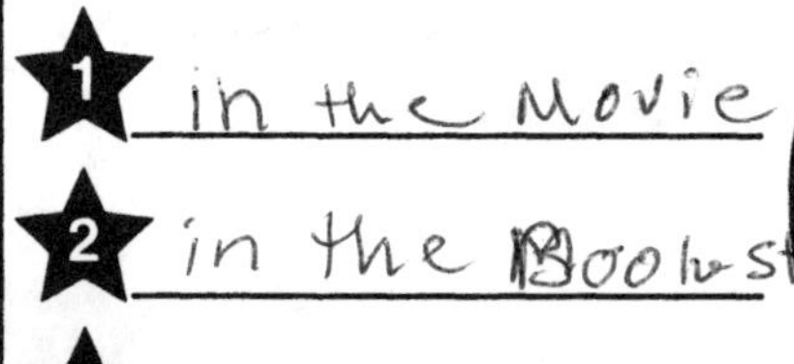

Attach Volume Dial Here

LOUD

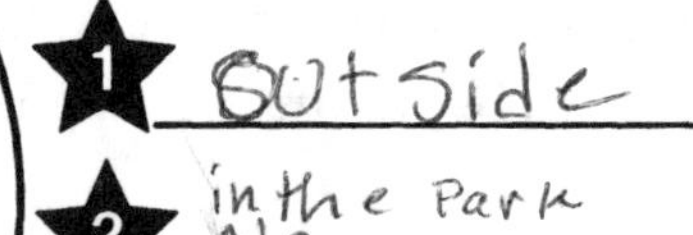

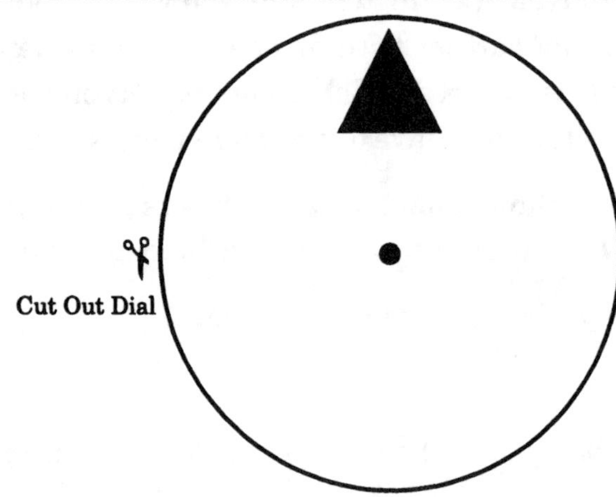

Lesson B

OBJECTIVE:

To demonstrate quiet, normal, and loud volumes

MATERIALS:

1. *Volume Dial* (Student copies from Lesson A)
2. *Volume* classroom poster (See page 13.)
3. *Thinking Skills Web* (See *Appendix T*; one per pair of students and one transparency.)
4. *Happy To Be Me* (See page 112; one per pair of students.)
5. *Quiet Symbols* (See page 113; choose one to enlarge for classroom display.)

PREPARATORY SET:

Place the *volume dials* in various areas of the room. Tell students that when you say "go," the partners from Lesson A should find their dial and sit down together. Challenge partners to see if they can find their dial in 30 seconds or less.

PLAN:

1. Review the definition and skill step for *volume* by referring the class to the *Volume* classroom poster.
2. Ask student pairs to take turns telling each other the skill step for volume. Follow the procedure described in step 8, Lesson A. (As an option, ask students to decide who will be "Martha Washington" and who will be "Betsy Ross.") Next, ask students to work with a partner to think of a situation when the use of soft, normal, and loud volume is important. Tell students that one or more pairs will be asked to share their situation. Have one or more pairs share their situation.
3. Read each situation that follows aloud. After each is read, ask the student pairs to move their dials to the appropriate volume level and hold them up.
   - Talking in the hallway when classes are going on
   - Talking in a library
   - Cheering at a basketball game when your team does something exciting

- Talking when someone is sleeping
- Talking during a movie in a theatre
- Calling for help in an emergency
- Answering a discussion question in class
- Asking to borrow a pencil from the person next to you during class

4. Distribute and display the *Thinking Skills Web.* Have students brainstorm reasons why educators sometimes ask students to use quiet voices when working in small groups. Write "quiet voices during small group activities" on the inside circle and the reasons for using quiet voices on the outside lines. Example reasons follow:

   - So one group does not disturb another group
   - So the classroom doesn't disturb another classroom
   - So the room doesn't get so loud that no one can hear anything
   - So you can be proud of using an appropriate volume

5. Distribute *Happy To Be Me* to each pair of students. Orally read the dialogue to students. Then ask all pairs to simultaneously read *Happy To Be Me* aloud. Explain that when you call out "quiet voices," students read quietly in their groups. When you call out "normal voices," students read using a normal volume, and when you call out "loud voices," students read using a loud volume.

6. Ask one group to demonstrate reading *Happy To Be Me* aloud using a quiet volume while the other groups listen. Ask a second group to demonstrate a normal volume while the other groups listen. Ask a third group to demonstrate a loud volume while the other groups listen. Continue this same procedure until all groups have had a chance to demonstrate one of the volumes.

7. Review the reasons for using quiet voices during group activities (on the *Thinking Skills Web*) and add any additional reasons students can think of. Remind students that their ideas are also reasons to talk quietly in other situations (e.g., a library, a theatre).

8. Show the *Quiet Symbol* that you chose. Explain that it will be displayed (and referred to during the school day) as a reminder to use quiet volume when appropriate. Provide students an opportunity to practice using quiet voices by holding up the *Quiet Symbol* and asking them to quietly say, "That is the quiet symbol."

9. Say with excitement to the class: *Each of you is a special, spectacular, marvelous, wonderful, magnificent social person!*

Names ________________________________

I am a special person!

There is only one me in the whole world!

I am happy to be me!

I know that I can do good things for myself.

**I can also do good things for my school,
my family, and my friends.**

I like who I am!

I am important!

I care about myself and my body.

I take good care of myself!

I know I can do great things!

I AM SPECIAL!

QUIET SYMBOLS

1	2	3	4	5	6

Use a 6-Inch Voice

Quiet as a Mouse

Lesson C

OBJECTIVES:

1. To learn why it's important to speak loudly enough in class
2. To demonstrate an appropriate volume for the classroom

MATERIALS:

1. *Thought Bubble* (See *Appendix O*; one for educator use.)
2. Figures of Victor Parra and Ms. Paula Hess (See *Appendix F*.)
3. *Checking Myself* (See *Appendix I*; one per student and one transparency.)

PREPARATORY SET:

Instruct students to take out pieces of scrap paper and pencils. Ask them to draw the symbol for the volume skill step.

PLAN:

1. Model use of the volume skill step while thinking aloud. A scripted example follows:

   Introduction

   I am going to pretend to be a student who is performing in the play "The Wizard of Oz." I know that I need to talk with a loud voice volume. I will show you a loud voice volume and tell you the thoughts I'm having. When I hold up this Thought Bubble, *you'll know the words I'm saying are actually what I am thinking.*

   Actual Model

   While holding up the *Thought Bubble* say, *When I say my part, I need to talk loud enough so everyone in the auditorium can hear.* Put down the *Thought Bubble* and say, using an appropriate volume, *I'm off to see the wizard, the wonderful Wizard of Oz.*

2. Discuss other situations when it is necessary to talk more loudly than normal so everyone can hear (e.g., answering questions during a class discussion, reading aloud to a group).

3. Tell students that you will be reading a script to them. Explain that the setting is at McKinley School and that Ms. Hess is having a discussion with her class. Using the figures of Victor and Ms. Hess, read the script that follows. While reading Victor's words "Bus, plane, car..." speak in a very quiet voice that cannot be heard.

   Ms. Hess: Yesterday we talked about ways people travel. Let's see how many forms of transportation you can name.

   Victor: *(raises his hand)*

   Ms. Hess: Victor, your hand is up. How many can you remember?

   Victor: Bus, plane, car...

   Ms. Hess: Victor, I can't hear you. Please speak more loudly.

4. Distribute and display the discussion guideline sheet called *Checking Myself.* Ask students to complete the goal statement with the words "think about an answer to each question asked," or use another classroom discussion goal more appropriate for your group (see page 26). Tell students that you will be asking questions about the script they just heard. Explain that after you ask each question, it's important for them to be thinking about an answer, even if they are not called on. Instruct them to put an "X" on their sheets each time they think about an answer to a question. It's important that the educator remember to provide enough "wait time" before calling on a student to orally answer each question.

5. Model use of the *Checking Myself* sheet while thinking aloud. A scripted example follows:

   Introduction

   I am going to pretend to be one of you completing this sheet during the discussion we will be having. I will tell you the thoughts I'm having while I'm completing the sheet. When I hold up this Thought Bubble, *you'll know the words I'm saying are actually what I'm thinking.*

   Actual Model

   While holding up the *Thought Bubble* say, *OK, the teacher just asked, "What kind of voice volume did Victor use?" I need to think of an answer.... He used a volume that was too quiet. I'll put an "X" on my paper because I just thought about an answer for that question.* Put the *Thought Bubble* down and mark an "X" on the transparency.

6. Proceed with the actual discussion by asking the questions that follow. During the discussion, periodically remind students to be thinking of answers to the questions and to mark their discussion guideline sheets.

   - What voice volume could Victor have used?
   - Why do you think Victor may have used a quiet volume?
   - Why is it important to speak loudly enough for everyone to hear during a class discussion?
   - Name another time when you might speak with a loud volume.

   After the discussion, have students complete the bottom of *Checking Myself.*

7. Process the use of the sheet by asking the following question or another one more appropriate for your group:

   - Why is it important to stay on task by thinking of answers to questions during a discussion?

   Process further by asking the following question:

   - Why is it sometimes hard to stay on task and think of answers?

8. Tell students that you are going to be calling on each of them to answer a fun question. They are to answer the questions using an appropriate volume for classroom discussion. Examples follow. (The educator may wish to substitute content questions.)

   - What is your favorite flavor of ice cream?
   - What is your favorite television show?
   - When is your birthday?
   - What month do you like best?
   - What does "supercalifragilisticexpealidoshes" mean?
   - What color do you think a clown's hair could be?

9. Write the following where everyone can see it: I CAN BE ESPECIALLY NICE TO OTHER PEOPLE BY USING GOOD SOCIAL SKILLS. Have the students say this aloud, in unison, with sincerity.

Lesson D

OBJECTIVE:

To verbalize important information about the social skill of *volume*

MATERIALS:

1. Disguise props for educator use (See Preparatory Set following.)
2. Tape recorders and blank cassette tapes (One per group of students)

PREPARATORY SET:

Tell students that you will be leaving the room for a few minutes and that while you are gone a guest speaker will be talking to them. Leave the room and return disguised and wearing a nametag with "Poor Volume Pat" written on it. Introduce yourself as "Poor Volume Pat." Speak to the class for a short period of time about the importance of using appropriate social skills, but purposely use inappropriate voice volumes while speaking. First, speak so quietly that no one can hear. When students indicate that they are unable to hear, speak with an uncomfortably loud volume. Say "good-bye" and leave the room. (Note: The students may recognize you as "Poor Volume Pat," but it doesn't matter. Also, if you are concerned about leaving the room unattended, slip into your disguise as quickly and as unobtrusively as you can while staying in the room.)

PLAN:

1. Return to the classroom and ask the class about the guest speaker. Allow students time to share their reactions and thoughts about "Poor Volume Pat."
2. Tell the class that you are concerned about the guest speaker's inappropriate volumes and would like them to give some constructive criticism to the speaker. (The educator could explain that *constructive criticism* means telling someone in a nice way how they can improve.) Ask students what helpful ideas they could give to the speaker about improving voice volume (e.g., talk loudly enough so everyone can hear; ask if people at the back of the room can hear you).
3. Group students using *Pick-A-Card Any Card* (see *Appendix P*). Distribute one tape recorder and one cassette tape to each group. Instruct each group to prepare a cassette tape to give to the guest speaker. The tapes might begin by thanking the speaker for coming and talking to the class. The tapes could include the students' ideas for improving voice volume and examples of volumes

which would be too soft, just right, and too loud when speaking to a class. Tell students that you will be playing the tapes so everyone can hear the groups' suggestions before giving the tapes to "Poor Volume Pat."

4. Allow ample time for production of the tapes as well as for sharing the tapes with the class. When multiple groups are simultaneously producing their tapes, they need to be careful not to create so much noise that the tapes become difficult to hear upon playback. Students should speak directly into the tape recorder microphones and groups should be spread apart as far as possible.

5. Say with a smile to the class: *I enjoy seeing each of you grow as individuals as you use new skills! You're terrific!* Tell them to think about how they've grown.

Lessons X, Y, and Z

Due to similarities in format, the final three lesson plans for each unit in *Social Star* are provided in *Appendix A*. Substitute the word "volume" whenever a "_____" appears in the lesson plans. Information specific to this unit follows.

LESSON X PREPARATORY SET:

Ask students to pretend that they are volume meters. Tell them to start out crouching near the floor, and that as your voice volume gets louder and louder, they should stand higher and higher. As it gets softer and softer, they should stand lower and lower. Tell a favorite story to students, varying your volume up and down.

LESSON Y PREPARATORY SET:

Darken the room, if you prefer, and ask students to visualize themselves correctly using this social skill by reading the following script:

> *Let's take a few moments to relax.... Make sure you are sitting in a comfortable position.... Close your eyes if you feel like it.... On the count of three, take a very slow, deep breath. One . . . two . . . three.... Breathe in deeply.... Now breathe out slowly.... Let your entire body relax. Now imagine yourself sitting in your classroom. You are working with a group of students and have been instructed to discuss some questions quietly. Students are beginning to use louder and louder voice volumes. You remind your group that it is important to use quiet voices. You continue to use a quiet voice during the time your group is working. The teacher congratulates your group on how quietly you worked! Think about how good you feel about remembering the skill of* volume. *Tell yourself what a nice job you did!*

LESSON Z PLOT SITUATION:

Ask students to pretend that they just got to school, will start class in 10 minutes, and realize they didn't do their homework.

LESSON Z ROADBLOCK EXAMPLES:

- Using a normal voice volume when angry
- Using an appropriate voice volume when the teacher calls on you to answer a question and you are uncertain about the answer

Name ____________________

Volume T-Chart

LOOKS LIKE...	SOUNDS LIKE...
volume doesn't look like anything (but it usually changes with different facial expressions and with personal space)	quiet • in a library • when someone is sleeping • when others are studying • when telling a secret
	normal • during a conversation with the principal • when speaking on the telephone to ask directions • when sharing information or asking questions in class

	loud • when talking to someone far away • when at a sports event • at recess • when you need help in an emergency

HOME

Pretend your mom or dad is watching something important on the news. Show the volume you would use to talk to your brother, who is in the same room.

SCHOOL

Pretend you are working in a group with three students. Your teacher tells the class to use "quiet voices." Show the correct volume to use when you say to your group, "Does everyone agree with that idea?"

COMMUNITY

Pretend you are cheering for your brother at his baseball game. Show the volume you will use so you can be heard.

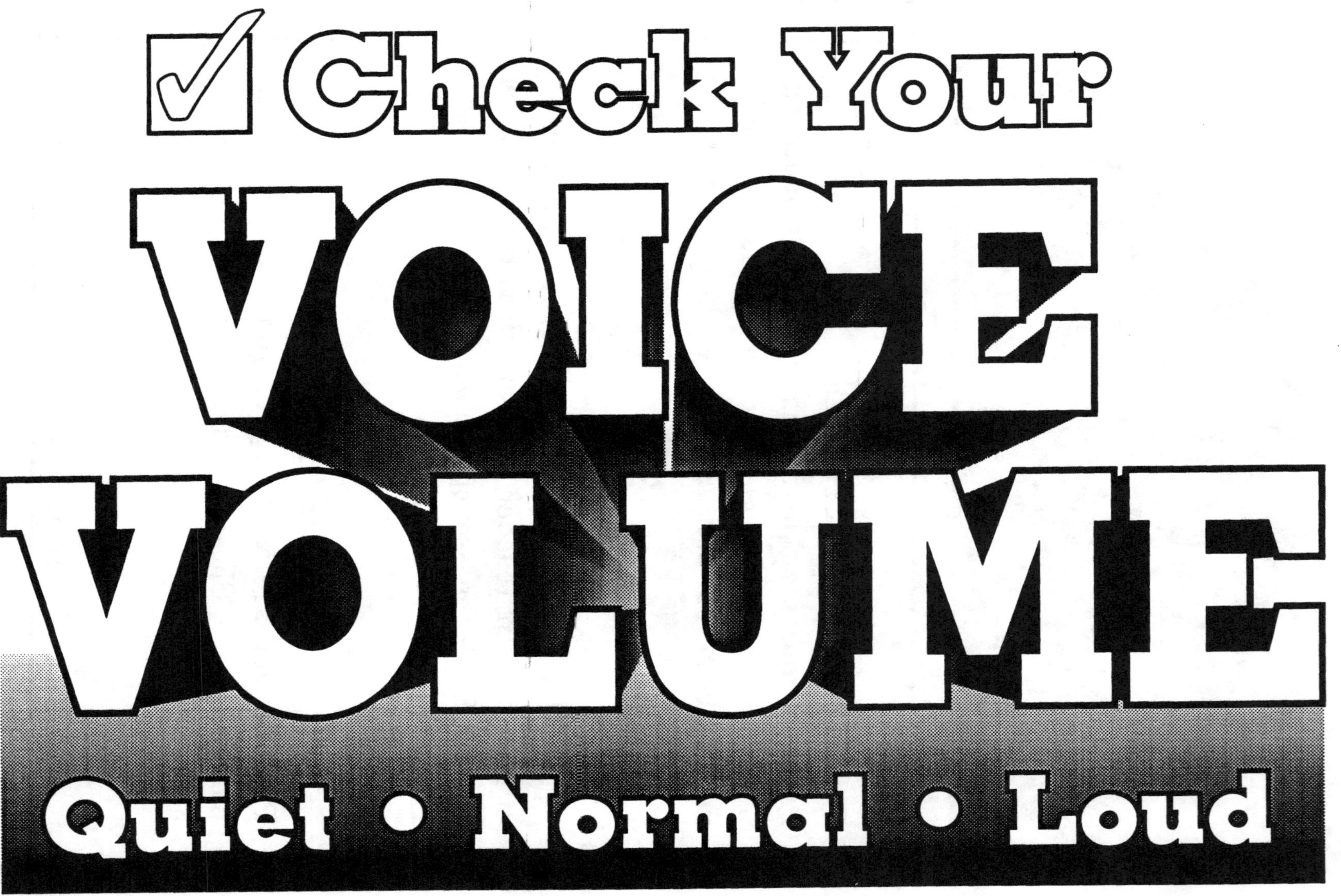
Check Your
VOICE
VOLUME
Quiet • Normal • Loud

HOME-A-GRAM

Dear Family,

At school, we have been talking about the social skill called

VOLUME

I learned that *voice volume* means how quietly or loudly I talk.

I know that whenever I want to talk, I need to ask myself, "What volume should I use (quiet, normal, or loud)?"

I learned that people may enjoy talking to me more when I use a volume that is right for the situation (quiet, normal, or loud). It brings a good feeling inside.

Below, I have written a situation appropriate for each voice volume.

QUIET VOLUME: like a Mouse ________________

____

NORMAL VOLUME: Talking Belly lown ________________

____

LOUD VOLUME: When You on the cell Phone ________________

____

I'll show you the difference between a quiet, normal, and loud volume at home. After I do, please sign my "Volume" badge so I can return it to school and become a SOCIAL SUPER STAR this week.

From: ________________

Tone of Voice

UNIT GOAL:

To demonstrate comprehension and use of appropriate tone of voice

EDUCATOR INFORMATION:

This unit teaches students that voice tones often give stronger messages than words. This unit teaches students to avoid inappropriate voice tones which may get them into trouble (e.g., braggy, whiney, bossy, sarcastic). The educator should exert sensitivity and care in generalizing rules about tone of voice into the children's home cultures.

RELATED ACTIVITIES:

1. Show video excerpts from an appropriate television show. Ask students to identify the various voice tones used by characters.
2. Ask the school secretary to talk to the class about the importance of using a polite tone of voice while answering the phone, greeting visitors, etc. The class may identify other jobs that require the use of polite voice tones.
3. Ask students to prepare a tape-recorded message about various tones of voice to be played over the morning announcements. The messages could include examples of various voice tones and the possible outcomes of using inappropriate tones.
4. Visit a radio station to observe and then talk to a broadcaster about the importance of voice tone.
5. Invite adults from different cultures to talk to the students about how their cultures' conventions for tone of voice compare with American common culture norms.

It is important for educators to provide opportunities for students to work in groups so they can experience social skills in contexts where social communication is needed. Therefore, educators are encouraged to have students complete the Related Activities in small groups whenever possible. Educators trained in cooperative learning could incorporate the five components (see page 34) into the group activity.

RELATED LITERATURE:

Happy Birthday, Delores (1989) by Barbara Samuels, Ill. by author, Orchard Books. (Picture book)

Ramona Forever (1984) by Beverly Cleary, Morrow. (Text) (pages 62, 146–148)

SOCIAL SKILLS ALL DAY LONG:

Look for opportunities to teach social skills throughout the day (incidental teaching). Four ways to reinforce good social skills and an example of each follow:

Encouragement

> *When you were telling about your new birthday presents, your voice sounded excited instead of braggy. Way to go!*

Personal Example

> *This morning I reminded my spouse to pick up something from the grocery store. I used a cheerful tone of voice instead of a bossy tone of voice.*

Prompting

> *In a few minutes, I'll be telling you which groups you'll be working in today. Remember to use a cheerful and energetic tone of voice when you get into your groups, so your group members might feel good about working with you.*

Corrective Feedback (must be positive, private, specific, and nonthreatening)

> *Lee, just now when I told you not to draw on your desk, you said, "OK," but your voice sounded sarcastic. If your voice had sounded respectful, then you would have sounded like you felt sorry for what you did. Sounding sarcastic can get you into just as much trouble as writing on a desk, and may even get you into more trouble.*

Lesson A

OBJECTIVES:

1. To state the meaning of *tone of voice* and tell why it is important
2. To tell the self-talk associated with correct use of the skill

MATERIALS:

1. *Thinking Skills Web* (See *Appendix T*; one transparency.)
2. *Tone of Voice* (See page 128; one per student and one transparency.)
3. *Thought Bubble* (See *Appendix O*; one for educator use.)

PREPARATORY SET:

Display the *Thinking Skills Web*. Write "Hi, my name is ____" on the inside circle. While covering your face with a piece of paper, say the statement with a happy tone of voice. Ask the students to tell how your voice sounded and write their responses on the outside lines. With your face covered again, read the statement a second time with an angry tone of voice. Again, ask the students to tell how you sounded and write their responses on the outside lines. Follow the same procedure using a scared and a sad tone of voice. Erase the statement from the inside circle. Tell the students that the words written on the outside lines have something in common—they describe tones of voice. Write "Tones of Voice" on the inside circle and tell students they will be learning about voice tones.

PLAN:

1. Distribute and display *Tone of Voice*. Discuss the definition. Explain the skill steps and the symbols next to them. (Don't spend much time discussing skill step #2, as it will be the focus of Lessons B and C.) Remind students that the symbols are there to help them visualize and remember the skill steps. Read and explain the reasons provided for using an appropriate tone of voice.
2. Model use of the tone-of-voice skill steps while thinking aloud. A scripted example follows:

   Introduction

   I am going to pretend that one of you brought a treat for the class. It is something that I do not care for. I will use an appropriate tone of voice and tell you the thoughts I'm having. When I hold up this Thought Bubble, *you'll know the words that I'm saying are actually what I'm thinking.*

Actual Model

While holding up the *Thought Bubble* say, *I really don't care for this treat so I won't take any.* Put the *Thought Bubble* down and say, *No thank you.* While holding up the *Thought Bubble* say, *How does my voice sound? It sounds polite—that's great!*

3. Read the story at the bottom of *Tone of Voice* aloud to students twice. The first time, the story should be read having Mike use a pleasant or cheerful tone of voice. The second time, the story should be read having Mike use a sad tone of voice. Have students write the voice tones used by Mike on the lines below the story. Discuss how the tone of voice Mike used each time reflected how Mike was feeling.

4. Pair students using the *Shoe Match* activity (see *Appendix P*).

5. Ask student pairs to take turns telling each other the meaning of *tone of voice* and why it's important to use the skill. Encourage students to use a cheerful tone of voice while completing this task. Students could be reminded that the information they are to say is printed on *Tone of Voice.*

   As an option to add structure to this activity (see *Appendix Q*), ask partners to come to an agreement about which person will be called "George Washington" and which person will be called "Abraham Lincoln." After students have made their decisions, ask "George" to tell "Abe" the definition of *tone of voice.* Next, ask "Abe" to tell "George" the definition. Ask the students to use the same procedure to tell each other the reasons for using an appropriate tone of voice.

6. Say sincerely to the class: *You are each important and capable people in this world! You can use your good social skills to get along with other people.*

Name ____________________

Tone of Voice

MEANING OF TONE OF VOICE: The way your voice sounds (which usually shows how you are feeling)

SKILL STEPS:

1. Ask myself: What tone of voice am I using?

2. Stop: If I think my voice tone may get me into trouble

REASONS FOR USING THIS SKILL:

Using appropriate voice tones helps you make a good impression and can keep you out of trouble. It helps you feel proud of yourself.

DIRECTIONS: Listen as your teacher reads this story about Mike and Ann two times. Write what tone of voice Mike uses each time the story is read.

Mike and Ann were waiting for the school bus. Ann said, "It sure is nice out today!" Mike replied, "Yeah, it's a great day." Ann asked Mike, "Did you get your homework done?" Mike answered, "Yeah, it's all finished." Ann said, "There's the bus. We'd better go."

Story #1 Tone: ____________________

Story #2 Tone: ____________________

Remember: When you change the way your voice sounds, you change the meaning of your words.

Lesson B

OBJECTIVES:

1. To identify inappropriate voice tones and explain why they are inappropriate
2. To substitute appropriate voice tones for inappropriate voice tones

MATERIALS:

1. *Tone of Voice* classroom poster (See page 13.)
2. *Thought Bubble* (See *Appendix O;* one for educator use.)
3. *Skill Step #2* (See pages 132–135; one set per pair of students and one transparency per page.)
4. Figures of Mr. Marcus Aaron, Jolisa Walker, Mrs. Corin Walker, Mr. Jesse Walker, Lee Vue, Victor Parra, Ann Olson, and Mr. Joe Jackson (See *Appendix F.)*

PREPARATORY SET:

Tell students you will say four statements two times each. Ask them to listen to how the meaning changes when you change your tone of voice. (Exaggerate the tones.) Assist students to label each tone of voice and to identify feelings which may cause each tone. The four statements and the tones to use for each follow:

- "Oh wow! I can hardly wait." (sarcastic, then excited)
- "Can I please have more milk?" (whiney, then polite)
- "I got to go skiing." (braggy, then happy)
- "You better put it down right now." (bossy, then firm)

PLAN:

1. Review the definition and skill steps for *tone of voice* by referring the class to the *Tone of Voice* classroom poster.
2. Model use of the tone-of-voice skill steps while thinking aloud. A scripted example follows:

Introduction

I am going to pretend that I'm one of you, and my mom says I have to stay home because we are having company. I really want to go to my friend's house instead. I will use an appropriate tone of voice and tell you the thoughts I'm having. When I hold up this Thought Bubble, *you'll know the words I'm saying are actually what I'm thinking.*

Actual Model

While holding up the *Thought Bubble* say, *Oh boy, I'm really angry! How does my tone of voice sound? I'd better not sound sarcastic or Mom will scold me. I'll let her know I'm a little disappointed, though.* Put the *Thought Bubble* down and say disappointedly, *OK Mom, I'll stay home.*

3. Pair students (see *Appendix P*). Distribute and display *Skill Step #2*. Using the figures of Jolisa and Mr. Aaron, perform Script #1 for the students. Use a sarcastic tone of voice when Jolisa says, "Yes, sir, Mr. Aaron."
4. Ask students to work with their partners to answer the three questions following Script #1. Then discuss answers as a class. (Answers could be written on the transparency.)
5. Instruct students to say the statement, "Yes, sir, Mr. Aaron," to their partners, first with a sarcastic tone of voice and then with a polite tone of voice.
6. Using the figures of Corin and Jesse, perform Script #2 for the students. Use a bossy tone of voice when Jesse says, "You'd better return your library books today or you'll have to pay a fine!" Use an annoyed tone of voice when Corin responds, "I know that, Jesse! I already have them out in the car."
7. With their partners, have students answer the questions following Script #2. Then, discuss the answers as a class. (Answers could be written on the transparency.)
8. Instruct students to say the statement, "You'd better return your library books today or you'll have to pay a fine!" to their partners, first with a bossy tone of voice and then with a friendly tone of voice.
9. Using the figures of Lee and Victor, perform Script #3 for the students. Use a braggy tone of voice when Victor says, "We went out for a movie and had pizza too!" Use an annoyed tone of voice when Lee says, "Good for you! But you don't have to brag about it."
10. With their partners, students answer the three questions following Script #3. Then, discuss the answers as a class. (Answers could be written on the transparency.)
11. Instruct students to say the statement, "We went out for a movie and had pizza too!" to their partners, first with a braggy tone of voice and then with an excited tone of voice.

12. Using the figures of Ann and her stepfather, Joe Jackson, perform Script #4 for the students. Use a whiney tone of voice when Ann speaks.

13. With their partners, have students answer the three questions following Script #4. Then, discuss the answers as a class. (Answers could be written on the transparency.)

14. Instruct students to say, “Can you help me?” to their partners, first with a whiney tone of voice and then with a normal tone of voice.

15. Ask student pairs to take turns telling each other the skill steps for tone of voice. Follow the procedure described in step 5 of Lesson A. (As an option, ask students to decide who will be “Sitting Bull” and who will be “Geronimo.”) Next, ask students to work with their partners to think of a situation when it’s important to use an appropriate tone of voice. Tell students that one or more pairs will be asked to share their situation. Have one or more pairs share their situation.

16. Write the following where everyone can see it: SOCIAL SKILLS, SOCIAL SKILLS! RAH! RAH! RAH! Have the students say this aloud, in unison, with spirit.

Names ______________________________

Skill Step #2

STOP: If I think my voice tone may get me into trouble

DIRECTIONS: Listen to each script and answer the questions.

SCRIPT #1

Characters: Jolisa Walker
Mr. Aaron

Scene: Mr. Aaron is teaching science. Jolisa is whispering to the student next to her.

Mr. Aaron:	Jolisa, you need to stop talking and listen.
Jolisa:	Yes, sir, Mr. Aaron!
Mr. Aaron:	Jolisa, you'll need to see me during recess.
Jolisa:	What? All I said was, "Yes sir!"

QUESTIONS:

1. Which word describes the inappropriate tone of voice Jolisa used when she said, "Yes, sir, Mr. Aaron"? Circle it.

   braggy   whiney   bossy   sarcastic

2. Why did Mr. Aaron ask Jolisa to see him during recess?

   ____

   ____

3. Why might Jolisa want to use a polite tone of voice next time?

   ____

   ____

Names ______________________________

Skill Step #2 (continued)

Braggy
Bossy
Whiney
Sarcastic

SCRIPT #2

Characters: Corin Walker
Jesse Walker

Scene: **Jesse is talking to his wife and is reminding her to return some library books.**

Jesse:	Are you running any errands today?
Corin:	Yes, after lunch. Why?
Jesse:	You'd better return your library books today or you'll have to pay a fine!
Corin:	I know that, Jesse! I already have them out in the car.

QUESTIONS:

1. Which word best describes Jesse's voice tone? Circle it.

   braggy whiney bossy sarcastic

2. How did Corin feel about her husband's tone of voice?

   ____

   ____

3. Why might Jesse want to use a friendly tone of voice next time?

   ____

   ____

Names ______________________________

Skill Step #2 (continued)

Braggy
Bossy
Whiney
Sarcastic

SCRIPT #3

Characters: Lee Vue
Victor Parra

Scene: Lee and Victor are talking about what they each did over the weekend.

Lee:	We went to see a movie Saturday afternoon. It was really good! What did you do?
Victor:	We went out for a movie and had pizza too!
Lee:	Good for you! But you don't have to brag about it!
Victor:	I'm not bragging! I just told you what we did!
Lee:	You sounded like you were bragging!

QUESTIONS:

1. Which word best describes the tone of voice Victor used when he said, "We went out for a movie...."? Circle it.

   braggy whiney bossy sarcastic

2. How did Lee feel about Victor's tone of voice?

   ____

   ____

3. Why might Victor want to use an excited tone of voice next time?

   ____

   ____

Names ______________________________

Skill Step #2 (continued)

SCRIPT #4

Characters: Ann Olson
Joe Jackson

Scene: Ann is asking her stepfather for help with her homework.

Ann:	Can you help me?
Joe:	With what?
Ann:	I need some help with this homework. I just don't understand it!
Joe:	You need to ask for help without whining!

QUESTIONS:

1. Which word best describes Ann's tone of voice? Circle it.

   braggy   whiney   bossy   sarcastic

2. How did Mr. Jackson feel about Ann's tone of voice?

   ____

   ____

3. Why might Ann want to use a normal tone of voice when she asks for help?

   ____

   ____

Lesson C

OBJECTIVE:

To identify self-talk that could be used to avoid using inappropriate voice tones

MATERIALS:

1. Figures of Ann Olson and Mrs. Mary Jackson (See *Appendix F.)*
2. *Tone of Voice* classroom poster (See page 13.)
3. *Self-Talk* (See page 139; one per pair of students.)
4. *Thought Bubble* (See *Appendix O*; two per pair of students and one transparency.)
5. *Checking Myself* (See *Appendix I*; one per student and one transparency.)

PREPARATORY SET:

Use the figures of Ann and her mother to perform a skit in which Mrs. Jackson asks Ann to do some chores. Ann should respond by saying, "Sure, Mom, I'd be glad to," using a sarcastic tone of voice. Mrs. Jackson should then ask Ann to go to her room until she is ready to use a polite tone of voice.

PLAN:

1. Refer to the skit and the *Tone of Voice* classroom poster to review the definition and skill steps for *tone of voice*. Remind students that the words "braggy," "whiney," "bossy," and "sarcastic" are used to describe voice tones that are usually inappropriate. Ask if they can think of other words used to describe these inappropriate voice tones (e.g. "sassy," "snotty").
2. Pair students (see *Appendix P).*
3. Distribute one copy of *Self-Talk* and two *Thought Bubbles* to each pair. Explain that they will be dealing with situations in which members of the Social Star Club need to remind themselves not to use inappropriate tones of voice.
4. After discussing the directions, read situation #1 on *Self-Talk* aloud.
5. Display the *Thought Bubble* transparency. Tell students that you will demonstrate how to fill in the *Thought Bubble*. Say: "Ann could be thinking that she shouldn't use a whiney tone of voice when she answers her mother. If she whines, she might not be able to go out even after her room is clean. In the

Thought Bubble, I'm going to write, 'I'd better not whine or Mom might get angry and not let me go out at all.' "

6. Read situation #2 aloud. Ask for volunteers to describe the self-talk they think might be used by Lee to remind himself not to brag. Write the words on the transparency.

7. Instruct student pairs to read the two remaining situations and complete a *Thought Bubble* for each. Tell students that there will be a discussion following the activity.

8. After all pairs have completed the *Thought Bubbles*, distribute and display the discussion guideline sheet called *Checking Myself.* Ask students to complete the goal statement with the words "raise my hand," or use another classroom discussion goal more appropriate for your group (see page 26). Tell students that you will be asking for pairs to share their self-talk ideas, and that it is important that everyone be willing to participate. Instruct them to put an "X" on their sheets each time they raise their hands to share information (even if they don't get called on).

9. Model use of *Checking Myself* while thinking aloud. A scripted example follows:

    Introduction

    I am going to pretend to be one of you completing this sheet during the discussion we will be having. I will tell you the thoughts I am having while I'm completing the sheet. When I hold up this Thought Bubble, *you'll know the words I'm saying are actually what I am thinking.*

    Actual Model

    While holding up the *Thought Bubble* say, *OK, the teacher is asking a question. I am going to raise my hand.... She called on someone else, but I'll put an "X" on my sheet because I raised my hand.* Put the *Thought Bubble* down and mark an "X" on the overhead transparency.

    During the discussion, periodically remind students to raise their hands to volunteer and to mark their discussion guideline sheets.

10. Proceed with the discussion by asking for volunteers to share the self-talk written in their *Thought Bubbles.* Ask for at least one example for each of the situations given; however, the educator may call on as many volunteers as time allows.

    After the discussion, ask students to complete the bottom of *Checking Myself.*

11. Process the use of the sheet by asking the following question or another one more appropriate for your group:

- Why do you think it's important to raise your hand to share ideas and answers during a discussion?

Process further by asking students who raised their hands but did NOT get called on the following question:

- What was appropriate about raising your hand even though you didn't get called on?

12. Say enthusiastically to the class: *You are dynamite, vibrant students! Thank you for using your smart brains!*

Names ______________________________

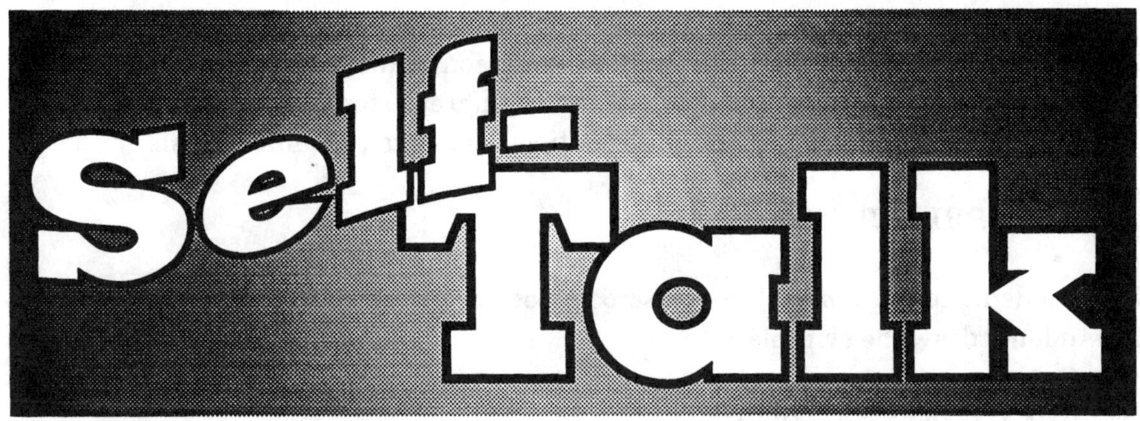

DIRECTIONS: Read each situation. In a *Thought Bubble,* write the self-talk that could be used.

1. Ann was just about to go outside to play. Her mother told her that she needed to clean her bedroom. Ann is upset because she really wants to go outside. In a *Thought Bubble,* write the self-talk she could use to remind herself not to use a whiney tone of voice.

2. Lee was the only person from his class chosen to be a participant in a district spelling contest. In a *Thought Bubble,* write the self-talk he could use to remind himself not to use a braggy tone of voice when he tells others about it.

3. Ann was having difficulty with her math problems. The teacher asked Jolisa to help Ann. In a *Thought Bubble,* write the self-talk that Jolisa could use to remind herself not to use a bossy tone of voice while helping Ann.

4. Mike's parents want him to apologize to his sister Ann. In a *Thought Bubble,* write the self-talk he could use to remind himself not to use a sarcastic tone of voice when he apologizes.

Lessons X, Y, and Z

Due to similarities in format, the final three lesson plans for each unit in *Social Star* are provided in *Appendix A*. Substitute the phrase "tone of voice" whenever a "_____" appears in the lesson plans. Information specific to this unit follows.

LESSON X PREPARATORY SET:

Refer students to the *Tone of Voice* classroom poster. Review the skill steps by having the students draw the symbols.

LESSON Y PREPARATORY SET:

Darken the room, if you prefer, and ask students to visualize themselves correctly using this social skill by reading the following script:

> *Let's take a few moments to relax.... Make sure you are sitting in a comfortable position.... Close your eyes if you feel like it.... On the count of three, take a very slow, deep breath. One . . . two . . . three.... Breathe in deeply.... Now breathe out slowly.... Let your entire body relax. Now imagine yourself at home early in the morning. The first thing your dad does is ask you to take out the garbage. You remember to use an appropriate tone of voice. You ask if you can take the garbage out after you finish eating and you don't sound whiney or sarcastic. You sound respectful. Think about how proud you feel because you used an appropriate tone of voice.*

LESSON Z PLOT SITUATION:

Ask students to pretend that they just finished recess and don't have a pencil but the teacher told them to work quietly at their desks.

LESSON Z ROADBLOCK EXAMPLES:

- Experiencing feelings that may bring about inappropriate voice tones, such as anger and a sarcastic voice tone or frustration and a whiney voice tone
- Being asked to apologize and sound sincere when you don't want to

Name ______________________

Tone of Voice T-Chart

LOOKS LIKE...	SOUNDS LIKE...
tone of voice doesn't look like anything (but it usually goes along with different facial expressions)	a tone that is appropriate for the situation ••••••••• a tone that will not cause you to get into trouble

HOME

Pretend your father asks you to help fix lunch. Show how to say, "Sure, Dad," using an appropriate tone of voice.

SCHOOL

Pretend your teacher says, "Good morning." Show how to say, "Hi," using a cheerful tone of voice.

COMMUNITY

Pretend you are at the library. Show how to ask a librarian for help using a polite tone of voice.

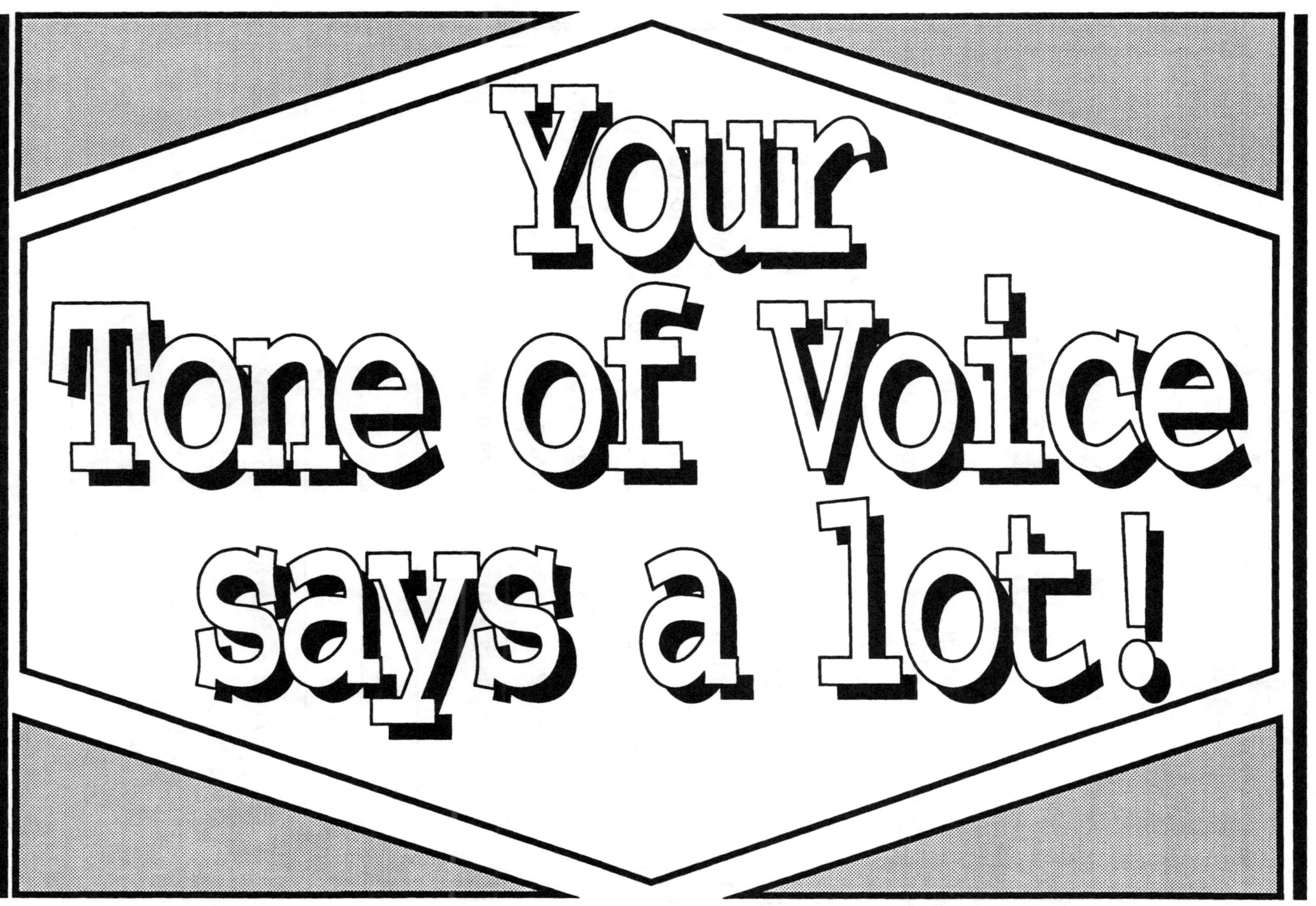
Your
Tone of Voice
says a lot!

HOME-A-GRAM

Dear Family,

At school, we have been talking about the social skill called

TONE OF VOICE

I learned that *tone of voice* means the way my voice sounds (which usually shows how I am feeling).

I know that using appropriate voice tones helps me make a good impression and keeps me out of trouble. It helps me feel proud of myself.

I learned that it is important to ask myself, "What tone of voice am I using?" and that I should stop if my voice can get me into trouble (e.g., whiney, bossy, sarcastic, or braggy).

Below, I have told what might happen if I use a bossy, whiney, braggy, or sarcastic tone of voice.

If I sound bossy, whiney, braggy, or sarcastic, then...

____

____

____

I'll show you a cheerful tone of voice when you ask me to do something for you at home. After I do, please sign my "Tone of Voice" badge so I can return it to school and become a SOCIAL SUPER STAR this week.

From: ____________________

Facial Expression

UNIT GOAL:

To demonstrate comprehension and use of appropriate facial expressions

EDUCATOR INFORMATION:

This unit was developed to teach students that people's facial expressions often give stronger and more accurate messages than their words. Many elementary students are developmentally at a stage where they show exactly how they feel. This unit, therefore, avoids more subtle issues such as when and why people might try to hide facial expressions that show sadness, hurt, or anger. This unit does teach students to avoid facial expressions which may get them into trouble (e.g., looking rude, stuck-up, or pouty). Students are encouraged to express their feelings calmly and honestly.

Educators need to be aware of cultural variations in norms for facial expressions. For instance, Cheng (1987) states that Asian Americans may remain composed when emotional and do not always exhibit facial expressions. The educator should exert sensitivity and care in generalizing rules about facial expression into the children's home cultures.

RELATED ACTIVITIES:

1. Ask students to practice an "ignoring" facial expression. Explain that this facial expression can be used when trying to ignore inappropriate behavior of others. Explain that the social skill of *ignoring* may be addressed in greater detail at a later time.
2. Watch television shows or videos without sound. Identify facial expressions displayed by characters.
3. Teach students new words to the song, "If You're Happy and You Know It." An example stanza follows:

   If you're happy and you know it, look like this.

   If you're happy and you know it, look like this.

   If you're happy and you know it, then your face will surely show it!

   If you're happy and you know it, look like this.
4. Arrange to visit the director of a community theatre group (or the director of the high school drama club) to find out how makeup is used to highlight the performer's face. Discuss the importance of facial expressions during a performance.

5. Have students take photographs of each other making a variety of facial expressions. Display the photographs in the classroom.
6. Invite adults from other cultures to talk to the students about how their cultures' conventions for facial expressions compare with American common culture norms.

It is important for educators to provide opportunities for students to work in groups so they can experience social skills in contexts where social communication is needed. Therefore, educators are encouraged to have students complete the Related Activities in small groups whenever possible. Educators trained in cooperative learning could incorporate the five components (see page 34) into the group activity.

RELATED LITERATURE:

An Angel for Solomon Singer (1992) by Cynthia Rylant, Ill. by Peter Catalanotto, Orchard Books. (Picture book)

Jamaica Tag-Along (1989) by Juanita Havill, Ill. by Anne Sibley O'Brien, Houghton Mifflin. (Picture book)

Meet the Austins (1960) by Madeleine L'Engle, Vanguard. (Text) (pages 13–14, 17–19)

Sam (1967) by Ann Herbert Scott, Ill. by Symeon Shimin, McGraw-Hill. (Picture book)

SOCIAL SKILLS ALL DAY LONG:

Look for opportunities to teach social skills throughout the day (incidental teaching). Four ways to reinforce good social skills and an example of each follow:

Encouragement

When your friend was telling you about his vacation, you used an interested facial expression. I bet that made your friend feel like you were really listening. Great job!

Personal Example

When I heard that the concert I planned on attending was cancelled, my face looked like this (demonstrate a disappointed facial expression). *I thought of some other fun things I could do instead of going to the concert and that helped me to feel a lot better. Then my face looked like this* (demonstrate a happy facial expression.)

Prompting

In a few minutes, I need to send three students to help in the computer room. Remember, not everyone can go. If you are not asked to help, you need to remember not to pout. If you are not chosen today, there will be other chances to help.

Corrective Feedback (must be positive, private, specific, and nonthreatening)

Maria, just now when I asked you to redo your paper, you rolled your eyes and said, "What's wrong with it?" What you could have done was to ask, "What's wrong with it?" using a sincere facial expression. Rolling your eyes can get you into trouble with adults.

Lesson A

OBJECTIVES:

1. To state the meaning of *facial expression* and tell why it is important
2. To tell the self-talk associated with correct use of the skill
3. To identify labels and possible causes for these facial expressions: confused, tired, sad, and surprised

MATERIALS:

1. *Facial Expression* (See page 150; one copy per student and one transparency.)
2. *Thought Bubble* (See *Appendix O*; one for educator use.)
3. *Spider Faces #1* (See page 151; one per pair of students and one transparency.)

PREPARATORY SET:

Show a few facial expressions and ask students to identify the feelings they think your face is showing. Be sure that only your face is used to express the feeling. A list of facial expressions you may choose to use includes surprised, sad, tired, confused, afraid, disappointed, happy, angry, bored, jealous, sorry, interested, disgusted, worried, guilty, and confident.

PLAN:

1. Distribute and display *Facial Expression*. Discuss the definition. Explain the skill steps and the symbols next to them. Remind students that the symbols are there to help them visualize and remember the skill steps. Discuss the reasons provided for using appropriate facial expressions.
2. Model correct use of facial expression skill step #1 while thinking aloud. A scripted example follows:

   Introduction

   I am going to pretend to be one of you apologizing for breaking a friend's yo-yo. I will use a sincere facial expression while I apologize and tell you the thoughts I'm having. When I hold up this Thought Bubble, *you'll know the words I'm saying are actually what I'm thinking.*

Actual Model

Say, *I'm sorry for breaking your yo-yo,* using a sincere facial expression. Hold up the *Thought Bubble* and say, *What is my face saying? My face looks like I am really sorry. My friend will know that I'm really sorry.*

3. Read the story at the bottom of *Facial Expression* aloud to students.

4. Pair students (see *Appendix P*). Direct the students' attention to the four pictures of Ann at the bottom of the page. Discuss the four facial expressions (confused, sad, tired, surprised). Ask student pairs to work together to complete the activity at the bottom of *Facial Expression.*

5. Display and distribute *Spider Faces #1* to each pair of students. Direct the students' attention to the "example" (the surprised spider) and discuss the synonyms and possible causes for the facial expression. Allow students to add ideas not listed. Ask students to work with their partners to think of synonyms and causes for the remaining spider expressions. Tell students you will be calling on one or more groups to share their answers.

6. After pairs have had time to complete the activity, ask them to share their synonyms and causes for each facial expression. Write their responses on the transparency as they are shared. If students are having difficulty thinking of synonyms, provide examples:

   Sad—miserable, depressed, down-in-the-dumps

   Tired—fatigued, exhausted, sleepy

   Confused—puzzled, mixed up, perplexed

   (This page will prepare students for the "Bingo" activity during Lesson E.)

7. Ask student pairs to take turns telling each other the meaning of *facial expression* and why it's important to use the skill. Encourage students to use happy facial expressions while completing this task. Students could be reminded that the information they are to say is printed on *Facial Expression.*

   As an option to add structure to this activity (see *Appendix Q*), ask partners to come to an agreement about which person will be called "Wolfgang Mozart" and which person will be called "Leonardo da Vinci." After students have made their decision, have "Wolfgang" tell "Leonardo" the definition of *facial expression.* Next, ask "Leonardo" to tell "Wolfgang" the definition. Ask students to use the same procedure to tell each other the reasons for using appropriate facial expressions.

8. Say sincerely to the class: *You are each unique individuals. I hope you enjoy what you've learned in class today!*

Name ____________________

Facial Expression

MEANING OF FACIAL EXPRESSION:

Showing how you feel by the look on your face

SKILL STEPS:

1. Ask myself: What is my face saying?
2. Stop: If my face can get me into trouble (rude, pouty, stuck-up)

REASONS FOR USING THIS SKILL:

If you avoid looking rude, pouty, or stuck-up, people will probably like you better. You'll feel proud.

DIRECTIONS: Listen to the story below. Decide which picture shows how Ann probably looked before school, during school, after school, and at bedtime. Write one word on each line: **BEFORE, DURING, AFTER, BEDTIME**.

Ann had a day of ups and downs. Before school, Ann's mom gave her a new barrette that matched her outfit exactly. During school, Mrs. Marrero gave directions that Ann couldn't understand. After school, Ann ripped her jacket. At bedtime, Ann could hardly wait to go to sleep. She'd had a long day.

Confused

____

Sad

____

Tired

____

Surprised

____

Names ______________________________

SPIDER FACES #1

DIRECTIONS: 1. Fill in as many spider legs on the **right** as you can with synonyms (words that mean the same).

2. Fill in the spider legs on the **left** with situations that might cause the spider's facial expression.

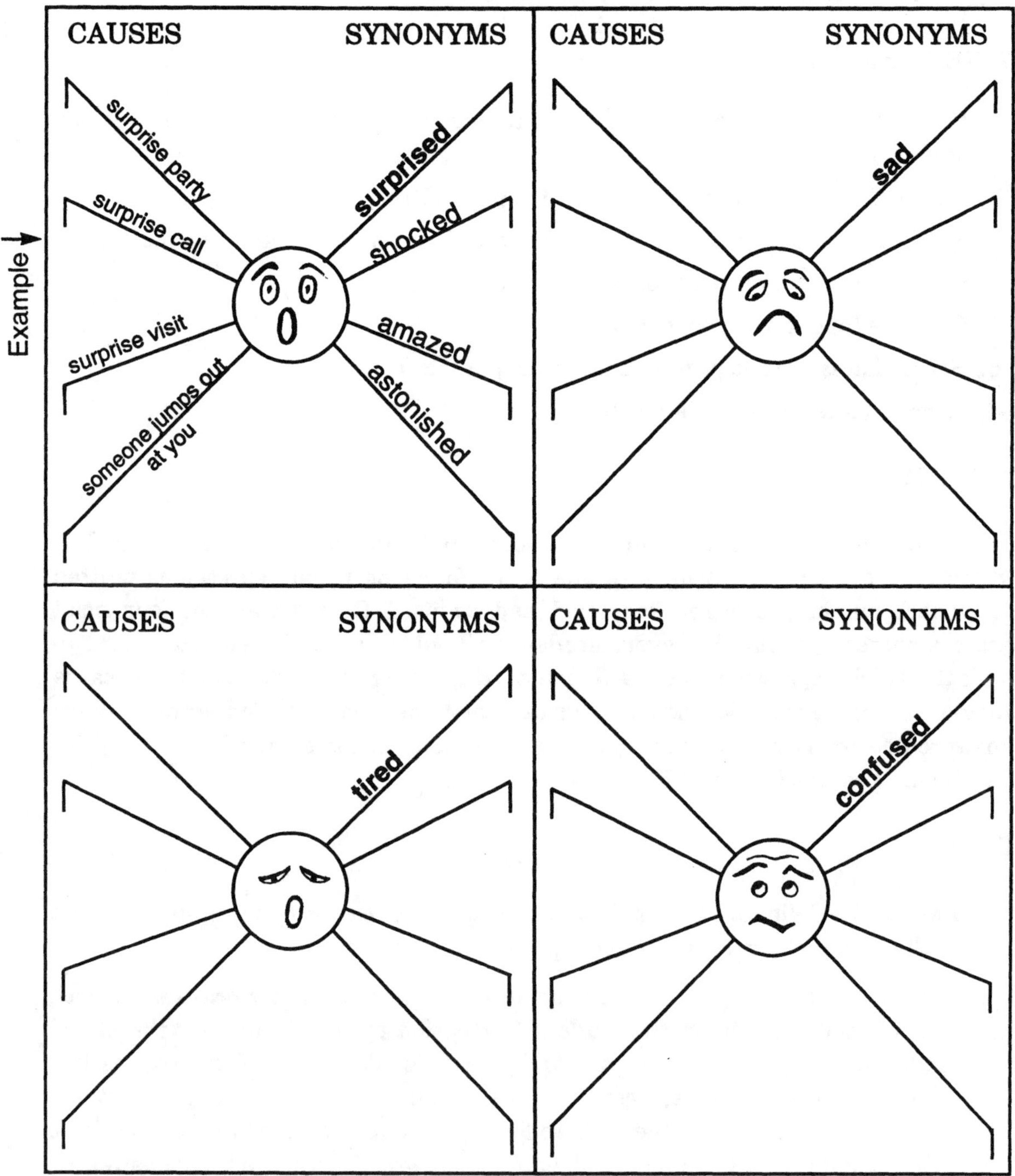

Lesson B

OBJECTIVES:

1. To identify labels and possible causes for these facial expressions: afraid, disappointed, happy, and angry
2. To identify how facial parts can look with different feelings

MATERIALS:

1. Four index cards, numbered from one to four with large numbers (One set per student)
2. *Facial Expression* classroom poster (See page 13.)
3. *Spider Faces #2* (See page 154; one per pair of students and one transparency.)
4. Cassette tape player (One for educator use)
5. Cassette tape of an upbeat song
6. *Spider Faces #1* (See page 151; one transparency.)
7. Mirrors (One per pair of students)

PREPARATORY SET:

Distribute one set of index cards to each student. Write the numbers one through four where everyone can see them, with one of the following facial expressions written below each number: surprised, sad, tired, and confused. Demonstrate the four facial expressions at random. Ask every student to hold up a numbered index card to indicate which expression you are demonstrating. The numbers on the index cards should be large enough so the educator can easily determine which students have answered correctly by scanning the room. The index cards should be retained for use during Lessons C, D, and E.

PLAN:

1. Review the definition and skill steps for *facial expression* by referring the class to the *Facial Expression* classroom poster.
2. Pair students (see *Appendix P*). Display and distribute *Spider Faces #2* to each pair of students. Direct the students' attention to the "example" (the afraid spider) and discuss the synonyms and possible causes for the facial expression. Allow students to add ideas not listed. Ask students to work with their partners to think of synonyms and then causes for the remaining spider facial expressions. Tell students you will be calling on one or more groups to share their answers.

3. After the pairs have had time to complete the activity, ask them to share the synonyms and causes for each facial expression. Write their responses on the transparency as they are shared. If students are having difficulty thinking of synonyms, provide examples:

   Disappointed—hurt, let down, sad

   Happy—joyful, merry, cheerful

   Angry—irate, furious, irritated

   (This page will prepare students for the "Bingo" activity during Lesson E.)

4. Introduce "Facial Aerobics" by saying the following: "Do you know that you have 90 muscles in your face? I will be playing a song and while it is playing, I want you to try to move as many of those 90 facial muscles as you can."

   Model first for students by making several exaggerated and goofy facial movements, so they will feel more comfortable during the activity. Proceed by playing "Facial Aerobics" with the upbeat music.

5. Ask student pairs to describe what happens to each facial part for the facial expressions shown on *Spider Faces #1* (confused, tired, sad, surprised) and on *Spider Faces #2* (disappointed, happy, afraid, and angry). Distribute the mirrors. Have student pairs take turns making each of the facial expressions while their partners observe and describe what each part of the face (i.e., eyes, eyebrows, nose, mouth, forehead, cheeks, jaws, and ears) is doing.

6. Ask student pairs to take turns telling each other the skill steps for facial expression. Follow the procedure described in step 7 of Lesson A. (As an option, ask students to decide who will be "Paul Revere" and who will be "Ben Franklin.") Next, ask students to work with their partners to think of a situation when it's important to use an appropriate facial expression. Tell students that one or more pairs will be asked to share their situation. Have one or more pairs share their situation.

7. Write the following where everyone can see it: I AM A SPECIAL PERSON. I CAN GET ALONG WELL WITH OTHERS. Have the students say this aloud, in unison, with enthusiasm.

Names ______________________________

SPIDER FACES #2

DIRECTIONS: 1. Fill in as many spider legs on the **right** as you can with synonyms (words that mean the same).

2. Fill in the spider legs on the **left** with situations that might cause the spider's facial expression.

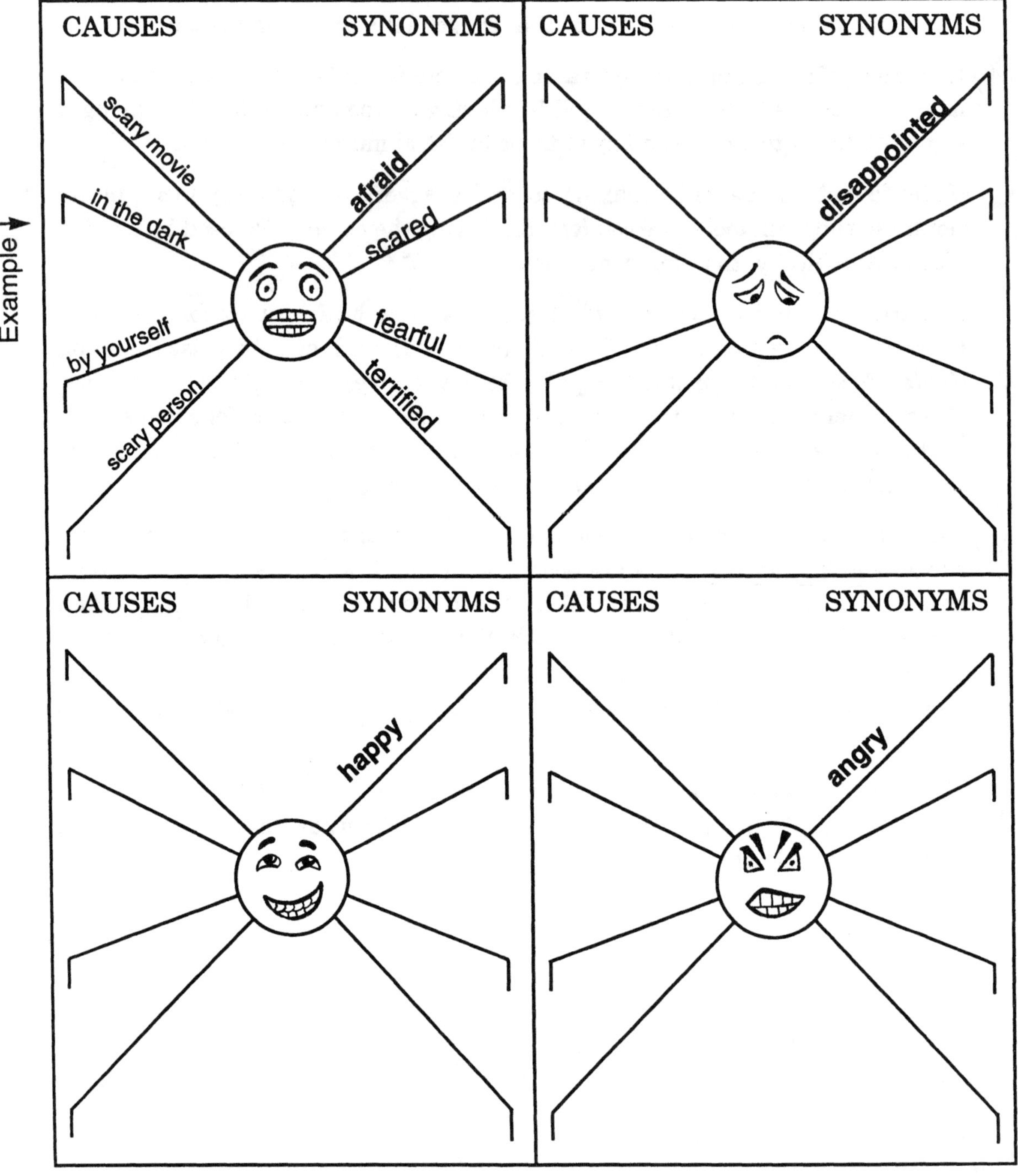

Lesson C

OBJECTIVES:

1. To identify labels and possible causes for these facial expressions: bored, jealous, sorry, and interested
2. To demonstrate awareness that facial expressions give stronger and more accurate messages than words (when facial expression and words don't match)
3. To identify inappropriate facial expressions

MATERIALS:

1. Index cards from Lesson B (One set per student)
2. *Spider Faces #3* (See page 159; one per pair of students and one transparency.)
3. *Facial Expression* classroom poster (See page 13.)
4. *Thought Bubble* (See *Appendix O*; one for educator use.)
5. *Skill Step #2* (See pages 160–162; one per student and one transparency.)
6. *Checking Myself* (See *Appendix I*; one per student and one transparency.)

PREPARATORY SET:

Ask for student volunteers to demonstrate facial expressions for angry, happy, afraid, and disappointed. Ask the other students to guess the feeling each volunteer shows, using the numbered index card system described in the Preparatory Set during Lesson B.

PLAN:

1. Pair students using the *Inside-Outside Circle* activity (see *Appendix P*). Display and distribute *Spider Faces #3* to each pair of students. Direct students' attention to the "example" (the bored spider) and discuss the synonyms and possible causes for the facial expression. Allow students to add ideas not listed. Ask students to work with their partners to think of synonyms and causes for the remaining spider facial expressions. Tell students you will be calling on one or more groups to share their answers.
2. After the pairs have had time to complete the activity, ask them to share their synonyms and causes for each facial expression. Write their responses on the

transparency as they are shared. If students are having difficulty thinking of synonyms, provide examples:

Jealous—envious, resentful, bitter

Sorry—apologetic, guilty, ashamed

Interested—alert, involved, curious

(This page will prepare students for the "Bingo" activity during Lesson E.)

3. Review the definition and skill steps for *facial expression* by referring the class to the *Facial Expression* classroom poster. Tell students that today's lesson will focus on skill step #2.

4. Model use of the facial expression skill step #2 while thinking aloud. A scripted example follows:

Introduction

I am going to pretend to be a student in class. I've just found out that I don't get to be partners with the person I was hoping for. I will show you the facial expression I decide to use and tell you the thoughts I'm having. When I hold up this Thought Bubble, *you'll know the words I'm saying are actually what I'm thinking.*

Actual Model

(Pause for a few seconds while showing a pouty facial expression.) While holding up the *Thought Bubble* say, *I wish I had gotten the partner I was hoping for! Oh, oh, my face looks pouty. I'd better stop. Pouting makes me look like a baby and it can get me into trouble. Also, I don't want to hurt my partner's feelings.* Put the *Thought Bubble* down, demonstrate a happy facial expression, and say, *OK, partner! We'd better get started.*

5. Distribute and display *Skill Step #2*. Read Cartoon A aloud to students.

6. Distribute and display the discussion guideline sheet called *Checking Myself*. Ask students to complete the goal statement with the words "use eye contact." Tell students that you will be having a discussion about the cartoon you just read to them. When a student is answering a question or making a comment during the discussion, it's important for everyone to give that student eye contact. Instruct them to put an "X" on their sheets each time they give eye contact to a student who is called on.

7. Model use of the *Checking Myself* sheet while thinking aloud. A scripted example follows:

Introduction

I am going to pretend to be one of you completing this sheet during the discussion we will be having. I will tell you the thoughts I'm having while I'm completing the sheet. When I hold up this Thought Bubble, *you'll know the words I'm saying are actually what I'm thinking.*

Actual Model

While holding up the *Thought Bubble* say, *OK, the teacher just called on Sharla. I'd better give her eye contact so she knows I'm listening to her answer. I'll put an "X" on my sheet because I gave her eye contact.* Put the *Thought Bubble* down and mark an "X" on the overhead transparency.

During the discussion, periodically remind students to give eye contact to the student who is answering or commenting and to mark their discussion guideline sheets.

8. Proceed with the discussion by asking these questions: (Cartoon A may need to be reread first.)

   - Why does Mr. Vue's face look worried and then angry in this cartoon?
   - What facial expressions does Lee use in this cartoon?
   - What facial expressions could Lee have used?

9. Display and read Cartoon B to students and then discuss it (continuing with the discussion guideline sheet procedure) using the following questions:

   - What facial expression does Jolisa use when Joshua gets called on?
   - Why do you think Mr. Aaron complimented the students who didn't pout?
   - What facial expressions could Jolisa have used?

10. Display and read Cartoon C to students and then discuss it (continuing with the discussion guideline sheet procedure) using the following questions:

    - What facial expression does Ann use when she meets the new girl?
    - Why do you think the new girl wants to invite Maria over but not Ann?
    - What facial expressions could Ann have used?

    After the discussion, have students complete the bottom of *Checking Myself*.

11. Process the use of the sheet by asking the following question or another one more appropriate for your group:

    - Why do you think it's important to give eye contact to the person who is speaking during a discussion?

Process further by asking the students who volunteered to speak during the discussion to share their answers to the following question:

- You answered one of the questions during our discussion. How did you feel when the other students gave you eye contact when you were talking?

12. Say with conviction to the class: *You are all great kids! I'm impressed with what you've learned in class today!*

Names ______________________________

SPIDER FACES #3

DIRECTIONS: 1. Fill in as many spider legs on the **right** as you can with synonyms (words that mean the same).

2. Fill in the spider legs on the **left** with situations that might cause the spider's facial expression.

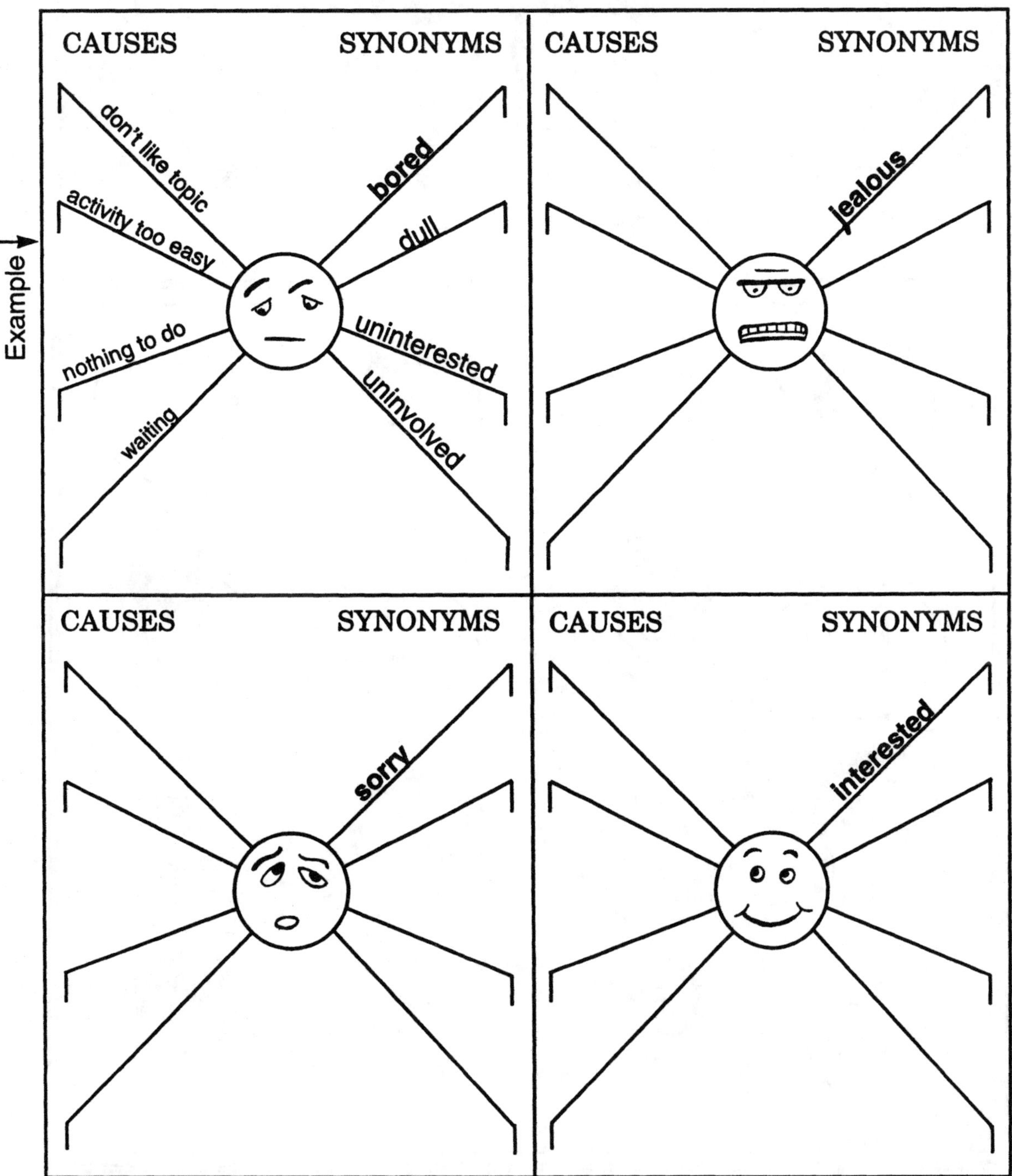

Name ______________________

SKILL STEP #2

STOP: If my face can get me into trouble
(rude, pouty, stuck-up)

CARTOON A

DIRECTIONS: Look at this cartoon about Mr. Vue and his son Lee.

Lee, you are two hours late! Where have you been?

I was with my friends.

You should have called! I've been worried!

I guess I should have.

You need to go to your room until you can talk nicely.

What did I say?

It's not what you said, it's the faces you've been making.

Oh.

Name ______________________

SKILL STEP #2 CONTINUED

CARTOON B

DIRECTIONS: Look at this cartoon about Mr. Aaron and his students.

Name ________________________

SKILL STEP #2 CONTINUED

CARTOON C

DIRECTIONS: Look at this cartoon about Maria, Ann, and Kris (a new girl).

Lesson D

OBJECTIVES:

1. To analyze inappropriate facial expressions
2. To identify labels and possible causes for these facial expressions: disgusted, worried, guilty, and confident
3. To prepare individualized *Facial Expression Bingo Cards,* which will be used as a learning tool

MATERIALS:

1. Index cards from Lesson B (One set per student)
2. Mirrors (One per pair of students)
3. *Spider Faces #4* (See page 165; one per pair of students and one transparency.)
4. *Bingo Pictures* (See page 166; one per student and one additional copy to be used by the educator.)
5. *Facial Expression Bingo Card* (See page 167; one per student.)
6. Scissors and glue (One per student)

PREPARATORY SET:

Ask for student volunteers to demonstrate facial expressions for bored, jealous, sorry, and interested. Ask the other students to guess the feeling each volunteer shows by using the numbered index card system described in the Preparatory Set during Lesson B.

PLAN:

1. Review the idea that inappropriate facial expressions can get a person in trouble by providing time for students to experience what it feels and looks like when making the three inappropriate facial expressions discussed in this unit (pouty, rude, and stuck-up).
2. Pair students (see *Appendix P*). Distribute the mirrors. Ask student pairs to take turns making a pouty facial expression. Have students analyze how the expression looks and feels by answering the following questions:

- When you pout, what do you do with your eyes and eyebrows? Your mouth and jaw? Your nose? Your ears? Your cheeks? Your forehead?

Ask students to experience rude and then stuck-up facial expressions by following the same procedure.

3. Display and distribute *Spider Faces #4* to each pair of students. Direct the students' attention to the "example" (the disgusted spider) and discuss the synonyms and possible causes for the facial expression. Ask students to add ideas not listed. Ask students to work with their partners to think of synonyms and causes for the remaining spider facial expressions. Tell students you will be calling on one or more groups to share their answers.

4. After the pairs have had time to complete the activity, ask them to share their synonyms and causes for each facial expression. Write their responses on the transparency as they are shared. If students are having difficulty thinking of synonyms, provide examples:

   Worried—anxious, frantic, troubled

   Guilty—ashamed, blamable, sorry

   Confident—secure, self-assured, sure

   (This page will prepare students for the "Bingo" activity during Lesson E.)

5. Distribute *Bingo Pictures, Facial Expression Bingo Card,* scissors, and glue. Ask each student to make a "Bingo Card" by following the directions printed on the top of *Bingo Pictures.* Monitor to see that each student's card is different from everyone else's in regard to the combination of faces in any given row or column on the card. After students have completed their individual *Facial Expression Bingo Cards,* collect them to redistribute during Lesson E. (The educator should also cut apart a set of the 16 facial expression pictures, and put them into a container to be used during the "Bingo" activity in Lesson E.)

6. Write the following where everyone can see it: I CAN CHOOSE TO USE STUPENDOUS, SPECTACULAR SOCIAL SKILLS! Have the students say this aloud, in unison, with energy.

Names ______________________________

SPIDER FACES #4

DIRECTIONS: 1. Fill in as many spider legs on the **right** as you can with synonyms (words that mean the same).

2. Fill in the spider legs on the **left** with situations that might cause the spider's facial expression.

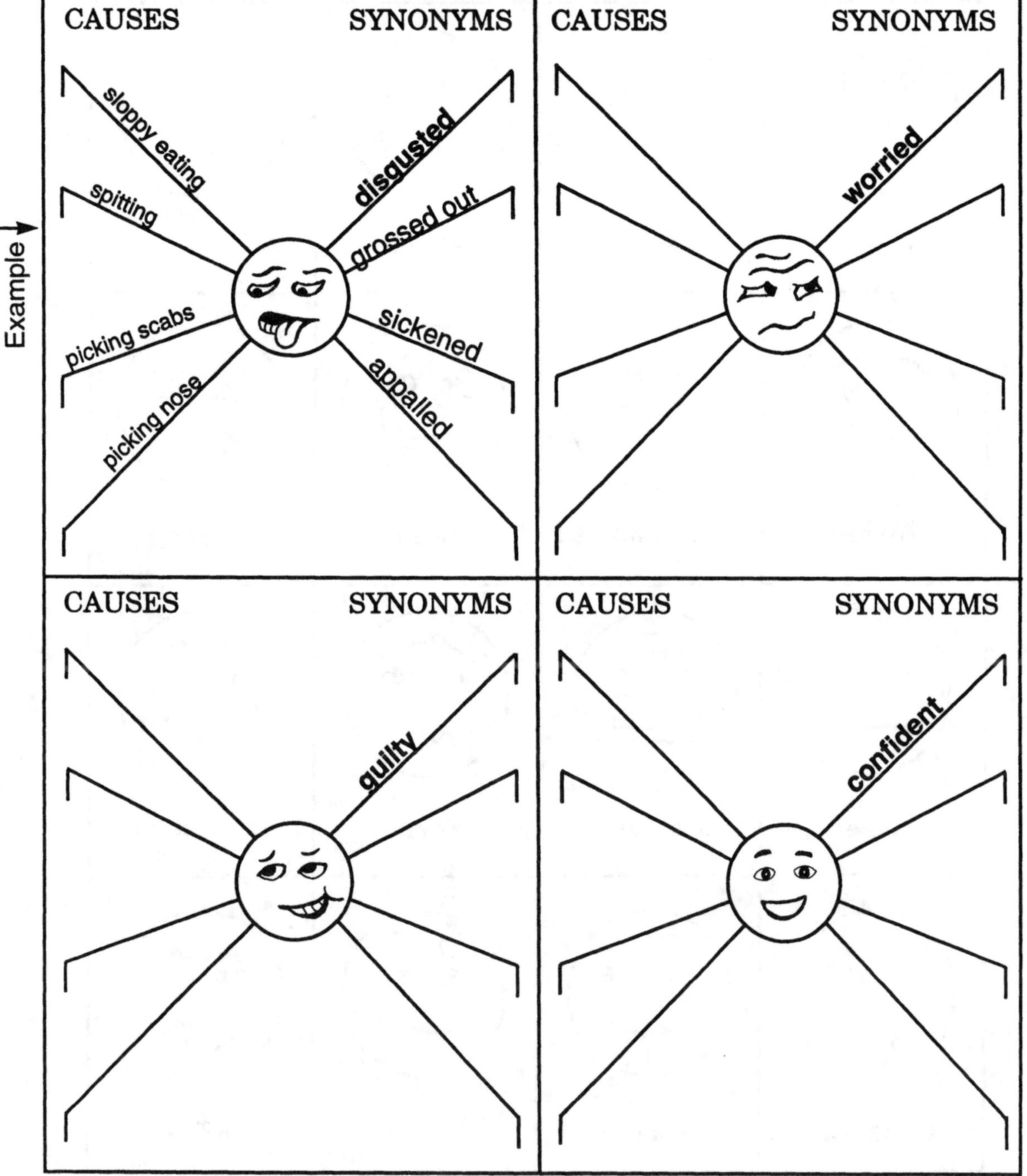

Name ____________________

BINGO PICTURES

DIRECTIONS: Before playing "Facial Expression Bingo," make a bingo card by:
1) Cutting apart the 16 pictures below.
2) Mixing up the pictures.
3) Gluing the pictures into the blank spaces on the bingo card.
The order of your pictures should be different from everyone else's.

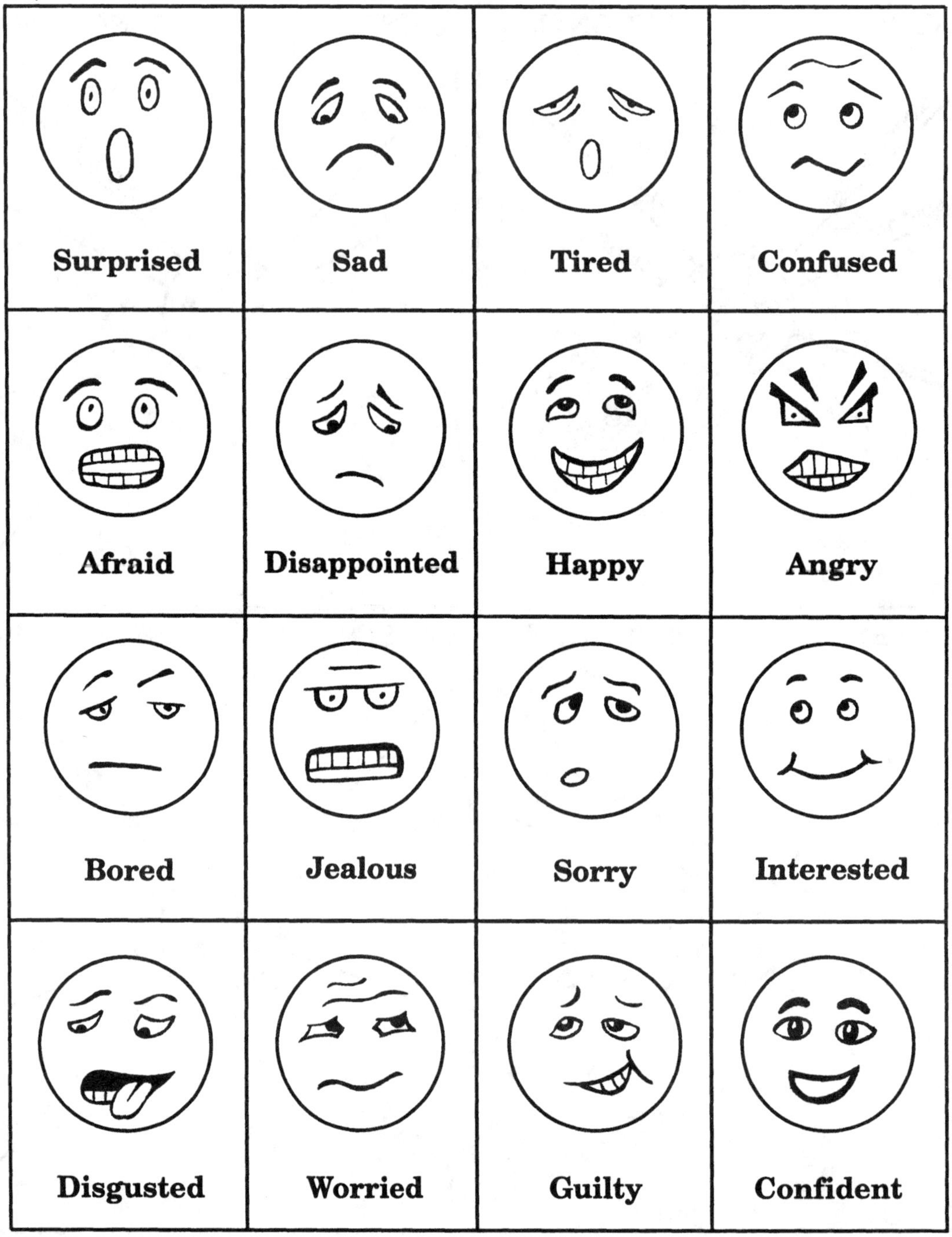

Surprised	**Sad**	**Tired**	**Confused**
Afraid	**Disappointed**	**Happy**	**Angry**
Bored	**Jealous**	**Sorry**	**Interested**
Disgusted	**Worried**	**Guilty**	**Confident**

Name ______________________

FACIAL EXPRESSION BINGO CARD

Lesson E

OBJECTIVES:

1. To review various facial expressions discussed during the unit
2. To demonstrate a variety of facial expressions

MATERIALS:

1. Index cards from Lesson B (One per student)
2. *Facial Expression Bingo Card* (Made during Lesson D; one per student)
3. 16 "Bingo" markers per student (e.g., chips, paper clips)
4. Container with 16 facial expression *Bingo Pictures* (Created by the educator during Lesson D)
5. Rewards for "Bingo" winners (Optional)

PREPARATORY SET:

Ask for student volunteers to demonstrate facial expressions for disgusted, worried, guilty, and confident. Ask the other students to guess the feeling each volunteer shows by using the numbered index card procedure described in the Preparatory Set during Lesson B.

PLAN:

1. Distribute an individualized *Facial Expression Bingo Card* and 16 markers to each student.
2. Review the rules for "Bingo" and then play the game (as often as time allows) by drawing *Bingo Pictures* from the container. As each picture is drawn, say the expression (or model it). Students need to find the appropriate expression on their *Facial Expression Bingo Cards* and cover it with a marker. "Bingo" is achieved by covering all expressions in a row vertically, horizontally, or diagonally. Vary the game by also including four corners to count as "Bingo." If desired, present a small reward to the "Bingo" winners.
3. Students could be asked to demonstrate each facial expression when they have "Bingo." Only the four expressions that won the "Bingo" need to be demonstrated. The winner could demonstrate all four expressions or could call on other students to help with the demonstrations.

4. **As an option to avoid a "winner-loser" feeling during the "Bingo" game, share a reward with each student for playing and participating.**

5. **Say with a smile to the class: *I enjoy seeing each of you grow as individuals as you use new social skills! You're terrific!* Ask them to think about how they've grown.**

Lessons X, Y, and Z

Due to similarities in format, the final three lesson plans for each unit in *Social Star* are provided in *Appendix A*. Substitute the phrase "facial expression" whenever a "_____" appears in the lesson plans. Information specific to this unit follows.

LESSON X PREPARATORY SET:

Tell the class that you will be reading the following situations to them. Pause after each and ask students to show the facial expression they would use.

- You are angry because your brother broke your skateboard.
- You are tired because it's getting late.
- You are surprised by the gift you just opened.

LESSON Y PREPARATORY SET:

Darken the room, if you prefer, and ask students to visualize themselves correctly using this social skill by reading the following script:

> *Let's take a few moments to relax.... Make sure you are in a comfortable position.... Close your eyes if you feel like it.... On the count of three, take a very slow, deep breath. One . . . two . . . three.... Breathe in deeply.... Now breathe out slowly.... Let your entire body relax.... Now imagine yourself during lunch asking your father if you can go to your friend's house. Your father says no. You are disappointed because you really wanted to go. You tell yourself, "I feel disappointed because I really wanted to go, so it's OK if I look disappointed at first, but there is no reason to pout for the rest of the day." You finish the meal without pouting. Think about how proud you are that you chose to use an appropriate expression.*

LESSON Z PLOT SITUATION:

Ask students to pretend that they are walking through the park and some older kids start following them and calling them names.

LESSON Z ROADBLOCK EXAMPLES:

- Using acceptable facial expressions when experiencing feelings such as anger, boredom, dislike, disappointment, pride
- Using appropriate facial expressions when talking with a person who is using inappropriate facial expressions

Name ____________________

Facial Expression T-Chart

LOOKS LIKE...	SOUNDS LIKE...
  	no sound

avoid looking like this...

HOME

Pretend you're eating dinner with your family. Your dad is talking about a trip he went on when he was a kid. Show an interested facial expression.

SCHOOL

Pretend you listened to directions about how to do a science experiment, but you didn't understand them. Show a confused facial expression you could use to let your teacher know you don't understand.

COMMUNITY

Pretend you are up to bat in a softball game. Show a confident facial expression you could show to the pitcher.

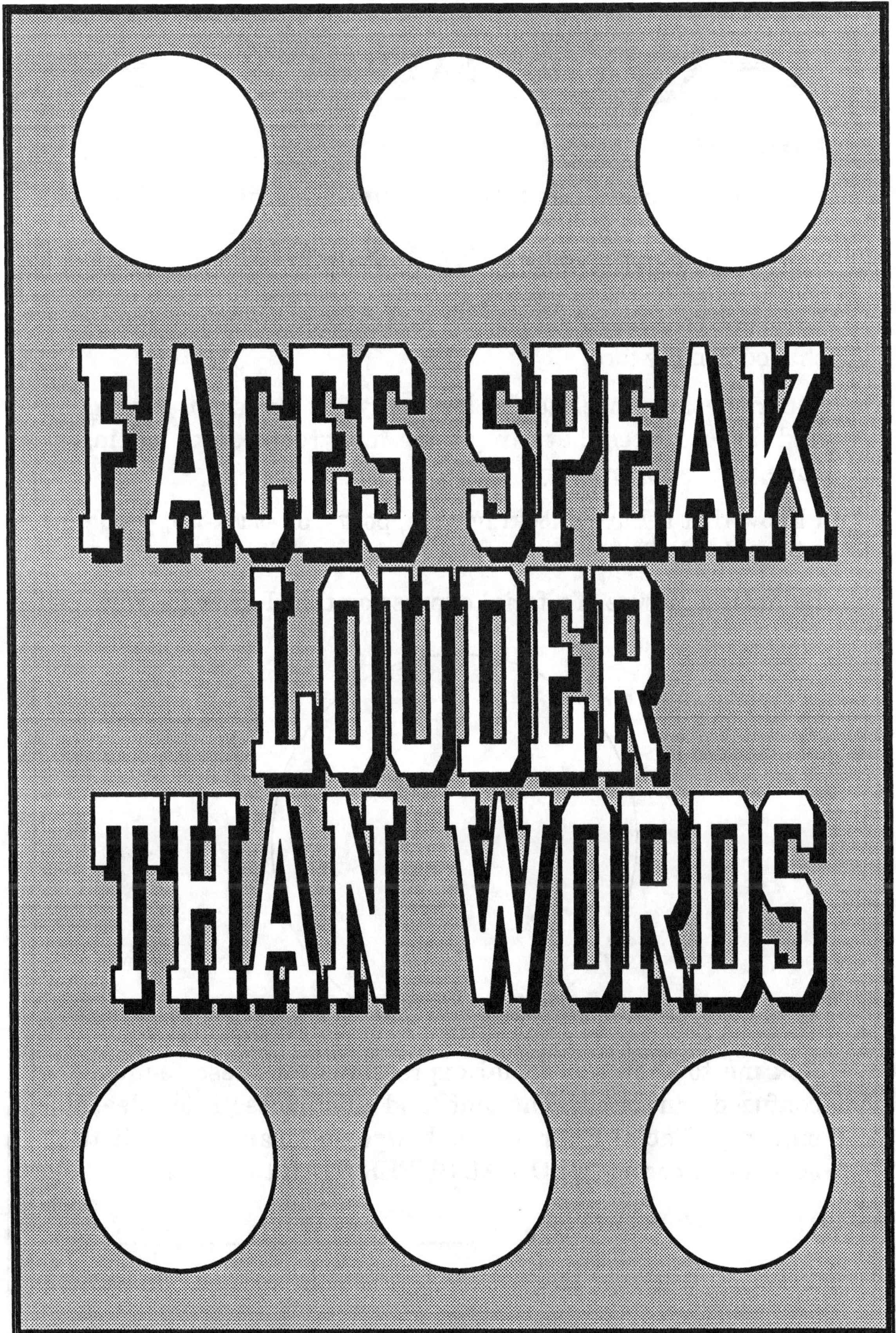
FACES SPEAK
LOUDER
THAN WORDS

HOME-A-GRAM

Dear Family,

At school, we have been talking about the social skill called

FACIAL EXPRESSION

I learned that *facial expression* means showing how I feel by the look on my face.

I learned that I need to think about what my face is saying, and not use faces that can get me into trouble, like looking rude, stuck-up, or pouty.

I know that if I avoid looking rude, pouty, or stuck-up, people will probably like me better and I'll feel proud.

Below is a picture of a facial expression that I drew for you.

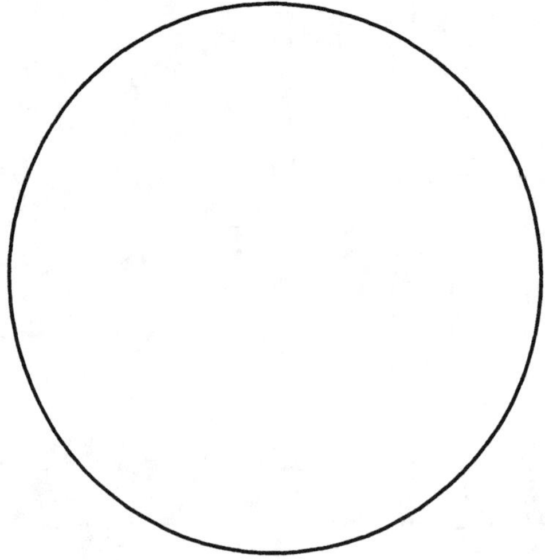

Ask me to show you facial expressions for these feelings: confused, surprised, confident, and tired. After I do, please sign my "Facial Expression" badge so I can return it to school and become a SOCIAL SUPER STAR this week.

From: ______________________________

Posture

UNIT GOAL:

To demonstrate comprehension and use of appropriate posture

EDUCATOR INFORMATION:

This unit emphasizes use of a standing or sitting posture which is appropriate to the situation. Students learn that in some situations, it is appropriate to stand or sit up straight, and in other situations it is acceptable to stand or sit in a more relaxed way. Students learn that their posture can send messages to other people about how they are feeling. The benefits of a using a confident posture (whether standing or sitting in a straight or more relaxed way) are addressed. The educator should exert sensitivity and care in generalizing rules about posture into the children's home cultures.

RELATED ACTIVITIES:

1. Have students study the skeletal system and how it provides the framework for body posture.
2. Have students visit a health care professional (e.g., a chiropractor, an x-ray technician) and view an x-ray machine and x-rays of the spine. Ask the health care professional to discuss ways of keeping a person's spine healthy.
3. Photograph students using confident standing and sitting appropriate postures. Display the photographs or give the photographs to the students.
4. Invite adults from different cultures to talk to the students about how their cultures' conventions for posture compare with American common culture norms.

It is important for educators to provide opportunities for students to work in groups so they can experience social skills in contexts where social communication is needed. Therefore, educators are encouraged to have students complete the Related Activities in small groups whenever possible. Educators trained in cooperative learning could incorporate the five components (see page 34) into the group activity.

RELATED LITERATURE:

Jamaica Tag-Along (1989) by Juanita Havill, Ill. by Anne Sibley O'Brien, Houghton Mifflin. (Picture book)

Mama One, Mama Two (1982) by Patricia MacLachlan, Ill. by Ruth Lercher Bornstein, Harper and Row. (Picture book)

Not So Fast, Songololo (1986) by Niki Daly, Ill. by author, Atheneum. (Picture book)

On My Honor (1986) by Marion Dave Bauer, Clarion. (Text) (pages 79, 84)

The Relatives Came (1985) by Cynthia Rylant, Ill. by Stephen Gammell, Bradbury. (Picture book)

Where's Our Mama? (1991) by Diane Goode, Ill. by author, Dutton. (Picture book)

SOCIAL SKILLS ALL DAY LONG:

Look for opportunities to teach social skills throughout the day (incidental teaching). Four ways to reinforce good social skills and an example of each follow:

Encouragement

During class today, you used appropriate posture by sitting up straight. That showed me you were paying attention and you were interested in what was going on. Super job!

Personal Example

When I was in a faculty meeting, I sat up straight. Using appropriate posture showed the principal that I was listening.

Prompting

Tomorrow when you tell the class about your project, use a posture that shows that you are confident and proud of your work.

Corrective Feedback (must be positive, private, specific, and nonthreatening)

Maria, when the speaker was talking, you were slouched in your seat and your head was on your desk. You could have sat up straight and looked alert. Using appropriate posture in class will make a good impression and can help you pay better attention.

Lesson A

OBJECTIVES:

1. To state the meaning of *posture* and tell why it is important
2. To tell the self-talk associated with correct use of the skill

MATERIALS:

1. *Posture* (See page 180; one per student and one transparency.)
2. *Thought Bubble* (See *Appendix O*; one for educator use.)
3. *Numbered Stones* (See *Appendix P*; one set per pair of students.)
4. *Checking Myself* (See *Appendix I*; one per student and one transparency.)

PREPARATORY SET:

Ask four students to come to the front of the class. Instruct the first student to sit with a straight posture, the second to sit with a more relaxed posture, the third to stand with a straight posture, and the fourth to stand with a more relaxed posture. Tell the class that each student is using a different posture. Inform students that in this unit they will be learning when it may be appropriate to use each type of posture.

PLAN:

1. Distribute and display *Posture.* Discuss the definition. Explain the skill step and the symbol next to it. Remind students that the symbol is there to help them visualize and remember the skill step. Discuss the reasons for using appropriate posture.
2. Model use of the posture skill step while thinking aloud. A scripted example follows:

   Introduction

   I am going to pretend to be a student your age. I am sitting in class listening to my teacher. I will show you appropriate posture for this situation and tell you the thoughts I'm having. When I hold up this Thought Bubble, *you'll know the words that I'm saying are actually what I'm thinking.*

Actual Model

While holding up the *Thought Bubble* say, *I want the teacher to know that I am paying attention. Am I using the right posture for this situation? Yes! I'm sitting up straight. The teacher will think that I'm alert.*

3. Pair students using *Numbered Stones*. Read the story at the bottom of *Posture* aloud to students.

4. Distribute and display the discussion guideline sheet called *Checking Myself.* Ask students to complete the goal statement with the words "use a straight sitting posture," or another classroom discussion goal more appropriate for your group (see page 26). Tell students that you will be having a discussion about the story they just heard. Explain that during a discussion it's important to use a posture that shows that you are paying attention. Instruct them to put an "X" on their sheets each time they discuss a question with their partners using a straight sitting posture.

5. Model use of the *Checking Myself* sheet while thinking aloud. A scripted example follows:

Introduction

I am going to pretend to be one of you completing this sheet during the discussion we will be having. I will tell you the thoughts I'm having while I'm completing the sheet. When I hold up this Thought Bubble, *you'll know the words I'm saying are actually what I'm thinking.*

Actual Model

While holding up the *Thought Bubble* say, *OK, my partner and I need to discuss the question the teacher just asked. I'm going to use a straight sitting posture that shows I am paying attention to what my partner is saying. I'll put an "X" on my sheet because I'm sitting up straight.* Put the *Thought Bubble* down and mark an "X" on the overhead transparency.

During the discussion, periodically remind students to sit up straight and mark their discussion guideline sheets.

6. Proceed with the discussion by asking these questions: (The story may need to be reread first.)

- What posture did Jolisa use when she was sitting in class?
- What posture did Jolisa use when she was sitting on the couch at home?

- What might happen if Jolisa slouches down in her desk at school like she does on her couch at home?
- What might happen if Jolisa sits up straight on her couch at home like she does in her desk at school? (The answer could include that she may not feel as relaxed.)

After the discussion, have students complete the bottom of *Checking Myself.*

7. Process the use of the sheet by asking the following question or another one more appropriate for your group:

   - Why do you think it's important to use a straight sitting posture when discussing a question with a partner at school?

8. Ask four students to come to the front of the class and assume the same postures as those used during the Preparatory Set. Ask students to brainstorm situations when each of the four postures would be appropriate. Try to elicit a home, school, and community situation for each one.

9. Ask student pairs to take turns telling each other the meaning of *posture* and why it's important to use the skill. Students could be reminded that the information they are to say is printed on *Posture.*

   As an option to add structure to this activity (see *Appendix Q*), ask partners to come to an agreement about which person will be called "Tom Sawyer" and which person will be called "Huckleberry Finn." After students have made their decisions, ask "Tom" to tell "Huckleberry" the definition of *posture.* Next, ask "Huckleberry" to tell "Tom" the definition. Ask the students to use the same procedure to tell each other the reasons for using appropriate posture.

10. Write the following where everyone can see it: I FEEL JAZZED AND TOTALLY MARVELOUS WHEN I USE MY SOCIAL SKILLS. Have the students say this aloud, in unison, with energy.

Name ____________________

Posture

MEANING OF POSTURE: How straight your body looks

SKILL STEPS:

1. Ask myself: Is my posture right for this situation?

REASONS FOR USING THIS SKILL:

Using a posture that is right for the situation will make a good impression on others and will help you feel more comfortable.

DIRECTIONS: Listen to the story below. Look at the pictures of Jolisa while you are listening.

When Jolisa was sitting in her desk listening to a guest speaker at school, she sat up straight. At home that evening, Jolisa sat back in a more relaxed position on the couch when she was watching TV.

Lesson B

OBJECTIVE:

To demonstrate confident standing and sitting postures (both straight and more relaxed)

MATERIALS:

1. *Posture* classroom poster (See page 13.)
2. *What Is His Posture Saying?* (See page 183; one per student and one transparency.)
3. Full-length mirror (One for class use)
4. *Thought Bubble* (See *Appendix O*; one for educator use and two per pair of students.)

PREPARATORY SET:

Tell students that taking care of the back is important to help maintain appropriate posture. Demonstrate the procedure recommended for lifting objects to avoid back injury. The procedure includes bending the knees and keeping the back straight while lifting.

PLAN:

1. Review the definition and skill step for *posture* by referring the class to the *Posture* classroom poster.
2. Discuss the meaning of *feeling confident* and the benefits of feeling that way. Distribute and display *What Is His Posture Saying?* Identify which two of Victor's three standing postures show confidence and which two of Victor's three sitting postures show confidence. Circle the sitting and standing postures in which Victor does not look confident. Ask students to brainstorm feelings that Victor may be experiencing which are causing his posture not to look confident in the two circled pictures (e.g., scared, bored, tired, sick, unsure).
3. Position the full-length mirror in a secure way that allows students to view themselves in both sitting and standing positions. Ask students to take turns viewing themselves using each of the following postures:
   - Standing confident and straight
   - Standing confident and more relaxed

- Sitting confident and straight
- Sitting confident and more relaxed

4. Pair students (see *Appendix P*). Distribute two *Thought Bubbles* to each pair. Ask students to pretend they are sitting at their school desks and feeling very tired. Ask students to work with their partners to write self-talk in one of their *Thought Bubbles* that could be used to convince themselves to use a confident sitting posture even though they are feeling tired. Call on pairs at random to come to the front of the class, hold up their *Thought Bubbles,* and read their self-talk examples. Next, ask students to pretend they have been asked to come up to receive an award during a school assembly, and they are feeling very unsure and nervous. Ask students to work with their partners to write self-talk in their second *Thought Bubbles* that could be used to convince themselves to use a confident standing posture even though they are feeling nervous. Call on pairs at random to come to the front of the class, hold up their *Thought Bubbles,* and read their self-talk examples.

5. Ask student pairs to take turns telling each other the skill step for posture. Follow the procedure described in Step 9 of Lesson A. (As an option, ask students to decide who will be "Davy Crockett" and who will be "Daniel Boone.") Next, ask students to work with their partners to think of a situation when the use of straight sitting posture would be appropriate and a situation when a more relaxed sitting posture would be appropriate. Tell students that one or more pairs will be asked to share their situations. Have one or more pairs share their situation.

6. Say sincerely to the class: *You are an awesome class! You make teaching social skills totally tremendous!*

Name ____________________

What Is His Posture Saying?

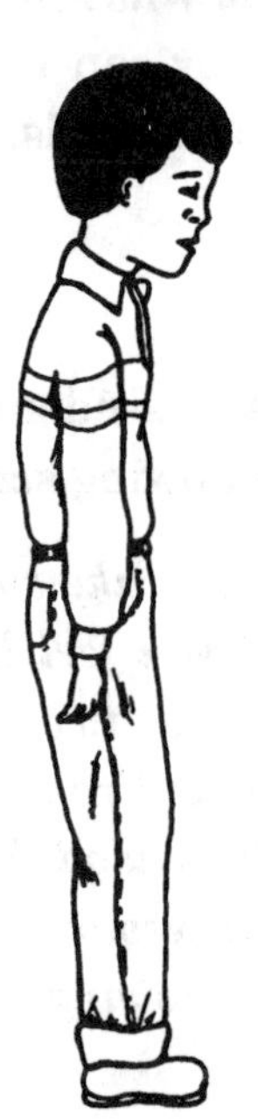

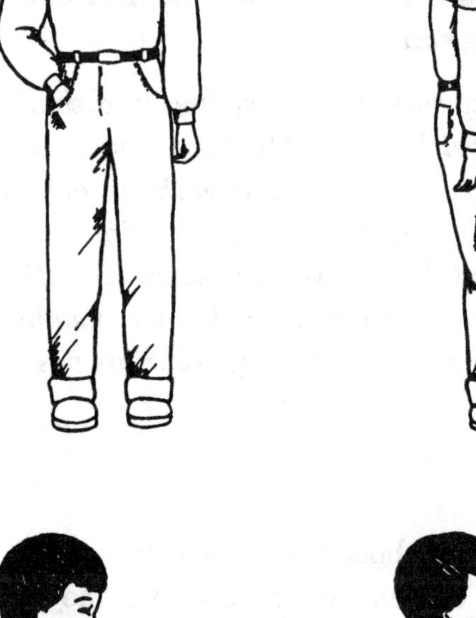

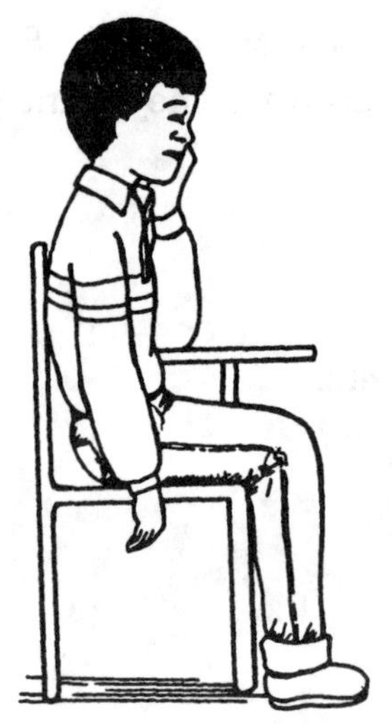

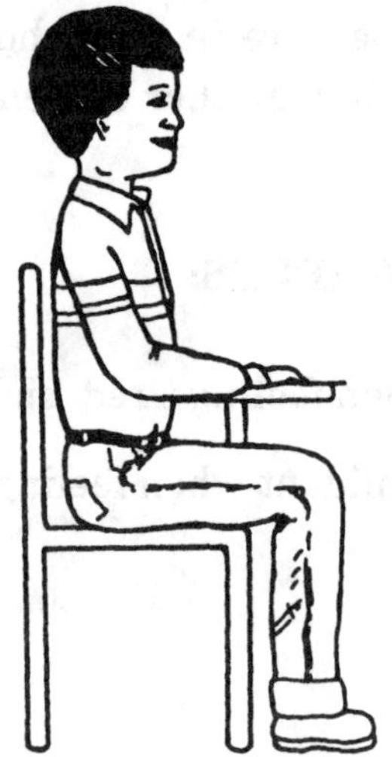

Lessons X, Y, and Z

Due to similarities in format, the final three lesson plans for each unit in *Social Star* are provided in *Appendix A*. Substitute the word "posture" whenever a "_____" appears in the lesson plans. Information specific to this unit follows.

LESSON X PREPARATORY SET:

Ask students to use a straight posture to balance a book on their heads while sitting and standing. Ask students to find out what happens to the book when they use a more relaxed posture. Tell students they can remember to use straight posture by picturing themselves with a book on their heads.

LESSON Y PREPARATORY SET:

Darken the room, if you prefer, and ask students to visualize themselves correctly using this social skill by reading the following script:

> *Let's take a few moments to relax.... Make sure you are sitting in a comfortable position.... Close your eyes if you feel like it.... On the count of three, take a very slow, deep breath. One . . . two . . . three.... Breathe in deeply.... Now breathe out slowly.... Let your entire body relax. Now imagine yourself meeting a new family in your neighborhood. Picture yourself using a confident posture. Think about the good impression you make on the new neighbors and the good feeling you get inside knowing you used an appropriate posture.*

LESSON Z PLOT SITUATION:

Ask students to pretend that they are in the school cafeteria eating lunch. Some other kids at their table are teasing another student in a mean way. They want you to tease the student too.

LESSON Z ROADBLOCK EXAMPLES:

- Using appropriate posture when feeling tired, sick, angry, etc.
- Using a posture that looks confident when feeling nervous

Name ____________________

Posture T-Chart

LOOKS LIKE...	SOUNDS LIKE...
straight  	no sound
more relaxed  	

HOME

Pretend that your mom is having some friends over. She is introducing you to her friends. Show the posture you could use to show you are confident and happy to meet them.

SCHOOL

Pretend your teacher has asked you to discuss a question with a partner. Show the posture you could use during the discussion to let your partner know you are interested in working together to find an answer.

COMMUNITY

Pretend you are standing while the national anthem is being sung. Show the posture you might use to make a good impression on people who see you.

PICK A POSTURE

that is right for the situation.

HOME-A-GRAM

Dear Family,

At school, we have been talking about the social skill called

POSTURE

I learned that *posture* means how straight my body looks when I am standing or sitting.

When I'm with others, I should ask myself, "Is my posture appropriate for this situation?"

When I use a posture that is right for the situation, I can make a good impression on others and feel comfortable inside.

A time when I could use a straight standing posture is:

____

____

A time when I could use a more relaxed standing posture is:

____

____

I will show you how I can use a posture that is appropriate for a situation which you describe to me. After I do, please sign my "Posture" badge so I can return it to school and become a SOCIAL SUPER STAR this week.

From: ________________________

Personal Space

UNIT GOAL:

To demonstrate comprehension and use of appropriate personal space

EDUCATOR INFORMATION:

1. This unit discusses the idea that varying amounts of personal space are appropriate in different situations. The unit teaches that although we all have different personal space comfort zones, many people in the American common culture feel comfortable being about an arm's length away from others in many situations. This unit discusses feelings associated with invasion of one's personal space and strategies to use when this occurs.

2. Rules for personal space vary among cultures. The Western culture is one of the few in which people stand apart from one another. In many cultures, two women or two men commonly walk arm in arm. According to Althen (1988), habits concerning "conversational distance" vary. For example, if an American is talking to a Greek, a Latino, or an Arab, the American may keep backing away because the other person keeps getting "too close." On the other hand, if the conversational partner is Japanese, the American may try to move closer because the Japanese insists on standing farther away. As the two people attempt to maintain a "normal" conversational distance, they are likely to be uncomfortable and may make negative judgments about each other. In the Hispanic English culture, touching is often observed between two people in conversation, while in the American English culture, touching is usually unacceptable and often carries sexual overtones (Taylor, 1993). The educator should exert sensitivity and care in generalizing rules about personal space into the children's home cultures.

RELATED ACTIVITIES:

1. Take students to a playground and ask them to practice using appropriate personal space while waiting in line to use various pieces of equipment (e.g., getting too close to the person in front while climbing can be dangerous; leaving too much space will cause others to wait longer for a turn.)

2. Photograph pairs of students demonstrating an appropriate personal space for most situations (an arm's length away). Display the photographs or give them to students to use as a reminder of the social skill.

3. Invite adults from different cultures to talk to the students about how their cultures' conventions for personal space compare with American common culture norms.

It is important for educators to provide opportunities for students to work in groups so they can experience social skills in contexts where social communication is needed. Therefore, educators are encouraged to have students complete the Related Activities in small groups whenever possible. Educators trained in cooperative learning could incorporate the five components (see page 34) into the group activity.

RELATED LITERATURE:

On My Honor (1986) by Marion Dave Bauer, Clarion. (Text) (pages 79, 84)

The Relatives Came (1985) by Cynthia Rylant, Ill. by Stephen Gammell, Bradbury. (Picture book)

Where's Our Mama? (1991) by Diane Goode, Ill. by author, Dutton. (Picture book)

SOCIAL SKILLS ALL DAY LONG:

Look for opportunities to teach social skills throughout the day (incidental teaching). Four ways to reinforce good social skills and an example of each follow:

Encouragement

When you came over to ask me a question, you stood about an arm's length away. I felt comfortable talking with you.

Personal Example

Whenever I need to speak to someone privately, I make sure that I stand close enough so others can't hear, but I try to leave enough personal space so that person can still feel comfortable.

Prompting

When you line up to come in from recess, think about personal space. Avoid bumping into and stepping on others.

Corrective Feedback (must be positive, private, specific, and nonthreatening)

Victor, when you asked to borrow an eraser from Ann, you stood very close to her. I could tell she felt uncomfortable because she backed away. If you had stood about an arm's length away, she may have felt more comfortable.

Lesson A

OBJECTIVES:

1. To state the meaning of *personal space* and tell why it is important
2. To tell the self-talk associated with correct use of the skill

MATERIALS:

1. *Personal Space* (See page 193; one per student and one transparency.)
2. *Thought Bubble* (See *Appendix O*; one for educator use.)

PREPARATORY SET:

Have students form two lines (lines A and B) that face one another and are at least eight feet apart. Each student should have a partner across from him or her in the opposite line. Ask students to identify who their partners are. Ask the students in line A to take one step (specify either a baby step, a medium step, or a giant step) toward their partners in line B. Ask the students in line B to take one step (specify which type) toward their partners in line A. Continue this procedure until students are too close to follow the instructions. Tell students that during this activity they were changing the distance between themselves and their partners. Explain that the distance is called *personal space,* which is the name of the unit they will be discussing in the next few lessons.

PLAN:

1. Distribute and display *Personal Space.* Discuss the definition. Explain the skill step and the symbol next to it. Remind students that the symbol is there to help them visualize and remember the skill step. Discuss the rationale for using appropriate personal space.
2. Model use of the personal space skill step while thinking aloud. A scripted example follows:

   Introduction

   I am going to pretend to be someone your age. I want to ask a student named Lee if I can borrow an eraser. I will show you an appropriate amount of personal space to use in this situation and tell you the thoughts I'm having. When I hold up this Thought Bubble, *you'll know the words that I'm saying are actually what I'm thinking.*

Actual Model

While holding up the *Thought Bubble* say, *I don't want Lee to feel uncomfortable because of the distance between us. Does my distance feel right in this situation? I think so. I'm standing about an arm's length away. I feel comfortable and Lee looks like he does too.*

3. Read the story at the bottom of *Personal Space* aloud to students.

4. Pair students (see *Appendix P*). Ask students to work with their partners to brainstorm situations when:

   - more than an arm's length of distance would probably feel comfortable.
   - about an arm's length of distance would probably feel comfortable.
   - less than an arm's length of distance would probably feel comfortable.

   Ask several student pairs to share their ideas with the class.

5. Ask student pairs to take turns telling each other the meaning of *personal space* and why it's important to use the skill. Students could be reminded that the information they are to say is printed on *Personal Space*.

   As an option to add structure to the activity (see *Appendix Q*), ask partners to come to an agreement about which person will be called "Eli Whitney" and which person will be called "George Washington Carver." After students have made their decisions, ask "Eli" to tell "George" the definition of *personal space*. Next, ask "George" to tell "Eli" the definition. Ask the students to use the same procedure to tell each other the reason for using the skill.

6. Say with a smile to the class: *I enjoy seeing each of you grow as individuals as you use new social skills! You're terrific!* Tell them to think about how they've grown.

Name ____________________

Personal Space

MEANING OF PERSONAL SPACE: The distance between two people

SKILL STEP:

1. Ask myself: Does my distance feel right in this situation?

REASON FOR USING THIS SKILL:

Using the right amount of personal space helps you and others feel comfortable.

DIRECTIONS: Listen to the story about Jolisa. Look at the pictures of Jolisa while you are listening.

When Jolisa was talking with Mr. Aaron, she stood about an arm's length away. At recess, Jolisa stood close to Ann while Ann was telling her a secret.

Lesson B

OBJECTIVES:

1. To tell how people may feel when their personal space comfort zones are violated
2. To tell what people can say or do when their personal space comfort zones are violated

MATERIALS:

1. Hula-Hoop
2. *Personal Space* classroom poster (See page 13.)
3. *Take A Look* (See page 197; one per student and one transparency.)
4. *Checking Myself* (See *Appendix I*; one per student and one transparency.)
5. *Thought Bubble* (See *Appendix O*; one for educator use.)

PREPARATORY SET:

Hold a Hula-Hoop around your waist. Tell students that the Hula-Hoop shows about how big a "comfort zone" is for many people, which means that in many situations people feel comfortable standing about that far apart. Give a few examples of exceptions, such as receiving a hug from someone special. Go on to explain that for many people in the common American culture, their comfort zone is about the size of a Hula-Hoop (about an arm's length away), but for some people it is closer and for others it is farther away. This would be an opportune time to discuss the information about cultural differences provided in the Educator Information section (see page 189). Explain to students that they can tell when someone is violating their personal space by standing too close because they will feel uncomfortable inside. They can also tell if they are violating someone else's personal space because the other person will look uncomfortable.

PLAN:

1. Review the definition and skill step for *personal space* by referring the class to the *Personal Space* classroom poster.
2. Distribute and display *Take A Look*. Tell students that each cartoon shows a way that others may use inappropriate personal space. Ask students to look at each cartoon as you read it aloud.

3. Distribute and display the discussion guideline sheet called *Checking Myself*. Ask students to complete the goal statement with the words "think about an answer to each question asked," or use another classroom discussion goal more appropriate for your group (see page 26). Tell students that you will be having a discussion about the cartoons. During the discussion, it is important that each of them think about an answer to each question, even if they are not called on. Instruct them to put an "X" on their sheets each time they think of an answer to a question. It's important that the educator provide enough "wait time" before calling on a student to orally answer each question.

4. Model use of the *Checking Myself* sheet while thinking aloud. A scripted example follows:

Introduction

I am going to pretend to be one of you completing this sheet during the discussion we will be having. I will tell you the thoughts I'm having while I'm completing this sheet. When I hold up this Thought Bubble, *you'll know the words I'm saying are actually what I'm thinking.*

Actual Model

While holding up the *Thought Bubble* say, *OK, the teacher just asked if Ann is using the right amount of personal space in the first cartoon. I need to think about the answer.... No, she isn't using the right amount. I'll put an "X" on my paper because I just thought of an answer for that question.* Put the *Thought Bubble* down and mark an "X" on the overhead transparency.

5. Proceed with the discussion by rereading each cartoon and then asking the following questions as a follow-up. During the discussion, periodically remind students to be thinking of answers and to mark their discussion guideline sheets.

Cartoon #1:

- Is Ann using an appropriate amount of personal space?
- How do you think Victor feels when she bumps into him again?
- What could Victor say to Ann to remind her about personal space?

Cartoon #2:

- Is Mike using an appropriate amount of personal space?
- How do you think Maria feels when she doesn't have room for her legs?
- What could Maria say to Mike to remind him about personal space?

Cartoon #3:

- Is Jolisa using an appropriate amount of personal space?
- How do you think Mike and Victor feel when Jolisa is sitting so far away from them?
- What could Mike and Victor say to remind Jolisa about personal space?

Ask students to think of other situations when their personal space comfort zones might be violated. Ask students to identify what they could say or do in each situation.

After the discussion, have students complete the bottom of *Checking Myself.*

6. Process the use of the sheet by asking the following questions or others more appropriate for your group:
   - Why is it important to think of answers to questions during a discussion?
   - Why is it that sometimes people don't think about answers to questions during discussion?
7. Pair students using *Line Up–Fold Up* (see *Appendix P*). Ask student pairs to take turns telling each other the skill step for personal space. Follow the procedure described in step 5 of Lesson A. (As an option, ask students to decide who will be "Louis Pasteur" and who will be "Jonas Salk.") Next, ask students to think of a situation when it would be appropriate to stand about an arm's length away from another person. Tell students that one or more pairs will be asked to share their situation. Have students share some of the situations.
8. Say sincerely to the class: *You are important and capable people in this world! You can use your good social skills to get along with other people!*

Name ____________________

TAKE A LOOK

CARTOON #1

CARTOON #2

CARTOON #3

Lessons X, Y, and Z

Due to similarities in format, the final three lesson plans for each unit in *Social Star* are provided in *Appendix A.* Substitute the words "personal space" whenever a "______" appears in the lesson plans. Information specific to this unit follows.

LESSON X PREPARATORY SET:

Ask students to position themselves in various spots around the classroom. Ask students to hold their arms out in front of them and turn to form an imaginary circle around themselves. Explain that the "circles" could be their comfort zones of personal space.

LESSON Y PREPARATORY SET:

Darken the room, if you prefer, and ask students to visualize themselves correctly using this social skill by reading the following script:

> *Let's take a few moments to relax.... Make sure you are sitting in a comfortable position.... Close your eyes if you feel like it.... On the count of three, take a very slow, deep breath. One . . . two . . . three.... Breathe in deeply.... Now breathe out slowly.... Let your entire body relax. Now imagine yourself during recess. Picture yourself leaving enough space between you and your friend when you climb up the ladder to the slide.... When you need to talk to the playground supervisor, you stand about an arm's length away. When you line up to go in, you are careful not to bump into the person in front of you. Think about how great it feels to use appropriate personal space.*

LESSON Z PLOT SITUATION:

Ask students to pretend that they are being blamed for something they did not do (e.g., being falsely accused for not bringing the playground ball back into the school).

LESSON Z ROADBLOCK EXAMPLES:

- Asking someone to move away, and the person doesn't move
- Being in a very crowded line, elevator, or bus
- Talking with someone from a culture with personal space rules different from your own

Name ______________________

Personal Space T-Chart

LOOKS LIKE...	SOUNDS LIKE...
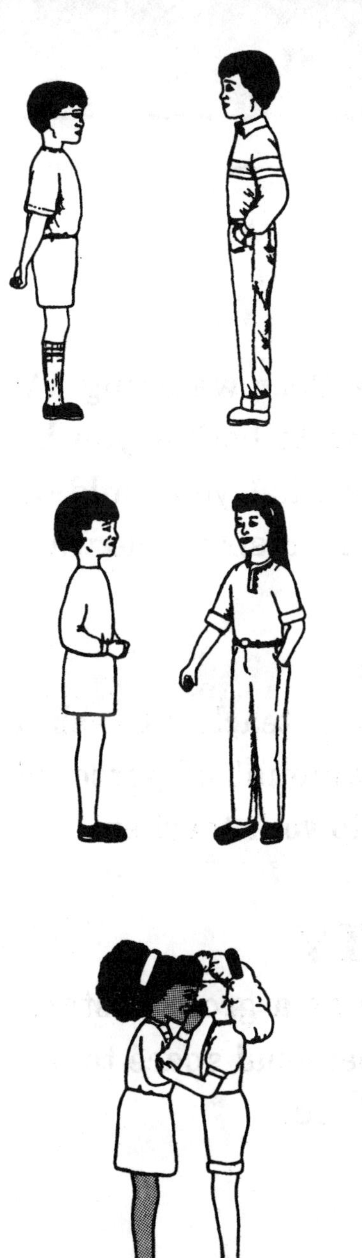	no sound

HOME

Pretend that you are lying on the floor watching TV with your brother. He keeps trying to bother you by not giving you enough space. Show what you could do or say to get more personal space in a responsible way.

SCHOOL

Pretend you want to walk up to your teacher to ask a question. Show the appropriate amount of personal space to use when you are talking to your teacher.

COMMUNITY

Pretend you are standing in line at a grocery store. Show the appropriate amount of personal space to use with the person waiting in front of you.

Think About
PERSONAL SPACE

HOME-A-GRAM

PERSONAL SPACE

I learned that *personal space* means the distance between two people.

Whenever I'm with other people, I should ask myself, "Does my distance feel right in this situation?"

I learned that using the right amount of personal space helps other people and me to feel comfortable.

I know that in many situations I should stand about an arm's length away from other people. But sometimes it's good to stand further away or closer together. Below, I wrote a situation for each one.

A time to stand more than an arm's length away:

____

____

A time to stand about an arm's length away:

____

____

A time to stand closer than an arm's length away:

____

____

Please sign my "Personal Space" badge after I tell you what I can do or say when someone is too close to me, so I can return it to school and become a SOCIAL SUPER STAR this week.

From: __________________________

Hygiene

UNIT GOAL:

To demonstrate comprehension and use of basic personal hygiene habits

EDUCATOR INFORMATION:

1. This unit was developed to teach students the importance of basic hygiene. The unit does not attempt to set a specific standard about how often hair should be washed or how often a child should take a bath. The authors recognize that some parents may choose not to have their children shower or bathe every day, etc. This unit advocates that students take baths or showers when they want to look and feel better. This unit emphasizes that people use basic hygiene to feel good, to make a positive impression on others, and to help in staying healthy.

2. The educator needs to be sensitive to the feelings of students in class who may not use good hygiene. If a student has poor hygiene due to parental neglect or purposely practices poor hygiene because of emotional problems, the educator should take special caution not to alienate the student during the class activities. The educator might work with the student privately to determine some changes that the child could make. This student would need to be reinforced for making improvements in hygiene, and the reinforcement should be delivered without the knowledge of other class members. Time for hygiene-related activities could be available to students upon arriving at school. Students may be given the opportunity to brush teeth, comb hair, wash hands and faces, or if necessary, shower.

3. It is interesting to note that hygiene practices vary in different cultures. For example, in India people regularly put oil in their hair and comb it through. In southeast Asia, people bathe several times a day due to the heat. Since they often have no running water, they bathe next to a large pool of water by dipping out water with a dish. Powder is used frequently. Children are often seen with white, powdered faces immediately after bathing. In Thailand, there are foot baths outside many houses. People who have been walking on dusty roads can wash their feet before entering the house. Althen (1988) notes that many foreigners feel that "Americans are hung up on body odor." Some cultures contend that a more "natural" smell is better. Interestingly, Americans themselves "smell bad" according to the stereotype that Japanese and others have of them. What smells "good" and what smells "bad" turns out to be a matter of personal and cultural experience. The educator should exert sensitivity and care in generalizing rules about hygiene into the children's home cultures.

RELATED ACTIVITIES:

1. Discuss how hygiene needs increase as children get older and bodies change.
2. Have a speaker from the health department talk to children about the rules and regulations governing restaurants in regard to hygiene and food preparation.
3. Have the class put together a "Hygiene Basket" (soap, shampoo, toothpaste, toothbrushes, dental floss, facial tissue). Keep the basket in the classroom for student use.
4. Have students write poems about hygiene using one of the formats that follow. (Students write one word on each line.) Example poems have been created:

Hygiene,
Keep Clean,
Wash Your Hair,
Smell Nice,
Hygiene.

Use
Good Hygiene.
Keep Healthy Now!
It's Cool!
Hygiene.

5. Have students investigate how people in other countries keep themselves clean.
6. Provide students with information on how to wash their own clothes or what strategies they can use if there are no clean clothes to put on.
7. Have students put on a hygiene/health fair and invite younger students.
8. As a lab activity, have students try a variety of hand soaps to compare their qualities (e.g., cleaning power, fragrance, feel).
9. Have students visit a local clinic, hospital, or dental office to find out what measures are taken to help prevent the spread of communicable diseases.
10. Invite adults from different cultures to talk to the students about how their cultures' conventions for hygiene compare with American common culture norms.

It is important for educators to provide opportunities for students to work in groups so they can experience social skills in contexts where social communication is needed. Therefore, educators are encouraged to have students complete the Related Activities in small groups whenever possible. Educators trained in cooperative learning could incorporate the five components (see page 34) into the group activity.

RELATED LITERATURE:

No More Baths (1980) by Brock Cole, Ill. by author, Doubleday. (Picture book)

Russel Rides Again (1985) by Johanna Hurwitz, Morrow. (Text)
Sister Elisa takes her bath first, then Russell was in the tub so long he looked like a raisin. (pages 28-40)

SOCIAL SKILLS ALL DAY LONG:

Look for opportunities to teach social skills throughout the day (incidental teaching). Four ways to reinforce good social skills and an example of each follow:

Encouragement

Your hair looks so clean. I'll bet that feels great!

Personal Example

Even though I'm not always dirty, I take a shower or bath almost every day because it helps me feel so good.

Prompting

Lots of students in our room have colds right now. Each of you can help stop the germs from spreading to others by covering your mouth when you cough and by washing your hands often.

Corrective Feedback (must be positive, private, specific, and nonthreatening)

Mike, you just took a drink out of Lee's can of soda. You need to remember not to share drinks because that is a way germs are spread.

Lesson A

OBJECTIVES:

1. To state the meaning of *hygiene* and tell why it is important
2. To tell the self-talk associated with correct use of the skill

MATERIALS:

1. A bag containing a variety of common hygiene items (e.g., soap, toothbrush, toothpaste, washcloth, towel, comb)
2. *Hygiene* (See page 208; one per student and one transparency.)
3. *Thought Bubble* (See *Appendix O*; one for educator use.)
4. *Thinking Skills Web* (See *Appendix T*; one per pair of students and one transparency.)

PREPARATORY SET:

Have all of the hygiene items in a bag before class. Give clues to students to help them identify a certain hygiene item. For example, the clues for *toothbrush* might include: It's 6–7 inches long, it's skinny, part of it's made of plastic, it has bristles, it's used in the mouth, etc. As soon as someone guesses the item, take the item out of the bag. Continue the activity until all the hygiene items have been identified. Explain to the class that these are items that people use to improve their hygiene so they can look and feel better. Tell the students that they will be learning about hygiene in the next few lessons.

PLAN:

1. Distribute and display *Hygiene*. Discuss the definition. Explain the skill step and the symbol next to it. Remind students that the symbol is there to help them visualize and remember the skill step. Discuss the reasons for using good hygiene.
2. Model use of the hygiene skill step while thinking aloud. A scripted example follows:

   Introduction

   I am going to pretend to be a student your age getting ready for school. I will show you how I use good hygiene and tell you the thoughts I'm having. When

I hold up this Thought Bubble, *you'll know the words I'm saying are actually what I'm thinking.*

Actual Model

While holding up the *Thought Bubble* say, *I'm going to school today. What do I need to do to look and feel good? I don't need to take a bath because I took one last night. I do need to brush my teeth, wash my face, and comb my hair though.*

3. Pair students (see *Appendix P*). Read the story at the bottom of *Hygiene* aloud to students. Ask students to work with their partners to find seven actions that Lee takes to have good hygiene. Call on pairs to share their answers until all seven actions have been identified.

4. Distribute and display *Thinking Skills Web*. Have students work with their partners to brainstorm things they could do to have good hygiene (e.g., brush teeth, take a bath). Write "good hygiene" on the inside circle and the ways to have good hygiene on the outside lines.

5. Tell the student pairs that tomorrow the class will be having a special guest speak to them about the importance of using good hygiene. Ask them to discuss with each other what questions about hygiene they might like to ask the speaker. Ask students to write their questions on paper. Call on pairs to share questions they wrote. Collect the questions and save them for Lesson B.

6. Ask student pairs to take turns telling each other the meaning of *hygiene* and why it's important to use the skill. Students could be reminded that the information they are to say is printed on *Hygiene.*

   As an option to add structure to this activity (see *Appendix Q*), ask partners to come to an agreement about which person will be called "Christopher Columbus" and which person will be called "Ferdinand Magellan." After the students have made their decision, ask "Christopher" to tell "Ferdinand" the definition of *hygiene.* Next, ask "Ferdinand" to tell "Christopher" the definition. Ask students to use the same procedure to tell each other the reasons for using good hygiene.

7. Write the following where everyone can see it: SOCIAL SKILLS, SOCIAL SKILLS! RAH! RAH! RAH! Have the students say this aloud, in unison, with spirit.

Name ___________________________

Hygiene

MEANING OF HYGIENE: Keeping your body and clothes clean

SKILL STEP:

1. Ask myself: What could I do right now to have good hygiene?

REASONS FOR USING THIS SKILL:

Good hygiene helps you look and feel better. It helps you to stay healthy. Also, people may be more comfortable being with you.

DIRECTIONS: Listen to the story below. Look at the picture of Lee while you are listening. Find seven things that Lee does to have good hygiene.

Lee has good hygiene. He takes a bath and washes his hair when he wants to look or feel better. Lee remembers to wash his hands before he eats and to wash up after he eats. He brushes his teeth after a snack or a meal and before he goes to bed. Lee combs his hair so that it looks neat. He picks clean clothes to wear when he goes to school.

Lesson B

OBJECTIVE:

To state some basic hygiene rules and to ask questions about hygiene

EDUCATOR INFORMATION:

In this lesson, a guest speaker talks to the class about hygiene. It would be most desirable to ask a person knowledgeable about hygiene (i.e., a school or public health nurse). If that is not possible, this lesson offers the option of using the figure of Dr. Juanita Parra to speak to the class about hygiene. A list of things the speaker should address is included in step 4 of the Plan. This list could be provided to the speaker prior to the presentation.

MATERIALS:

1. A small contest prize (See Preparatory Set below.)
2. *Hygiene* classroom poster (See page 13.)
3. Questions for the guest speaker (Created in Lesson A)
4. *Thank You!* (See page 211; one transparency.)
5. Figure of Dr. Juanita Parra (See *Appendix F*, if a guest speaker was not found.)

PREPARATORY SET:

Discuss the idea that doctors and nurses are very interested in hygiene because people who practice good hygiene habits don't get sick as often. Ask students to guess how many physicians are listed in the phone book. Give a small prize to the student whose guess comes closest.

PLAN:

1. Review the definition and skill step for *hygiene* by referring the class to the *Hygiene* classroom poster.
2. Ask students to think about who they were partners with in Lesson A. Challenge them to see if they can all get with their partners in 30 seconds or less. Distribute the questions written during Lesson A. Ask students to set their questions aside until later in the lesson. Ask partners to take turns telling each other the skill step for hygiene. Follow the procedure described in step 6 of

Lesson A. (As an option, ask students to decide who will be "Florence Nightingale" and who will be "Marie Curie.") Next, ask students to work together with their partners to think of a situation when the use of hygiene is important. Tell students that one or more pairs will be called on to share their situation. Have one or more pairs share their situation.

3. Remind students that a guest speaker will be talking to them about hygiene. Encourage careful listening while the speaker is talking. After the speaker is finished, they will have a chance to ask any questions they wrote during Lesson A which were not answered.

4. Introduce the guest speaker (or hold up the figure of Dr. Parra and introduce her to the class). Have the speaker begin the presentation by telling students that using good hygiene is very important in keeping themselves healthy. The presenter could continue by discussing the hygiene rules that follow:

   - Wash your hands before eating.
   - Wash up after meals.
   - Bathe or shower when you want to look, feel, or smell better.
   - Brush your teeth after eating and before going to bed.
   - Use dental floss on a regular basis.
   - Wash your hair when you want it to look, feel, or smell better.
   - Flush the toilet and wash your hands after going to the bathroom.
   - Don't drink from other people's glasses.
   - Don't share combs and brushes with others.
   - Cover your mouth when you cough.
   - Blow your nose in a tissue.

5. Ask student pairs to check the questions they wrote in Lesson A. Any questions not answered should be asked at this time.

6. Give farewells to the guest speaker.

7. Display *Thank You*! Explain that the class will write a letter thanking the speaker for coming. Read the part of the letter already printed and then ask students to work with their partners to list things the speaker said. Explain that each pair will be asked to share their answers. After partners have completed their task, call on students to share their answers and write them on the *Thank You!* transparency.

8. Say sincerely to the class: *Each of you is a special, spectacular, marvelous, wonderful, magnificent, social person!*

Thank You!

Dear ________________________,

Thank you for visiting our class to talk about hygiene. You helped us to understand the importance of good hygiene. We will remember to:

____

____

____

____

____

____

____

____

____

____

____

____

Sincerely,

____

Lesson C

OBJECTIVES:

1. To identify possible consequences of poor hygiene
2. To self-evaluate personal hygiene habits
3. To create posters about use of good hygiene for schoolwide display

MATERIALS:

1. *Hygiene Charade Cards* (See page 215; one set cut apart.)
2. *Checking Myself* (See *Appendix I*; one per student and one transparency.)
3. *Thought Bubble* (See *Appendix O*; one for educator use.)
4. Figures of Ann Olson, Lee Vue, Ms. Paula Hess, Mike Olson, and Jolisa Walker (See *Appendix F.*)
5. *Clean Machine* (See page 216; one per student and one transparency.)
6. Poster paper and a variety of markers for each student

PREPARATORY SET:

Tell students that they are going to play "Hygiene Charades." Call on one student at a time to come to the front of the room, pick a *Hygiene Charade Card*, and then act out what is on the card for the class to guess. (Use four of the cards during this lesson; save the other four for Lesson X of this unit.)

PLAN:

1. Pair students (see *Appendix P*). Display and distribute the discussion guideline sheet called *Checking Myself.* Ask students to complete the goal statement with the words "listen to others," or use another classroom discussion goal more appropriate for your group (see page 26). Tell students that you will be asking them questions about hygiene. First, they will be discussing the answers with their partners and then partners will be called on to share answers with the entire class. During this activity when a student is answering a question or making a comment, it's important for students to listen appropriately by giving eye contact, nodding their heads, asking relevant questions, and/or making relevant comments. Instruct them to put an "X" on their sheets each time someone new talks and they were listening.

2. Model use of the *Checking Myself* sheet while thinking aloud. A scripted example follows:

Introduction

I am going to pretend to be one of you completing this sheet during the discussion we will be having. I will tell you the thoughts I'm having while I'm completing the sheet. When I hold up this Thought Bubble, *you'll know the words I'm saying are actually what I'm thinking.*

Actual Model

While holding up the *Thought Bubble* say, *Lee is telling one of his answers. I'll listen appropriately by looking at him and nodding my head.... I'll put an "X" on my sheet because I am listening to Lee.* Put the *Thought Bubble* down and mark an "X" on the overhead transparency.

During the discussion, periodically remind students to listen appropriately and to mark their discussion guideline sheets.

3. Proceed with the discussion by reading the following situations and asking partners to discuss the follow-up questions. Then, call on partners to share answers with the entire group. Hold up figures of the characters as situations are presented.

- Ann checks her clothes to make sure they look clean before she gets dressed. What might happen if Ann wears dirty clothes to school?
- Lee flushes the toilet and washes his hands after going to the bathroom. Why does he flush the toilet and wash his hands after going to the bathroom?
- Ms. Hess has a student who doesn't cover her mouth when she sneezes or coughs. Why is it important for her to remember to cover her mouth?
- When Mike's hair looks and smells dirty, he washes it to look and feel better. What might other people think if Mike didn't wash his hair when it was dirty?
- Jolisa brushes her teeth after eating and before going to bed. Why is it important that she brush her teeth after a meal or snack and before going to bed?
- Ms. Hess has a student who wipes his nose on his sleeve. What could the student do when his nose is running? Tell why.

After the discussion, have students complete the bottom of *Checking Myself.*

4. Process the use of the sheet by asking the following question or another one more appropriate for your group:

- Why do you think it's important to listen appropriately during a discussion?

5. Display and distribute *Clean Machine.* Explain that you will be reading each statement about hygiene aloud and that students should mark an "X" in the box that best describes themselves. Tell students that this activity is a chance for them to decide how they are personally doing with use of hygiene and that they will not be required to share their answers with anyone. Read each statement aloud as students mark their checklists. Ask students to look over their sheets and decide if there is an area where they could improve. Offer extra credit to students who take *Clean Machine* home to complete with their parents.

6. Remind students about the importance of flushing the toilet and washing hands after using a restroom. Distribute poster paper and markers to each pair. Ask students to make posters about use of good hygiene in bathrooms. The completed posters could be hung in the school restrooms.

7. Write the following where everyone can see it: THIS CLASS IS EXTRAORDINARY. I'M LEARNING A LOT ABOUT SOCIAL SKILLS! Have the students say this aloud, in unison, with spirit.

HYGIENE CHARADE CARDS

BLOWING YOUR NOSE WITH A TISSUE	BRUSHING YOUR TEETH
COVERING YOUR MOUTH WHEN YOU COUGH	TAKING A BATH
CLIPPING YOUR FINGERNAILS	WASHING YOUR HANDS
WASHING YOUR FACE	TAKING A SHOWER
WASHING YOUR HAIR	COMBING YOUR HAIR

Name ____________________

CLEAN MACHINE

DIRECTIONS: Complete the following checklist. Add up your points and check your score below.

	Almost always	Sometimes	Hardly ever
1. I wash my hair when it is dirty.		✓	
2. I take a bath or shower when I look, feel, or smell dirty.	✓		
3. I brush my teeth after meals and snacks.	✓	✓	
4. I wash my hands before I eat.	✓		
5. I flush the toilet after using it.	✓		
6. I drink from my glass only.	✓		
7. I wear clothes that look and smell clean.	✓		
8. I brush or comb my hair each day.	✓		
9. I use a tissue to blow my nose.	✓		
10. I cover my mouth when I cough or sneeze.	✓		
11. I wash up after meals.	✓		

SCORING: Give yourself one point for each "Almost always" answer you marked.

8–11 points	Great job! You are a clean machine!
5–7 points	Doing OK, but there's room for improvement!
0–4 points	You need to use better hygiene!

Lesson D

OBJECTIVES:

1. To list positive qualities of people besides use of good hygiene habits
2. To list ways of improving hygiene

MATERIALS:

1. A tape recorder and a cassette tape prepared by the educator and called "The Sounds of Hygiene" (The tape should be prepared by the educator so it contains sounds associated with basic hygiene habits, e.g., toilet flushing, water running, brushing teeth, blow dryer blowing.)
2. *Card Match* cards (See *Appendix P*.)
3. *Pig-Pen* (See page 219; one per student and one transparency.)
4. *Inside Qualities* (See page 220; one per pair of students and one transparency.)

PREPARATORY SET:

Tell students that they will be hearing a tape called "The Sounds of Hygiene." Play each individual sound from the tape. Ask students to guess the sounds they hear.

PLAN:

1. Pair students using the *Card Match* activity.
2. Distribute and display *Pig-Pen.* After reading the cartoon, ask students to discuss with their partners why they think he has that nickname. Ask student pairs to share their thoughts.
3. Remind students that *Pig-Pen* is a cartoon character. Ask why, in real life, it is not appropriate to give others nicknames such as "Pig-Pen" or "Stinky" regardless of how the person looks or smells.
4. Display and distribute *Inside Qualities.* Tell students that even though Pig-Pen does not use good hygiene, he may have many positive inside qualities like being trustworthy or being honest. Ask partners to work together to list other positive inner qualities that Pig-Pen might have on their copy of *Inside Qualities.* After the partners have completed their tasks, ask them to share their ideas with the class. Print appropriate responses on the transparency.

5. Tell students they'll have an opportunity to help Pig-Pen by giving him some advice about hygiene. Ask students to work with their partners to write a letter to Pig-Pen in which they explain the importance of hygiene and give him some hygiene tips that might help so others will stop calling him Pig-Pen.

6. Ask student pairs who finish before others to share their letters with another partnership who also finished the task early. Collect the letters from all pairs when everyone is finished. Select several to read to the whole group.

7. Tell students that you received a phone call from the person who spoke to the class in Lesson B, asking for their advice about a problem. Explain that the speaker knows a student their age from a different school. He is a nice young man, but is embarrassed at school because he often has dirty clothes. He is allowed to take only one shower a week. His parents do not do the laundry on a regular basis and he often has nothing clean to wear. Some of the kids are teasing him. Explain that the speaker wonders if they have any ideas about how to help the boy look cleaner at school and how to convince students to stop teasing him. Ask students to discuss ideas with their partners. Call on students to share their ideas and write appropriate responses where everyone can see them.

8. Read the following statement aloud:

   Everyone on earth is a unique, special person! We are all important because we are human beings. Hygiene is important! Everyone can work at having better hygiene. It is not appropriate to call people mean names because of the way they look or smell. It is our responsibility to help other people improve and to look for their good qualities too!

9. Say sincerely to the class: *You are important and capable people in this world! You can use your good social skills to get along with other people!*

Name ______________________

PIG-PEN

GOOD GRIEF! HE DIDN'T EVEN CHANGE CLOTHES!

I CAN'T BELIEVE IT!

YOU'RE NOT GOING TO VIOLET'S BIRTHDAY PARTY LOOKING LIKE THAT?!!

SO WHAT'S WRONG?

SO WHAT'S WRONG?! YOU'RE A MESS, THAT'S WHAT'S WRONG!!

THEY WON'T EVEN LET YOU IN THE HOUSE, PIG-PEN! THEY'LL BAR YOU AT THE DOOR!

OH I DON'T THINK SO...
OF COURSE, THEY WILL! YOU WON'T BE WELCOME AT ALL! YOUR APPEARANCE WILL BE INSULTING! IT WILL BE...

WELL! PIG-PEN! COME IN! COME ON IN! HOW NICE TO SEE YOU! HOW NICE OF YOU TO COME!

OH, THANK YOU! YOU SHOULDN'T HAVE!

THE **PRESENT** WAS CLEAN!
SCHULZ

Names ______________________________

Inside Qualities

Lessons X, Y, and Z

Due to similarities in format, the final three lesson plans of each unit in *Social Star* are provided in *Appendix A*. Substitute the word "hygiene" whenever a "______" appears in the lesson plans. Information specific to this unit follows.

LESSON X PREPARATORY SET:

Play "Hygiene Charades" using the cards remaining from Lesson C.

LESSON Y PREPARATORY SET:

Darken the room, if you prefer, and ask students to visualize themselves correctly using this social skill by reading the following script:

> *Let's take a few moments to relax.... Make sure you are sitting in a comfortable position.... Close your eyes if you feel like it.... On the count of three, take a very slow, deep breath. One . . . two . . . three.... Breathe in deeply. Now breathe out slowly.... Let your entire body relax. Now imagine yourself at home getting ready for bed. Picture yourself taking a bath . . . brushing and flossing your teeth . . . and clipping your nails to help yourself look and feel better.... Now picture yourself picking out clean clothes to wear to school tomorrow. Think how good you feel about keeping your body clean and healthy.*

LESSON Z PLOT SITUATION:

Ask students to pretend that someone in a group they are working in is being bossy and not letting others participate.

LESSON Z ROADBLOCK EXAMPLES:

- Using good hygiene when hygiene items are not available (out of shampoo, soap, or toothpaste)
- Using good hygiene when your parents are unwilling or unable to help (laundry is not done regularly; you are not allowed to shower or bathe often)

Name ______________________

Hygiene T-Chart

LOOKS LIKE...	SOUNDS LIKE...
washing • hands and face • body and hair	water running
brushing and flossing your teeth	brushing noise
drinking from your own glass	swallowing
flushing the toilet	flushing sound
washing clothes	washer and dryer running
clipping and/or filing nails	clipping and rubbing
covering your mouth when you cough	muffled cough
using tissue to clean your nose	blowing

HOME

Pretend you've been playing outside and your grandmother says she'd like to take you out to eat. Show what you'll say to yourself to check for good hygiene and then what you will do. (Your face and hands are dirty and your hair needs combing.)

SCHOOL

Pretend you are in your desk at school. Your teacher has said to help yourself to tissue on the counter whenever you need one. Show how to blow your nose politely.

COMMUNITY

Pretend you're at the mall. You've just gone to the bathroom and flushed the toilet. Show what you'll do next to have good hygiene.

Be A
Clean
Machine
Use Good Hygiene!

HOME-A-GRAM

Dear Family,

At school, we have been talking about the social skill called

HYGIENE

I learned that *hygiene* means keeping my body and clothes clean.

I learned that I should ask myself, "What do I have to do right now to have good hygiene?" and that I need to follow through and do what I decided.

I know that when I use good hygiene, I'll feel better, I'll be healthier, and I invite people to feel more comfortable when they are with me.

I have written three ways that I can have good hygiene to feel better and stay healthy.

1. ______________________________

2. ______________________________

3. ______________________________

Please sign my "Good Hygiene" badge when you see me doing something for good hygiene so I can return it to school and become a SOCIAL SUPER STAR this week.

From: ____________________

Body Talk

UNIT GOAL:

To demonstrate knowledge and use of the components of body talk and the messages our bodies send

EDUCATOR INFORMATION:

1. "Body talk" (body language, body basics) is a term used to describe various components of the human body which can be used in different ways to communicate various messages. This unit emphasizes the following body-talk components: eye contact, facial expression, posture, personal space, hygiene, volume, tone of voice, body movements, breathing, and speed. Each of these components (except for body movements, breathing, and speed) are units in and of themselves within *Social Star*. They don't all need to be taught prior to teaching this unit. *Body Talk* must, however, be taught prior to teaching the remaining units (units 9–15) in *Social Star,* because body talk is incorporated as a skill step in all of those units.
2. Body talk is used to communicate feelings. Body talk helps convey a clearer meaning for the listener when it is paired with an oral message. Body talk is usually an honest reflection of how someone is thinking and/or feeling.
3. This unit is designed to help students understand the power they have within their own bodies (intra-body talk). They can use their bodies to help bring about certain emotions (e.g., if they are feeling sad, smiling and getting active may help them feel better). The unit advocates that it is OK to feel sad, angry, etc. However, when students wish to start feeling better, they can use their body talk to help bring about this goal.
4. This unit also emphasizes that students have control over their own bodies. It helps students recognize that there are times when they will need to demonstrate self-control with their bodies.
5. The educator should exert sensitivity and care in generalizing rules about body talk into the children's home cultures.

RELATED ACTIVITIES:

1. Teach students about the art of mime and have them watch a demonstration. Have students develop a mime with a partner and present it to other students. Students could identify the emotions expressed by the mime.

2. Have students write body-talk lyrics to a familiar melody. An example follows:

   (Sung to the melody of "Are You Sleeping?")

   Body talk, body talk,
   Sends a message, sends a message.
   What are you saying, with your body talk?
   Ask yourself, ask yourself.

3. Have students identify specific body-talk gestures, facial expressions, etc. that are used by a variety of famous people (e.g., a football player who consistently waves his arms the same way when he makes a touchdown, or a singer who often uses a specific facial expression).

4. Play a variety of songs. Ask students to move their bodies to portray the feeling or mood they associate with each song.

5. Have students visit some place in the community (e.g., shopping mall) where they can observe people. Have students record the various messages people are sending with their body talk.

6. Have students create mobiles about body talk. Key words, phrases, or concepts related to body talk might be hung from the mobile. Alternatively, students could draw small illustrations depicting appropriate body talk and these could be attached to the mobile.

7. Invite adults from different cultures to talk to the students about how their cultures' conventions for body talk compare with American common culture norms.

It is important for educators to provide opportunities for students to work in groups so they can experience social skills in contexts where social communication is needed. Therefore, educators are encouraged to have students complete the Related Activities in small groups whenever possible. Educators trained in cooperative learning could incorporate the five components (see page 34) into the group activity.

RELATED LITERATURE:

Alfie Lends a Hand (1983) by Shirley Hughes; Ill. by author; Lothrop, Lee and Shepard. (Picture book)

The Fourth-Grade Four (1989) by Marilyn Levinson, Henry Holt. (Text)
Alex's body language tells how he feels when he goes to the eye doctor to be tested for glasses. (pages 1–9)

I Dance in My Red Pajamas (1982) by Edith Thacher Hurd, Ill. by Emily Arnold McCully, Harper and Row. (Picture book)

Ragtime Tumpie (1989) by Alan Schroeder; Ill. by Bernie Fuchs; Little, Brown and Co. (Picture book)

Sam (1967) by Ann Herbert Scott, Ill. by Symeon Shimin, McGraw-Hill. (Picture book)

SOCIAL SKILLS ALL DAY LONG:

Look for opportunities to teach social skills throughout the day (incidental teaching). Four ways to reinforce good social skills and an example of each follow:

Encouragement

Lee, you're sitting up straight, you're looking at me, and your face looks interested. Your body talk tells me you're excited about learning! Wonderful!

Personal Example

This morning when I came to school, I was feeling tired. I know I have control over my body. I wanted to feel more awake, so I started breathing and moving my body like I do when I'm awake and energetic. My strategy worked great because I felt more awake right away.

Prompting

(At the end of recess) *There are times when you want your body talk to be active. There are other times when your body talk needs to be more calm. Remember, you're in control of your body. Before you go back into school, your bodies need to get more relaxed and calm. Take a few seconds right now to get your body calmed down.*

Corrective Feedback (must be positive, private, specific, and nonthreatening)

Mike, just now you were pushing other kids in the line. You could have used appropriate body talk by keeping your arms at your side. When you use appropriate body talk, other children might enjoy being with you.

Lesson A

OBJECTIVE:

To state the meaning of *body talk* and tell why it is important

MATERIALS:

1. *Body-Talk Parts* (See page 231; one transparency.)
2. *I Know...* (See page 232; one per pair of students and one transparency.)
3. *Body Talk* (See page 233; one per student and one transparency.)
4. *Thought Bubble* (See *Appendix O*; one for educator use.)

PREPARATORY SET:

Demonstrate a variety of different body-talk messages (e.g., look cheerful, look tired, look sad, look bored). For each, have students identify the feeling message you are sending with your body.

PLAN:

1. Pair students using the *Line Up–Fold Up* activity (see *Appendix P*). Have students line up according to height. Tell students that you will be discussing different parts of the body and the messages they can give. Explain that these messages are called "body talk."
2. Display *Body-Talk Parts* and read each of the 10 components of body talk without defining them. Distribute and display *I Know...* to each student pair. Instruct students to write "Body Talk" on the line above "I Know" and on the line above "I Learned." Have students work as pairs to write everything they already know about the body-talk components listed on *Body-Talk Parts* in the first column. Model this by saying, "I know a lot about facial expression so I might write, 'how my face looks.' " (Keep *Body-Talk Parts* displayed while students are writing.) They should leave the second column of *I Know...* blank. (Collect the sheets to be completed during Lesson E.)
3. Distribute and display *Body Talk*. Discuss the definition. Explain the skill step and the symbol next to it. Remind students that the symbol is there to help them visualize and remember the skill step. Discuss the reasons for being aware of one's body talk.

4. Model the skill step for body talk while thinking aloud. A scripted example follows:

   Introduction

   I am going to pretend to be a student out on the playground at recess. I will show you appropriate body talk and tell you the thoughts I'm having. When I hold up this Thought Bubble, *you'll know the words that I'm saying are actually what I'm thinking.*

   Actual Model

   While holding up the *Thought Bubble* say, *What is my body saying? I'm smiling, I'm standing up straight, and I'm looking right at the kids I'm talking to. That's good, because other kids will know I'm confident.*

5. Read the story at the bottom of *Body Talk* aloud to students.

6. Have student pairs discuss answers to the following questions with their partners:

   - Why did Ms. Hess think Victor was happy?
   - What do you think Victor was happy about?

   Call on various student pairs to share their answers with the class.

7. Ask student pairs to take turns telling each other the meaning of *body talk* and why it's important to use the skill. Encourage students to use energetic body talk (sit up straight, smile, use eye contact, and produce a happy tone of voice) while completing this task. Students could be reminded that the information they are to say is printed on *Body Talk*.

   As an option to add structure to this activity (see *Appendix Q*), ask partners to come to an agreement about which person will be called "Alice in Wonderland" and which person will be called "Robin Hood." After students have made their decisions, ask "Alice" to tell "Robin" the definition of *body talk*. Next, ask "Robin" to tell "Alice" the definition. Ask students to use the same procedure to tell each other the reasons for using appropriate body talk.

8. Write the following where everyone can see: I CAN CHOOSE TO USE STUPENDOUS, SPECTACULAR SOCIAL SKILLS! Have the students say this aloud, in unison, with energy.

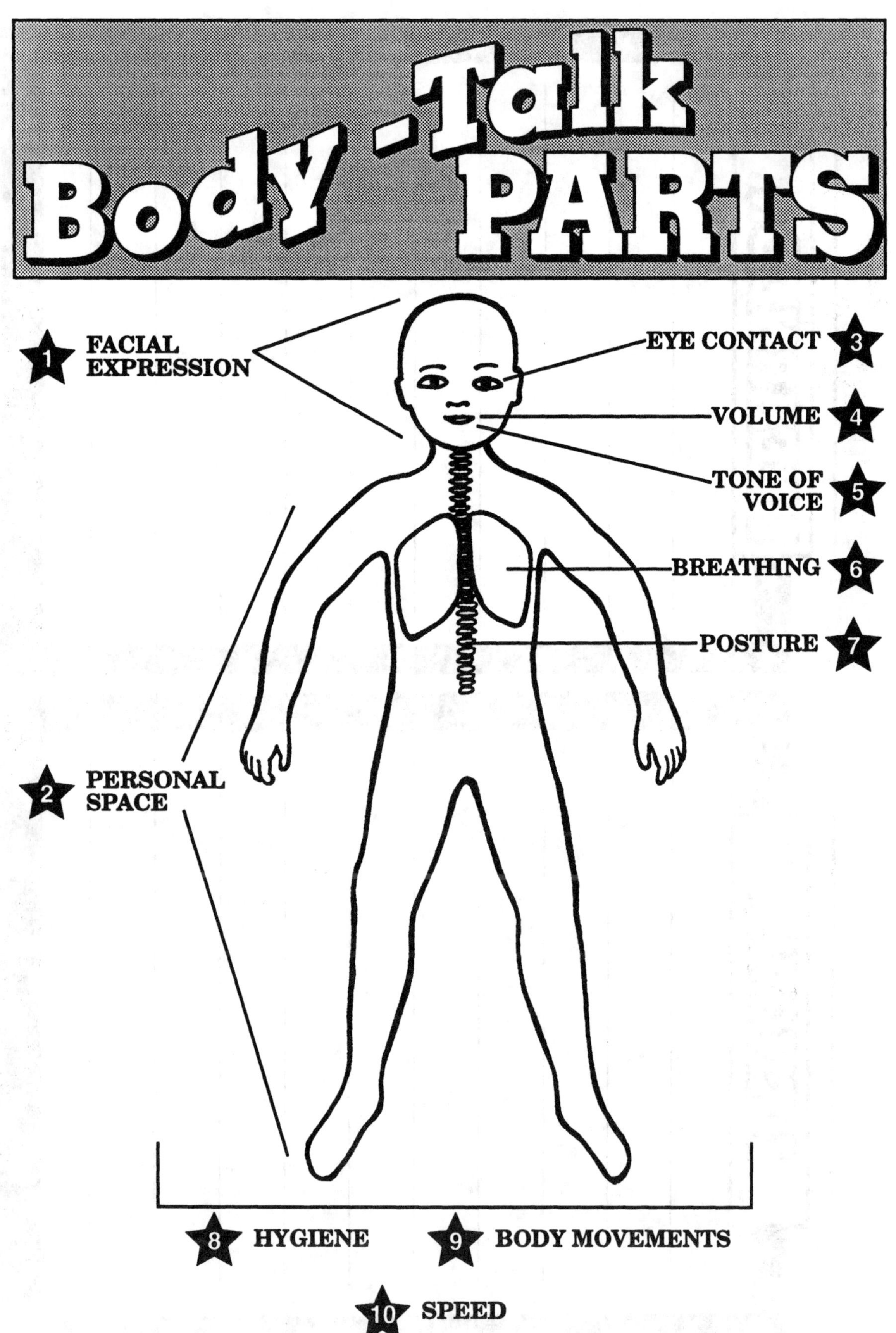
Body -Talk PARTS
1 FACIAL EXPRESSION
2 PERSONAL SPACE
EYE CONTACT 3
VOLUME 4
TONE OF VOICE 5
BREATHING 6
POSTURE 7
8 HYGIENE
9 BODY MOVEMENTS
10 SPEED

Names
I KNOW...
I LEARNED...

Name ____________________

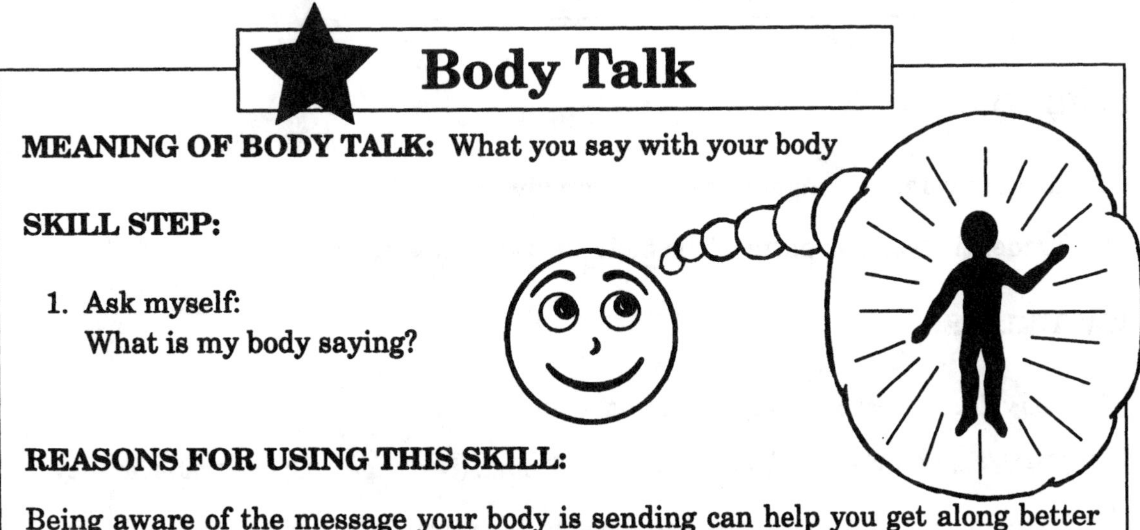

Body Talk

MEANING OF BODY TALK: What you say with your body

SKILL STEP:

1. Ask myself:
   What is my body saying?

REASONS FOR USING THIS SKILL:

Being aware of the message your body is sending can help you get along better with others. It can help you feel good about yourself too.

DIRECTIONS: Listen to the story below. Look at the picture of Victor while you are listening.

Victor came into the room with a big smile on his face. His head was up, his shoulders were back, and he walked with a light bounce. Ms. Hess said, "Victor, you sure look happy today." Victor thought to himself, "She's right. I am happy."

Lesson B

OBJECTIVES:

1. To state some messages our bodies can give
2. To identify various parts of the body that give messages

MATERIALS:

1. *Body Talk* classroom poster (See page 13.)
2. *The Messages You Give to Others Come From...* (See page 236; one transparency.)
3. Large pieces of butcher paper to draw body outlines (One piece per student)
4. Markers or crayons for each student
5. *Body-Talk Parts* (See page 231; one transparency.)

PREPARATORY SET:

Use some common gestures and facial expressions that send specific messages as some of the following listed:

Come here	Yes	Yuk
Hello	No	Good-bye
Sit down	I don't know	I don't like it
Quiet	I can't hear you	I'm confused

Ask students to guess what message your body talk is sending.

PLAN:

1. Review the definition and skill step for *body talk* by referring the class to the *Body Talk* classroom poster.
2. Pair students (see *Appendix P*). Ask student pairs to take turns telling each other the skill step for body talk. Follow the procedure described in step 7 of Lesson A. (As an option, ask students to decide who will be "Robert E. Lee" and who will be "Ulysses S. Grant.") Next, ask students to work with their partners to think of a situation when the use of happy body talk is important. Tell students that one or more pairs will be asked to share their situation. Have one or more pairs share their situation.

3. Display *The Messages You Give to Others Come From...* Discuss the concept that body talk plays a major role in communicating with others. In most cases, people's body talk probably gives a truer indication of their feelings than do words.

4. Give each student pair two large pieces of butcher paper. Tell students to trace each other's body outlines. Tell students they can make different formations with their bodies if the paper is wide enough (i.e., they don't have to lie straight).

5. Display *Body-Talk Parts.* Discuss each of the 10 components in detail. Give a definition of each component and discuss what the component usually does, sounds like, and/or looks like during various emotions or states (while providing students with frequent demonstrations). Ask students to write the 10 components of body talk on their body outlines while you are talking. Depending on past experience, some components will have to be discussed in greater detail than others. Afterwards, hang the body outlines all over the classroom to be left up as a reminder of the components of body talk, or let students take them home.

6. Have students walk around the classroom in a circle. Shout out various instructions such as the following:

   - "Walk like you are happy."
   - "Now, walk like you are really tired and worn out."
   - "Walk like you are really excited and you're feeling great!"

   The educator may need to prompt students even further (by asking questions such as, "What would you do with your eyes, your face, your speed, your shoulders?") if students do not know what types of body movements or facial expressions to use to represent the various emotions.

7. Say enthusiastically to the class: *You are a great class! I can see you cooperating with one another more each day!* (Give a recent example of cooperation.)

The Messages You Give to Others Come From...

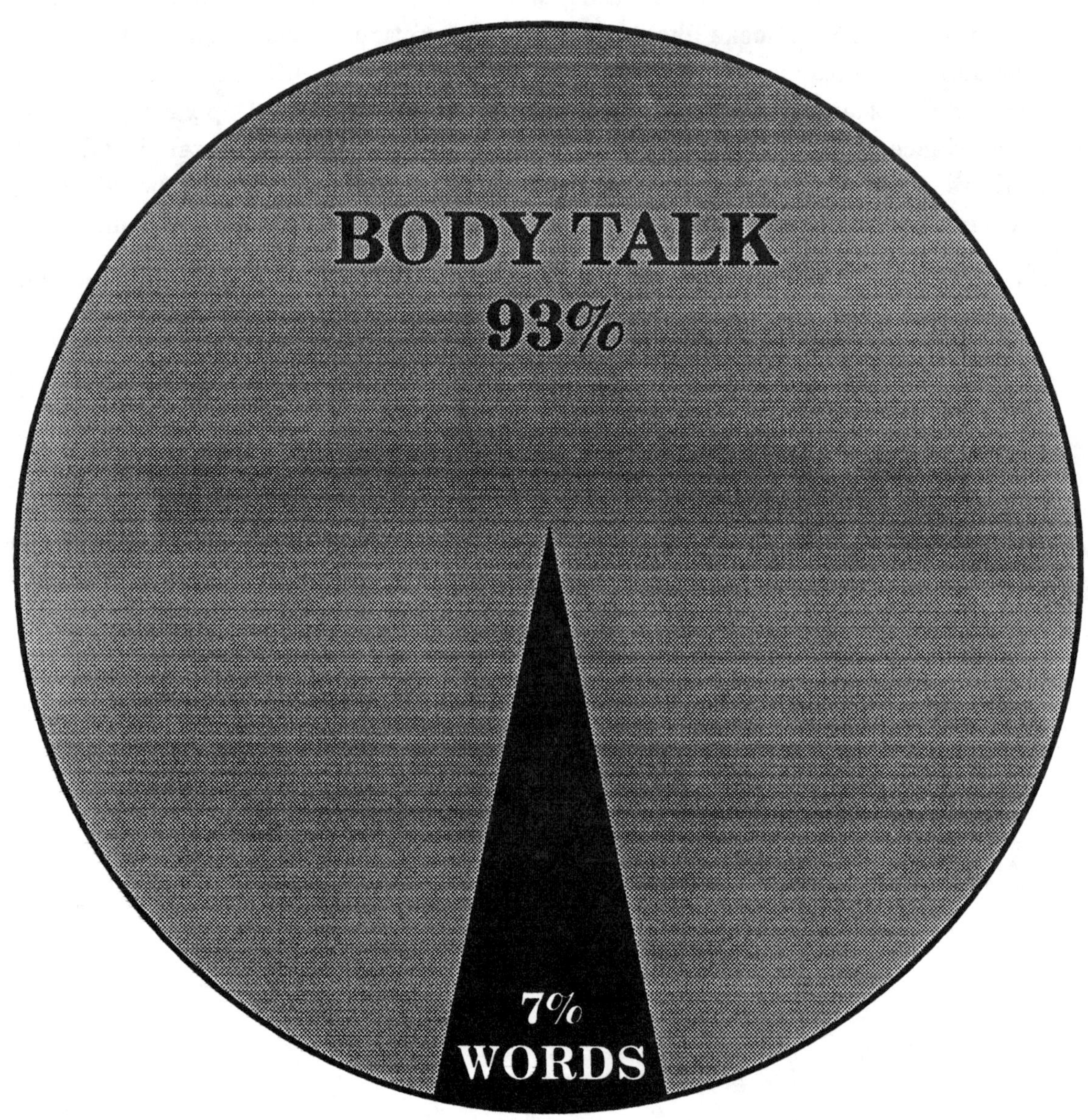

Lesson C

OBJECTIVE:

To demonstrate various components of body talk

MATERIALS:

1. *Dominoes* (See *Appendix U*; one set cut apart per pair of students, and one set of transparency dominoes.)

PREPARATORY SET:

(Prepare two students before doing this role play.) Ask the first student to walk into the room slowly, looking sad, with shoulders hunched and head down. Next, ask the second student to briskly walk in with head held high, shoulders back, and a huge smile. Have the class identify differences in specific body-talk components between the two students.

PLAN:

1. Tell students they will be playing a game called "Body-Talk Dominoes."
2. Model specifically how to play dominoes using an overhead and the transparency *Dominoes.*
3. Pair students (see *Appendix P*). Distribute a set of dominoes to each pair.
4. Write the numbers 1–6 on the board. Next, choose six of the body-talk components that follow and write each one next to a number:
   - Eye Contact (e.g., look right at your partner, showing you feel confident)
   - Facial Expression (e.g., show a happy facial expression)
   - Posture (e.g., sit up straight and lean forward slightly, showing you are interested)
   - Personal Space (e.g., sit an arm's length away from your partner, showing that you feel confident)
   - Hygiene (e.g., check to be certain your clothes are straight, showing you care about how you look)
   - Volume (e.g., use a normal volume when you say your name, showing you feel confident)

- Tone of Voice (e.g., sound cheerful when you say, "This is a great game!")
- Body Movements (e.g., show what you would do with your arms when you feel very excited and happy)
- Breathing (e.g., breathe deeply, showing you feel energetic)
- Speed (e.g., walk briskly, showing you feel happy)

Each time students match dominoes, have them demonstrate some component of body talk. When a student matches a "1," have that student demonstrate some aspect of the body-talk component listed by number "1" on the board and so on for numbers 2–6.

5. Write the following where everyone can see it: I AM A SPECIAL PERSON! I CAN USE MY TALENTS TO GET ALONG WITH OTHERS. Have the students say this aloud, in unison, until they sound like they really mean it.

Lesson D

OBJECTIVES:

1. To identify which parts of body talk are inappropriate in various situations
2. To identify the possible negative consequences of using inappropriate body talk

MATERIALS:

1. *Body Talk* classroom poster (See page 13.)
2. *Thought Bubble* (See *Appendix O*; one for educator use.)
3. Index cards (A set of 10 cards numbered 1–10, per pair of students)
4. *Body-Talk Parts* (See page 231; one transparency.)

PREPARATORY SET:

Use body talk that would not ordinarily be appropriate to use when starting class (e.g., mean, angry body talk; silly, giggly body talk; sad, crying body talk) and say "Let's get class started." Afterwards, discuss why the body talk used was inappropriate.

PLAN:

1. Review the definition and skill step for ***body talk*** by referring the class to the ***Body Talk*** classroom poster.
2. Model the skill step for body talk while thinking aloud. A scripted example is provided below.

   Introduction

   I am going to pretend to be a student your age. I'm at home and my parents just told me that I can't go to a movie with my friends. I will show you the body talk I decide to use and tell you the thoughts I'm having. When I hold up this Thought Bubble, *you'll know the words that I'm saying are actually what I'm thinking.*

   Actual Model

   Say, *Fine, I won't go!* while demonstrating inappropriate body talk (e.g., rude tone of voice, crossing arms, rolling eyes). While holding up the *Thought Bubble* say, *What is my body saying? I know I'm using rude body talk, but I just feel so angry that I can't go! I'd better change the way I look and sound, or I'll get sent to my room.* Put the *Thought Bubble* down and demonstrate taking a deep breath and using more appropriate body talk as a result.

3. Inform students that during today's lesson they will be looking at how body talk can sometimes get people into trouble.
4. Pair students (see *Appendix P*).
5. Distribute a set of 10 numbered index cards to each pair, and display *Body-Talk Parts.*
6. Tell students that you will be telling them five short stories about people who use inappropriate body talk. After each story, they should work with their partners to decide which two body-talk components the character in the story could change to demonstrate more appropriate body talk. The partners should hold up the numbered index cards which correspond to the correct body-talk components listed on *Body-Talk Parts*. Next, ask partners to discuss an answer to each story's follow-up question. The stories and their follow-up questions follow:

Story A

Victor decided to go to his neighbors' houses to let them know that he would be willing to do lawn work, if they were interested in hiring him. Victor felt nervous talking to the first neighbor. He stood up straight and used appropriate eye contact, but his face looked like he was angry about something. He hadn't bathed in a few days and his clothes were dirty.

- Which two body-talk components could Victor change before he talks to more neighbors?
- What could happen if Victor doesn't change his body talk?

Story B

Jolisa went to visit her aunt in another city. While she was there, she felt like she didn't have anything do. Then some kids from her aunt's neighborhood came by and asked Jolisa if she wanted to play. Jolisa said, "OK," and went outside with them. While she was outside, she stood far away from the kids and talked so quietly that no one could really hear what she was saying.

- Which two body-talk components could Jolisa change?
- What could happen if Jolisa doesn't change her body talk?

Story C

Mike's pet fish died and he felt very sad. Mike knew it would be better to feel happy whenever he thought about his fish, but he just couldn't. Whenever he thought about his fish, Mike's breathing was shallow and he slouched his shoulders and head.

- Which two body-talk components could Mike change to feel better?
- What could happen if Mike doesn't change his body talk?

Story D

Mr. Parra asked Victor to clean up his room right away. Victor said, "I'm going, I'm going," with a sarcastic tone of voice. Victor took slow, tiny steps to his room and then slowly picked up one object at a time to put away.

- Which two body-talk components could Victor change?
- What could happen if Victor doesn't change his body talk?

Story E

Lee asked Maria if she would share her candy bar with him. Maria looked at the floor, held out her candy bar and said, "Here, take some," with a rude tone of voice.

- Which two body-talk components could Maria change?
- What could happen if Maria doesn't change her body talk?

7. Write the following where everyone can see it: I CAN BE ESPECIALLY NICE TO OTHER PEOPLE BY USING GOOD SOCIAL SKILLS. Have the students say this aloud, in unison, with sincerity.

Lesson E

OBJECTIVES:

1. To tell how body language differs between a tired person, a happy person, and an angry person
2. To demonstrate how communication can be changed by changing body talk

MATERIALS:

1. An audiotape, compact disk, or record of an upbeat, cheerful popular song that students know and equipment to play the song
2. *Checking Myself* (See *Appendix I*; one per student and one transparency.)
3. *Thought Bubble* (See *Appendix O*; one for educator use.)
4. *Victor, Ann, and Jolisa* (See page 245; one per student.)
5. *I Know...* (See page 232; use half-completed pages from Lesson A.)

PREPARATORY SET:

Play a cheerful song. Tell students to move around the room while moving their bodies in a happy, cheerful manner. Be certain to join the fun! Point out to students that their bodies are sending happy messages.

PLAN:

1. Distribute and display the discussion guideline sheet called *Checking Myself.* Ask students to complete the goal statement with the words "use interested body talk," or use another classroom discussion goal more appropriate for your group (see page 26). Tell students that you will be having a discussion about some pictures. Encourage students to demonstrate body talk that shows they are interested in the discussion (e.g., sitting up in chair, leaning slightly forward, nodding head, giving eye contact). Tell students that during the discussion they should ask themselves if their body talk says, "I'm interested in this discussion." Instruct students to put an "X" on their sheets if they are using interested body talk each time a new person begins to speak.
2. Model use of the *Checking Myself* sheet while thinking aloud. A scripted example follows:

Introduction

I am going to pretend to be one of you completing this sheet during the discussion we will be having. I will tell you the thoughts I'm having while I'm completing the sheet. When I hold up this Thought Bubble, *you'll know the words I'm saying are actually what I'm thinking.*

Actual Model

While holding up the *Thought Bubble* say, *A different person just started talking. Am I using interested body talk? Yes, I am sitting up straight and giving eye contact. I'll put an "X" on my sheet.* Put the *Thought Bubble* down and mark an "X" on the overhead transparency.

3. Distribute *Victor, Ann, and Jolisa* to each student. Discuss the following questions and periodically remind students to mark their sheets when a new person begins talking:

   - How do you think Victor is feeling? (happy, excited)
   - What parts of Victor's body help us know how he is feeling?
   - How do you think Ann is feeling? (tired, sad)
   - What parts of Ann's body help us know how she is feeling?
   - How do you think Jolisa is feeling? (angry, frustrated)
   - What parts of Jolisa's body help us know how she is feeling?

   After the discussion, have students complete the bottom of *Checking Myself.*

4. Process the use of the sheet by asking the following questions or others more appropriate for your group:

   - Why do you think it's important to have interested body talk during a class discussion?
   - What might happen if you don't use interested body talk?

5. Tell students to make their bodies look like they are feeling happy. Say, "Make your bodies look like they would when you are feeling really happy. Stand up straight. Put your shoulders back. You're really excited. Get a big smile on your face. Move your body like you're really feeling excellent."

6. Next say, "Now, make your body look like you are really tired. You feel like you are going to fall asleep. Hang your head, slouch your shoulders. How would you move if you were so tired? You can barely keep your eyes open. You feel so tired."

7. Next say, "Now make your body look like you would if you were angry. Make your body tense. Clench your fists. Make your face look angry. You are just furious. How would you look if you were angry?"

8. Have students sit down. Discuss that we can change how we are feeling by changing what we are doing with our bodies. Ask students what they could do with their bodies if they are feeling bored and tired and don't want to feel that way. Tell students that by doing something as simple as smiling and breathing deeply, they can make themselves feel better.

9. Model use of the skill step for body talk while thinking aloud. A scripted example follows:

   Introduction

   I am going to pretend to be feeling tired and bored. I will then tell you the thoughts I'm having and show you more appropriate body talk. When I hold up this Thought Bubble, *you'll know the words that I'm saying are actually what I'm thinking.*

   Actual Model

   Demonstrate body talk typical of a tired and bored person. While holding up the *Thought Bubble* say, *I feel so tired and bored and I don't like it! What is my body talk saying? No wonder I feel this way! I'm hardly breathing, I'm frowning, and I'm all slumped over. I've got to change my body talk so I can feel better.* Put the *Thought Bubble* down and demonstrate energized, alert body talk.

10. Hand out *I Know...*, which was collected during Lesson A. Using the same student pairs, have them complete the "I Learned" column together. This provides an opportunity to review all key ideas in the unit.

11. Write the following where everyone can see it: IT'S FUN LEARNING ABOUT SOCIAL SKILLS! IT'S TOTALLY DYNAMITE! Have the students say this aloud, in unison, enthusiastically.

Name ______________________

VICTOR, ANN, AND JOLISA

Lessons X, Y, and Z

Due to similarities in format, the final three lesson plans for each unit in *Social Star* are provided in *Appendix A.* Substitute the words "body talk" whenever a "______ " appears in the lesson plans. Information specific to this unit follows.

LESSON X PREPARATORY SET:

Tell students to sit up straight at their desks. Tell them to show how their bodies could look if they are really excited and interested in what the teacher is saying. Next, have students show the body talk they could use if they don't understand something that the teacher is explaining. Explain why it is helpful to the teacher when students use a baffled or perplexed look.

LESSON Y PREPARATORY SET:

Darken the room, if you prefer, and ask students to visualize themselves correctly using this social skill by reading the following script:

> *Let's take a few moments to relax.... Make sure you are sitting in a comfortable position.... Close your eyes if you feel like it.... On the count of three, take a very slow, deep breath. One . . . two . . . three.... Breathe in deeply.... Now breathe out slowly.... Let your entire body relax. Now imagine yourself giving a report in class. You're a little nervous so you take a deep breath. You stand up straight so your posture says you are confident. You think about how glad you are that you combed your hair after recess so it looks good. You remember to look at all the students listening to you and keep a smile on your face. You speak loudly enough so everyone can hear and use a pleasant tone of voice. When you finish your report, your teacher compliments you on the nice job that you did. You are proud of yourself for remembering to use the body talk skills that you learned.*

LESSON Z PLOT SITUATION:

Ask students to pretend that they are at the store and their parents will not buy them something that they want.

LESSON Z ROADBLOCK EXAMPLES:

- Forgetting to remind yourself to change your body talk to help yourself feel better
- Having difficulty controlling your inappropriate body talk if it's a habit (e.g., if you're used to hitting when you're angry)

Name ____________________

Body Talk T-Chart

LOOKS LIKE...	SOUNDS LIKE...
eye contact	voice volume
facial expression	voice tone
posture	
personal space	
hygiene	
body movements	
breathing	
how fast/slow you move your body	

HOME

Pretend that you broke something of your mom's. Show how your body talk could look when you are apologizing and are truly sorry.

SCHOOL

Pretend you are walking into school in the morning. Show how your body talk could look if you are feeling great.

COMMUNITY

Pretend you've just been introduced to your friend's cousin. Show body talk that shows you are feeling confident and glad to meet the cousin.

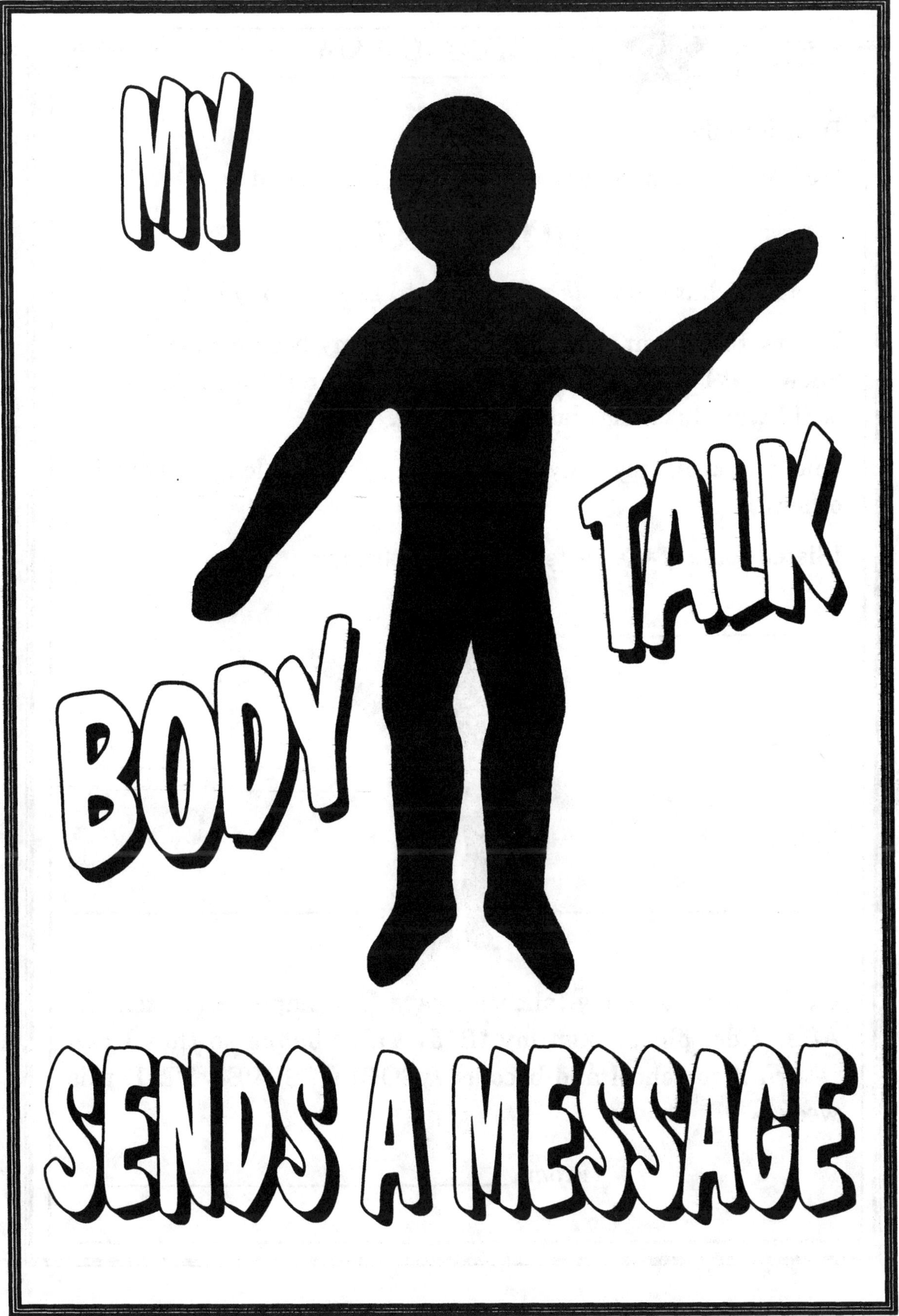
MY
BODY
TALK
SENDS A MESSAGE

HOME-A-GRAM

Dear Family,

We have been talking about the social skill called

BODY TALK

I learned that *body talk* means what I say with my body.

I know that I can ask myself, "What is my body saying?" I also know that I can change my body talk if it can get me into trouble or if I want to change how I'm feeling.

Knowing about my body talk can help me get along better with others.

I listed some of the parts of body talk below:

1. ____________________

2. ____________________

3. ____________________

4. ____________________

I will show you body talk that says "I'm happy and excited." After I do, please sign my "Body Talk" badge so that I can return it to school and become a SOCIAL SUPER STAR this week.

From: ____________________________

Manners

UNIT GOAL:

To demonstrate comprehension and use of respectful manners

EDUCATOR INFORMATION:

This unit was developed to teach students that using appropriate manners is important when interacting with others. It stresses that there are socially appropriate ways of behaving in both informal and formal settings. The unit emphasizes that people tend to be more relaxed with manners when around family members or close friends, but that it is important to show respect for everyone through the use of polite behaviors. A variety of manners is discussed (e.g., saying "Please" and "Thank you," saying "Excuse me," asking politely for things). The educator should exert sensitivity and care in generalizing rules about manners into the children's home cultures.

RELATED ACTIVITIES:

1. Have students interview the principal about a schoolwide manners program. Schedule a planning session to discuss how such a program might be implemented.
2. Have each student write a thank-you note to someone (e.g., parent, friend) for something nice that person recently said or did for the student.
3. Have students write a song or poem about using appropriate manners.
4. Have students work together to write a book about manners, and then have them bind it. Put the book in the school's library.
5. Prepare a treat (e.g., muffins and juice). Visit a home for the elderly, and have a party with some of the residents. Beforehand, discuss various manners that might be used during the party.
6. Invite adults from different cultures to talk to the students about how their cultures' conventions for manners compare with American common culture norms.

It is important for educators to provide opportunities for students to work in groups so they can experience social skills in contexts where social communication is needed. Therefore, educators are encouraged to have students complete the Related Activities in small groups whenever possible. Educators trained in cooperative learning could incorporate the five components (see page 34) into the group activity.

RELATED LITERATURE:

The Hot and Cold Summer (1984) by Johanna Hurwitz, Morrow. (Text)
Rory and Derek are ordered to play host to Bolivia, a 10-year-old girl visiting neighbors. (pages 20–28)

Miss Nelson Is Missing (1977) by Harry Allard, Ill. by James Marshall, Houghton Mifflin. (Picture book)

Russell Sprouts (1987) by Johanna Hurwitz, Morrow. (Text) (pages 9–18, 45–47)

SOCIAL SKILLS ALL DAY LONG:

Look for opportunities to teach social skills throughout the day (incidental teaching). Four ways to reinforce good social skills and an example of each follow:

Encouragement

Lee, you just used great manners when you said "Thank you" to Maria. Great job!

Personal Example

A few months ago, my son was saying things like, "I want more juice," or "Give me some gravy." We've been working with my son on learning to ask for things in a polite way instead of just demanding things.

Prompting

We'll be going into the auditorium soon. It will probably be crowded. You will have a good opportunity to demonstrate your manners. If you accidentally bump into someone or can't get past someone, you can say "Excuse me."

Corrective Feedback (must be positive, private, specific, and nonthreatening)

Victor, just now when Lee gave you a treat, you didn't say anything. If you had used respectful manners by saying "Thank you," people might enjoy being around you more.

Lesson A

OBJECTIVES:

1. To state the meaning of *manners* and tell why they are important
2. To tell the self-talk associated with correct use of the skill
3. To identify a variety of manners that are used in different situations

MATERIALS:

1. *Manners* (See page 255; one per student and one transparency.)
2. *Thought Bubble* (See *Appendix O*; one for educator use.)
3. *Animal Cards* (See *Appendix P.*)
4. *Mind Map* (See *Appendix V*; one per pair of students and one transparency.)

PREPARATORY SET:

Bump lightly into the desk of a student and say, "Watch it, move out of my way!" Then look confused and say, "That's not what I'm supposed to say, is it?" Call on students to help you remember to say "Excuse me," "I'm sorry," or "Pardon me." Say, "Let me try again." Bump into the desk again and say, "Excuse me" or another appropriate response. Use this activity to introduce the *Manners* unit.

PLAN:

1. Distribute and display *Manners.* Discuss the definition. Explain the skill step and the symbol next to it. Remind students that the symbol is there to help them visualize and remember the skill step. Discuss the reasons for using appropriate manners. Refer to the body-talk symbol in the left-hand margin. Remind students that appropriate body talk is important when using manners.
2. Model use of the skill step for using appropriate manners while thinking aloud. A scripted example follows:

   Introduction

   I am going to pretend to be a student who needs to borrow something from a classmate. I will show you how I use appropriate manners and tell you the thoughts that I'm having. When I hold up this Thought Bubble, *you'll know the words that I'm saying are actually what I'm thinking.*

Actual Model

While holding up the *Thought Bubble* say, *I want to borrow Victor's scissors. How can I be polite? I could say "please," using a polite tone of voice.* Put the *Thought Bubble* down and politely say, *Victor, can I borrow your scissors, please?*

3. Read the story at the bottom of *Manners* aloud to students. Have students complete the bottom of *Manners* as directed and share their responses.

4. Pair students using the *Animal Cards*.

5. Display and distribute the *Mind Map*. Write the heading "Manners" in the largest oval on the *Mind Map*. Ask students to tell some situations when they would need to use appropriate manners (e.g., at a restaurant, at grandmother's house). Write the students' responses in circles attached to the heading. Assign one of the situations to each pair of students. Have the student pairs work together to complete their *Mind Maps* by coming up with examples of manners that one might use in their assigned situation. Here is an example of a *Mind Map* completed by a pair of students.

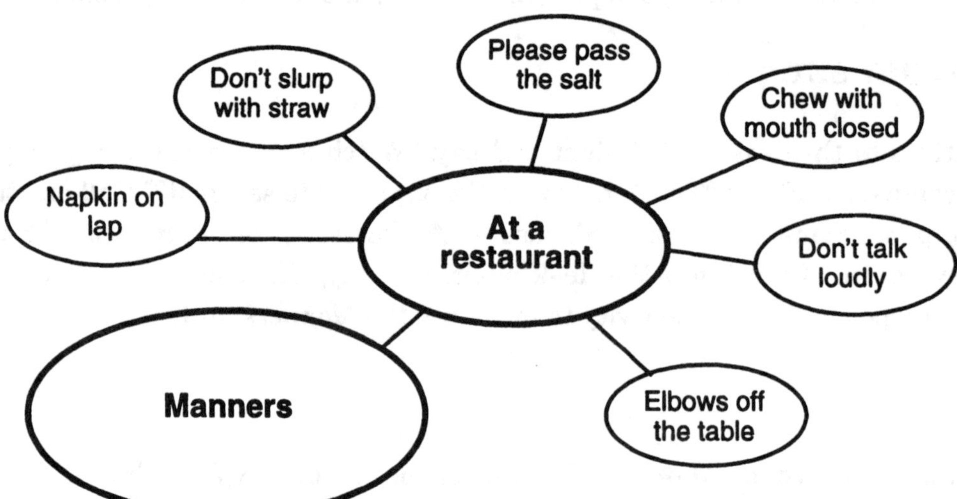

6. Ask student pairs to take turns telling each other the meaning of *manners* and why it is important to use the skill. Students could be reminded that the information they are to say is printed on *Manners*.

   To add structure to this activity (see *Appendix Q*), ask partners to come to an agreement about which person will be called "Harriet Tubman" and which person will be called "Frederick Douglass." After students have made their decisions, ask "Harriet" to tell "Frederick" the definition of *manners*. Next, ask "Frederick" to tell "Harriet" the definition. Ask students to use the same procedure to tell each other the reasons for using appropriate manners.

7. Say sincerely to the class: *You are each unique and wonderful people. I hope you enjoy using what you've learned in class today!*

Name ____________________

Manners

MEANING OF MANNERS: Being polite and respectful

Some examples of appropriate manners are saying "Please" and "Thank you"; saying "Excuse me" or "I'm sorry"; and using appropriate table manners.

SKILL STEP:

1. Ask myself: What manners could I use?

REASONS FOR USING THIS SKILL:

When you use appropriate manners, kids and adults enjoy being with you, and you feel good about yourself.

DIRECTIONS: Listen to the story below. Write the words Lee used to show appropriate manners.

Lee was at a restaurant with his father. He wanted another glass of juice. When the waiter went by, Lee said, "Excuse me, could I please have more orange juice?"

____

____

____

Lesson B

OBJECTIVES:

1. To identify words or actions which result in appropriate manners
2. To observe and describe use of appropriate manners by others

MATERIALS:

1. *Manners* classroom poster (See page 13.)
2. *Thought Bubble* (See *Appendix O*; one for educator use.)
3. Figure of Ann Olson (See *Appendix F*.)
4. *Ann's Manners* (See page 259; one per pair of students and one transparency.)
5. *Checking Myself* (See *Appendix I*; one per student and one transparency.)
6. *Manners Hunt* (See page 260; one per student.)

PREPARATORY SET:

Begin class by playing a game of "Hangman" with students for the word "thanks." Tell them the word they are guessing is associated with manners.

PLAN:

1. Review the definition and skill step for *manners* by referring the class to the *Manners* classroom poster.
2. Pair students (see *Appendix P*). Ask student pairs to take turns telling each other the skill step for manners. Follow the procedure described in step 6 of Lesson A. (As an option, ask students to decide who will be "Johann Sebastian Bach" and who will be "Ludwig van Beethoven.") Next, ask students to work with their partners to think of a situation when the use of manners is important. Tell the students that one or more pairs will be asked to share their situation. Have several student pairs share their situations.
3. Model use of respectful manners while thinking aloud. A scripted example follows:

   Introduction

   I am going to pretend to be eating at my aunt's house. I will show respectful manners and tell you the thoughts I'm having. When I hold up this Thought Bubble, *you'll know the words I'm saying are actually what I'm thinking.*

Actual Model

While holding up the *Thought Bubble* say, *I'd really like ketchup for my French fries. What could I do to show appropriate manners? I'll ask politely and say "please."* Put the *Thought Bubble* down and ask, *Could I please have some ketchup for my French fries?*

4. Hold up the figure of Ann and tell students they will be learning more about the manners that Ann uses.
5. Distribute and display *Ann's Manners.* Read the directions aloud and complete the first question with students. Instruct students to complete the remainder of the page with their partners.
6. When students have finished, distribute and display the discussion guideline sheet called *Checking Myself.* Ask students to complete the goal statement with the words "listen to others," or use another classroom discussion goal more appropriate for your group (see page 26). Tell students that you will be having a discussion about *Ann's Manners,* which they just completed. When a student is answering a question or making a comment during the discussion, it's important for everyone to be polite by listening to that student. Tell students they can show they are listening by giving eye contact, nodding their heads, asking relevant questions, or making relevant comments. Instruct them to put an "X" on their sheets each time someone new talks and they are listening.
7. Model use of the *Checking Myself* sheet while thinking aloud. A scripted example follows:

   Introduction

   I am going to pretend to be one of you completing this sheet during the discussion we will be having. I will tell you the thoughts I'm having while I'm completing the sheet. When I hold up this Thought Bubble, *you'll know the words I'm saying are actually what I'm thinking.*

   Actual Model

   While holding up the *Thought Bubble* say, *Jill is telling one of her answers. I'll be polite by looking at her when she's talking and smile at her so she knows I'm listening.... I'll put an "X" on my sheet because I listened to Jill.* Put the *Thought Bubble* down and mark an "X" on the overhead transparency.

8. Proceed with the discussion by having students share their responses to the questions on *Ann's Manners.*
9. After the discussion, have students complete the bottom of *Checking Myself.*

10. Process the use of the sheet by asking the following question or another one more appropriate for your group:

    - Why do you think it's important to listen to others while they are talking?

    Process further by asking the students who volunteered to speak during the discussion to share their answers to the following questions:

    You shared one of your answers during the discussion. How could you tell which people were listening to you? How did you feel to know others were listening?

11. Distribute *Manners Hunt* and read the directions for its completion with students. Be sure to discuss the example provided. Tell students that during the next lesson, they will be sharing the manners they found.

12. Say with conviction to the class: *You are better than excellent kids! I'll bet you feel proud of yourselves when you use good social skills!* (Encourage kids to pat themselves on their backs.)

Names ______________________________

DIRECTIONS: Read each situation below. Answer each question.

1. Ann accidentally burped in class. What might she say to be polite?

____

____

2. Ann politely asked her father for more pickles. What words do you think Ann used?

____

____

3. Ann didn't mean to, but she bumped into Jolisa. What could Ann say to be polite?

____

____

4. Ann received a gift from a friend. What can she say to her friend to be polite?

____

____

5. Ann and Maria both got to the drinking fountain at the same time. What could Ann do or say to show appropriate manners?

____

____

Name ____________________

MANNERS HUNT

DIRECTIONS: Be on the lookout for appropriate manners! When you see or hear someone using manners that are appropriate, mark the information on the chart below. Look at the example.

WHO	MANNERS USED
★1 My friend Steve	Said "please" when he asked for a pencil
★2	
★3	
★4	

Lesson C

OBJECTIVES:

1. To differentiate between a polite request and a demand
2. To practice making a polite request
3. To identify how others feel about manners that are inappropriate or disrespectful

MATERIALS:

1. Props to simulate a game show (e.g., upbeat music, a bell, a decorated contestant's table with four chairs, an emcee costume, a microphone)
2. *Ask Politely Game Show Questions* (See pages 263–264; one for educator use.)
3. *Would You Invite Victor To Your House?* (See pages 265–266; one per student and one transparency.)
4. Figures of Mrs. Mary Jackson (Mike's mother), Mike Olson, and Victor Parra (See *Appendix F.*)

PREPARATORY SET:

Ask students to share examples of appropriate manners they observed and recorded on *Manners Hunt,* as assigned in Lesson B. After the examples have been shared, thank the students and say in a theatrical voice, "And now, let's play the TV game show called 'Ask Politely'!"

PLAN:

1. Ask students if they have ever seen a TV game show and ask for examples. Tell students that today they will be contestants on a game show called "Ask Politely." Before the game begins, place students into groups of three or four. Ask students to number off from one to three or four within their groups. Check to be certain everyone remembers his or her number by saying something like, "All the one's raise your hands," etc.
2. Explain the purpose of the game by saying, "During the game, I will be reading some situations. Each situation tells about a person who wants to ask for something. Your job is to tell the polite way for the person to ask. Sometimes during the game, I will be telling you what someone said. Your job is to decide if the person asked politely or demanded impolitely. For example, if a person says 'Give me that cookie,' (say it rudely) that's not asking, that's telling or demanding, and that's not appropriate manners."

3. Put on the emcee costume, hold the microphone, turn on the music, and say in a theatrical voice, "Welcome to the game show called 'Ask Politely,' the game show filled with fun and excitement! Without further ado, would all the three's please raise your hands? Congratulations and COME ON DOWN, three's! You're our first contestants on 'Ask Politely.' Take a seat at our contestant's table."

4. While the three's are being seated, write a number between 1 and 50 on a piece of paper so no one can see it. Ask each three to quickly pick a number between 1 and 50. Say to whoever comes closest to your number, "_____," congratulations! You get to answer the first question on 'Ask Politely.' "

5. Read the first situation from the *Ask Politely Game Show Questions.* Allow a comfortable period of time for the student to answer. The student can consult with the other three's before answering. You might ring a bell after the answer is completed to signal a transition.

6. Ask all the three's to go back to their seats, and then ask all the two's (or one's or four's) to COME ON DOWN. Continue playing using the same procedure as described above as long as time allows. Devise a scoring system only if it's necessary to maintain students' interest.

7. Distribute and display *Would You Invite Victor To Your House?* Display the characters while reading the script. After reading the script, the class can discuss the questions that follow it.

8. Write the following where everyone can see it: I FEEL JAZZED AND TOTALLY MARVELOUS WHEN I USE MY SOCIAL SKILLS. Have the students say this aloud, in unison, with energy.

ASK POLITELY
GAME SHOW QUESTIONS

1. Ann would like her mother to get her some juice. Tell the words Ann might say to ask politely.
2. Decide if this is a polite request or a demand: "I want my breakfast now!"
3. Listen to this demand: "Help me with this!" Change that demand into a polite request.
4. Victor wants to ask his dad if he can go to his friend's house. Tell the words Victor could say to ask politely.
5. Decide if this is a polite request or a demand: "Could I please have some more salad?"
6. Listen to this demand: "Give it to me!" Change that demand into a polite request.
7. Mike wants to ask if he can ride his friend's bike. Tell the words Mike might say to ask politely.
8. Decide if this is a polite request or a demand: "Would you mind if I borrowed your ball?"
9. Listen to this demand: "You have to let me go to his house." Change that demand into a polite request.
10. Jolisa wants to ask her dad for a neat pencil she saw at the store. Tell the words Jolisa can say to ask politely.
11. Decide if this is a polite request or a demand: "Let me stay up later so I can finish this book."
12. Listen to this demand: "Let me wear your shirt to school tomorrow." Change that demand into a polite request.
13. Lee wants to ask his teacher for a new worksheet because he lost his copy. Tell the words Lee could say to ask politely.
14. Decide if this is a polite request or a demand: "Let me have a pair of your socks. Mine are all dirty."
15. Listen to this demand: "Don't touch it or you'll break it." Change that demand into a polite request.

16. Maria wants to ask her neighbor if she can borrow an egg for her mom. Tell the words Maria could say to ask politely.
17. Decide if this is a polite request or a demand: "Can I please get a haircut? My bangs are in my eyes."
18. Listen to this demand: "Don't come in my room. I'm changing." Change that demand into a polite request.

Name ____________________

Would You Invite Victor To Your House?

DIRECTIONS: Read the script and answer the questions.

Characters: Mike Olson
Mrs. Jackson (Mike's mother)
Victor Parra

Setting: Mike has invited Victor to eat at his house.
(The boys are watching television.)

Mrs. Jackson: Boys, it's time to eat!

Victor: OK, I'll fill my plate and bring it out here so I can finish watching this show.

Mike: We always turn off the TV and eat at the table.

Victor: That's dumb! What's to eat? I hope it's good.

Mrs. Jackson: Chicken, potatoes, gravy...

Victor: *(Interrupting)* Do you have something else? Is there dessert?

Mrs. Jackson: Yes, Victor, we have dessert for later.

(At the table)

Mike: Mom, could you please pass the potatoes?

Mrs. Jackson: Sure, Mike.

Victor: Toss me one of those rolls, Mike!

Mike: *(Looking embarrassed, while passing the basket of rolls to Victor)* Here you go.

Victor: I think I'll take three right away. *(Victor burps loudly and reaches way across the table for more potatoes without asking. He knocks over the gravy.)* Oops! You'd better get a paper towel!

Mrs. Jackson: *(Looking annoyed)* Is there anything else I can get you, Victor?

Victor: Can I have two pieces of dessert?

(Mrs. Jackson rolls her eyes.)

Name ______________________

Would You Invite Victor To Your House?

DIRECTIONS: Answer these questions.

1. What things did Victor do to show poor manners?

____

____

____

2. What things could Victor have done to show better manners?

____

____

____

3. What thoughts do you think Mrs. Jackson had about Victor's table manners?

____

____

____

4. What thoughts do you think Mike had about his friend's manners?

____

____

____

5. What could happen because Victor chose to use poor manners?

____

____

____

Lesson D

OBJECTIVES:

1. To determine whether or not appropriate, respectful manners are used in various given situations
2. To demonstrate use of appropriate, respectful manners while preparing the game "Skateboard to Mannerland"

MATERIALS:

1. A skateboard (For educator use)
2. *Skateboard to Mannerland Cards* (See pages 270–271; one for educator use and one set per student.)
3. *Mannerland Questions* (See pages 272–273; one for educator use.)
4. *Skateboard to Mannerland Game Board* (See page 274; one per student.)
5. Light-colored markers or crayons (An assortment for each pair of students)
6. Scissors and paper clips (One per student)
7. *Mannerland Game Pieces* (See page 275; one per student.)
8. Business-size envelopes or larger (One per student)

PREPARATORY SET:

Skateboard across the front of the classroom to get students' attention. Tell students that they are going to be making a game called "Skateboard to Mannerland" to play with a partner at school and to take home to play with their families.

PLAN:

1. Pair students (see *Appendix P*). Tell students you will be reading through the *Skateboard to Mannerland Cards* with them so that when they play the game during the next lesson, they will already have some experience with the cards. Read the first statement (card A) from *Skateboard to Mannerland Cards,* omitting the consequence statement at the end (e.g., Lose 1 turn). Have students put their thumbs up if the statement shows appropriate manners and their thumbs down if the statement shows inappropriate manners. Ask the corresponding question from *Mannerland Questions* and ask students to discuss an answer

with their partners. Call on one pair of students to share their answer. A demonstration opportunity is suggested after each question as well. (The educator may choose to ask just the follow-up question. If the demonstration opportunity is also used, it is critical to model for students first.)

2. Follow the same procedure for cards B, C, and D.

3. Tell students, "Let's take a break from these game cards, so you can make the game board for 'Skateboard to Mannerland.' I will be giving each of you a copy of the game board and markers to color it. Be sure to write your name on your game board. I will be watching for people using appropriate manners while you are coloring. What are some examples of things you might say or do to show appropriate manners while you are working?" Encourage the students to share examples.

4. Distribute markers and *Skateboard to Mannerland Game Board.* Allow five minutes for students to complete their task.

5. Follow the same procedure as described in step 1 of this Plan for cards E, F, G, and H.

6. Tell students, "Let's take another break from these game cards so you can continue preparing your game. I will be giving each of you a copy of the game cards, a pair of scissors to cut them apart, and a paper clip to clip the cards together. I will be watching for people using appropriate manners while you are cutting."

7. Distribute scissors, paper clips, and *Skateboard to Mannerland Cards.* Allow five minutes for students to complete their task.

8. Follow the same procedure as described in step 1 of this Plan for cards I, J, K, and L.

9. Tell students, "Let's take another break from these game cards so you can continue preparing your game. I will be giving each of you a copy of the game pieces to color and cut apart. When you are finished cutting them apart, fold the playing pieces in half on the dotted lines so they form tents."

10. Distribute *Mannerland Game Pieces.* Allow five minutes to cut them apart and fold them.

11. Follow the same procedure as described in step 1 of this Plan for cards M, N, O, and P.

12. Tell students, "Now we are finished going through all of the game cards. I will be giving each of you an envelope. Please write your name on it. Next, put your game cards which are paper clipped together and your playing pieces which are folded inside the envelope."

13. Distribute one envelope to each student. Collect the envelopes and the game boards after students have finished.
14. Discuss respectful manners that both the educator and students observed during this lesson.
15. Say with conviction to the class: *You are all great kids! I'm impressed with what you learned in class today!*

SKATEBOARD TO MANNERLAND CARDS

You burped loudly and forgot to say "Excuse me."

Lose 1 turn.

When you bumped into a man at the store, you did not say anything to him.

Stay on your space.

You forgot to say "Please" when you asked your sister for a piece of gum.

Stay on your space.

You asked politely for a drink of water at your friend's house.

Flip the coin again.

On a field trip, you were talking to others while the leader was talking.

Stay on your space.

You said "Please" when you asked your grandfather for some cake.

Move ahead 1 space.

You stood in line for a ride at the park. You did not cut into line.

Move ahead 1 space.

You said "Thank you" when your friend's father gave you a ride home.

Move ahead 3 spaces.

SKATEBOARD TO MANNERLAND CARDS
(Continued)

You said "Please" when you asked your brother to pass the milk during dinner.

Move ahead 1 space.

When your friend thanked you for helping, you said "You're welcome."

Flip the coin again.

At your friend's house, you took a drink out of the refrigerator without asking.

Stay on your space.

The teacher brought treats to class. You didn't like the treat so you politely said "No, thank you."

Flip the coin again.

There was only one cookie left. You told your brother he could have it.

Move ahead 3 spaces.

You said you were sorry when you accidentally got your friend's shirt dirty.

Move ahead 1 space.

You jumped on the couch at your grandparent's house.

Stay on your space.

You were quiet at the movie so other people could hear.

Flip the coin again.

MANNERLAND QUESTIONS

A. What might people think if you do not excuse yourself for burping?
Show what you can say to be polite if you accidentally burp.

B. What might people think if you don't say "Excuse me"?
Show what you could say if you accidentally bump into someone.

C. Why is it important to say "Please" when you ask for something?
Show how you can politely ask for a piece of gum.

D. How might your friend's parents feel about you if you use appropriate manners?
Show how you can politely ask for a drink of water.

E. Why is it not polite to talk when you should be listening?
Show the body talk you could use to listen politely.

F. How might your grandparents feel when you use respectful manners?
Show how you can politely ask for some cake.

G. Why is it polite to wait your turn in line?
Show how you can wait your turn in line.

H. What might your friend's father think about you if you don't say "Thank you"?
Show how you can thank a friend's parent for a ride.

I. Why is it important to use table manners at home?
Show how you can politely ask your brother to pass the milk.

J. Why is it polite to say "You're welcome" when someone thanks you?
Show how you can say "You're welcome" to your friend.

K. What might your friend and friend's family think if you get a drink from the refrigerator without asking?
Show how you can politely ask for something to drink.

L. How might the teacher have felt if you had said, "Yuck. I don't like those"?
Show how to say "No, thank you" in a polite way.

M. Why is it polite to offer the last piece of something to someone else?
Show how to politely offer the last of something to another person.

N. Why is it polite to say "I'm sorry" when something happens accidentally?
Show how to politely say "I'm sorry" for getting your friend's shirt dirty.

O. Why might your grandparents feel upset when you jump on their furniture?
Show how you can politely sit on a couch.

P. Why is it polite to be quiet at a movie?
Show how you can sit quietly while watching a movie.

Name ______________________

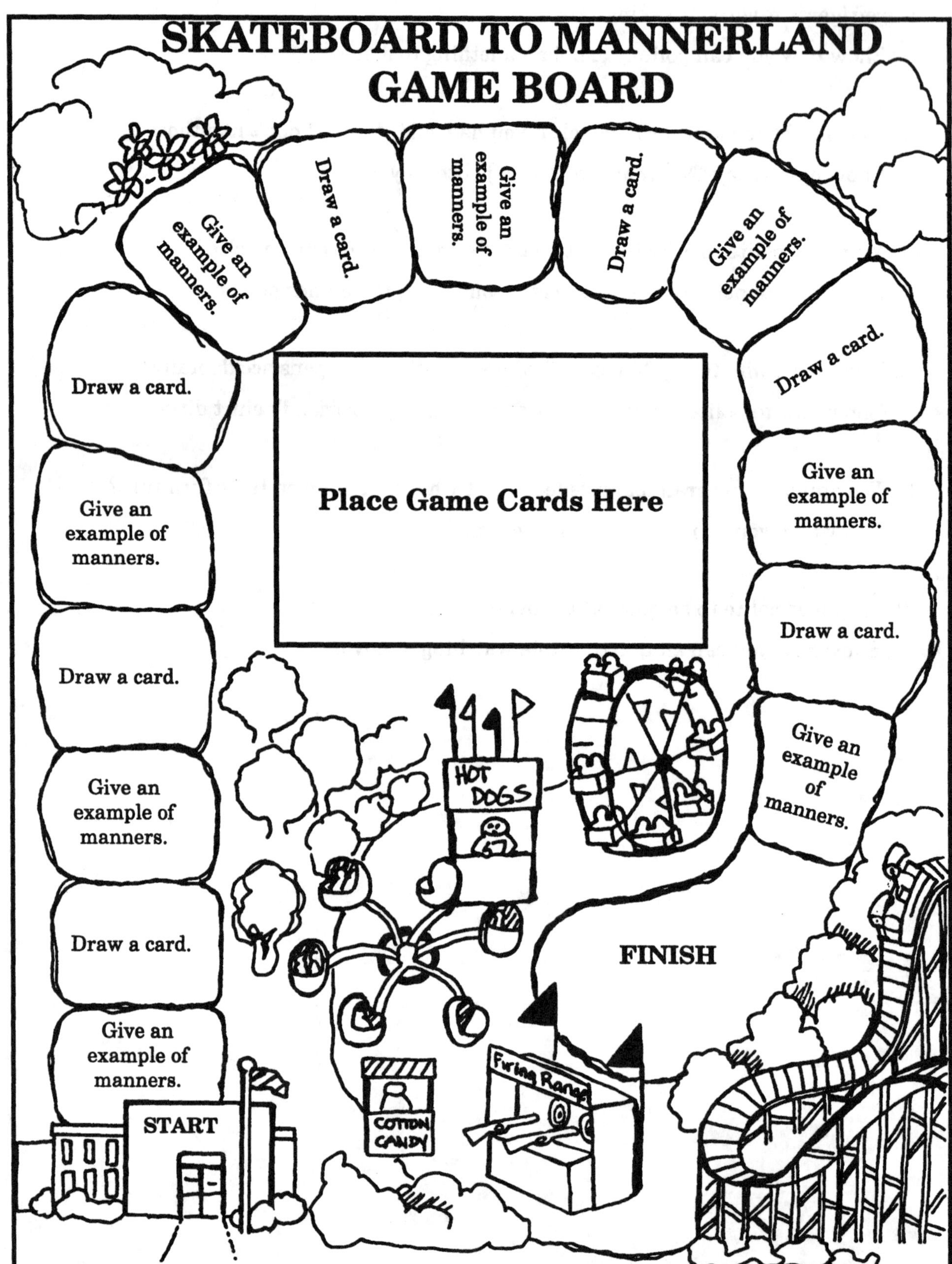
SKATEBOARD TO MANNERLAND
GAME BOARD
Give an example of manners.
Draw a card.
Give an example of manners.
Draw a card.
Give an example of manners.
Draw a card.
Give an example of manners.
Draw a card.
Give an example of manners.
Draw a card.
Give an example of manners.
Draw a card.
Give an example of manners.
Draw a card.
Give an example of manners.
Place Game Cards Here
START
HOT DOGS
COTTON CANDY
Firing Range
FINISH

Name ____________________

MANNERLAND GAME PIECES

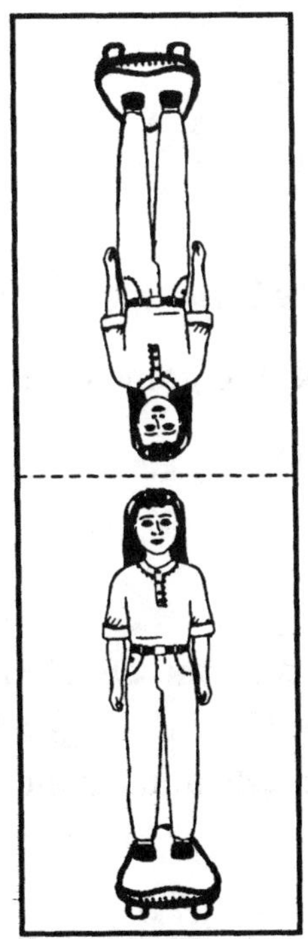
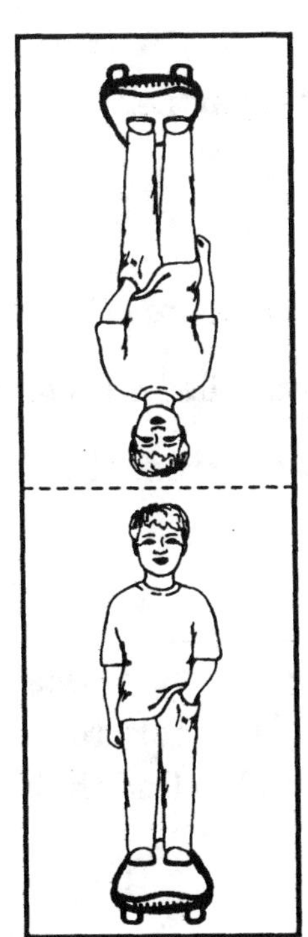
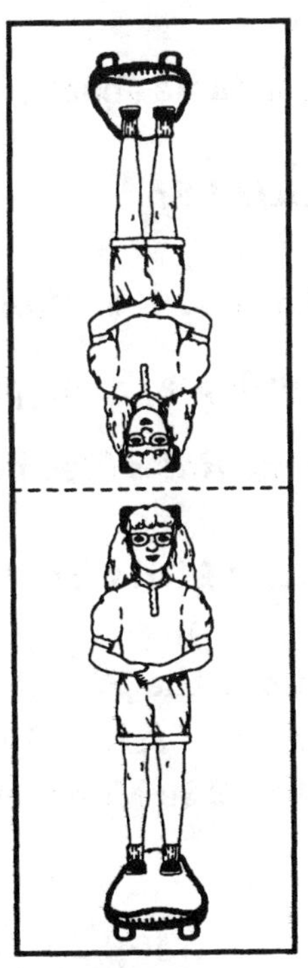

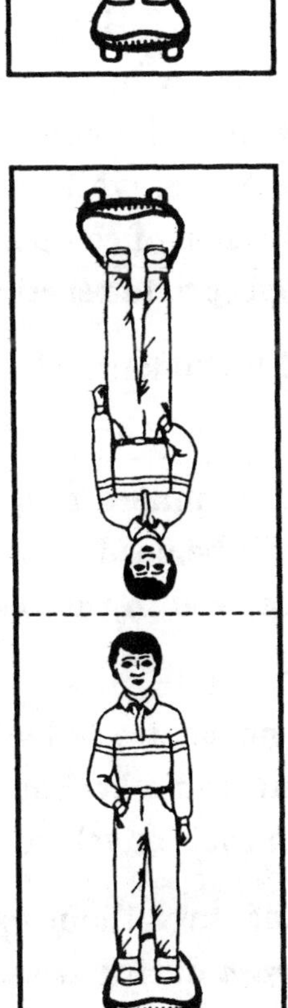
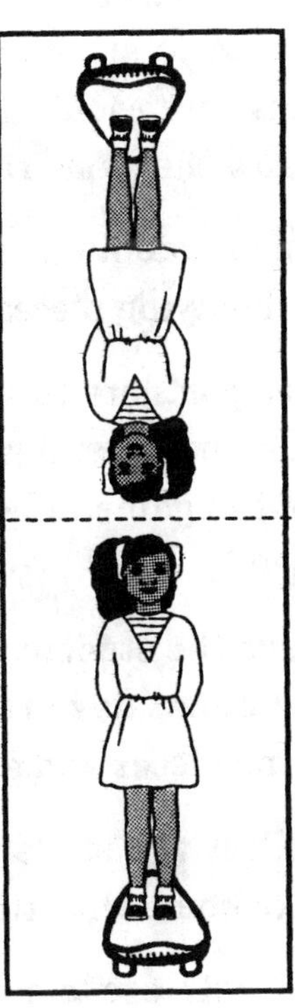

Lesson E

OBJECTIVE:

To play a game about manners with a partner

MATERIALS:

1. *Skateboard to Mannerland Game Boards* (From previous lesson)
2. Envelopes (From previous lesson, filled with game cards and game pieces)
3. *Game Rules* (See page 277; one per student.)

PREPARATORY SET:

Spread out the *Skateboard to Mannerland Game Boards* and the envelopes on a counter or a table. In an excited manner, tell students that they get to play "Skateboard to Mannerland" today and to find their game boards and envelopes.

PLAN:

1. Distribute *Game Rules*. As a class, read and discuss the rules for "Skateboard to Mannerland." After reading over the rules, ask students to tell things they can do to show appropriate manners while playing the game with a partner. (Answers could include expectations of competitive situations, e.g., take turns, follow the game rules, show appropriate reactions to winning and losing.)
2. Pair students (see *Appendix P*). Students should each have their game board and playing pieces.
3. Ask partners to use respectful manners to quickly determine which person's game board and game pieces will be used to play the game. (There may be time for the game to be played twice, and in that case both people's games could be used.)
4. Have the students play the game as directed with their partners and when they are done, have them fold their game boards and place them, as well as the game pieces and game cards, in their envelopes.
5. Collect the students' games and save them to be redistributed to students to take home with the *Home-A-Gram* during Lesson Y.
6. Say with excitement to the class: *Each of you is a special, spectacular, marvelous, wonderful, magnificent social person!*

Name ____________________

GAME RULES

1. Place the game cards on the space indicated on the game board. Choose one of the Socialville characters as your game piece and place it on the picture of the school.
2. Get a coin and place it near the game board.
3. The player who is the youngest goes first.
4. Player #1 flips the coin. *Heads* means move 1 space on the game board and *tails* means move 2 spaces. If "Give an example of manners" is written on the space landed on, the player tells any appropriate example of manners. Then, play advances to the next player. If the player lands on a "Draw a card" space, the player reads the top game card aloud and follows the direction given on the card (e.g., "Move ahead 1 space," "Lose 1 turn," etc.).
5. To enter "Mannerland Amusement Park," a player must flip the exact number needed (e.g., if a player has 1 space to go, a heads must be flipped on the coin).
6. The first player to get to "Mannerland Amusement Park" is the winner.
7. Reshuffle the game cards if needed.

Lessons X, Y, Z

Due to similarities in format, the final three lesson plans for each unit in *Social Star* are provided in *Appendix A*. Substitute the word "manners" whenever a "_____" appears in the lesson plans. Information specific to this unit follows.

LESSON X PREPARATORY SET:

Tell students that when you went to school, you knew a teacher with the nickname "Mr. Impolite." Ask students to tell things the teacher might have done to get that nickname.

LESSON Y PREPARATORY SET:

Darken the room, if you prefer, and ask students to visualize themselves correctly using this social skill by reading the following script:

> *Let's take a few moments to relax.... Make sure you are sitting in a comfortable position.... Close your eyes if you feel like it.... On the count of three, take a very slow, deep breath. One . . . two . . . three.... Breathe in deeply.... Now breathe out slowly.... Let your entire body relax. Now imagine yourself in the lunch line. You say "Yes, please" when the cook offers you food you want, and you say "No, thank you" when the cook offers you food you do not care for. When you eat your lunch, you chew with your mouth closed. Think about what a good impression you are making and how good you feel because you are using appropriate manners.*

LESSON Z PLOT SITUATION:

Ask students to pretend that one of their siblings just accidentally broke a favorite toy that belongs to them.

LESSON Z ROADBLOCK EXAMPLES:

- Using appropriate manners when you are around people who are being rude
- Using appropriate manners when experiencing feelings such as anger, sadness, frustration

Name ____________________

Manners T-Chart

LOOKS LIKE...	SOUNDS LIKE...
using appropriate body talk • looking at the person who is talking • nodding your head • using an interested facial expression	saying • "Please" • "Thank you" • "Excuse me" • "Pardon me"
table manners • elbows off the table	using appropriate tone of voice
	using correct voice volume

HOME

Pretend your family is eating dinner. Show what you could say to politely ask for more bread.

SCHOOL

Pretend you accidentally knock a pencil off a classmate's desk when you walk by. Show what you might say and do to be polite.

COMMUNITY

Pretend you are in the middle of a row at the movie theatre. You need to leave to use the restroom. Show what you would say to politely get past people.

BE
POLITE
WITH
MANNERS

HOME-A-GRAM

Dear Family,

At school, we have been talking about the social skill called

MANNERS

I learned that *using manners* means acting in a polite, respectful way.

It will help me feel good about myself when I use appropriate manners, and others will be impressed.

I know that whenever I'm at home, school, other people's homes, and other places, I should ask myself, "What manners could I use?"

I have written down one way I can use respectful manners in each of the following places.

At home: ____

____

In other people's homes: __________________________

____

At school: _______________________________________

____

I am bringing home a game about manners for us to play. If I politely ask you to play the game, please sign my "Manners" badge so I can return it to school and become a SOCIAL SUPER STAR this week.

From: ______________________________

Listening Basics

UNIT GOAL:

To demonstrate comprehension and use of basic listening skills

EDUCATOR INFORMATION:

1. This unit was developed to teach students that listening is a crucial communication skill. Of the four major communication processes (reading, writing, speaking, and listening), 55 percent of communication time is spent listening (Werner, 1975). This unit does not attempt to encompass the entire topic of listening, but focuses on basic listening skills. It teaches students to show others that they are listening and the positive consequences of doing so. Educators should emphasize the importance of thinking about what is being said in order to be listening appropriately.

2. Educators need to note that there are cultural variations in the use of body talk in the listening process. According to Althen (1988), for example, people from certain parts of India typically move their heads in a sort of figure-eight motion when they are listening to someone talk. To the Indians, this gesture means "I am listening, I understand." Americans do not have a similar gesture. In addition, the head movement of the Indians is not the same as the one Americans use to indicate agreement (the head goes up and down) or disagreement (the head goes side to side). The Indian movement involves moving the head around in a fashion that is likely to suggest to Americans that the Indian has a sore neck. Black Americans have a preference for indirect eye contact during listening; common culture Americans prefer direct eye contact (Taylor, 1993). The educator should exert sensitivity and care in generalizing rules about listening into the children's home cultures.

RELATED ACTIVITIES:

1. During silent reading time, play different types of music. Students could vote on the type of music easiest to listen to (if any) while reading and explain their choice.

2. Videotape students listening to a classmate speaking in front of the group. Ask students to view the videotape to analyze the messages their body talk may have given the speaker during the presentation.

3. Have students tape record themselves having a conversation with a friend. Ask students to analyze their individual communication style. They may want to evaluate skills specific to listening (e.g., staying on topic, asking questions to

keep the topic going, taking turns talking and listening, using appropriate body talk such as volume or tone).

4. Invite a person with a hearing impairment to speak to the class about adapting to life situations. A person with a visual impairment could discuss the increased reliance on listening when adapting for a visual handicap.
5. Have students make tapes containing a variety of sounds or noises (at least 10). The students may switch tapes and try to guess the sounds their partner taped.
6. Take students on a "no-talk walk." Lead the class through the school and then around outside the school. Ask students to listen to the sounds they hear. Discuss with students the variety of sounds heard in each environment.
7. Have students visit an office receptionist to discover the importance of listening skills for that job. They might visit other workers as well (e.g., a custodian, a guidance counselor).
8. Invite adults from different cultures to talk to the students about how their cultures' conventions for listening compare with American common culture norms.

It is important for educators to provide opportunities for students to work in groups so they can experience social skills in contexts where social communication is needed. Therefore, educators are encouraged to have students complete the Related Activities in small groups whenever possible. Educators trained in cooperative learning could incorporate the five components (see page 34) into the group activity.

RELATED LITERATURE:

Mama One, Mama Two (1982) by Patricia MacLachlan, Ill. by Ruth Lercher Bornstein, Harper and Row. (Picture book)

One to Grow on (1969) by Jean Little; Little, Brown and Co. (Text) (pages 3–11)

S.O.R. Losers (1984) by Avi, Bradbury. (Text) (pages 4–6)

SOCIAL SKILLS ALL DAY LONG:

Look for opportunities to teach social skills throughout the day (incidental teaching). Four ways to reinforce good social skills and an example of each follow:

Encouragement

When Jack was telling you about his Boy Scout meeting, you really looked like you were listening. I'll bet he enjoyed talking to you. Super!

Personal Example

Last night I needed to go to a class. I was having a hard time listening because I was tired, so I sat up straight, told myself to listen, and gave the teacher eye contact. Doing that really helped me to be a good listener.

Prompting

In a few minutes, we'll be having a fire drill. You need to listen carefully to what I'm going to say, so you'll know what to do.

Corrective Feedback (must be positive, private, specific, and nonthreatening)

Ann, just now when I was giving directions, you were reading a book. If you had listened, you might have learned how to complete the activity.

Lesson A

OBJECTIVES:

1. To state the meaning of *listening basics* and tell why the skill is important
2. To tell the self-talk associated with correct use of the skill

MATERIALS:

1. *Listening Basics* (See page 289; one per student and one transparency.)
2. *Thought Bubble* (See *Appendix O*; one for educator use.)
3. *Look Alive!* (See page 290; one transparency.)

PREPARATORY SET:

Tell students that they are going to try to guess a word. (The answer is LISTEN.) Explain that the word has six letters. Ask students to try to guess the word, using the clues that follow, and then explain that they will be learning more about listening in the next lessons.

- You do it to make a good impression.
- You could give eye contact when you do this.
- It helps you to understand things.
- You do it with your ears and brain.

PLAN:

1. Distribute and display *Listening Basics.* Discuss the definition. Explain the skill steps and the symbols next to them. Remind students that the symbols are there to help them visualize and remember the skill steps. Remind students that during the first skill step, they need to use what they know about body talk. Read and explain the reasons provided for using basic listening skills.
2. Model use of the first listening skill step while thinking aloud. A scripted example follows:

   Introduction

   I am going to pretend to be a student your age. My art teacher is giving directions for today's project. I will tell you the thoughts I'm having while I listen. When I hold up this Thought Bubble, *you'll know the words that I'm saying are actually what I'm thinking.*

Actual Model

While holding up the *Thought Bubble* say, *The teacher is talking. Does my body talk show I am listening? Yes, I'm looking at the teacher and nodding my head.*

3. Read the story at the bottom of *Listening Basics.*
4. Pair students using *Inside-Outside Circle* (see *Appendix P*). Tell students that you will be reading the story again. Ask student pairs to look at the story and underline the things Mike did to show that he was really listening.
5. Display *Look Alive!* Tell students that each listed body part plays a different role in the listening process. Ask students to think about what each part listed does to show someone that they are listening. Ask for student volunteers to write their responses on the transparency. Suggested responses include:

   Head: It nods.

   Ears: They hear the words the people are saying.

   Brain: It thinks—"Do I look like I'm really listening?"
   "What is the person saying?"
   "Do I understand this?

   Eyes: They look at the person.
   They don't roll.
   They stay open.

   Mouth/Voice: It is quiet while someone else is talking.
   It doesn't yawn.
   It takes turns talking.

   Body: It faces the person you are talking with.
   It doesn't move around too much.
   It uses appropriate posture.

   Proceed with this discussion by asking the student pairs to tell each other the answers to the following questions:

   - Why is it important to use listening skills in class?
   - What might happen if you don't listen in class?

6. Ask student pairs to take turns telling each other the meaning of *listening basics* and why it's important to use the skill. Ask students to use basic listening

skills while completing this task. Students could be reminded that the information they are to say is printed on *Listening Basics.*

As an option to add structure to this activity (see *Appendix Q*), ask partners to come to an agreement about which person will be called "Pocahontas" and which person will be called "Captain John Smith." After students have made their decisions, ask "Pocahontas" to tell "Captain Smith" the definition of *listening basics.* Next, ask "Captain Smith" to tell "Pocahontas" the definition. Ask the students to use the same procedure to tell each other the reasons for using listening skills.

7. Write the following where everyone can see it: THIS CLASS IS EXTRAORDINARY. I LEARN A LOT EVERY DAY! Have the students say this aloud, in unison, vibrantly.

Name ____________________

Listening Basics

MEANING OF LISTENING BASICS: Hearing and thinking about what someone is saying

SKILL STEPS:

1. Ask myself: Does my body talk show that I'm listening?
2. Think: Do I understand what is being said?

REASONS FOR USING THIS SKILL:

If you listen, people might like talking to you more. You will hear and understand information that you need. You will feel good about your listening skills.

DIRECTIONS: Listen to the story below. Look at the pictures of Mr. Aaron and Mike. Underline the things that Mike did to show that he was really listening.

When Mr. Aaron was talking, Mike looked at him. He stood still and nodded his head to let Mr. Aaron know he was listening. Mike thought about what Mr. Aaron was saying. He listened until Mr. Aaron finished talking before he asked a question. Mr. Aaron could see that Mike was really listening.

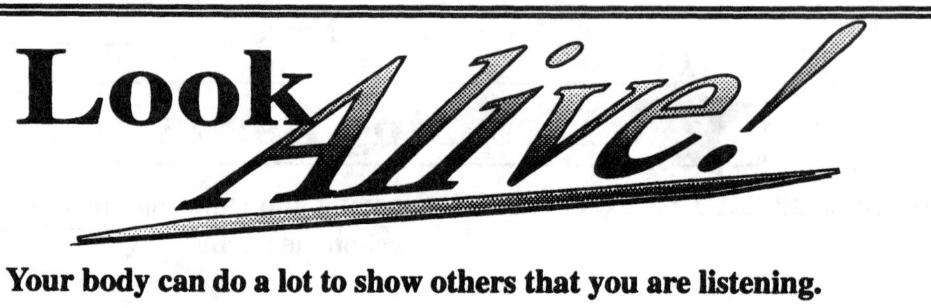

Your body can do a lot to show others that you are listening.

DIRECTIONS: On the lines provided, fill in things that can be done to show others that you are listening.

Head: ____________________

Brain: ____________________

Eyes: ____________________

Mouth/Voice: ____________________

Ears: ____________________

Body: ____________________

Lesson B

OBJECTIVE:

To practice listening to, and then thinking about, what is being said

MATERIALS:

1. *Listening Basics* classroom poster (See page 13.)
2. *Thought Bubble* (See *Appendix O*; one for educator use.)
3. Drawing paper (One piece per student)
4. Crayons, markers, or colored pencils (A variety for each student)
5. *Listen Up!* (See page 293; one per student and one transparency.)

PREPARATORY SET:

Ask students to sit in a circle. Play the game of "Telephone." Begin by whispering a "nonsense" statement into one student's ear (e.g., "ran, ren, rin, ron, run"). That student then whispers the message into the ear of the next student, and so forth, until the message travels around the circle. The last person to hear the message says it aloud. Ask students the following questions:

- Who heard the message that was whispered into their ears?
- Who understood the message that was whispered into their ears?

Discuss the difference between hearing what is said and understanding what is said in the listening process.

PLAN:

1. Review the definition and skill steps for *listening basics* by referring the class to the *Listening Basics* classroom poster.
2. Pair students (see *Appendix P*). Ask student pairs to take turns telling each other the skill steps for listening basics. Follow the procedure described in step 6 of Lesson A. (As an option, ask the students to decide who will be "John Henry" and who will be "Casey Jones.") Next, ask students to work with their partners to think of a situation when the use of listening basics is important. Tell students that one or more pairs will be asked to share their situation. Have one or more pairs share their situation.

3. Model use of the listening basics skill steps while thinking aloud. A scripted example follows:

   Introduction

   I am going to pretend to be listening to my soccer coach. I am having a hard time listening because I am feeling nervous about the game. I will tell you the thoughts I'm having while I listen. When I hold up this Thought Bubble, *you'll know the words I'm saying are actually what I'm thinking.*

   Actual Model

   While holding up the *Thought Bubble* say, *It's OK to be nervous about the game, but the coach is telling us some important directions. Is my body talk showing I'm listening? No. I'd better change it.* (Stand up tall, look alert, and nod your head.) *Now I need to think about what he is saying so I know what to do.*

4. Distribute the drawing paper and crayons, markers, or colored pencils. Instruct students to draw a picture of a wish they would like to come true.

5. When the pictures are complete, tell students that they will be telling their partners about their drawings and will be rating themselves on how well they listen during the activity. Display *Listen Up!* and read aloud the criteria by which students will be rating themselves.

6. Have Partner 1 begins by telling Partner 2 about the picture drawn. Partner 2 is directed to show Partner 1 that he is really listening and is thinking about what is being said. When Partner 1 is finished telling about her picture, Partner 2 tells about his. Partner 1 then becomes the listener. Tell students that it is especially important that they think about what is being said because one or more students will be called on to tell about their partner's picture. After students have shared their pictures, ask for students at random to tell about their partner's picture.

7. Distribute *Listen Up!* Tell partners that they will be rating the listening skills they each just used. Read the directions from *Listen Up!* aloud. Direct students' attention to #1 on the sheet. Read it aloud. Ask students, "For you, is this 'mostly yes' or 'mostly no'? If it was mostly yes, put an 'X' in this box. (Point to the "mostly yes" box on the transparency.) If it was mostly no, put an 'X' in this box." (Point to the "mostly no" box on the transparency.) Continue in the same fashion, reading aloud #2, #3, and #4 and allowing students to put an "X" in the appropriate box after each.

8. Ask students to list words that describe how they feel when they know others are listening to what they have to say.

9. Say enthusiastically to the class: *You are dynamite, vibrant students! Thank you for using your smart brains!*

Name ______________________

LISTEN UP!

DIRECTIONS: Decide how well you listened by putting an "X" in the box that was most true for you.

While I listened to my partner,	**MOSTLY YES**	**MOSTLY NO**
1. I used body talk that showed I was listening.		
2. I was thinking about what my partner was saying.		
During our class discussion,		
3. I looked at the person who was talking.		
4. I was thinking about what the person was saying.		

Lesson C

OBJECTIVES:

1. To recognize negative consequences of using inappropriate listening basics
2. To identify distractions that may interfere with the listening process

MATERIALS:

1. *Listen Please!* (See page 298; one per student and one transparency.)
2. *Checking Myself* (See *Appendix I*; one per student and one transparency.)
3. *Thought Bubble* (See *Appendix O*; one for educator use.)
4. One treasure box containing a treasure that can be divided equally among students (e.g., stickers, certificates, food items) hidden in the room before class
5. Treasure hunt cassette tape (See step 6 of the Plan below; recorded prior to class. Be sure that the tape includes at least one clue for each student who will be participating—if there will be five students participating, the tape should include at least five clues.)
6. Small pieces of paper with one number written on each (If five students will be participating, prepare five pieces of paper containing one number from 1 to 5. If 21 students will be participating, prepare 21 pieces of paper containing one number from 1 to 21.)
7. Cassette tape player (One for educator use)
8. Radio (One for educator use)

PREPARATORY SET:

Tell students that you will be reading some situations aloud. Ask them to show the "thumbs up" sign if the person showed appropriate listening basics and the "thumbs down" sign if the person did not show appropriate listening basics. Proceed by reading aloud the following situations:

- Jolisa looked at the TV the whole time that her dad was talking to her.
- Lee nodded his head to show he understood when Mrs. Marrero asked if the class understood the assignment.
- Victor jiggled his chair back and forth when Ms. Hess was talking to him.
- Ann looked at her stepfather and smiled when he was telling her a funny joke.

- Mike waited until Lee was finished telling his story before he began telling his own story.
- At practice, Victor sat still on the bench and thought about what the coach was saying.

PLAN:

1. Distribute and display *Listen Please!* Tell students that they should look at the cartoon while you read it aloud.
2. Distribute and display the discussion guideline sheet called *Checking Myself.* Ask students to complete the goal statement with the words "use eye contact," or use another classroom discussion goal more appropriate for your group (see page 26). Tell students that you will be having a discussion about the cartoon they just saw and heard. When a person is answering a question or making a comment during the discussion, it's important to give that person eye contact. Instruct them to put an "X" on their sheets each time they give eye contact to a student who is called on.
3. Model use of the *Checking Myself* sheet while thinking aloud. A scripted example follows:

   Introduction

   I am going to pretend to be one of you completing this sheet during the discussion we will be having. I will tell you the thoughts I'm having while I'm completing the sheet. When I hold up this Thought Bubble, *you'll know the words I'm saying are actually what I'm thinking.*

   Actual Model

   While holding up the *Thought Bubble* say, *OK, the teacher just called on Trish. I'd better look at Trish so she knows I'm listening to her answer. I'll put an "X" on my sheet because I gave her eye contact.* Put the *Thought Bubble* down and mark an "X" on the overhead transparency.

   During the discussion, periodically remind students to give eye contact and to mark their discussion guideline sheets.
4. Proceed with the discussion by asking these questions: (The cartoon may need to be reread first.)
   - Was Mrs. Jackson using basic listening skills?
   - How did Mike know that his mother was not really listening?
   - How do you think Mike felt when he walked away?

- What could Mike have said or done to let his mom know that he really needed her to listen?

After the discussion, have students complete the bottom of *Checking Myself.*

5. Process the use of the sheet by asking the following question or another one more appropriate for your group:

   - What effect did using eye contact have on your listening?

   Process further by asking the students who volunteered to speak during the discussion to share their answers to the following question:

   - You answered one of the questions during our discussion. How did you feel when the other students gave you eye contact when you were talking?

6. Be certain you hide a box filled with a "treasure" somewhere in the classroom before class begins. Prerecord a cassette tape giving directions for locating the treasure. An example script follows. It will need to be modified to fit your classroom situation. There should be one or more clues for each person who will be participating. (Not all students need to participate; the number of students participating will depend on the amount of class time available and the size of your class.)

   Clue for Person 1: Stand in the corner of the room by the windows. Walk until you reach Sue's desk. Stop.

   Clue for Person 2: From Sue's desk, turn right and take 3 large steps to the chalkboard.

   Clue for Person 3: From the chalkboard, turn left and take baby steps until you are standing under the clock.

   Clue for Person 4: From the clock, take 2 steps toward the science table. Then face the opposite direction.

   Clue for Person 5: From there, take a giant step backwards. You will be standing near the bookshelf. Look behind the book that is sideways on the shelf. Congratulations, the treasure is yours to share with your class!

7. Tell students that some of them will be taking turns to follow directions. Tell them if they follow the directions accurately, they will find a secret treasure. Explain that you might be making some noises but they need to do the best that they can do. Without being able to see the numbers, each participating student draws one piece of paper. Ask the person who drew the paper with #1 written on it to listen carefully to the tape and to follow the direction given.

8. Play the first clue from the prerecorded treasure hunt tape. As the clue is given, make it difficult for the student to listen to the tape by causing distractions (e.g., turn radio up loudly, call out a student's name and ask the student to come see what is going on out the window, drop a book, hum or sing loudly). Stop the tape after the first clue. Ask the person who drew the paper with #2 written on it to stand in the spot where #1 finished and to listen to the next clue. Again cause distractions. Stop the tape after the second clue. If the students ask for repetitions of their directions, ask "What's wrong? I played the direction. Why couldn't you follow it?" as a lead-in to the discussion about distractions in step 9. Continue in the manner described with the person who has drawn #3. Cause distractions that make it impossible for the students to hear their clues.

9. After students are obviously unable to proceed with the treasure hunt, ask them to sit down. Tell students that you were doing things called "distractions." (Explain that you will play the tape again at the end of the lesson without distractions.) Explain that distractions often interfere when trying to listen. Ask students to name the things that distracted them and to tell some of the feelings they had while being distracted. Ask students to tell about things that may distract them:

   - when they are listening to the teacher talk in the classroom.
   - when they are having a conversation with a friend at lunch.
   - when they are having a conversation with someone in their family.

   Call on students to share their responses to the above questions.

10. Play the tape without distractions. When the treasure is found, instruct that it be divided equally among all classmates.

11. Write the following where everyone can see it: I AM A SPECIAL PERSON. I CAN GET ALONG WELL WITH OTHERS. Have the students say this aloud, in unison, with enthusiasm.

Name ____________________

LISTEN Please!

DIRECTIONS: Look at this cartoon while it is read aloud.

Characters: Mike Olson

Mrs. Jackson (Mike's mother)

Setting: Mike arrives home from school and would like to talk to his mother. She is reading the paper.

Lesson D

OBJECTIVE:

To identify strategies for overcoming listening distractions

MATERIALS:

1. *Distractions Mind Map* (See page 300; one transparency.)
2. *Distractions* (See page 301; one per student and one transparency.)

PREPARATORY SET:

Pair students (see *Appendix P*). Announce that they will be learning more about distractions to their listening.

PLAN:

1. Display *Distractions Mind Map*. Talk through the *Distractions Mind Map* from the center (i.e. Distractions—Things that can stop me from listening) outward.
2. Ask student pairs to work together to identify a few more inside and outside distractions and share them with the class. Write additional examples on the transparency.
3. Distribute and display *Distractions*. Have student pairs work with their partners to complete their sheets as directed. Call on partners at random to share their ideas and write the ideas on the transparency.
4. Display *Distractions Mind Map* and discuss strategies for overcoming the inside and outside distractions listed.
5. Write the following where everyone can see it: SOCIAL SKILLS, SOCIAL SKILLS! RAH! RAH! RAH! Have the students say this aloud, in unison, with spirit.

DISTRACTIONS MIND MAP

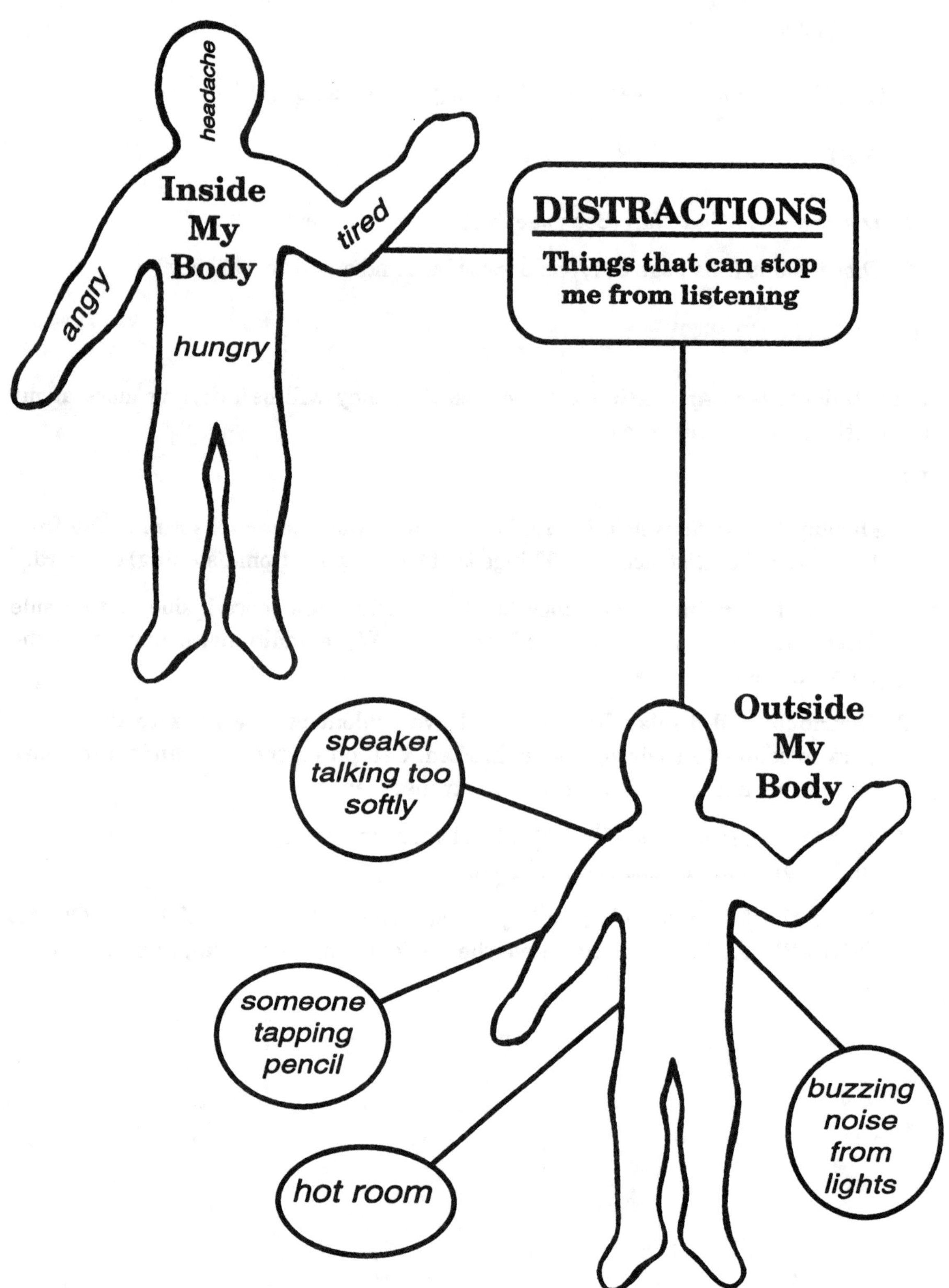

Name ____________________

DiStrACTiOns

DIRECTIONS: Each person in the situations below has a listening distraction. Decide what each person can do to listen.

1. Mr. Vue is listening to the news on the radio. He's distracted because he keeps thinking about all the yard work he has to do when he gets home. What could Mr. Vue say to himself in order to listen better?

____

____

____

2. Lee is trying to listen to the announcements at school. Lee is distracted because the student sitting behind him keeps tapping a pencil loudly. What could Lee do or say aloud to stop the distraction?

____

____

____

3. Ann wants to be a good listener when she is in the art room. She is distracted because the room is cold. What could Ann do to avoid having the distraction the next time she goes to the art room?

____

____

____

Lessons X, Y, and Z

Due to similarities in format, the final three lesson plans for each unit in *Social Star* are provided in *Appendix A*. Substitute the words "listening basics" whenever a "________" appears in the lesson plans. Information specific to this unit follows.

LESSON X PREPARATORY SET:

Play the game "Simon Says." Ask students to listen carefully to directions that you say. Explain that they should follow only the directions which begin with the words "Simon says." Examples follow:

- Stand up.
- Simon says, "Stand up."
- Jump on one foot.
- Simon says, "Jump on one foot."

LESSON Y PREPARATORY SET:

Darken the room, if you prefer, and ask students to visualize themselves correctly using this social skill by reading the following script:

> *Let's take a few moments to relax.... Make sure you are sitting in a comfortable position.... Close your eyes if you feel like it.... On the count of three, take a very slow, deep breath. One . . . two . . . three.... Breathe in deeply.... Now breathe out slowly.... Let your entire body relax.... Now imagine yourself in the classroom. The teacher is giving important directions. You look at the teacher, you stay still, you think about what is being said. You ignore distractions. Think about how fantastic you feel because you are listening.*

LESSON Z PLOT SITUATION:

Ask students to pretend that they are alone at home and that a stranger is knocking on the door. (The authors do not advocate leaving children alone. Unfortunately, this situation occurs and thus the topic warrants discussion.)

LESSON Z ROADBLOCK EXAMPLES:

- Experiencing feelings that may make it difficult to listen (e.g., tired, scared, bored)
- Listening while experiencing external distractions
- Listening while experiencing internal distractions

Name ____________________

Listening Basics T-Chart

LOOKS LIKE...	SOUNDS LIKE...
using appropriate body talk • looking at the person who is talking • nodding your head • using an interested facial expression	listening feedback • "Uh huh" • "OK, yes" • "I understand"

HOME

Pretend you are listening to your mother. She is talking with you about one of your cousins. Show the listening basics you would use.

SCHOOL

Pretend you are listening to the principal. He is telling your class about some new rules in the cafeteria. Show the listening basics you would use.

COMMUNITY

Pretend you are listening to your friend's father. He is telling you about a trip your families will be going on together. Show the listening basics you would use.

Listening
It's Important

HOME-A-GRAM

Dear Family,

At school, we have been talking about the social skill called

LISTENING BASICS

I learned that *listening basics* means hearing and thinking about what is being said.

I learned that it is important to ask myself, "Does my body talk show that I'm listening?" and "Do I understand what is being said?"

When I use listening basics, I will hear and understand information that I need and people might like talking with me more.

I learned that there are things I can do to show others that I am listening. Below, I have listed some of those things:

____

____

____

____

While I listen to people in my family tonight, I'll demonstrate some of the things listed above. After I do, please sign my "Listening Basics" badge so I can return it to school and become a SOCIAL SUPER STAR this week.

From: ______________________________

Staying on Topic/Switching Topics

UNIT GOAL:

To demonstrate comprehension and use of the ability to stay on topic and switch topics appropriately

EDUCATOR INFORMATION:

This unit teaches what a topic is and how to stay on topic in conversations with others. It is not to be confused with the study skill of staying on task. The unit also addresses what it means to switch topics. Because elementary-age students change topics frequently, this unit describes two techniques for switching topics politely. The first technique (for those at a lower level) is to say at least one thing about the current topic before talking about something different. The second technique (for those at a higher level) is to give a warning (transition statement) before switching topics. The educator should exert sensitivity and care in generalizing rules about staying on topic/switching topics into the children's home cultures.

RELATED ACTIVITIES:

1. Have students choose a topic of current interest in the media and start a scrapbook of clippings related to that topic.
2. Have students make a list of topics they would like to talk about with a favorite hero or heroine.
3. Have students research a library card catalog database to find the number and variety of topics listed. Students may choose a topic of particular interest and read books referenced in the library.
4. Discuss the importance of staying on topic when writing (e.g., writing a story, writing an answer).
5. Visit the local newspaper office. Talk to a staff member about the importance of staying on topic in newspaper articles.
6. Discuss how to tell when you've stayed on one topic too long and the conversation is no longer interesting to the listener.
7. Invite adults from different cultures to talk to the students about how their cultures' conventions for staying on topic/switching topics compare with American common culture norms.

It is important for educators to provide opportunities for students to work in groups so they can experience social skills in contexts where social communication is needed. Therefore, educators are encouraged to have students complete the Related Activities in small groups whenever possible. Educators trained in cooperative learning could incorporate the five components (see page 34) into the group activity.

RELATED LITERATURE:

Beans on the Roof (1988) by Betsy Byars, Delacorte. (Text)
George and his mother discuss why Anna can sit on the roof to write her poem but George can't. (pages 1–5)

Dear Mr. Henshaw (1983) by Beverly Cleary, Morrow. (Text) (pages 68–72, 74–78)

Sarah, Plain and Tall (1985) by Patricia MacLachlan, Harper and Row. (Text) (pages 17–20, 40–43)

Skinnybones (1982) by Barbara Park, Knopf. (Text)
Alex exchanges words with the camera operator (and God) who is to take the pictures of a Little League game. (pages 68–70)

Strides (1991) by Beverly Cleary, Morrow. (Text)
Leigh calls his dad for help in building a fence for his dog Strider. (pages 138–144)

SOCIAL SKILLS ALL DAY LONG:

Look for opportunities to teach social skills throughout the day (incidental teaching). Four ways to reinforce good social skills and an example of each follow:

Encouragement

Hey, great job staying on the topic while we were talking! It's fun to talk to someone who knows how to stay on topic! Pat yourself on the back!

Personal Example

I was just talking to the principal. Before I switched topics, I remembered to say, "I need to switch topics for a minute."

Prompting

It's time to go to lunch now. Remember, when you're talking with a friend, practice switching topics politely. Let me know how you did when you come back from lunch.

Corrective Feedback (must be positive, private, specific, and nonthreatening)

Lee, just now you switched topics without giving us any warning. You could have made a comment about the homework assignment we are talking about. When you get off the topic, the other students and I think you are not listening.

Lesson A

OBJECTIVES:

1. To state the meanings of *staying on topic* and *switching topics* and tell why they are important
2. To tell the self-talk associated with correct use of the skill
3. To sort comments and questions according to topic

MATERIALS:

1. *Staying on Topic/Switching Topics* (See page 311; one per student and one transparency.)
2. *Thought Bubble* (See *Appendix O*; one for educator use.)
3. *Picture Puzzles* (See *Appendix P*; one per pair of students.)
4. *Topic Cards* (See pages 312–314; cut apart one set of 16 small and 4 large cards for each pair of students.)

PREPARATORY SET:

Ask students to think about and then name things they like to talk about. List their ideas and explain that each one could be a topic for a conversation. Quickly choose one of the topics. Ask students to think of a few statements they could make and questions they could ask which would relate to that topic. For example, if the topic chosen is a circus, a statement about the topic could be, "Clowns juggle at the circus." A question about the topic could be, "Have you ever been on an elephant ride at a circus?"

PLAN:

1. Distribute and display *Staying on Topic/Switching Topics*. Discuss the definitions. Explain the skill steps and the symbols next to them. Remind students that the symbols are there to help them visualize and remember the skill steps. Discuss the reasons for staying on topic and switching topics appropriately. Refer to the body-talk symbol in the left-hand margin. Remind students that appropriate body talk is important when staying on topic and switching topics.
2. Model use of the first two skill steps for staying on topic/switching topics while thinking aloud. A scripted example follows:

Introduction

I am going to pretend to be having a conversation with a friend. I will show you how I stay on topic and tell you the thoughts that I'm having. When I hold up this Thought Bubble, *you'll know the words that I'm saying are actually what I'm thinking.*

Actual Model

While holding up the *Thought Bubble* say, *Steve is talking about his rock collection. I need to make a comment or ask a question about his rock collection so he knows I'm interested.* Put the *Thought Bubble* down and say, *I'd like to see your collection sometime.*

3. Complete the bottom half of *Staying on Topic/Switching Topics* as directed.
4. Pair students using the *Picture Puzzles* activity.
5. Distribute one set of large *Topic Cards* (trip to the zoo, computer games, carnival or amusement park rides, sports) to each pair of students. (If you are working with younger or academically lower students, modify by choosing only two of the large *Topic Cards* to distribute.) Ask each pair to lay the cards face up in a line in front of them. Read aloud the name of the topic printed on each large card. Distribute one set of small *Topic Cards* to each pair of students. Tell students that each of the small cards has a comment or question written on it about one of the topics. Instruct students to sort their small cards by laying them next to the large topic cards they relate to. (For older or more capable students, you may ask them to sort their cards without providing the large cards.)
6. If time allows, ask students to share other comments and questions which would relate to the topics on their large cards.
7. Ask student pairs to take turns telling each other the meaning of *staying on topic/switching topics* and why it is important to use the skill. Students could be reminded that the information they are to say is printed on *Staying on Topic/Switching Topics.*

   As an option to add structure to this activity (see *Appendix Q*), ask partners to come to an agreement about which person will be called "Anne Sullivan" and which person will be called "Helen Keller." After students have made their decisions, ask "Anne" to tell "Helen" the definition of *staying on topic/switching topics*. Next, ask "Helen" to tell "Anne" the definition. Ask the students to use the same procedure to tell each other the reasons for staying on topic or switching topics politely.
8. Say with pride to the class: *I feel honored to have the opportunity to teach such talented students. You worked very hard today!*

Name ____________________

Staying on Topic/Switching Topics

MEANING OF STAYING ON TOPIC: Talking about the same idea

MEANING OF SWITCHING TOPICS: Talking about a new idea

SKILL STEPS:

1. Ask myself: What is the topic?

2. Make a comment or ask a question about the topic

● or ?

OR

3. Change the topic appropriately

REASONS FOR USING THIS SKILL:

If you stay on topic or switch topics politely, people will like having conversations with you. You'll feel confident talking to others.

DIRECTIONS: Read the cartoon below. It shows Jolisa and her mother having a conversation. Decide what the topic of their conversation is.

Topic Cards

I went on the Loop-the-Loop roller coaster.	Did you feel dizzy after you got off?
I thought the rides were expensive.	Were you afraid on any of the rides?
I love to play hockey!	What is your favorite sport to play?
I felt great when I blocked the ball!	Does your team wear uniforms?

Topic Cards

I really like my new joystick!	How did your joystick get broken?
I hope I get Space Raiders for my birthday.	Have you ever seen my brother play Space Raiders?
The bear climbed to the top of the tree!	Did you see the polar bears go in the water?
The peacock didn't open its feathers.	Did you hear the parrots talk?

Topic Cards

CARNIVAL OR AMUSEMENT PARK RIDES

TRIP TO THE ZOO

SPORTS

COMPUTER GAMES

Lesson B

OBJECTIVE:

To differentiate between comments and questions which are on and off topic

MATERIALS:

1. *Staying on Topic / Switching Topics* classroom poster (See page 13.)
2. Figures of Jolisa Walker and Maria Parra (See *Appendix F*.)
3. *Checking Myself* (See *Appendix I*; one per student and one transparency.)
4. *Thought Bubble* (See *Appendix O*; one for educator use.)
5. *On or Off?* (See page 318; one transparency.)
6. Index cards (Two per student: one with ON written on it and one with OFF written on it.)

PREPARATORY SET:

Review the definition and skill steps for *staying on topic / switching topics* by referring the class to the classroom poster. Ask for volunteers to draw the skill step symbols where everyone can see them.

PLAN:

1. Pair students (see *Appendix P*). Ask student pairs to take turns telling each other the skill steps for staying on topic/switching topics. Follow the procedure described in step 7 of Lesson A. (As an option, ask students to decide who will be "Neil Armstrong" and who will be "John Glenn.") Next, ask students to work with their partners to think of a situation when the use of staying on topic/switching topics is important. Tell students that one or more pairs will be asked to share their situation. Have one or more pairs share their situation.
2. Tell students today's lesson will focus on skill step #2. Model self-talk for that step by thinking aloud. A scripted example follows:

   Introduction

   I am going to pretend to be having a conversation with my uncle. I will stay on topic and tell you the thoughts I'm having. When I hold up this Thought Bubble, *you'll know the words I'm saying are actually what I'm thinking.*

Actual Model

While holding up the *Thought Bubble* say, *He's talking about his broken leg. To stay on topic, I need to ask a question or make a comment about his leg.* Put the *Thought Bubble* down and ask, *How do you take a shower with that cast on?*

3. Tell students that you will be reading a script to them. Explain that Jolisa is excited about her birthday. She is talking to Maria about her party. Using the figures of Jolisa and Maria, read the script below. Sound angry while reading Jolisa's words, "Maria, you're not listening to me!"

   Jolisa: My birthday party is in three days. I can't wait!

   Maria: I can't wait for summer vacation!

   Jolisa: You're coming to the party, right?

   Maria: Yeah. Oh! I think Mom is taking me to see that new movie tonight.

   Jolisa: I hope everyone will have fun at the party. We've got some new games planned!

   Maria: Fun? Do you remember how fun the popcorn party at school was?

   Jolisa: *(sounding angry)* Maria, you're not listening to me!

4. Distribute and display the discussion guideline sheet called *Checking Myself.* Ask students to complete the goal statement with the words "think about an answer to each question asked," or use another classroom discussion goal more appropriate for your group (see page 26). Tell students that you will be asking questions about the script they just heard. Explain that after you ask each question, it's important for them to be thinking about an answer, even if they are not called on. Instruct them to put an "X" on their sheets each time they think about an answer to a question. It's important that the educator remember to provide enough "wait time" before calling on a student to orally answer each question.

5. Model use of the *Checking Myself* sheet while thinking aloud. A scripted example follows:

   Introduction

   I am going to pretend to be one of you completing this sheet during the discussion we will be having. I will tell you the thoughts I'm having while I'm completing the sheet. When I hold up this Thought Bubble, *you'll know the words I'm saying are actually what I'm thinking.*

Actual Model

While holding up the *Thought Bubble* say, *OK, the teacher just asked if Maria stayed on topic. Let me think. No, she didn't. I'm going to raise my hand to answer the question.* Put the *Thought Bubble* down, raise your hand, and mark an "X" on the transparency.

6. Proceed with the actual discussion by asking the questions that follow. (The script may need to be reread first.) During the discussion, periodically remind students to participate by thinking about answers and to mark their discussion guideline sheets.

   - What topic was Jolisa talking about?
   - Did Maria stay on topic?
   - How do you know?
   - What thoughts do you think Jolisa was having about Maria?
   - What could Maria have said or asked to stay on topic?

   After the discussion, have students complete the bottom of *Checking Myself.*

7. Process the use of the sheet by asking the following questions or others more appropriate for your group:

   - Why do you think it's important to think about answers to participate in a discussion?
   - How many of you thought about an answer, then raised your hand more often than you usually do? How did it feel?

8. Display *On or Off.* Distribute a set of ON and OFF index cards to each student. Complete the activity page together by having students hold up their ON cards if they think a sentence is on topic and their OFF cards if they think a sentence is off topic. Have someone write ON or OFF on the overhead next to the sentences that are on the topic or off the topic. If there is not a group consensus, ask students who answered correctly to explain their answers.

9. Write the following where everyone can see it: USING GOOD SOCIAL SKILLS HELPS ME GET ALONG BETTER WITH OTHERS! Have the students say it aloud, in unison, with conviction.

ON OR OFF?

DIRECTIONS: Read each situation below and the four sentences that follow. When the sentence stays on the topic, write **ON**. When the sentence is off the topic, write **OFF**.

1. Your friend says to you, "Last night I had a funny dream."

   ________ 1. My dreams are really funny, too.

   ________ 2. I wish it wasn't raining today.

   ________ 3. What was your dream about?

   ________ 4. Where are you going this weekend?

2. Your mother says at dinner, "It should be a good football game on TV tonight!"

   ________ 1. What's for dessert?

   ________ 2. I hope I get my homework done so I can watch part of the game!

   ________ 3. I hope my blue shirt is clean so I can wear it.

   ________ 4. Who's playing?

3. Your teacher says, "The field trip to the space lab is on Thursday."

   ________ 1. My mom went on a business trip last week.

   ________ 2. Next time can we go to the petting zoo?

   ________ 3. What time are we leaving?

   ________ 4. We went to the space lab last summer.
   It has a neat computer section!

Lesson C

OBJECTIVE:

To practice asking questions that stay on topic

MATERIALS:

1. Figures of Victor Parra, Grandma Mika Vue, Mr. Marcus Aaron, and Ms. Paula Hess (See *Appendix F.*)
2. *Who? What? When? Where? Why? How?* cards (See page 321; cut apart one set of cards for each student.)

PREPARATORY SET:

Show the figure of Victor. Tell students that Victor is a writer for his school's newspaper. Discuss what some of his duties probably are.

PLAN:

1. Write the following words where all students can see them: Who? What? When? Where? Why? and How? Explain that as a newspaper writer, Victor must be thorough and stay on the topic when he writes an article. If an article does not stay on topic, it will not be interesting to read. One way he can be thorough and stay on topic is to answer who, what, when, where, why, and how questions about his topic. (Refer students to the words written where all can see them.)
2. Tell students that Victor can write an article about one of the following topics (show each character):
   - Mika Vue is honored as school cook of the year.
   - Mr. Aaron takes his students on a field trip to the local toy factory.
   - Ms. Hess has her students build a model spaceship.
3. Ask students to vote on one topic they think Victor should write about. Ask them to develop as a group some who, what, when, where, why, and how questions that Victor could answer in his article. Write their questions where all students can see them.
4. Tell students it's not always easy to think of questions to ask someone during a conversation. Explain that they will be working in groups to play a card game that will give them practice asking questions that relate to a topic.

5. Distribute *Who? What? When? Where? Why? How?* cards to each student and then put students into groups of three (see *Appendix P*).

6. Ask each group to come to an agreement about what topic they would be interested in discussing. If students are having difficulty thinking of a topic, the educator may provide suggestions (e.g., fast food restaurants, video games, the local zoo, robots). When the group has agreed upon a topic, group members begin taking turns thinking of who, what, when, where, why, or how questions they could ask during a conversation about their chosen topic. If the first group member thinks of a "what" question to ask (e.g., "What is your favorite kind of burger?"), that member's "what" card is laid down and then it's the next group member's turn to think of a question to ask. The game continues until no group member has cards left. Questions cannot be duplicated.

7. Say enthusiastically to the class: *You are a great class! I can see you using social skills and cooperating with one another more each day!* Give a recent example of cooperation.

WHO? WHAT? WHEN? WHERE? WHY? HOW?

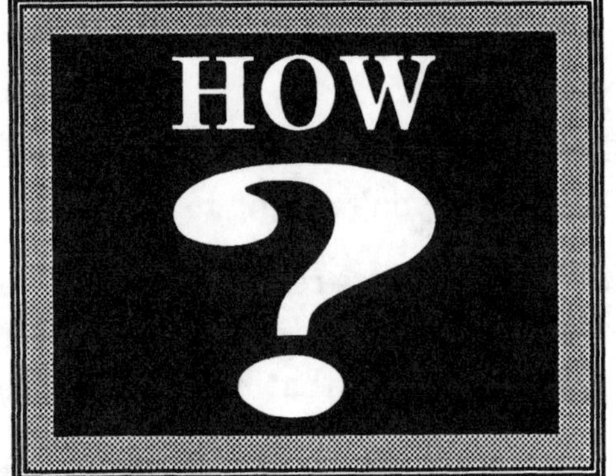

Lesson D

OBJECTIVE:

To practice making transition statements before switching topics

MATERIALS:

1. *Time for a Change* (See page 324; one per student and one transparency.)
2. *Topic Change Tents* (See pages 325–326; cut apart one set per pair of students.)

PREPARATORY SET:

Tell students to pretend that a spell has been cast upon the classroom. The only topic the students can talk about is "green beans." Allow students a few minutes to get up and talk with each other, but remind them that they may only discuss green beans. Afterwards, discuss what it was like to be able to discuss only one subject. Tell the students that it is OK to change topics if it is done politely.

PLAN:

1. Say to the students, "If a friend is talking to you about a new toy, you might be rude if you all of a sudden say, 'We're going on a trip this weekend.' It would probably be better to say something about your friend's toy first and then start talking about your trip. Let's take a look at how some of the people from Socialville switch topics politely."
2. Distribute and display *Time for a Change*. Have students read the cartoon about Lee and Mike. Discuss how Lee changed the subject. He made a comment about the topic (i.e., the new basketball) before switching to another. Further discuss how Mike probably didn't mind that Lee switched topics. Mike could tell that Lee was listening to him by the comment he made about the basketball.
3. Share with students that an even better way to switch topics is to warn someone that you're going to do it.
4. Have students read the cartoon about Mr. Ho Vue and Grandma Mika Vue. Ask students to identify the words Mr. Vue used (i.e., "That reminds me") to warn Grandma Vue that he was going to switch topics.
5. Ask students to read the phrases that can be used to warn someone that a topic change is going to happen. The phrases are printed at the bottom of *Time for a*

Change. Model saying each one and provide the students time to practice saying the words for each aloud.

6. Pair students (see *Appendix P*) and ask partners to position themselves across from each other at a table or on opposite sides of a desk top.
7. Distribute *Topic Change Tents*. Ask students to fold each of the four cards on the dotted lines to form tents, with the writing on the outside.
8. Tell students to determine which partner will be Person 1 and which partner will be Person 2. Situate each tent so "side 1" faces Person 1 and "side 2" faces Person 2.
9. Tell students that they will be practicing saying things to warn their partners that they will be switching topics during a conversation.
10. Tell students that for each of the four tents, Person 1 begins by reading aloud the statement or question on "side 1" of the tent. Person 2 responds by reading aloud the statement or question on "side 2" of the tent (this will contain a statement warning Person 1 that Person 2 wants to change the topic). Demonstrate this with another student, using one of the situation tents.
11. After students have read through each situation one time, the partners switch roles, with Person 1 becoming Person 2 and Person 2 becoming Person 1. The partners read through each situation again. (This will provide each partner the opportunity to practice saying statements considered acceptable for switching topics.)
12. Write the following where everyone can see it: I'M A SOCIAL SUPER STAR! Have the students say this aloud, in unison, with excitement.

Name ____________________

Time for a Change

Here are some other things you can say to warn someone that you're going to change the topic:

1. "This is changing the topic, but..."
2. "Oh, that reminds me..."
3. "This is off the topic, but..."
4. "Would it be OK if I talked to you about..?"

TOPIC CHANGE TENTS

1 We went camping a lot last summer.

2 I'll bet that was fun! This is about something different, but can I get a ride home with you after practice?

1 How did you like the movie we saw in class today?

2 It was pretty good. Oh, by the way, there's a great movie on TV tonight!

Topic Change Tents

1 Why weren't you in school yesterday afternoon?

2 I was at the dentist. Oh, that reminds me, are we still having a substitute teacher next week?

1 So, did you get your new dog?

2 No, not yet. This is switching topics, but what's for hot lunch today?

Lessons X, Y, and Z

Due to similarities in format, the final three lesson plans for each unit in *Social Star* are provided in *Appendix* A. Substitute the phrase "staying on topic/switching topics" whenever a "_____" appears in the lesson plans. Information specific to this unit follows.

LESSON X PREPARATORY SET:

Tell students that Lee just did a great job staying on topic during a conversation with Mr. Aaron. Ask for volunteers to stand with a *Thought Bubble*, pretend to be Lee, and say some self-talk Lee could use to reward himself.

LESSON Y PREPARATORY SET:

Darken the room, if you prefer, and ask students to visualize themselves correctly using this social skill by reading the following script:

> *Let's take a few moments to relax.... Make sure you are in a comfortable position.... Close your eyes if you feel like it.... On the count of three, take a very slow, deep breath. One . . . two . . . three.... Breath in deeply.... Now breath out slowly.... Let your entire body relax.... Now imagine your friend is talking to you about a fishing derby that will be held soon. You ask questions about the derby to let your friend know you are interested. Now you would like to tell your friend a funny joke. You tell yourself, "I know I can change the topic politely." You decide to say, "This is changing the topic, but I have a great joke to tell you." Think about how good you feel because you remembered the skill of* staying on topic/switching topics. *Imagine how good your friend feels because you showed an interest in the fishing derby by asking questions.... Give yourself a pat on the back for the nice job that you did!*

LESSON Z PLOT SITUATION:

Your friend asks if you would like to sleep over this weekend. You don't want to stay overnight.

LESSON Z ROADBLOCK EXAMPLES:

- Staying on topic when you are not interested or can't think of anything to say or ask about the topic
- Remembering to switch topics politely when you have something really exciting that you want to say about another topic

Name ____________________

Staying on Topic/Switching Topics T-Chart

LOOKS LIKE...	SOUNDS LIKE...
using appropriate body talk	staying on topic could be if a friend is talking about a magician she saw, then...

- saying
  "I'd love to see a magician someday."
- asking
  "Which trick did you like best?"

switching topics could be

- saying
  "This is changing the topic, but..."

  "Oh, that reminds me..."

  "This is about something different, but..."
- asking
  "Can I talk to you about something else?"

HOME

Pretend your brother says, "We are having a computer programmer visit our class today." Show how you can stay on topic by asking a question or making a comment.

SCHOOL

Pretend your teacher is talking about dinosaurs during science. Show how you can stay on topic by asking a question or making a comment.

COMMUNITY

Pretend your neighbor is talking to you about his dog. You want to tell him that you placed second in a school race. Show how you can change the topic politely.

STAY ON
TOPIC

or

CHANGE IT
POLITELY

HOME-A-GRAM

Dear Family,

At school, we have been talking about the social skills called

STAYING ON TOPIC AND SWITCHING TOPICS

I learned that *staying on topic* means talking about the same idea. I also learned that *switching topics* means talking about a new idea.

I learned that whenever I talk with another person, I should ask myself, "What is the topic?" Then I should make a comment or ask a question about the topic or change the topic appropriately.

I know that if I stay on topic or switch topics politely, people might like having conversations with me.

Below is a comment I could make and a question I could ask if you said to me, "We have lots to do before our summer vacation!"

COMMENT: ______________________________

____

QUESTION: ______________________________

____

I learned that there is a polite way to change topics. There are things I can say to warn someone that I'm going to switch topics. One thing I can say is:

____

Start a conversation with me and I'll show you I can stay on topic by asking a question or making a comment. After I do, please sign my "Staying On Topic/Switching Topics" badge so I can return it to school and become a SOCIAL SUPER STAR this week.

From: ______________________________

Conversations

UNIT GOAL:

To demonstrate comprehension and use of appropriate conversational skills

EDUCATOR INFORMATION:

1. This unit discusses how to participate appropriately in a conversation. The emphasis is on politely beginning, maintaining, and ending conversations.
2. Units in *Social Star* closely related to *Conversations* include *Staying On Topic/Switching Topics* and *Being Formal or Casual*. The *Staying On Topic/Switching Topics* unit helps students make relevant comments and ask relevant questions. It also teaches ways to change the topic of a conversation politely. The *Being Formal or Casual* unit helps students understand how and when to speak and act formally and casually.
3. Taylor (1993) compares conversational tendencies between Black English, Hispanic English, and Standard American English as follows:
   - In Black English, indirect eye contact while listening and direct eye contact while speaking shows attention and respect. In Standard American English, the reverse is generally true.
   - In Black English, asking questions about jobs, family, etc., to a person being met for the first time is not proper. In Standard American English, the reverse is generally true.
   - In Black English, interruptions during a conversation occur, and the most assertive person generally gains "access to the floor." In Standard American English, one person generally has the floor until all points are made.
   - In Black English, it is generally inappropriate for a third person to add comments to a conversation that is already taking place between two people. In Standard American English, these added comments are generally viewed as helpful.
   - In Hispanic English, it is generally acceptable to gain attention during a conversation by hissing. In Standard American English, hissing is generally viewed as being impolite and contemptuous.
   - In Hispanic English, business conversations are preceded by a great deal of small talk. In Standard American English, people generally get to the point in business conversations.

The educator should exert sensitivity and care in generalizing rules about conversations into the children's home cultures.

RELATED ACTIVITIES:

1. Connect computers or create an E-Mail system so that students can have "computer conversations" with one another by typing and reading their greetings, comments, questions, and farewells.
2. Investigate sign language by introducing students to signs used for greetings, farewells, and various actions and objects. Ask students to attempt to have conversations with each other using only sign language.
3. Ask students to have conversations with each other while pretending to be famous historical people familiar to the students.
4. Ask students to investigate how various animals communicate with each other (e.g., fireflies communicate through the duration of their lights). The way that bees communicate is discussed in Lesson A of this unit.
5. Have students visit another class (at their school or a different school). Ask each student to have a conversation with someone from the other class to find out about hobbies, families, favorite foods, etc.
6. Invite adults from different cultures to talk to the students about how their cultures' conventions for conversations compare with American common culture norms.

It is important for educators to provide opportunities for students to work in groups so they can experience social skills in contexts where social communication is needed. Therefore, educators are encouraged to have students complete the Related Activities in small groups whenever possible. Educators trained in cooperative learning could incorporate the five components (see page 34) into the group activity.

RELATED LITERATURE:

Eddie's Menagerie (1978) by Carolyn Haywood, Morrow. (Text)
(pages 46–50)

Tuck Everlasting (1975) by Natalie Babbitt, Farrar Straus Giroux. (Text)
(pages 37–41, 111–115)

SOCIAL SKILLS ALL DAY LONG:

Look for opportunities to teach social skills throughout the day (incidental teaching). Four ways to reinforce good social skills and an example of each follow:

Encouragement

I heard you end your conversation with Mr. Aaron by saying, "Good-bye, I'll see you tomorrow." You did an excellent job ending your conversation politely!

Personal Example

When I telephoned my friend, her sister answered the phone. I don't know her sister very well, so I began the conversation by telling her my name. Since she doesn't know me, she would not have recognized my voice.

Prompting

Tonight when you have a conversation with one of your parents, be sure to take turns talking and listening. Your parents will be impressed!

Corrective Feedback (must be positive, private, specific, and nonthreatening)

Victor, just now when I was talking with you, you started talking before I finished. You could have listened until I was done, and then taken your turn to talk. If you remember to take turns talking and listening, more people may enjoy having conversations with you.

Lesson A

OBJECTIVES:

1. To state the meaning of *having a conversation* and tell why it's important
2. To tell the self-talk associated with correct use of the skill

MATERIALS:

1. *Conversations* (See page 337; one per student and one transparency.)
2. *Thought Bubble* (See *Appendix O*; one for educator use.)

PREPARATORY SET:

Ask students to play "Hangman" by guessing the word "conversations." Give them the clue that the word they are guessing is the social skill they will be learning about in this unit.

PLAN:

1. Distribute and display *Conversations.* Discuss the definition. Explain the skill steps and the symbols next to them. Remind students that the symbols are there to help them visualize and remember the skill steps. Refer to the body-talk symbol in the left-hand margin. Remind students that appropriate body talk is important when having a conversation. Read and explain the reasons provided for having good conversations.
2. Model use of appropriate body talk during a conversation while thinking aloud. A scripted example follows:

   Introduction

   I am going to pretend to be having a conversation with someone I'm meeting for the first time. I will show you appropriate body talk and tell you the thoughts I am having. When I hold up this Thought Bubble, *you'll know the words I'm saying are actually what I'm thinking.*

   Actual Model

   While holding up the *Thought Bubble* say, *I want to use appropriate body talk during this conversation. I need to use a pleasant tone of voice, the right volume, and eye contact.* Put the *Thought Bubble* down and demonstrate these three components of body talk while saying, *It's nice to meet you.*

3. Pair students (see *Appendix P*). Read the cartoon at the bottom of *Conversations.* Ask students to work with their partners to write the number of the skill step being used below each frame in the cartoon.

4. Explain how bees have conversations (a picture of a bee appears on several pages within this unit) by paraphrasing the following example:

   When a worker bee called a "scout" finds nectar (which is needed to make honey), she goes back to her hive and tells the other bees the exact location of the nectar by dancing a figure-8 pattern on the honeycomb. The more quickly the bee dances, the closer the nectar is located. The imaginary line between the loops of the figure-8 indicates the position of the nectar in relation to the sun.

5. Ask student pairs to take turns telling each other the meaning of *conversations* and why it's important to use the skill. Students could be reminded that the information they are to say is printed on *Conversations.*

   As an option to add structure to this activity (see *Appendix Q*), ask partners to come to an agreement about which person will be called "Babe Ruth" and which person will be called "Jackie Robinson." After students have made their decisions, ask "Babe" to tell "Jackie" the definition of *conversations.* Next, ask "Jackie" to tell "Babe" the definition. Ask students to tell each other the reasons for using this social skill.

6. Write the following where everyone can see it: IT'S FUN LEARNING ABOUT SOCIAL SKILLS! IT'S TOTALLY DYNAMITE! Have the students say this aloud, in unison, enthusiastically.

Name ___________________________

Conversations

MEANING OF CONVERSATIONS: Talking with others

SKILL STEPS:

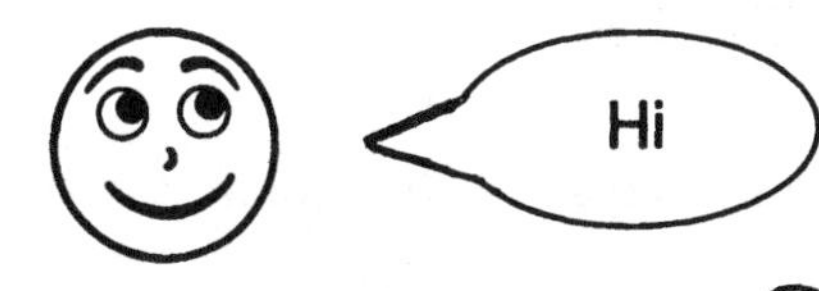

1. Start with a greeting
2. Take turns talking and listening
3. End with a farewell

REASONS FOR USING THIS SKILL:

If you have good conversations, more people will enjoy talking with you and you can feel proud.

DIRECTIONS: Look at the cartoon below. Listen to the conversation between Lee and Victor. Write the number of the skill step being used inside each frame.

Lesson B

OBJECTIVE:

To practice starting a conversation by using a greeting and the person's name

MATERIALS:

1. *Conversations* classroom poster (See page 13.)
2. *Thought Bubble* (See *Appendix O*; one for educator use.)
3. *Skill Step #1* (See page 340; one per student and one transparency.)
4. Figures of Jolisa Walker, Mrs. Cora Marrero, Mike Olson, Grandma Mika Vue, and Mr. Marcus Aaron (See *Appendix F.)*
5. Masking tape

PREPARATORY SET:

Greet several students using greetings from various languages (e.g., French—"Bon jour," German—"Guten tag," English—"Hello," Italian—"Buon giorno," Spanish—"Buenos dias"). Tell students you have just shown how to begin a conversation in several different languages.

PLAN:

1. Review the definition and skill steps for *having a conversation* by referring students to the *Conversations* classroom poster. Tell students that the focus of today's lesson is on the first skill step.
2. Model the first skill step while thinking aloud. A scripted example follows:

   Introduction

   I am going to pretend to be someone your age. I am just getting home from school and want to have a conversation with my dad. I will start the conversation correctly and tell you the thoughts I'm having. When I hold up this Thought Bubble, *you'll know the words I'm saying are actually what I'm thinking.*

   Actual Model

   While holding up the *Thought Bubble* say, *There's Dad. I want to talk to him. I'll remember to start with a greeting.* Put the *Thought Bubble* down and say, *Hi, Dad! How's it going?*

3. Pair students using *Shoe Match* (see *Appendix P*).
4. Distribute and display *Skill Step #1* and read the skill step at the top of the page.
5. After reading the greeting examples and the first cartoon, discuss the idea that some greetings depend on the time of day and the formality or casualness of the situation. Ask students to work with their partners to brainstorm other greetings that might be used to start a conversation. Call on students to share their ideas and write them on the transparency.
6. After reading the title examples and the second cartoon, discuss the idea that when talking with peers, usually just first names are used, but that when talking with adults, titles are frequently used. Ask students to work with their partners to brainstorm other titles that could be added to the list on *Skill Step #1.* Call on students to share their ideas and write them on the transparency.
7. Tape the five figures to a chalkboard in a line approximately two feet apart from each other. For the first figure, call on a student to supply a greeting and the title and/or name that could be used when beginning a conversation with that Socialville character. Write the greeting above the figure. Follow the same procedure for the remaining figures.
8. Have students line up at one end of the chalkboard. Tell students that as they pass each figure, they should say the greeting written above it, as if they were going to start a conversation with the Socialville character. (The purpose of this activity is to provide drill and practice for beginning conversations.)
9. Ask student pairs to take turns telling each other the skill steps for conversations. Follow the procedure described in step 5 of Lesson A. (As an option, ask students to decide who will be "Rembrandt" and who will be "Pablo Picasso.") Next, ask students to work with their partners to think of a situation when it's necessary to have a conversation. Tell students that one or more pairs will be asked to share their situation. Have one or more pairs share their situation.
10. Write the following where everyone can see it: I FEEL JAZZED AND TOTALLY MARVELOUS WHEN I USE MY SOCIAL SKILLS. Have the students say this aloud, in unison, with energy.

Name ____________

SKILL STEP #1

"Bee" sure to
START WITH A GREETING

There are many greetings you can use in the English language. Here are some examples:

Hi Hello Good morning Good afternoon

The cartoon below shows Mike beginning a conversation with his sister Ann.

If you are beginning a conversation with an adult, and you want to use the adult's name, it is polite to use a title. Here are some examples:

Mr. Mrs. Dr. Uncle Grandma

The cartoon below shows Jolisa beginning a conversation with Dr. Parra.

Lesson C

OBJECTIVE:

To take turns talking and listening during a conversation

MATERIALS:

1. Bouncing balls (One per pair of students)
2. *Skill Step #2* (See page 344; one per student and one transparency.)
3. *Thought Bubble* (See *Appendix O*; one for educator use.)
4. *Checking Myself* (See *Appendix I*; one per student and one transparency.)
5. *Asking a Question* (See page 345; one transparency.)

PREPARATORY SET:

Ask for two student volunteers to come to the front of the room and bounce a ball back and forth to each other a few times. After the volunteers have returned to their seats, tell the students that having a conversation is like bouncing a ball back and forth and that by the end of the lesson they will understand how they are similar. Tell students that the focus of today's lesson is on skill step #2.

PLAN:

1. Distribute and display *Skill Step #2.* Read the skill step at the top of the page.
2. Model skill step #2 while thinking aloud. A scripted example follows:

   Introduction

   I am going to pretend to be having a conversation with my good friend. I will show you how I take turns listening and talking, and tell you the thoughts I'm having. When I hold up this Thought Bubble, *you'll know the words I'm saying are actually what I'm thinking.*

   Actual Model

   Hold up the *Thought Bubble* and say, *Julia is talking now, so I need to listen. When she is done talking about her new computer, I want to tell her about what happened to my computer.* Put down the *Thought Bubble,* nod your head as if listening to Julia and then say, *Your new computer sounds great! Did you know my computer got struck by lightning?*

3. Read the first cartoon conversation between Mike and Lee.
4. Display and distribute the discussion guideline sheet called *Checking Myself.* Tell students that you will be having a discussion about the first cartoon on *Skill Step #2.* Encourage students to use appropriate body talk during the discussion. Ask students to name ways that they could use appropriate body talk during the discussion. Choose one of the responses and have students complete the goal statement words appropriate for the body talk chosen (e.g., if the body talk chosen for this discussion was "use appropriate body posture," those words should be written on the sheets), or use another classroom discussion goal more appropriate for your group (see page 26).

   During the discussion, periodically remind students to mark their discussion guideline sheets whenever they find themselves using the chosen body-talk goal.
5. Reread the cartoon and ask students the following questions:
   - Did the boys take turns talking and listening in this conversation?
   - What thoughts do you think Lee had when Mike did not give him a chance to talk?
   - How do you feel when someone talks to you but doesn't listen?
6. Read the second cartoon conversation between Maria and Victor. Continue your class discussion and use of the *Checking Myself* sheet by asking the following questions:
   - Did Victor talk very much during his conversation with Maria?
   - What thoughts do you think Maria had when Victor did not say very much to her?
   - How do you feel when you try having a conversation with someone and the person doesn't say very much?

   After the discussion, ask students to complete the bottom of *Checking Myself.*
7. Process use of the sheet by asking the following question or another one more appropriate for your group:
   - Why do you think it is important to use appropriate body talk during a discussion?
8. Display and discuss *Asking a Question.* Ask students how they feel when they talk to people who are only interested in talking about themselves.
9. Pair students (see *Appendix P*) and distribute one ball to each partnership. Remind students that taking turns talking and listening during a conversation

is like bouncing a ball back and forth with another person. Ask students to have a conversation with their partners about favorite foods. The first person to speak during the conversation should be the person holding the ball. When that person finishes, the ball is bounced to the partner who then takes a turn talking while continuing the conversation about favorite foods. Ask students to continue their conversations in this manner until their ball has been bounced back and forth at least five times. Model this procedure with another student first.

10. Say sincerely to the class: *You are each unique individuals. I hope you enjoy using what you've learned in class today!*

Name ____________________

SKILL STEP #2

It is no fun having a conversation with someone who doesn't listen and doesn't let you talk! In the conversation below, Mike does not follow skill step #2 when he talks to Lee.

It is also no fun having a conversation with someone who does not say much. In the conversation below, Victor does not follow skill step #2 when Maria talks to him.

Asking a Question
Asking a
question is a good
way to keep a
conversation going. When
you ask a
question,
the other
person
feels that you
are interested
in what is
being said.

Lesson D

OBJECTIVES:

1. To practice ending a conversation smoothly by making a farewell statement
2. To illustrate the skill steps for having a conversation

MATERIALS:

1. *Skill Step #3* (See page 348; one per student and one transparency.)
2. *Thought Bubble* (See *Appendix O*; one for educator use.)
3. *Mixed-Up Conversation* (See page 349; one per pair of students.)
4. Scissors (One per pair of students)
5. Figures of Grandma Mika Vue, Lee Vue, Jolisa Walker, and Maria Parra (See *Appendix F.*)
6. *Cartoon Strip* (See page 350; one per pair of students.)

PREPARATORY SET:

Say farewells to several students using words from various languages (e.g., French—"Au revoir," German—"Auf Wiedersehen," English—"See you later," Italian—"Arrivederci," Spanish—"Adios"). Tell students that you have just shown how to end a conversation in several different languages. Tell students that the focus of today's lesson is on skill step #3.

PLAN:

1. Distribute and display *Skill Step #3*. Read the skill step at the top of the page.
2. Model skill step #3 while thinking aloud. A scripted example follows:

   Introduction

   I am going to pretend to be a student your age. I need to end a conversation with my aunt so I can meet my friends on time. I will show you how I end the conversation politely and tell you the thoughts I'm having. When I hold up this Thought Bubble, *you'll know the words I'm saying are actually what I'm thinking.*

Actual Model

Hold up the *Thought Bubble* and say, *If I don't leave soon, I'll be late; I need to end this conversation.* Put the *Thought Bubble* down and say (using a polite tone of voice), *Aunt Marcie, I'd better get going. I told my friends I'd meet them soon. See you later!*

3. Pair students (see *Appendix P*). After reading the farewell examples and the cartoon on *Skill Step #3*, discuss the idea that some farewells depend on the time of day and the formality or casualness of the situation. Ask students to work with their partners to brainstorm other farewells that might be used to end a conversation. Call on students to share their ideas and write them on the transparency.

4. Read the middle paragraph and the script at the bottom of *Skill Step #3* using the characters. Ask students to discuss with their partners the answers to the following questions:

   - Did Maria end her conversation with Jolisa politely?
   - What thoughts do you think Maria had when Jolisa ran off?
   - What could Jolisa have said to end the conversation politely?

5. Distribute *Mixed-Up Conversation* and a pair of scissors to each pair of students. Ask students to cut apart *Mixed-Up Conversation* and then work with their partners to put the conversation in order. Review the three conversation skill steps before they begin.

6. When the partners have the conversation in order, instruct them to take the parts of Grandma Vue and Lee and read the conversation aloud with their partners. (The figures of Grandma Mika Vue and Lee can be used.)

7. Distribute *Cartoon Strip* to each pair of students. Ask students to work with their partners to create a cartoon showing a good conversation between two people. Tell students that the characters in their cartoon strips must follow all three steps. If any student pairs need more than four frames for their conversation, supply an additional *Cartoon Strip* page for their continuation frames. (The focus of this activity is on the three conversation skill steps. Do not spend an inordinate amount of time having students draw their characters. If necessary, encourage students to draw stick figures.)

8. Write the following where everyone can see it: THIS CLASS IS EXTRAORDINARY. I LEARN A LOT EVERY DAY! Have the students say this aloud, in unison, vibrantly.

Name ____________________

SKILL STEP #3

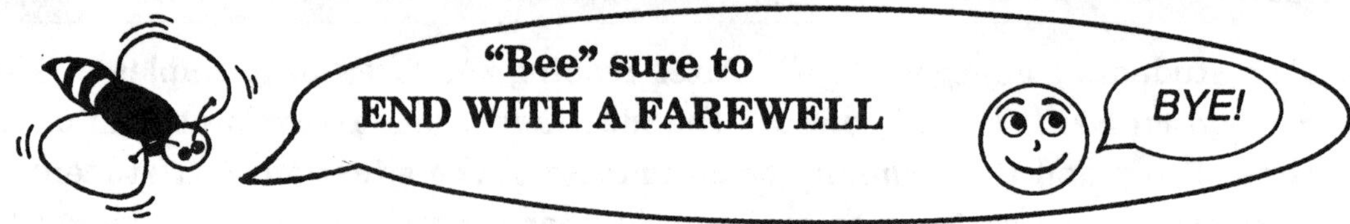

There are many farewells you can use in the English language. Here are some examples:

See you later   I'd better get going   So long   Bye

The cartoon below shows Victor ending a conversation with his mom.

Having a conversation with someone who does not end a conversation with a farewell can feel uncomfortable. In the script below, Maria and Jolisa are having a conversation about their school carnival. Maria does not follow skill step #3.

Jolisa: I hope they have the cakewalk again this year!

Maria: Oh yeah! That was fun! I hope they have the pie-throwing stand too! Last year I got Mr. Aaron right in the face.

Jolisa: Our class is in charge of tickets this year.

Maria: *(runs over to Victor when she sees him)* Hi, Victor!

Jolisa: *(feeling angry)* Maria!

Names ____________________

MixEd-Up CONVERSATION

DIRECTIONS: This conversation between Lee and his grandmother is all mixed up. Put the conversation in the correct order.

Mika: What did they talk to you about?

Mika: I don't know. How can you tell if the batteries are working?

Lee: Hi, Grandma! I'm home!

Mika: Hi, Lee! How was your day?

Lee: They talked about checking the batteries in our smoke detectors at home. Are our batteries working?

Mika: That sounds easy! I need to go next door now. Let's check our batteries when I get back.

Lee: To check the batteries, they said to push the button and see if the alarm buzzes.

Lee: My day was great! Some firefighters came to talk to our class.

Lee: OK. See you later, Grandma!

Mika: Good-bye, Lee.

Names ______________________________

CARTOON STRIP

DIRECTIONS: Make a cartoon showing a conversation between two people. Make sure they follow all three skill steps.

Lessons X, Y, and Z

Due to similarities in format, the final three lesson plans for each unit in *Social Star* are provided in *Appendix A*. Substitute the word "conversations" whenever a "______" appears in the lesson plans. Information specific to this unit follows.

LESSON X PREPARATORY SET:

Divide students into small groups. Provide each group with a ball of yarn. Tell students that each group will be given a few minutes to have a conversation. The person who starts the conversation permanently holds onto the end of the yarn and then passes the ball of yarn to another student. The second student wraps the yarn around a wrist, makes the next conversational comment, and then passes the ball of yarn to another student. The passing should not always be done to students who are side by side since conversational turns don't naturally occur that way. Rather, encourage students to pass the ball across the group too so the end result is an entanglement of yarn. The conversation continues until each group member has had an opportunity to talk more than once. (This activity is a fun way for students to be able to visualize the interaction of a conversation.)

LESSON Y PREPARATORY SET:

Darken the room, if you prefer, and ask students to visualize themselves correctly using this social skill by reading the following script:

> *Let's take a few moments to relax.... Make sure you are sitting in a comfortable position.... Close your eyes if you feel like it.... On the count of three, take a very slow, deep breath. One . . . two . . . three.... Breathe in deeply.... Now breathe out very slowly. Let your entire body relax.... Now imagine yourself having a conversation with a teacher after school.... Picture yourself beginning the conversation with a greeting.... Imagine the two of you taking turns talking and listening to each other.... You are both interested in what the other person is saying. Picture yourself ending your conversation with a farewell.... Think about the proud feeling you have inside because you had a good conversation.*

LESSON Z PLOT SITUATION:

Ask students to pretend they are having a hard time listening to a friend because they are upset about an argument they had with a parent.

LESSON Z ROADBLOCK EXAMPLES:

- Remembering all the steps to having a polite conversation when you are nervous, tired, angry, or in a hurry
- Having to have a conversation with someone who does all of the talking or with someone who does not say much

Name ___________________

Conversation T-Chart

LOOKS LIKE...	SOUNDS LIKE...
using appropriate body talk • eye contact • facial expression • posture • personal space • body movements	greeting someone • "Hi, Bill." • "Hello, Mrs. Joyce." taking turns talking and listening • "I went to a movie last night." • "Oh, really? Which one did you go to?" • "It was called ______." saying farewell to someone • "Ooh, there's my bus. I've gotta go. Bye." • "Good-bye, Mr. Davis."

HOME

Pretend that you just got home from school. Show how you could have a conversation with one of your parents about one of your teachers.

SCHOOL

Pretend you are having lunch at school. Show how you could have a conversation with one of your friends about a new girl at school.

COMMUNITY

Pretend you just got to soccer practice. Show how you could have a conversation with your coach about an upcoming game.

Enjoy a good conversation!

A GREETING

TALKING AND LISTENING

A FAREWELL

HOME-A-GRAM

Dear Family,

At school, we have been talking about the social skill called

CONVERSATIONS

I learned that *having a conversation* means talking with others.

I learned three steps to follow when I'm having a conversation:

1. Start with a greeting
2. Take turns talking and listening
3. End with a farewell

I learned that when I have good conversations, more people will enjoy talking with me and I can feel proud.

Below, I've drawn a picture of me having a conversation with someone. Can you guess who I'm having the conversation with?

I'm going to have a conversation with you and show that I can follow all three steps. After I do, please sign my "Conversations" badge so I can return it to school and become a SOCIAL SUPER STAR this week.

From: ______________________________

Interrupting

UNIT GOAL:

To demonstrate comprehension and use of interrupting appropriately

EDUCATOR INFORMATION:

1. This unit teaches students the importance of differentiating between when it is and is not necessary to interrupt. The unit also teaches students how to interrupt politely (when interrupting is necessary). Educators may choose to discuss perspective taking with students before embarking on this unit. Interrupting may be viewed differently depending on whose perspective is taken—the person doing the interrupting or the person being interrupted. In appropriate interruptions, both people view the message delivered as urgent or important. The educator should exert sensitivity and care in generalizing rules about interrupting into the children's home cultures.
2. This unit provides an acronym called GAG, which serves two purposes: (1) students think of a gag to help stop themselves from interrupting when it is not necessary; and (2) students use the letters G, A, and G to remember the three steps for interrupting appropriately (Get the person's attention, Apologize for interrupting, and Give the reason for interrupting).

RELATED ACTIVITIES:

1. Have students count the number of times the educator is interrupted. The interruptions may be staged within a short time or they may occur naturally over a longer period. As a math activity, have students chart or graph the results.
2. Brainstorm situations in which the principal of the school might be interrupted (e.g., an important phone call, an emergency in the building).
3. Have students write a letter to an imaginary friend who interrupts too often and impolitely. The letter could include tips about not interrupting and about interrupting politely.
4. Have students design a poster for the school office that is a reminder to interrupt the school secretary politely.
5. Visit an office. Speak to the staff about typical interruptions during the workday. Ask about the procedures that are followed when interruptions occur.
6. Invite adults from different cultures to talk to the students about how their cultures' conventions for interrupting compare with American common culture norms.

It is important for educators to provide opportunities for students to work in groups so they can experience social skills in contexts where social communication is needed. Therefore, educators are encouraged to have students complete the Related Activities in small groups whenever possible. Educators trained in cooperative learning could incorporate the five components (see page 34) into the group activity.

RELATED LITERATURE:

Willy Is My Brother ([1963] 1989) by Peggy Parish, Ill. by Jacqueline Rogers, Delacorte. (Picture book)

Winnie the Pooh ([1926] 1961) by A.A. Milne, Dutton. (Text)
Owl interrupts Pooh, who is on his way to give Eeyore a birthday present. (pages 81, 153, and 156)

SOCIAL SKILLS ALL DAY LONG:

Look for opportunities to teach social skills throughout the day (incidental teaching). Four ways to reinforce good social skills and an example of each follow:

Encouragement

Victor, I noticed that you decided not to interrupt when you saw me talking with Maria. Instead, you waited until we were finished talking. Fantastic!

Personal Example

Last night, I wanted to ask my spouse a question. My spouse was busy talking on the phone. I didn't interrupt. I waited until the phone conversation ended before I asked my question.

Prompting

While I'm teaching this group of students, I prefer that I not have any interruptions. If you absolutely need to interrupt me, stand near me until I see you and then say, "Excuse me for interrupting."

Corrective Feedback (must be positive, private, specific, and nonthreatening)

Ann, when the principal asked to speak to me in the hallway for a few minutes, you interrupted to ask what was for lunch. It seems that question could have waited until I got back into the classroom. Next time, you could ask yourself, "Do I need to interrupt right now, or can what I have to say wait?" You'll make a positive impression on people if you interrupt only when it's necessary.

Lesson A

OBJECTIVES:

1. To state the meaning of *interrupting* and tell why it is important
2. To tell the self-talk associated with correct use of the skill

MATERIALS:

1. *Lee's Maze* (See page 362; one per student and one transparency.)
2. *Interrupting* (See page 363; one per student and one transparency.)
3. *Checking Myself* (See *Appendix I*; one per student and one transparency.)
4. *Thought Bubble* (See *Appendix O*; one for educator use.)
5. *To Interrupt or Not to Interrupt* (See page 364; one per pair of students and one transparency.)

PREPARATORY SET:

Display *Lee's Maze* and discuss the instructions. Distribute *Lee's Maze* to students, face down. Tell them that when you say "go" they should turn their papers over and complete their mazes in one minute. Set a timer so students can hear and/or see time passing. Purposely interrupt students, making it difficult for them to complete their mazes. After the minute is over, use this experience to introduce this unit on interrupting.

PLAN:

1. Distribute and display *Interrupting.* Discuss the definition. Explain the skill steps and the symbols next to them. Remind students that the symbols are there to help them visualize and remember the skill steps. (The symbols will make better sense after completing lessons B and C.) Discuss the reasons for interrupting appropriately. Refer to the body-talk symbol in the left-hand margin. Remind students that appropriate body talk is important when interrupting appropriately.
2. Model use of interrupting skill step #1 while thinking aloud. A scripted example follows:

   Introduction

   I am going to pretend to be a student waiting to talk to a teacher. I will show you how I know if I could interrupt by telling you the thoughts I'm having.

When I hold up this Thought Bubble, *you'll know the words that I'm saying are actually what I'm thinking.*

Actual Model

While holding up the *Thought Bubble* say, *I need to ask the teacher about tomorrow's assignment but she's talking to someone in the hall. Do I really need to interrupt right now? No, it can wait until later.*

3. Read aloud the story at the bottom of *Interrupting* and then ask students to circle the self-talk that Jolisa used. Circle the words on the transparency.
4. Distribute and display the discussion guideline sheet called *Checking Myself.* Ask students to complete the goal statement with the phrase "use eye contact," or use another classroom discussion goal more appropriate for your group (see page 26). Tell students that you will be having a discussion about the story they just heard. Explain that when a student is answering a question or making a comment during the discussion, it's important for everyone to give the student eye contact. Instruct them to put an "X" on their sheets each time they give eye contact to a student who is called on.
5. Model use of the *Checking Myself* sheet while thinking aloud. A scripted example follows:

   Introduction

   I am going to pretend to be one of you completing this sheet during the discussion we will be having. I will tell you the thoughts I'm having while I'm completing the sheet. When I hold up this Thought Bubble, *you'll know the words I'm saying are actually what I'm thinking.*

   Actual Model

   While holding up the *Thought Bubble* say, *OK, the teacher just called on Frances. I'd better give her eye contact so she knows I'm listening to her answer.... I'll put an "X" on my sheet because I gave her eye contact.* Put the *Thought Bubble* down and mark an "X" on the transparency.

   During the discussion, periodically remind students to give eye contact to the student who is answering or commenting and mark their discussion guideline sheets.
6. Proceed with the discussion by asking these questions: (The story may need to be reread first.)
   - What did Jolisa want to ask her teacher?
   - What did Jolisa ask herself while deciding if she could interrupt?

- Why did she decide not to interrupt?
- What might have happened if Jolisa had interrupted the teachers while they were talking?

After the discussion, have students complete the bottom of *Checking Myself.*

7. Process the use of the sheet by asking the following question or another one more appropriate for your group:

   - Why do you think it's important to give eye contact to the person who is speaking during a discussion?

8. Pair students (see *Appendix P*). Distribute and display *To Interrupt or Not to Interrupt.* Have students work with their partners to complete it as directed. Tell students you will be calling on several pairs to share their answers.

9. Ask student pairs to take turns telling each other the meaning of *interrupting* and why it is important to use the skill. Students could be reminded that the information they are to say is printed on *Interrupting.*

   As an option to add structure to this activity (see *Appendix Q*), ask partners to come to an agreement about which person will be called "Aladdin" and which person will be called "Ali Baba." After students have made their decisions, ask "Aladdin" to tell "Ali Baba" the definition of *interrupting.* Next, ask "Ali Baba" to tell "Aladdin" the definition. Ask the students to use the same procedure to tell each other the reasons for interrupting appropriately.

10. Say with conviction to the class: *You are all great kids! I'm impressed with what you learned in class today!*

Name ______________________

LEE'S MAZE

DIRECTIONS: Help Lee find his home. When you finish, help Lee find the flower, trees, sun, star, or bird.

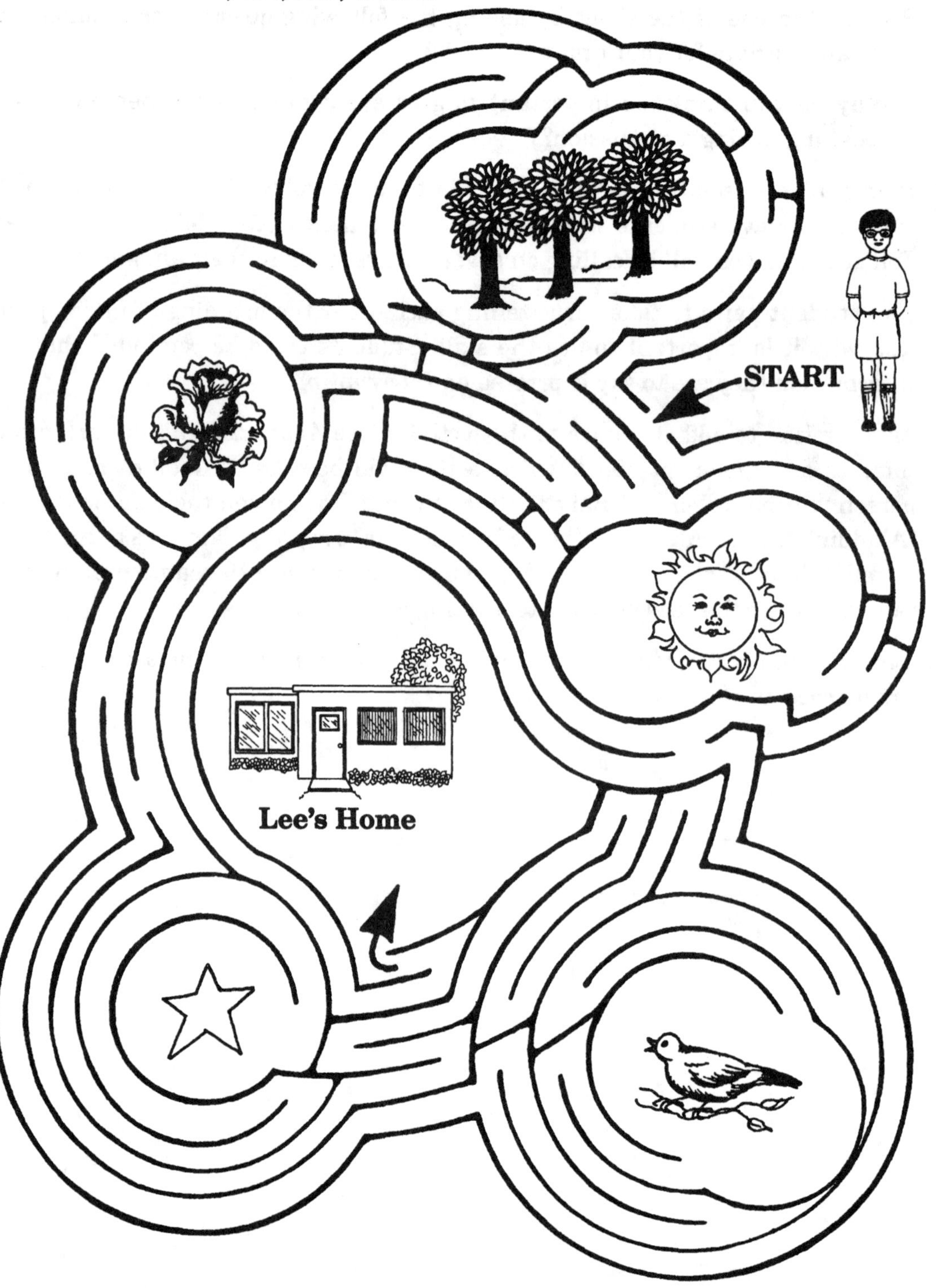

Name ________________________

Interrupting

MEANING OF INTERRUPTING: Intruding in someone's conversations or actions

SKILL STEPS:

1. Ask myself: Should I interrupt right now?
2. If yes: Interrupt politely

REASONS FOR USING THIS SKILL:

Knowing when and how to interrupt will make a good impression on others and will bring you a proud feeling.

DIRECTIONS: Listen to the story below. Look at the picture of Jolisa while you listen. Circle the self-talk Jolisa used when deciding whether or not to interrupt.

Jolisa needs to ask the teacher for help on math. She sees that Mr. Aaron is talking with Mrs. Marerro. Jolisa thinks: "Mr. Aaron is busy. I'll see if I can do the math problem by myself, or I'll wait until he's finished talking."

Names ______________________

To Interrupt or Not to Interrupt

DIRECTIONS: Read each situation below and discuss the questions that follow.

1. When Ann gets home from school, her brother Mike is on the phone. Ann wants to ask Mike if she can take his stamp collection to show her class at school tomorrow.
   - Should Ann interrupt or should she wait?
   - Why?

2. Mike has a stomachache and needs to go to the bathroom. He sees that Mrs. Marrero is busy working at her desk.
   - Should Mike interrupt or should he wait?
   - Why?

3. Lee wants to ask his teacher for help with a spelling word. Ms. Hess is giving an oral test to the other spelling group.
   - Should Lee interrupt or should he wait?
   - Why?

4. Jolisa is looking in the library for a book about rocks and needs help. The librarian is behind his desk reading a magazine.
   - Should Jolisa interrupt or should she wait?
   - Why?

Lesson B

OBJECTIVES:

1. To practice a technique to use to keep from interrupting when it is not necessary
2. To identify situations at school when it is not OK to interrupt

MATERIALS:

1. Figures of Jolisa Walker, Dr. Parra, and Ms. Hess (See *Appendix F*.)
2. *Interrupting* classroom poster (See page 13.)
3. *Numbered Stones* (See *Appendix P*; one per student.)
4. *G.A.G.* (See page *368*; one transparency.)
5. *Thought Bubble* (See *Appendix O*; one for educator use.)
6. *Thinking Skills Web* (See *Appendix T*; one per pair of students and one transparency.)

PREPARATORY SET:

Ask a student volunteer to assist you with the following skit. Have the student hold up the characters of Dr. Parra and Ms. Hess, while you hold up Jolisa.

Dr. Parra should be talking with Ms. Hess. Jolisa should say: "Hey, there's my doctor. I wonder what she's doing at school. I'll go and ask her. But wait! Should I interrupt right now?"

Ask students whether or not they think Jolisa should interrupt Dr. Parra and Ms. Hess. Help students understand that, in this case, Jolisa could wait until Dr. Parra finishes talking with Ms. Hess.

PLAN:

1. Review the definition and skill steps for *interrupting* by referring the class to the *Interrupting* classroom poster.
2. Pair students using *Numbered Stones*. Ask student pairs to take turns telling each other the skill steps for interrupting. Follow the procedure described in step 9 of Lesson A. (As an option, ask the students to decide who will be "Anne Frank" and who will be "Marie Antoinette.") Next, ask students to work with their partners to think of a situation when they would need to interrupt

appropriately. Tell the students that one or more pairs will be asked to share their situation. Have one or more pairs share their situation.

3. Display *G.A.G.* Discuss the sheet with students so they understand what a gag is and how picturing a gag can help stop a person from interrupting when it is not necessary.

   (Warn students about the dangers of actually gagging themselves or someone else.)

4. Model use of interrupting skill step #1 while thinking aloud. A scripted example follows:

   Introduction

   I'm going to pretend to be someone your age. I want to ask my mom to sign a permission slip that's due next week, but she's on the phone. I will show you the thoughts I'm having about interrupting. When I hold up this Thought Bubble, *you'll know the words I'm saying are actually what I'm thinking.*

   Actual Model

   Say, *Hey, Mom. Will you....* Then quickly put your hands over your mouth. While holding up the *Thought Bubble* say, *I want to ask her to sign this slip but she's on the phone. Should I interrupt right now? No, I don't need the slip right now. I'll wait until she's done.*

5. Have students practice making a gag with their hands over their mouths in a dramatic, fun manner after you read each of the following situations:

   - You really want to ask me for help, but you know you should wait until I'm finished helping another student.
   - You really want to ask your dad what you're having for dinner, but you know you should wait until he gets off the phone.

   Let students know that they do not actually have to put their hands over their mouths to stop themselves from interrupting. Ask students to practice visualizing themselves with their hands over their mouths after reading each of the following situations:

   - You really want to ask your mom if you can have a treat, but you know you should wait until she finishes talking to a person at the front door.
   - You really want to tell a joke, but you know you should wait until your friend finishes telling his joke.

   Now that the first skill step symbol will make better sense to students, refer to the symbol on the *Interrupting* classroom poster.

6. Distribute and display the *Thinking Skills Web*. Write "Don't Interrupt at School" in the center circle of the web, and ask students to do the same. Ask students to work with their partners to identify situations at school when students should not interrupt another person and to write their ideas on the lines of the web. The following are examples:

   - Asking for help before reading the directions
   - Asking to sharpen a pencil while the teacher is talking to the principal
   - Asking what the date is when the teacher is giving directions

   Call on several pairs to share their ideas with the class.

7. Write the following where everyone can see it: I CAN BE ESPECIALLY NICE TO OTHER PEOPLE BY USING GOOD SOCIAL SKILLS. Have the students say this aloud, in unison, with sincerity.

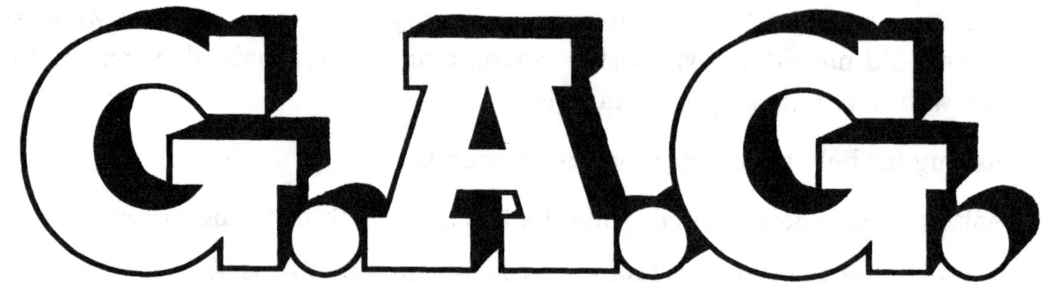

When what you want to say or ask can wait, it is important not to interrupt. But that can be very difficult!

Here is an idea for something you can try, to stop yourself from interrupting when you shouldn't:

A *gag* is something put over the mouth to prevent talking or making sounds.

PRETEND YOU HAVE A GAG OVER YOUR MOUTH, SO THAT EVEN IF YOU TRIED TO INTERRUPT, YOU COULDN'T.

Lesson C

OBJECTIVES:

1. To identify and practice an appropriate way to interrupt
2. To identify and practice three ways to get a person's attention when interrupting

MATERIALS:

1. *GAG—The Right Way* (See page 371; one per student and one transparency.)
2. *Interrupting* classroom poster (See page 13.)
3. *GAG—What To Do #1, #2,* and *#3* (See pages 372–374; one set per pair of students and one transparency.)

PREPARATORY SET:

Enthusiastically start a chant or cheer by clapping and saying the following: "Interrupt! Interrupt! Interrupt the right way!" Ask students to join in and repeat the chant several times. Tell students that in this lesson they will be learning more about skill step #2 for interrupting.

PLAN:

1. Display and distribute *GAG—The Right Way*. Remind students that remembering the G.A.G. symbol can help them to stop and think before interrupting someone. Tell them that the word "GAG" can help them remember the three steps for interrupting appropriately when they need to do so.

   Ask students to fill in their sheets as you write the three steps for interrupting appropriately on the transparency.

   G = Get the person's attention

   A = Apologize for interrupting

   G = Give the reason for interrupting

2. Now that it will make sense to students, refer them to the symbol for skill step #2 on the *Interrupting* classroom poster.
3. Model use of the interrupting skill steps while thinking aloud. A scripted example follows:

Introduction

I am going to pretend to be a student who needs to interrupt the school secretary. I will show how to interrupt appropriately and tell you the thoughts I'm having. When I hold up this Thought Bubble, *you'll know the words I'm saying are actually what I'm thinking.*

Actual Model

While holding up the *Thought Bubble* say, *She's busy typing. Do I need to interrupt her? Yes, my teacher asked me to give this note to her right away! I have to remember GAG. I'll get her attention by saying "Excuse me."* Put the *Thought Bubble* down and say, *Excuse me, Mrs. Jones.* While holding up the *Thought Bubble* say, *I need to apologize for interrupting and give the reason.* Put the *Thought Bubble* down and say, *I'm sorry for interrupting, but my teacher asked me to give this to you right away.*

4. Pair students (see *Appendix P*). Tell students they will be practicing three different ways of getting a person's attention before interrupting.
5. Distribute and display *GAG—What To Do #1*. Read the cartoon and the comments beside each frame. Ask students to take turns with their partners, pretending to be Lee, getting Mr. Aaron's attention by knocking on the door.
6. Distribute and display *GAG—What To Do #2*. Read the cartoon and the comments beside each frame. Ask students to take turns with their partners, pretending to be Victor, getting the teachers' attention by standing close enough to be seen.
7. Distribute and display *GAG—What To Do #3*. Read the cartoon and the comments beside each frame. Ask students to take turns with their partners, pretending to be Jolisa, getting Mrs. Marrero's attention by saying her name or by saying, "Excuse me."
8. Ask student pairs to take turns telling each other the three steps for interrupting appropriately. Instruct students not to interrupt each other during this activity. Students could be reminded that the information they are to say is printed on *GAG—The Right Way*. Follow the procedure described in step 9 of Lesson A. (As an option, ask students to decide who will be called "Hans Christian Andersen" and who will be called "Captain Hook.")
9. Write the following where everyone can see it: I'M A SOCIAL STAR! Have the students say this aloud, in unison, with excitement.

Name ______________________

GAG The Right Way

G = ______________________________________

____

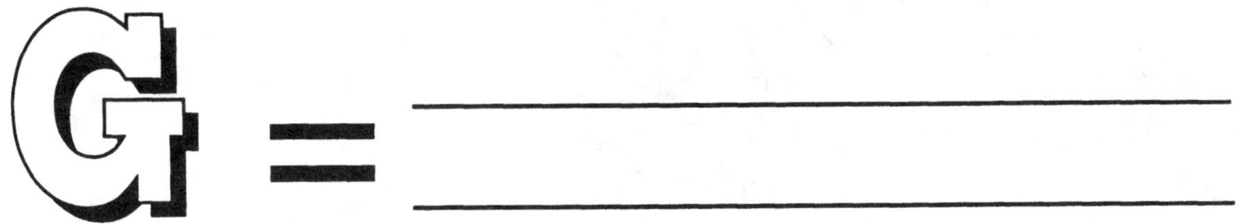

Names ____________________

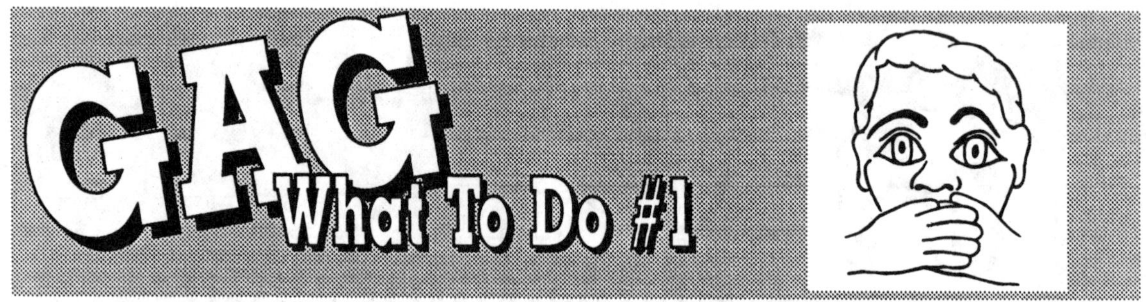

Get the person's attention by knocking on the door.

Apologize for interrupting.

Give the reason for interrupting.

Names ______________________________

Get the person's attention by standing close enough for them to see you, and wait for a break.

Apologize for interrupting.

Give the reason for interrupting.

Names ______________________________

Get the person's attention by saying the person's name (or by saying "excuse me").

Apologize for interrupting.

Give the reason for interrupting.

Lesson D

OBJECTIVES:

1. To tell the appropriate way to interrupt
2. To tell emergency situations when one should interrupt immediately and what to say

MATERIALS:

1. *GAG—The Right Way* (See page 371; one transparency.)
2. *Lee's Interruption* (See page 377; one per pair of students and one transparency.)

PREPARATORY SET:

Tell students you will be reading some situations (provided below) to them describing interruptions. They should put their thumbs up if the interruption was necessary. They should put their thumbs down if the interruption was unnecessary.

- While Jolisa's dad was talking on the telephone, she interrupted him to ask if they could go to the mall now.
- Mrs. Marerro was correcting papers in the classroom during recess. Mike interrupted to tell her that Maria fell and hurt herself on the playground.
- The clerk at the grocery store was helping a customer find a grocery item. Ann was thirsty and eager to buy a bottle of juice so she interrupted the clerk and the customer.
- Ann was telling Mike how to play a new card game. Before Ann was finished, Mike interrupted and said, "Lookout! There's a bee on your head!"

Tell students they will be learning more about appropriate interruptions in this lesson.

PLAN:

1. Display *GAG—The Right Way*. Review the three steps to interrupting politely.
2. Pair students (see *Appendix P*). Distribute and display *Lee's Interruption*. Read the script as a class. Have student pairs rewrite the script so that Lee interrupts in a polite way. Ask several pairs to perform their scripts for the class.

3. Have students brainstorm emergency situations in which students need to get help immediately and not worry about how they interrupt. Some examples follow:
   - If someone's hurt or sick
   - If there's a fire
   - If there's some type of danger
   - If the teacher tells them to get help immediately
4. Tell students that they could say, "This is an emergency" to alert people right away when someone needs help. Have them think of other ways to tell people there's an emergency.
5. Say with excitement to the class: *Each of you is a special, spectacular, marvelous, wonderful, magnificent, social person!*

Names ______________________________

LEE'S INTERRUPTION

Characters: Lee Vue and Mrs. Walker

Setting: Mrs. Walker is the teacher's assistant in Lee's classroom. She is checking some papers. Lee wants to interrupt her for help on his science project.

Lee: Mrs. Walker, help me with my science project now!

Mrs. Walker: *(looking upset)* Lee, you interrupted me! You'll have to sit down and wait until I'm finished with this work!

DIRECTIONS: Rewrite the script. Tell what Lee could do or say to interrupt politely.

Lee: (Get Mrs. Walker's attention.) ______________________________

____

____

Mrs. Walker: Yes, Lee?

Lee: (Apologize for interrupting.)______________________________

____

____

Mrs. Walker: That's OK. How can I help you?

Lee: (Give the reason for interrupting.)______________________________

____

____

Mrs. Walker: Thanks for interrupting politely. I'll be with you in just a minute.

Lee: Thanks, Mrs. Walker.

Lessons X, Y, and Z

Due to similarities in format, the final three lesson plans for each unit in *Social Star* are provided in *Appendix A*. Substitute the word "interrupting" whenever a "_______" appears in the lesson plans. Information specific to this unit follows.

LESSON X PREPARATORY SET:

Ask students to take out a piece of paper and a pencil and draw the GAG symbol for the first skill step. Ask them to make the face look as silly as they can. Ask for volunteers to show their pictures to the class and explain how the GAG symbol can help them remember the steps for interrupting.

LESSON Y PREPARATORY SET:

Darken the room, if you prefer, and ask students to visualize themselves correctly using this social skill by reading the following script:

> *Let's take a few moments to relax.... Make sure you are sitting in a comfortable position.... Close your eyes if you feel like it.... On the count of three, take a very slow, deep breath. One . . . two . . . three.... Breathe in deeply.... Now breathe out slowly.... Let your entire body relax.... Now imagine yourself needing to interrupt two lifeguards who are talking. You get their attention appropriately by saying, "Excuse me." You apologize for interrupting and then you tell them you're interrupting because you are supposed to call home and you lost your money for calling. The lifeguards smile at you because you interrupted so politely. They let you use the phone in the office. Think about how proud you feel because you interrupted appropriately.*

LESSON Z PLOT SITUATION:

Ask students to pretend that their good friend just said, "I hate you and I'm not going to be your friend anymore" and they don't know why it was said.

LESSON Z ROADBLOCK EXAMPLES:

- Not knowing if the reason for interrupting is important enough or if it can wait
- Not knowing if the other person is busy
- Waiting to interrupt someone and the person doesn't acknowledge you

Name ______________________

Interrupting T-Chart

LOOKS LIKE...	SOUNDS LIKE...
using appropriate body talk • looking at the person, trying to make eye contact • standing where the person can see you • waiting at the door	knocking on the door saying • "Excuse me..." • "Pardon me..." • "I'm sorry for interrupting..."

HOME

Pretend your parents are having a conversation during breakfast. Show how you could politely interrupt to tell your dad that you need a permission slip signed for school today.

SCHOOL

Pretend the school secretary is working on the computer. Show how you could politely interrupt to give the secretary an important note from your teacher.

COMMUNITY

Pretend you are at the grocery store and can't find an item on your parent's list. Show how you could politely interrupt a clerk to ask for help.

Sorry for interrupting, but...
INTERRUPT POLITELY

HOME-A-GRAM

Dear Family,

At school, we have been talking about the social skill called

INTERRUPTING

I learned that *interrupting* means intruding in someone's conversations or actions.

I learned that sometimes I should interrupt and sometimes I should not.

If I need to interrupt, I should:

G = Get the person's attention

A = Apologize for interrupting

G = Give the reason for interrupting

If I know when and how to interrupt, I will make a good impression on others, and I'll feel proud.

I have drawn a picture of myself on the back of this page. It shows me with my hands over my mouth (like a GAG) to remind me to stop and think before I interrupt someone. The word "GAG" helps me to remember the three steps when I do need to interrupt.

I'll show you how I would interrupt someone politely. After I do, please sign my "Interrupting" badge so I can return it to school and become a SOCIAL SUPER STAR this week.

From: ______________________________

Right Time and Place

UNIT GOAL:

To demonstrate comprehension and use of the ability to choose the right time and place

EDUCATOR INFORMATION:

This unit assists students in determining the right time and place to do and say various things. Children often have a difficult time understanding why it's OK to do something in one situation while it's not OK to do the exact same thing in a different situation. This unit does not address interrupting at the right time and place; however, the *Interrupting* unit does. The educator should exert sensitivity and care in generalizing rules about right time and place into the children's home cultures.

RELATED ACTIVITIES:

1. Have students write a poem about doing things at the right time and place. An example follows:

   Blow bubbles outside, but not in school!

   Choosing the right time and place is cool!

2. Discuss the phrase, "I was at the right place at the right time" (and variations of the phrase).

3. Take a field trip to the courthouse (or another government building) and then to a park. Before going, ask students to complete the following statements: "When I am at the courthouse, it will be the right time and place to..." and "When I am at the park, it will be the right time and place to..."

4. Invite adults from different cultures to talk to the students about how their cultures' conventions for time and place compare with American common culture norms.

It is important for educators to provide opportunities for students to work in groups so they can experience social skills in contexts where social communication is needed. Therefore, educators are encouraged to have students complete the Related Activities in small groups whenever possible. Educators trained in cooperative learning could incorporate the five components (see page 34) into the group activity.

RELATED LITERATURE:

Muggie Maggie (1990) by Beverly Cleary, Morrow. (Text) (pages 7–12)

Ramona Forever (1984) by Beverly Cleary, Morrow. (Text) (pages 28–31)

Where's Our Mama? (1991) by Diane Goode, Ill. by author, Dutton. (Picture book)

SOCIAL SKILLS ALL DAY LONG:

Look for opportunities to teach social skills throughout the day (incidental teaching). Four ways to reinforce good social skills and an example of each follow:

Encouragement

> *You waited until the end of class to ask about tomorrow's field trip. Thanks for not interrupting the class. You chose the right time and place to ask. I appreciate that!*

Personal Example

> *I need to talk to the principal about something. I think I'll wait until tomorrow because I know the principal has a very busy schedule today. I want to choose the right time and place because then the principal will be more interested in what I want to talk about.*

Prompting

> *The right time and place to bounce a ball might be outside during recess. Remember not to bounce your ball until you get outside!*

Corrective Feedback (must be positive, private, specific, and nonthreatening)

> *Ann, you just told a joke in the middle of class. We were discussing something different and we wanted your participation. The right time and place to tell a joke might be during lunch or recess. If you choose the right time and place to tell jokes, more people can enjoy them.*

Lesson A

OBJECTIVES:

1. To state the meaning of *right time and place* and tell why it's important
2. To tell the self-talk associated with correct use of the skill

MATERIALS:

1. Personal hygiene items (e.g., toothbrush, toothpaste, hand lotion, hairbrush or comb, mirror)
2. *Right Time and Place* (See page 388; one per student.)
3. *Thought Bubble* (See *Appendix O*; one for educator use.)
4. *Checking Myself* (See *Appendix I*; one per student and one transparency.)

PREPARATORY SET:

Start class by brushing or combing your hair, etc. Do this for a minute or two (students may giggle, look confused, and/or be surprised). Introduce the new social skill by discussing why it was not the right time or place for you to be doing personal grooming.

PLAN:

1. Distribute *Right Time and Place*. Discuss the definition. Explain the skill step and the symbol next to it. Remind students that the symbol is there to help them visualize and remember the skill step. Refer to the body-talk symbol in the left-hand margin. Remind students that appropriate body talk is needed to do or say something at the right time and place. Discuss the reasons for choosing the right time and place.
2. Model use of the right time and place skill step while thinking aloud. A scripted example follows:

   Introduction

   I am going to pretend to be someone your age. I'm at a restaurant with my family. My brother's trying to kick me under the table. I will show you the thoughts I'm having about right time and place. When I hold up this Thought Bubble, *you'll know the words that I'm saying are actually what I'm thinking.*

Actual Model

While holding up the *Thought Bubble* say, *Is this the right time or place to be goofing around with my brother? No! I'll tell him to stop.* Put the *Thought Bubble* down and say, *Stop that! I don't want to goof around in here!*

3. Read the story at the bottom of *Right Time and Place* aloud to students.

4. Distribute and display the discussion guideline sheet called *Checking Myself.* Ask students to complete the goal statement with the phrase "use eye contact," or use another classroom discussion goal more appropriate for your group (see page 26). Tell students that you will be having a discussion about the story they just heard. When a person is answering a question or making a comment during the discussion, it's important to give that person eye contact. Instruct them to put an "X" on their sheets each time they give eye contact to the person who is speaking during the discussion.

5. Model use of the *Checking Myself* sheet while thinking aloud. A scripted example follows:

   Introduction

   I am going to pretend to be one of you completing this sheet during the discussion we will be having. I will tell you the thoughts I'm having while I'm completing the sheet. When I hold up this Thought Bubble, *you'll know the words I'm saying are actually what I'm thinking.*

   Actual Model

   While holding up the *Thought Bubble* say, *OK, the teacher is asking a question. I'd better give eye contact so the teacher knows I'm listening. I'll put an "X" on my sheet because I just gave eye contact to the teacher.* Put the *Thought Bubble* down and mark an "X" on the overhead transparency. While holding up the *Thought Bubble* say, *Oh, now the teacher has called on Tolly. I'll give Tolly eye contact so she knows I'm listening.* Put the *Thought Bubble* down and mark an "X" on the overhead transparency.

   During the discussion, periodically remind students to give eye contact to the person who is answering or commenting and to mark their discussion guideline sheets.

6. Proceed with the discussion by asking these questions: (The story may need to be reread first.)

   - Why do you think Mike decided not to run around?
   - How might Mike's parents have felt if Mike would have gotten silly?

- When would it be an appropriate time and place to run around and be silly?

After the discussion, have students complete the bottom of *Checking Myself.*

7. Process the use of the sheet by asking the following questions or others more appropriate for your group:

   - Why do you think it's important to give eye contact to the person who is speaking during a discussion?

   - How do you think teachers feel when students give them eye contact?

8. Pair students (see *Appendix P*). Ask students to take turns telling each other the meaning of *right time and place* and why it's important to use the skill. Students could be reminded that the information they are to say is printed on *Right Time and Place.*

   As an option to add structure to this activity (see *Appendix Q*), ask partners to come to an agreement about which person will be called "Louisa May Alcott" and which person will be called "Mark Twain." After students have made their decisions, ask "Louisa" to tell "Mark" the definition of *right time and place.* Next, ask "Mark" to tell "Louisa" the definition. Ask the students to use the same procedure to tell each other the reasons for using the skill of *right time and place.*

9. Say with conviction to the class: *You are better-than-excellent kids! I'll bet you feel proud of yourselves when you use good social skills!* (Encourage kids to pat themselves on their backs.)

Name ______________________

Right Time and Place

MEANING OF RIGHT TIME AND PLACE:
Doing and saying things that are appropriate for the time and place you are at

SKILL STEP:

1. Ask myself: Is this a good time and place to _____?

REASONS FOR USING THIS SKILL:

Choosing the right time and place helps you stay out of trouble and get along better with others. You will feel proud inside.

DIRECTIONS: Listen to the story below. Look at the picture of Mr. and Mrs. Jackson and their son Mike while you are listening.

Mike was at the shopping mall with his parents. He felt energetic and kind of silly and wanted to run around. He thought about where he was and decided he'd better not get silly or run around in the mall.

Lesson B

OBJECTIVES:

1. To identify situations when it would and would not be the right time and place for various actions and words
2. To discuss the consequences of doing or saying something at the wrong time and place

MATERIALS:

1. *Opposites Match* cards (See *Appendix P.*)
2. *Right Time and Place* classroom poster (See page 13.)
3. *Thought Bubble* (See *Appendix O*; one for educator use.)
4. Characters of Victor and Maria Parra, Ann and Mike Olson, Lee Vue, and Jolisa Walker (See *Appendix F.*)

PREPARATORY SET:

Pair students using the *Opposites Match* cards. These same pairs will work together during steps 2 and 4 of this Plan.

PLAN:

1. Review the definition and skill step for *right time and place* by referring the class to the *Right Time and Place* classroom poster.
2. Ask student pairs to take turns telling each other the skill step for right time and place. Follow the procedure described in step 8 of Lesson A. (As an option, ask students to decide who will be "Wilbur Wright" and who will be "Orville Wright.") Next, ask students to work with their partners to think of a situation when it would be the right time and place to talk quietly. Tell students that one or more pairs will be asked to share their situation. Have one or more pairs share their situation.
3. Model the right time and place skill step while thinking aloud. A scripted example follows:

   Introduction

   I am going to pretend to be a student sitting at my desk in school. I will tell you the thoughts I'm having about right time and place. When I hold up this Thought Bubble, *you'll know the words I'm saying are actually what I'm thinking.*

Actual Model

While holding up the *Thought Bubble* say, *I think I'll play with my cars on my desk. Wait—is this the right time and place to play with my cars? No! The teacher might not like it. I'll wait until recess to show the kids my cars.*

4. Tell students you will be holding up each of the student characters from McKinley School in Socialville, one at a time, and telling what each character wants to do or say (scripts follow). Tell them it's their job to work with their partners to identify a situation when it would be the right time and place and a situation when it would be the wrong time and place for the character to do or say what was mentioned. They should also discuss possible negative consequences of choosing the wrong time and place. Tell students that you will be calling on several pairs to share their ideas with the entire class.
   - While holding up Victor, say, "Victor is chewing a piece of watermelon bubble gum. He wants to blow a bubble."
   - While holding up Maria, say, "Maria wants to do something silly to get one of her friends to giggle."
   - While holding up Ann, say, "Ann wants to tell a funny joke to one of her friends."
   - While holding up Mike, say, "Mike wants to offer help to a classmate."
   - While holding up Lee, say, "Lee wants to talk loudly."
   - While holding up Jolisa, say, "Jolisa wants to lay her head on her desk."
5. Write the following where everyone can see it: I AM A SPECIAL PERSON! I CAN USE MY TALENTS TO GET ALONG WITH OTHERS. Have the students say this aloud, in unison, until they sound like they really mean it.

Lesson C

OBJECTIVES:

1. To identify actions and words which would and would not be appropriate in various situations
2. To experience the feelings of being with a person who is making inappropriate time and place choices

MATERIALS:

1. Telephone (One for educator use)
2. *Telephone Faces* (See page 393; one per pair of students and one transparency.)
3. Characters of Ms. Paula Hess; Maria, Victor, and Mr. Ricardo Parra; Mrs. Cora Marrero; Jolisa Walker; and Mike and Ann Olson (See *Appendix F.*)
4. 40 miniature marshmallows and two spoons

PREPARATORY SET:

Tell students that sometimes children get in trouble at home for doing or saying something at the wrong time and place because their parents are on the phone. Pretend to be a parent talking on the phone. While talking, make gestures and faces at an imaginary child, indicating that the child is doing something inappropriate for the time and place. Ask students if their parents have ever made faces like that at them.

PLAN:

1. Pair students (see *Appendix P*). Distribute and display *Telephone Faces.* Ask students to work with their partners to write examples of things they might do or say while their parents are on the phone that their parents would judge to be happening at the wrong time and place. Ask several pairs to share their ideas and write them on the transparency.
2. Tell students you will be holding up some of the characters from Socialville, one at a time, and describing the situation each character is in (descriptions follow). Ask them to work with their partners to identify actions and words which would be appropriate for each situation and then actions and words which would not be appropriate. Tell students that you will be calling on several pairs to share their ideas with the entire class.

- While holding up Ms. Hess and Maria, say, "There are only five minutes left until the morning bell rings for class to begin. Maria walks into the classroom and sees Ms. Hess hurrying around trying to complete several tasks before class begins. What might be appropriate and inappropriate actions and words for Maria to choose at this given time and place?"
- While holding up Mr. Parra and Victor, say, "Mr. Parra is trying to finish preparing dinner and setting the table so the family can eat in 15 minutes. Victor wants to spend some time with his dad, so he goes into the kitchen. What would be appropriate and inappropriate actions and words for Victor to choose at this given time and place?"
- While holding up Mrs. Marrero and Jolisa, say, "Mrs. Marrero is telling her students about their next small group task and is giving several important directions. Jolisa is in her class. What would be appropriate and inappropriate actions and words for Jolisa to choose at this given time and place?"
- While holding up Mike and Ann, say, "Mike has been asked by his parents to lie down on the couch in the family room because he has a headache. Ann is in the family room too. What would be appropriate and inappropriate actions and words for Ann to choose at this given time and place?"

3. Divide the class into two teams. The educator should be on one of the teams. Have the two teams stand in lines. This activity will need to be done in an area where students can walk a distance of at least 8–10 feet. Divide the 40 marshmallows into two equal piles. Give the first person in each line a spoon. Tell students that they must work in relay fashion to carry one marshmallow in the spoon to a designated spot, drop it, and carry the spoon back to give it to the next person in line, who repeats the same procedure. They continue in this fashion until all the marshmallows are carried to the designated spot.

4. Get the kids excited about doing the relay. Stand close to the front of your line. After the relay starts and it is your turn, take your time, saying, "Just a minute, I have to get a tissue." Each time it is your turn, do something else which is inappropriate for the time and place of being in a relay.

5. Discuss how the team members felt when they were in a hurry and you were making poor time and place choices. Relate this to how Ms. Hess, Mr. Parra, Mrs. Marrero, and Mike might have felt if the other person in their situations had made poor time and place choices.

6. Say enthusiastically to the class: *You are dynamite, vibrant students! Thank you for using your smart brains!*

Names ______________________________

TELEPHONE FACES

Lessons X, Y, and Z

Due to similarities in format, the final three lesson plans for each unit in *Social Star* are provided in *Appendix A*. Substitute the phrase "right time and place" whenever a "______" appears in the lesson plans. Information specific to this unit follows.

LESSON X PREPARATORY SET:

Tell students you will be reading some situations (provided below) to them. They should put their thumbs up if the person did something at the right time and place. They should put their thumbs down if the person did not do something at the right time or place.

- Jolisa was chewing gum and blowing bubbles during class.
- Jolisa was chewing gum and blowing bubbles while walking home from school.
- Mike was making silly faces at Victor during the music recital.
- Mike was making silly faces at Victor when they were outside during recess.

LESSON Y PREPARATORY SET:

Darken the room, if you prefer, and ask students to visualize themselves correctly using this social skill by reading the following script:

> *Let's take a few moments to relax.... Close your eyes if you feel like it.... On the count of three, take a very slow, deep breath. One . . . two . . . three.... Breathe in deeply.... Now breath out slowly.... Let your entire body relax.... Now imagine that you want to ask your parents if you can sleep over at a friend's house. When you walk into your house, you hear your parents arguing. You ask yourself, "Is this the best time and place to ask them?" Picture yourself thinking no and deciding to wait until later to ask. You are glad that you decide to wait.*

LESSON Z PLOT SITUATION:

Ask students to pretend that a friend told them about a relative who physically hurts them but asks you not to tell anybody.

LESSON Z ROADBLOCK EXAMPLES:

- Feeling like it's fun to do certain things even if they're at the wrong time and place
- Having difficulty reading other people's body language to know if it's the right time and place to do something

Name ____________________

Right Time and Place T-Chart

LOOKS LIKE...	SOUNDS LIKE...
using appropriate body talk • eye contact • facial expression • posture • personal space • body movements	saying • "Can I ask a question or should I wait?" • "When can you help me with this?"
a person looking around to see what's happening in the situation	sounds and words that are right for the situation • laughing at a party • whispering when someone is sleeping nearby
actions that are right for the situation • running on a field house track • walking in the school halls	

HOME

Pretend your grandparents are at your house. Show how you could ask when it would be a good time and place for you to show them your photo album.

SCHOOL

Pretend you go to school with a pack of gum. Think about the right time and place to offer some gum to your friends. Say your thoughts aloud.

COMMUNITY

Pretend you're at the store with your friend. Your friend is being loud and silly. Show how you could tell your friend that it's not the right time and place to act goofy.

Choose
the
Right Time
and Place

HOME-A-GRAM

Dear Family,

At school we have been talking about the social skill called

RIGHT TIME AND PLACE

I learned that *right time and place* means doing and saying things that are good for the time and place you are at.

I know that before I do or say anything, I should ask myself, "Is this a good time and place for me to ____?"

I learned that choosing the right time and place helps me stay out of trouble, get along better with others, and feel proud inside.

Below, I wrote an appropriate and then an inappropriate time and place for me to ask you what we're having for dinner.

APPROPRIATE TIME AND PLACE:

____

____

INAPPROPRIATE TIME AND PLACE:

____

____

I'll show you what I know about right time and place by talking with you about what would be good things to do and say when you are in a real hurry. After I do, please sign my "Right Time and Place" badge so I can return it to school and become a SOCIAL SUPER STAR this week.

From: ______________________

Being Formal or Casual

UNIT GOAL:

To demonstrate knowledge of when and how to be formal or casual

EDUCATOR INFORMATION:

This unit teaches students that in some situations it is appropriate to be more formal, while in other situations it is appropriate to be more casual. The unit demonstrates how certain behaviors (e.g., dress, language, aspects of body talk) may change in formal versus casual situations. The educator should also help students realize that a formal situation may still permit casual language (e.g., while being more formally dressed for a wedding, children would probably still use casual language with their cousins) and a casual situation may demand more formal language (e.g., while being dressed more casually in play clothes, children would probably still use formal language if a police officer stopped them to ask a question). The educator should exert sensitivity and care in generalizing rules about being formal or casual into the children's home cultures.

RELATED ACTIVITIES:

1. Have students plan a formal "tea" for staff. Brainstorm several ways to make the tea more formal (e.g., send out formal invitations, wear more formal clothes, use cloth linens and a sterling tea service, serve the staff, use more formal table manners, use more formal language).
2. Visit a more formal restaurant. Discuss with the manager all the things they do to make the restaurant more formal.
3. Ask students to find pictures showing examples of formal/traditional clothes and casual clothes for various cultures throughout the world. (*National Geographic* would be an excellent source.)
4. Invite adults from different cultures to talk to the students about how their cultures' conventions for being formal or casual compare with American common culture norms.

It is important for educators to provide opportunities for students to work in groups so they can experience social skills in contexts where social communication is needed. Therefore, educators are encouraged to have students complete the Related Activities in small groups whenever possible. Educators trained in cooperative learning could incorporate the five components (see page 34) into the group activity.

RELATED LITERATURE:

Aldo Ice Cream (1981) by Johanna Hurwitz, Morrow. (Text)
Aldo's respect for adults is shown by the way he addresses them: Mr. Puccini, Mrs. Thomas, Mrs. Nardo. (pages 41–42)

Alexander and the Terrible, Horrible, No Good, Very Bad Day (1972) by Judith Viorst, Ill. by Ray Cruz, Atheneum. (Picture book)

Bridge to Terabithia (1977) by Katherine Paterson, Crowell. (Text) (pages 78–82)

From the Mixed-Up Files of Mrs. Basil E. Frankweiler (1967) by E.L. Konigsburg, Atheneum. (Text) (pages 13–14, 119)

Hi, Cat! (1970) by Ezra Jack Keats, Ill. by author, Macmillan. (Picture book)

Shiloh (1991) by Phyllis Reynolds Naylor, Atheneum. (Text) (pages 120–128)

SOCIAL SKILLS ALL DAY LONG:

Look for opportunities to teach social skills throughout the day (incidental teaching). Four ways to reinforce social skills and an example of each follow:

Encouragement

When Mrs. Jones, the president of the school board, visited our classroom, you stood up straight and said, "Mrs. Jones, thank you for coming." Spectacular job being more formal!

Personal Example

Yesterday, when I got home from work, we decided to have a picnic in our backyard. I put on a pair of jeans and a T-shirt so I could be more comfortable. We were very casual. We ate all finger foods because that was quick and simple, and then we played volleyball.

Prompting

Tomorrow we are going on a field trip to meet some adults who work at the bank. Remember, this will be a formal situation, so we'll need to be more proper and respectful. What can we all do to be more formal?

Corrective Feedback (must be positive, private, specific, and nonthreatening)

Ann, just now you called the principal by his first name. It would be better to be more formal and call him "Mr. Brown." That way he might be impressed and feel good about the respect that you show him.

Lesson A

OBJECTIVES:

1. To state the meanings of *formal* and *casual* and tell why the social skill is important
2. To tell the self-talk associated with correct use of the skill
3. To compare and contrast being formal and casual

MATERIALS:

1. A set of casual clothes (jeans and sweatshirt) and a set of formal clothes (suit, dress) (or pictures of casual and formal clothes)
2. *Thought Bubble* (See *Appendix O*; one for educator use.)
3. *Being Formal or Casual* (See page 404; one per student.)
4. *Venn Diagram* (See *Appendix W*; two transparencies.)
5. A plum and an orange

PREPARATORY SET:

Hold up the sets (or pictures) of formal and casual clothes. Ask students to tell how the clothes are alike and how they are different. Tell students that "formal" is a term that can be used to describe the dress-up clothes and that "casual" is a term that can be used to describe the everyday clothes. Explain that just like there are more formal and more casual clothes, there are also more formal and more casual ways of talking and acting. Tell students that during this unit, they will be learning how and when to be more formal and more casual.

PLAN:

1. Distribute and display *Being Formal or Casual*. Discuss the definitions. Explain the skill step and the symbol next to it. Remind students that the symbol is there to help them visualize and remember the skill step. Refer to the body-talk symbol in the left-hand margin. Remind students that appropriate body talk is needed in both formal and casual situations. Discuss the reasons for knowing when and how to be formal or casual. Students should be made aware that there may be situations when they need to act and talk more formally even though they are dressed casually, and vice versa.

2. Model use of the being formal or casual skill step while thinking aloud. A scripted example follows:

   Introduction

   I am going to pretend to be someone your age. My family is eating dinner at someone else's house. I will show you how to use the being formal or casual skill step and tell you the thoughts I'm having. When I hold up this Thought Bubble, *you'll know the words that I'm saying are actually what I'm thinking.*

   Actual Model

   While holding up the *Thought Bubble* say, *Should I be more formal or more casual?... I think I can be more casual because we're eating pizza in the family room while watching a movie. I can eat with my hands and sit on the floor, but I still need to use appropriate manners, like using a napkin and saying "please" and "thank you" when I ask for more pizza.*

3. Pair students (see *Appendix P*). Display the *Venn Diagram*. Tell students that the *Venn Diagram* is a fun way to show how things are alike and how they are different. Say, "Here is a plum and here is an orange (hold up the fruit for all students to see). Let's use the *Venn Diagram* to compare plums and oranges." Write "plums" above the left circle and "oranges" above the right circle. Ask, "How are plums and oranges alike?" (Answers might include: they are round; they are fruit.) As answers are provided, write them in the middle overlapping area of the diagram. Then ask, "How are plums and oranges different?" (Answers might include: oranges are orange and plums are purple; oranges are bigger and plums are smaller.) As answers are provided, write them on their respective areas on the diagram (e.g., "color is purple" written in the left section; "color is orange" written in the right section).

4. Read the story about Mike at the bottom of *Being Formal or Casual*. Display another *Venn Diagram*. Tell students they will be working with their partners to compare being more formal to being more casual and that they can use the story about Mike to help them come up with ideas. Write "Being more formal" above the left circle and "Being more casual" above the right circle.

5. Ask student pairs to begin by comparing the words Mike used in the two situations. (Answers might include: Talked formally by using titles and more proper words. Talked casually by using first names only and more slang.) Call on student pairs to share their answers. Record appropriate responses in the *Venn Diagram*. Proceed by asking student pairs to compare Mike's clothes and his posture in the two situations. Again, record appropriate responses in the *Venn Diagram*. (Keep the *Venn Diagram* for use in Lesson B.)

6. Ask student pairs to think about how being more formal and being more casual are the same. (Answers might include: You shouldn't be rude in either situation.) Call on student pairs to share their similarities and write them in the overlapping section of the diagram.

7. Ask student pairs to take turns telling each other the meanings of *formal* and *casual* and why it's important to use the skill. Students could be reminded that the information they are to say is printed on *Being Formal or Casual*.

   As an option to add structure to this activity (see *Appendix Q*), ask partners to come to an agreement about which person will be called "Zeus" and which person will be called "Odysseus." After students have made their decision, ask "Zeus" to tell "Odysseus" the definitions for *formal* and *casual*. Next, ask "Odysseus" to tell "Zeus" the definitions. Ask the students to use the same procedure to tell each other the reasons for knowing when and how to be formal or casual.

8. Write the following where everyone can see it: I AM A SPECIAL PERSON. I CAN GET ALONG WELL WITH OTHERS. Have the students say this aloud, in unison, with enthusiasm.

Name ____________________

Being Formal or Casual

MEANING OF FORMAL: Being more proper and respectful

MEANING OF CASUAL: Being more natural, relaxed, or informal

SKILL STEP:

1. Ask myself: Should I be more formal or casual?

REASONS FOR USING THIS SKILL:

If you know when and how to be formal or casual, you can make a good impression and feel proud.

DIRECTIONS: Listen to the story below. Look at the pictures of Mike while you are listening.

On Saturday, Mike went outside to play with his friends. He wore blue jeans and a T-shirt, and said things like, "Hi, Lee. Hi, Victor. How's it goin'?" and "What do you guys wanna do?" He didn't spend much time thinking about how he was standing or sitting, but he made certain not to do or say anything that was rude. Later that day, Mike went to a wedding with his parents. He wore a shirt and tie, and said things like, "Hello, how are you?" and "Thank you for inviting me." He remembered to have a straight posture during the wedding ceremony and while he was walking through the receiving line. Mike made certain not to do or say anything that was rude.

Lesson B

OBJECTIVES:

1. To differentiate between formal and casual illustrations
2. To practice the components of being formal

MATERIALS:

1. *Go Together Cards* (See *Appendix P*; one set per pair of students.)
2. *Being Formal or Casual* classroom poster (See page 13.)
3. *Puzzles* (See pages 407–408; one transparency of each page of puzzles, one set of puzzles cut apart per pair of students.)
4. Construction paper (Two pieces per pair of students)
5. Glue and markers (One of each per pair of students)
6. *Venn Diagram* (Transparency from Lesson A)

PREPARATORY SET:

Pair students using *Go Together* cards. Explain that student pairs will be making posters together from puzzle pieces.

PLAN:

1. Review the definition and skill step for *being formal or casual* by referring the class to the *Being Formal or Casual* classroom poster.
2. Ask student pairs to take turns telling each other the skill step for being formal or casual. Follow the procedure described in step 7 of Lesson A. (As an option, ask students to decide who will be "Poseidon" and who will be "Pandora.") Next, ask students to work with their partners to think of a more formal situation. Tell students that one or more pairs will be called on to share their situation. Have one or more pairs share their situation.
3. Distribute *Puzzles.* Ask student pairs to put together all six two-piece puzzles.
4. Display the *Puzzles* transparency showing clothes, posture, and words. Ask students to look at their two-piece puzzle labeled "clothes" and to decide which puzzle piece shows Lee in more formal clothes and which shows Lee in more casual clothes. Call on one pair to share their answer. On the transparency, write

"F" in the upper left corner of the formal puzzle piece and "C" in the upper right corner of the casual puzzle piece. Ask students to do the same on their puzzle pieces.

5. Proceed as described above for the remaining five two-piece puzzles.

6. Distribute two pieces of construction paper, glue, and a marker to each pair of students. Tell students they will be making two posters—one for being formal and one for being casual. Ask them to write "Being More Formal" at the top of one piece of construction paper and "Being More Casual" at the top of the second piece. Next, ask students to glue all the casual puzzle pieces to the casual poster and all the formal puzzle pieces to the formal poster. (The completed posters could be displayed throughout the school.)

7. Display the *Venn Diagram* from Lesson A. Work with students to add statements about the differences between personal space, hygiene, and table manners.

8. Ask students to visualize and practice the six formal/casual components discussed during this lesson as you read the following script to them:

   Pretend that you have won an award. You have been invited to a special awards breakfast at school with the school principal. The breakfast is going to be a more formal situation. Close your eyes and picture yourself at home getting ready for the breakfast. Picture yourself washing up, carefully fixing your hair, and putting on nice clothes. Now picture yourself arriving at school and meeting the principal. Since this is a formal situation, you decide to stand an arm's length away and use more proper and respectful words when you greet the principal. One thing you might say is, "Good morning, Mr. / Mrs. ______." When I say "go," actually say, "Good morning, Mr. / Mrs. ________" with a cheerful tone of voice.... Go. (pause) *Now, picture yourself sitting and eating breakfast. Since this is a formal situation, you decide to sit up straight and use extra polite table manners. Picture yourself putting your napkin on your lap and keeping your elbows off the table. Pretend you would like more milk. Since this is a formal situation, you decide to use more proper and respectful words when you ask for the milk. One thing you might say is, "Excuse me, may I please have more milk?" When I say "go," actually say, "Excuse me, may I please have more milk?".... Go.* (pause) *Now, pretend the breakfast has ended and it is time for you to walk up to receive your award. Picture yourself smiling and standing up straight as you walk to the front of the room. Since this is a formal situation, the principal reaches out to shake your hand. Picture yourself shaking hands and thanking the principal for the award. Experience the good feeling you might have inside because you know what type of personal space, hygiene, table manners, clothes, posture, and words would be appropriate in this formal situation.*

9. Say with pride to the class: *I feel honored to have the opportunity to teach such talented students. You worked very hard today!*

PUZZLES

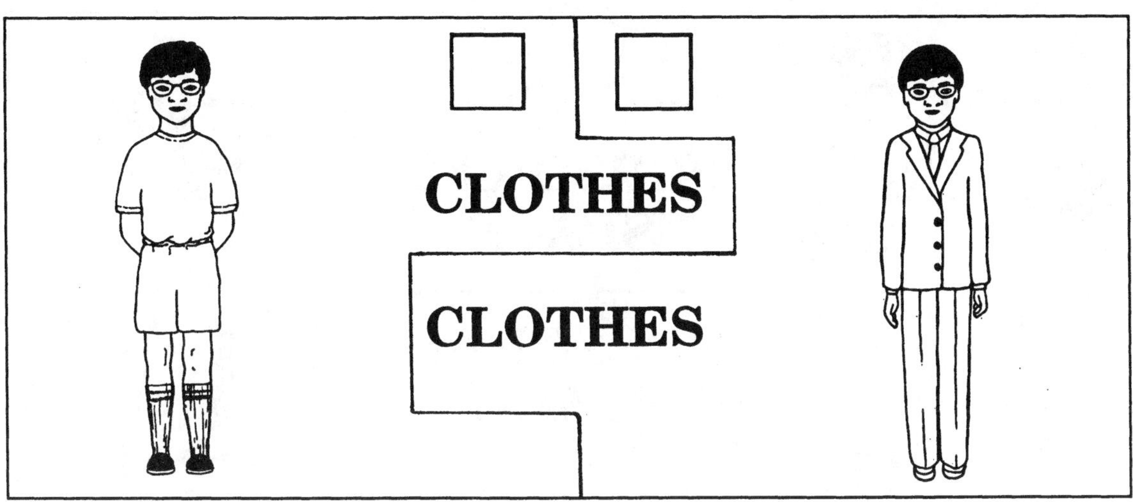
CLOTHES
CLOTHES

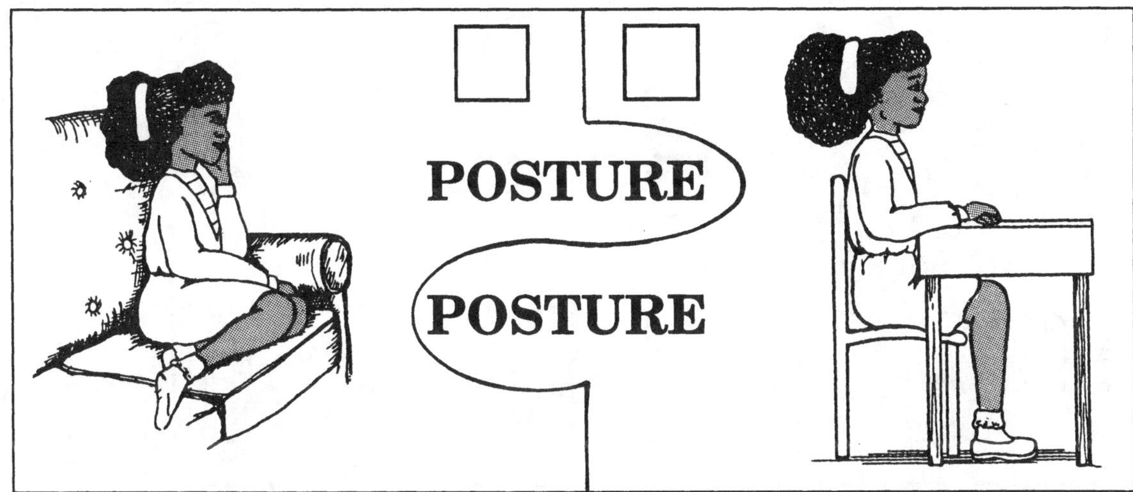
POSTURE
POSTURE

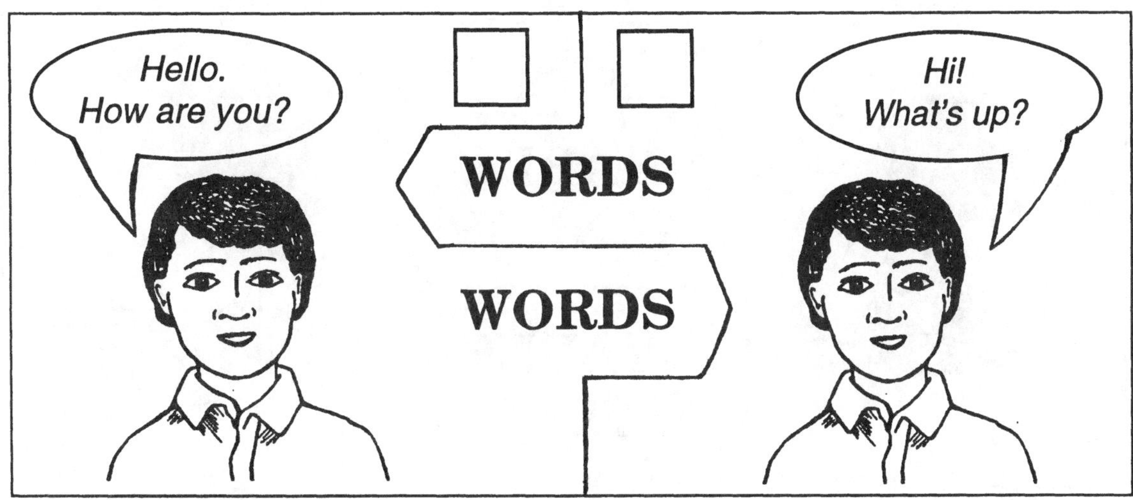
Hello.
How are you?
WORDS
WORDS
Hi!
What's up?

PUZZLES

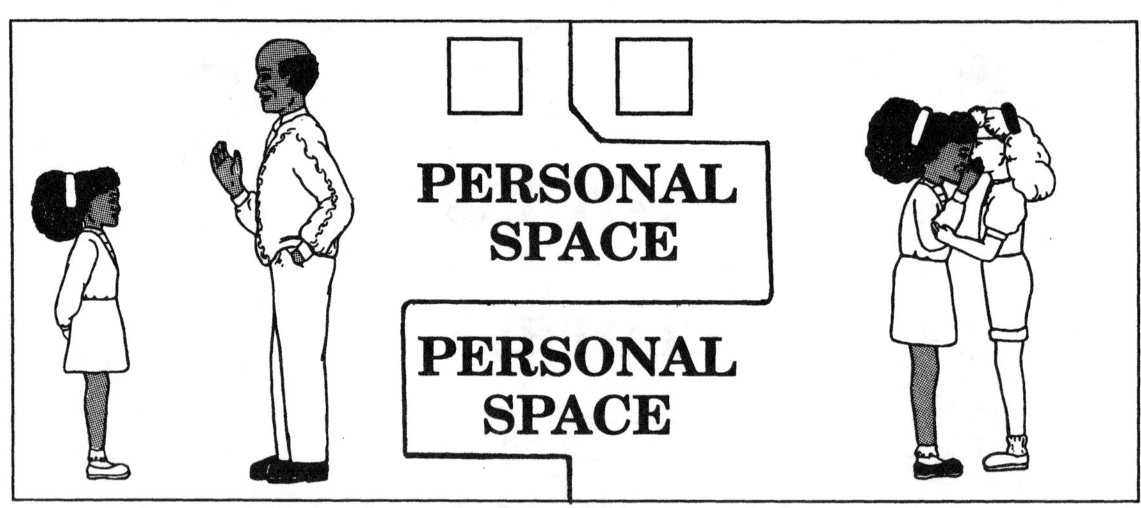
PERSONAL
SPACE
PERSONAL
SPACE

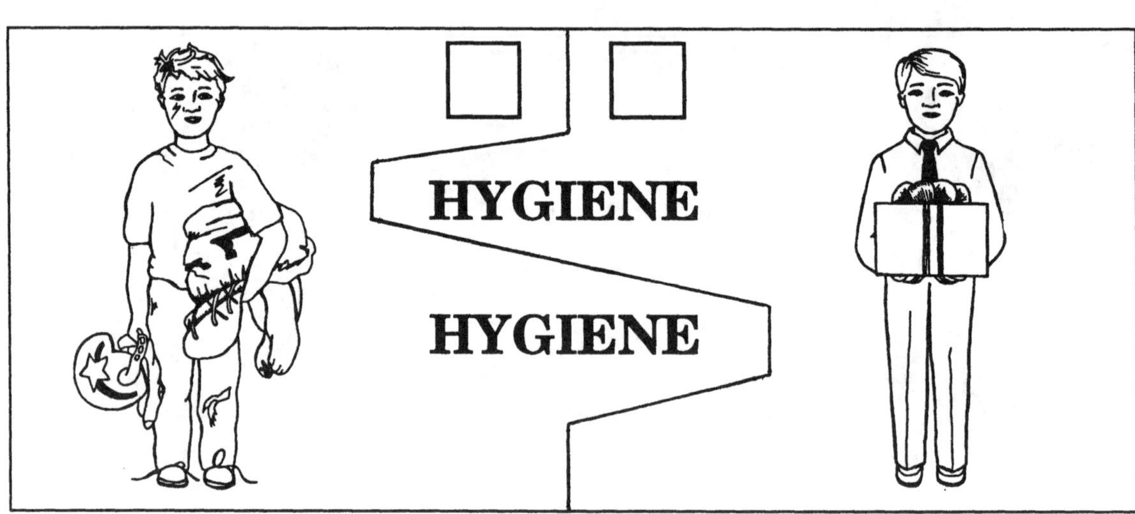
HYGIENE
HYGIENE

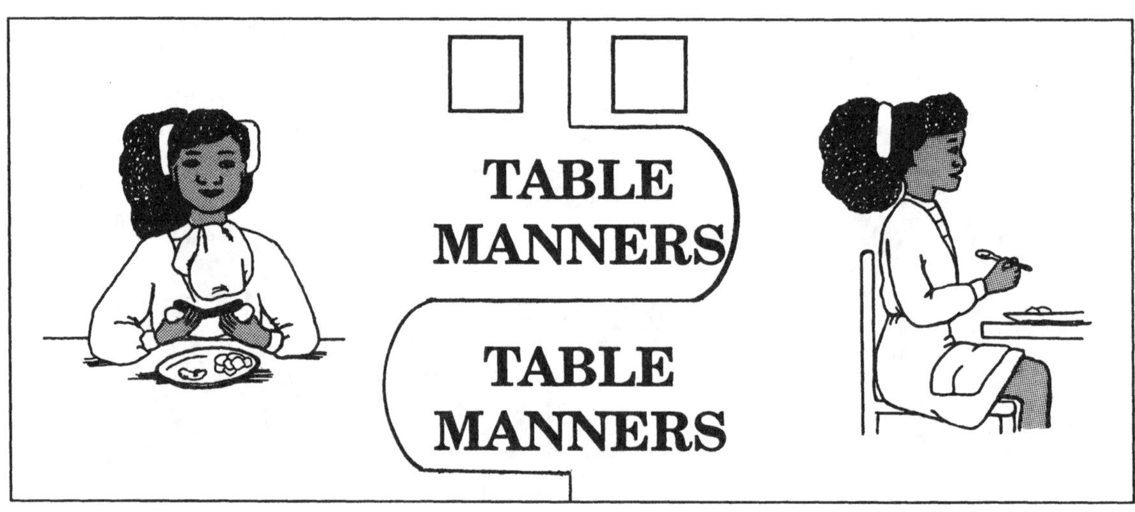
TABLE
MANNERS
TABLE
MANNERS

Lesson C

OBJECTIVE:

To differentiate between more formal and more casual situations

MATERIALS:

1. *Checking Myself* (See *Appendix I*; one per student.)
2. *Thought Bubble* (See *Appendix O*; one transparency.)
3. *Formal or Casual Situation Cards* (See page 412; one per pair of students and one transparency.)
4. Scissors (One per pair of students)
5. *Tick-Tack-Toe* (See page 413; one per pair of students.)

PREPARATORY SET:

Pair students (see *Appendix P*). Quickly review the rules for tick-tack-toe and then ask pairs to play a game of tick-tack-toe with each other. Tell students you wanted to make certain they knew how to play this game because they will be playing a similar game called "Formal or Casual Tick-Tack-Toe" later in this lesson.

PLAN:

1. Distribute and display the discussion guideline sheet called *Checking Myself*. Ask students to complete the goal statement with the words "raise my hand," or use another classroom discussion goal more appropriate for your group (see page 26). Tell students that you will be having a discussion about being formal or casual. Explain that the questions you will be asking have no certain right or wrong answers. Tell students that it's important that they share their thoughts. Instruct them to put an "X" on their sheets each time they raise their hands.
2. Model use of the *Checking Myself* sheet while thinking aloud. A scripted example follows:

   Introduction

   I am going to pretend to be one of you completing this sheet during the discussion we will be having. I will tell you the thoughts I'm having while I'm completing this sheet. When I hold up this Thought Bubble, *you'll know the words I'm saying are actually what I'm thinking.*

Actual Model

While holding up the *Thought Bubble* say, *OK, the teacher just asked, "Have you ever been with a good friend in a more formal situation?" Let's see.... I sat next to a good friend when my sister graduated last year, and that was a more formal situation. I'm raising my hand so the teacher knows that I have an answer. I'll put an "X" on my paper.* Put the *Thought Bubble* down and mark an "X" on the transparency.

3. Proceed with the discussion by asking the following questions:

   - When have you ever been with a good friend in a more formal situation?
   - What can you do if you are in a situation and you aren't sure if you should be more formal or more casual?
   - Who are some adults with whom you usually need to be more formal?
   - Who are some adults with whom you can usually be more casual?

   The purpose of this discussion is for students to gain an understanding that it's not just the age of the person they are with that determines whether a situation is formal or casual. When students are unsure of whether to be more formal or casual, encourage them to watch and to listen awhile to learn what other people are doing and saying and then to follow suit.

   After the discussion, have students complete the bottom of *Checking Myself.*

4. Process the use of this sheet by asking the following question or another one more appropriate for your group:

   - Why do you think that it's important to raise your hand to share your ideas during a discussion?

5. Distribute and display *Formal or Casual Situation Cards.* Read aloud the two situations in row one. Ask students to work with their partners to decide which of the two situations is more formal and which is more casual. Call on a pair of students to share their answers. Write the letter "F" for "formal" in the upper left box of the formal situation, and the letter "C" for "casual" in the upper left box of the casual situation. Ask students to mark their sheets the same way. Follow the same procedure for rows two through five.

6. Distribute the scissors. Ask partners to cut out their cards along the dotted lines.

7. Instruct students to separate the cards into two piles—formal and casual. Each player chooses a set of cards.

8. Distribute *Tick-Tack-Toe.* Tell students they will be playing "Formal or Casual Tick-Tack-Toe," only they will be using the F's and C's written on their situation

cards instead of marking X's and O's. Instruct students to play using the following procedure:

a. Tell students that the person who chose the "casual" cards will be first.

b. Player 1 chooses a card from his or her pile and reads the situation aloud. The player then gives an example of something that would be appropriate to do or say in the casual situation (e.g., suppose the card says, "Playing cards with your brother," the student could say, "I could have a casual posture while I'm sitting"). After making the statement, Player 1 places the card on the tick-tack-toe board.

c. Player 2 chooses a card from her or his pile and reads the situation aloud. The player then gives an example of something that would be appropriate to do or say in the formal situation (e.g., suppose the card says, "Receiving an award," the player could say, "I could use more formal words by saying, 'Thank you very much for this award' "). After making the statement, Player 2 places the card on the tick-tack-toe board.

d. Play continues until one of the students in the pair gets a tick-tack-toe, or until the game ends in a "draw."

e. Players may then switch piles of cards and play another game as directed above.

(The game can also be played without having students tell an appropriate thing to do or say. After sorting the cards into piles, the students could simply play tick-tack-toe, using their respective formal or casual cards.)

9. Say sincerely to the class: *You are an awesome class! You make teaching social skills totally tremendous!*

Names ______________________________

FORMAL OR CASUAL SITUATION CARDS

1.	☐ Eating at a fancy restaurant	☐ Eating at a fast food restaurant
2.	☐ Greeting a good friend at a store	☐ Greeting a police officer at a bike safety class
3.	☐ Taking a phone message from your dad's boss	☐ Taking a phone message from your sister's friend
4.	☐ Going roller skating	☐ Going to a graduation ceremony
5.	☐ Having a guest speaker in your classroom	☐ Having your favorite teacher in your classroom

Names ______________________________

TICK-TACK-TOE

Lessons X, Y, and Z

Due to similarities in format, the final three lesson plans for each unit in *Social Star* are provided in *Appendix A*. Substitute the phrase "being formal or casual" whenever a "______" appears in the lesson plans. Information specific to this unit follows.

LESSON X PREPARATORY SET:

Tell students you will be reading the following situations to them. They should put their thumbs up if the person in the situation is being appropriate according to the formality or casualness of the situation. They should put their thumbs down if the person is not being appropriate.

- Maria wears old shorts and a T-shirt to a graduation ceremony.
- Lee says, "Good morning, Victor. It is such a great pleasure to see you this morning," when he sees his best friend before school.
- Jolisa sits up straight during her aunt's wedding ceremony.
- Ann eats her food with her fingers at a fancy restaurant.

LESSON Y PREPARATORY SET:

Darken the room, if you prefer, and ask students to visualize themselves correctly using this social skill by reading the following script:

> *Let's take a few moments to relax.... Make sure you are sitting in a comfortable position.... Close your eyes if you feel like it.... On the count of three, take a very slow, deep breath. One . . . two . . . three.... Breathe in deeply.... Now breathe out slowly.... Let your entire body relax.... Now imagine yourself getting home from school. You wore nice clothes to school because it was picture day. Your friends have asked you to come outside to play. You ask yourself, "Will playing with my friends be more formal or more casual?" You know it will be more casual, so you decide to change and put on play clothes. Think about how proud you feel for remembering to take off your good clothes before going outside to play.*

LESSON Z PLOT SITUATION:

Ask students to pretend that a friend is angry at them and they don't know why.

LESSON Z ROADBLOCK EXAMPLES:

- Deciding what to say or do when you aren't sure if a situation is formal or informal
- Remembering to be polite and respectful whether the situation is formal or casual
- Being in a formal situation that you have never been in before

Name ______________________

Being Formal T-Chart

LOOKS LIKE...	SOUNDS LIKE...
using appropriate body talk • standing or sitting more straight than casual	saying • "Hello, Mr. _______." • "Good morning, Mrs. _______." • "Thank you very much." • "Please, may I...?"

Name ______________________

Being Casual T-Chart

LOOKS LIKE...	SOUNDS LIKE...
using appropriate body talk • standing or sitting in a relaxed position	saying • "Hi!" • "Whatcha doin'?" • "What's new?"

HOME

Pretend your mom's boss stops by to drop off some papers for you to give to her when she gets home. Show the posture, personal space, and words you could say in this more formal situation.

SCHOOL

Pretend your teacher is introducing you to an adult who is a guest speaker in your class. Show the posture, personal space, and words you could say in this more formal situation.

COMMUNITY

Pretend you are eating at a fancy restaurant. Show the posture, table manners, and words you could say in this more formal situation.

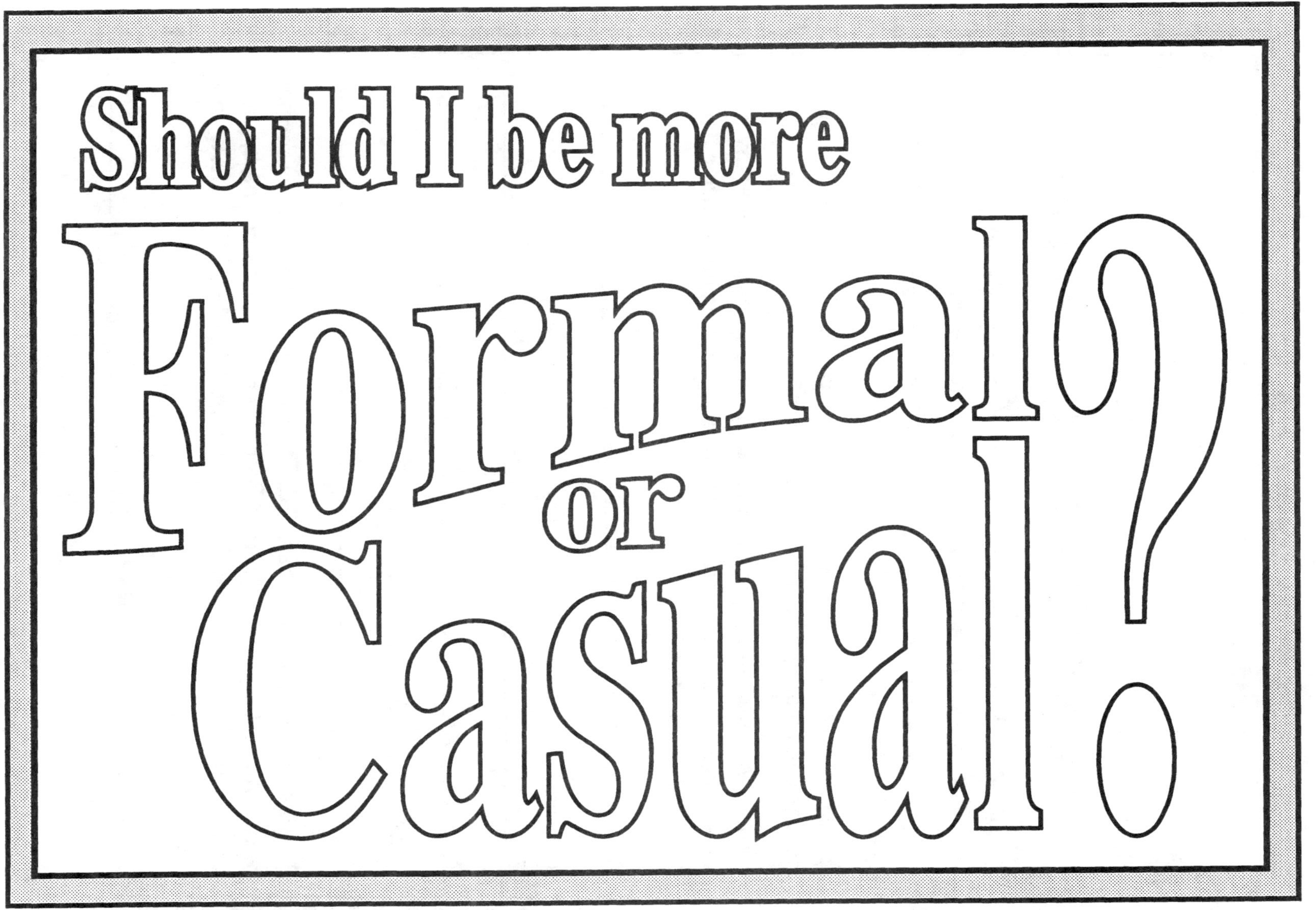
Should I be more
Formal
or
Casual?

HOME-A-GRAM

Dear Family,

At school, we have been talking about the social skill called

BEING FORMAL OR CASUAL

I learned that *being formal* means being more proper and respectful and *being casual* means being more natural, relaxed, or informal.

I know that when I'm with other people I should ask myself, "Should I be more formal or casual?"

If I know how and when to be formal or casual, I can make a good impression on others, and I can feel proud.

I know that my clothes, my words, my posture, my hygiene, my personal space, or my manners can change depending on whether I'm in a formal or casual situation.

An example of a more formal situation is: ______________________

____

____

An example of a more casual situation is: ______________________

____

____

I will tell you how I can say, "Hi. How's it goin'?" in a more formal way. After I do, please sign my "Being Formal or Casual" badge so I can return it to school and become a SOCIAL SUPER STAR this week.

From: ______________________________

Lesson X

OBJECTIVE:

To observe the appropriate use of _____ in a home, school, or community role play

MATERIALS:

1. _____ classroom poster (See page 13.)
2. _____ *T-Chart* (One per student and one transparency of page within the unit)
3. *Blank T-Chart* (See *Appendix L*; one per student and one transparency.)
4. _____ *Show Time* (One transparency of page found within the _____ unit)
5. *Thought Bubble* (See *Appendix O*; one for teacher and student use.)

PREPARATORY SET:

Follow the Preparatory Set described for Lesson X within the _____ unit.

PLAN:

1. Quickly review the definition and skill step(s) for _____ by referring to the _____ classroom poster.
2. Distribute and display the _____ *T-Chart*. Tell students it is a chart showing what a person looks and sounds like when appropriately using the social skill of _____ . Review the information listed in the chart and encourage students to make additions. Although time consuming, *T-Charts* can be more effective if students create their own with the educator, then compile the information on a single *T-Chart* for all to see. If you choose this option, use the *Blank T-Chart*.
3. Display _____ *Show Time*. Discuss each situation and explain that everyone will be role playing these situations during the _____ *Show Time* activity in the next lesson. Today will be a rehearsal for their _____ *Show Time*.
4. Model each situation and verbalize self-talk using the *Thought Bubble*. (For units 9–15, remind students that use of inappropriate body talk can sabotage any social skill.)
5. Choose a student to role play one of the situations twice (see pages 18–20). The first time, the student should verbalize self-talk using the *Thought Bubble*. The second time, the student should not verbalize self-talk.
6. Remind students that the next lesson will be _____ *Show Time*.

Lesson Y

OBJECTIVE:

To demonstrate use of _____ in a home, school, or community situation

MATERIALS:

1. _____ *Show Time* (One transparency of page found within the _____ unit)
2. _____ *Show Time* sign (One or more per student; found in _____ unit immediately after _____ *Show Time.*)
3. Markers or crayons for each student

PREPARATORY SET:

Ask students to visualize by reading the script provided for Lesson Y within the _____ unit.

PLAN:

1. Display _____ *Show Time.* Review the home, school, and community situations which students will be role playing during today's _____ *Show Time* activity.
2. Distribute markers or crayons and a copy or copies of _____ *Show Time* sign to each student. Tell students that you will be calling on them to role play the _____ *Show Time* situations. While they are waiting their turns to role play, students should decorate their _____ *Show Time* signs so that they can be hung in predetermined locations throughout the school during Lesson Z. Encourage students to avoid interrupting so that you may observe the _____ *Show Time* role plays.
3. Students may be called to role play individually or in pairs. (For additional information on role playing, see pages 18–20.) If a pair is role playing, one person can be the observer while the other student role plays with the educator. The students should then switch roles. It is important to provide feedback to students. (For additional information on feedback, see page 21.)
4. If time allows, ask students which past social skills they have used successfully. Have students identify how they feel when they use their social skills appropriately. Ask students which social skills they might like to improve.
5. Collect _____ *Show Time* signs to hang during Lesson Z.

Lesson Z

OBJECTIVES:

1. To review and practice cognitive planning techniques
2. To identify and discuss _____ roadblocks
3. To prepare an activity to transfer use of _____ into the home

MATERIALS:

1. *Cognitive Planning Formula* chart (See page 12.)
2. *Secret Formula Pages* (See *Appendix N*; one of the two pages per student.)
3. *Self-Management Sheet* (See *Appendix H*; one of the 10 choices per student and one transparency.)
4. *Roadblock Sheet* (See *Appendix R*; one per student and one transparency.)
5. _____ *Home-A-Gram* (See page found in the _____ unit; one per student and one transparency.)
6. _____ badge (See *Appendix S*; one per student.)
7. *Social Super Stars* display (See page 13.)
8. Completed *Show Time* signs (Colored during Lesson Y)

PREPARATORY SET:

To foster internalization of the cognitive planning steps called STOP, PLOT, GO, SO, ask students to participate in a "Beat the Clock" activity (see pages 53–54).

PLAN:

1. Display the *Cognitive Planning Formula* chart and remind students that they can use the four steps to solve problems they may have in their lives. As an option to reinforce this concept, have students complete one of the two *Secret Formula Pages* by addressing a real-life problem they need to solve or just recently solved. (These pages do not need to be used in every Lesson Z but should be used occasionally. They may also be used at any time when a student is trying to solve a problem. This shows the usefulness of the STOP, PLOT, GO, SO strategy across all areas of daily living.)

2. Review STOP with students by reminding them that STOP means stay calm and use self-control. Review what *self-control* means and why it's important. Ask students to practice one of the strategies for staying calm and using self-control by reading one of the six scripts on pages 48–49.

3. Review PLOT by reminding students that in whatever situations they find themselves, they should:

   - Decide exactly what the problem is
   - Brainstorm choices
   - Think about what might happen after each choice (consequences)
   - Pick a choice
   - Think about social skills needed

4. Have students practice the five steps to PLOT by asking them to pretend that... (use the plot situation described for Lesson Z within the _____ unit). Students can work individually, with partners, in small groups, or as a whole class.

5. Review GO by reminding students that after they pick a choice, they need to actually go ahead with the plan by doing it.

6. Review SO by reminding students that after they use their choice, they should ask themselves "So, how did my plan work?" If the plan worked well, they could praise or reward themselves. If the plan did not work, they could think about why it didn't work or what they would do differently next time.

7. Bring the discussion back to the specific social skill of _____. Tell students it's important for them to check how they are doing at using _____ during and outside of class. Distribute the chosen *Self-Management Sheet* and give directions for its use. (See pages 24–25 for a general discussion of self-management strategies.)

8. Distribute and display the *Roadblock Sheet*. Tell students that it will sometimes be difficult to use _____ because of roadblocks. Explain that a roadblock is something that may get in the way of successful use of a social skill. Remind students not to become discouraged if use of their social skills does not always turn out right. Suggest to students that when a roadblock occurs, they may need to take a "detour" rather than give up. Make students aware that a roadblock situation is an opportunity for them to use the SO step of STOP, PLOT, GO, SO. They could ask themselves questions such as how they did, what might have gone wrong, and how the roadblock could be dealt with in a more positive way next time. Examples of _____ roadblocks are described in Lesson Z within each specific social skill unit. Give students the opportunity to think of additional roadblocks that may occur.

9. Distribute the _____ *Home-A-Gram* and a _____ badge to each student. Have students complete the *Home-A-Gram* as directed (see pages 23–24).

10. Point to the *Social Super Stars* display. Remind students that their badges will be added to the display once they are brought back signed.

11. Distribute the completed _____ *Show Time* signs and ask students to hang them in the predetermined location(s).

Appendix B

Social Communication Skills Rating Scale

(Adult Form—General Interaction Skills)

Name of Student: ______________________ Grade: ________

Age: ____________ Date rating scale completed: ______________

Name of person completing rating scale: ______________________

Relationship with student (e.g., parent, case manager, regular education teacher): ______________________

DIRECTIONS: Rate this student on how well he or she uses the following social skills. Circle:

1—if the skill is **SELDOM** used correctly.

2—if the skill is **SOMETIMES** used correctly.

3—if the skill is **ALMOST ALWAYS** used correctly.

For example, a student who usually speaks too loudly would be rated as follows:

VOLUME—Uses a speaking volume appropriate for the situation.	①	2	3

Please give examples or comments when appropriate (e.g., if you give a low rating for volume, explain if the student speaks too loudly or too softly).

	RATING		
SOCIAL COMMUNICATION SKILL	**SELDOM**	**SOMETIMES**	**ALMOST ALWAYS**
1. EYE CONTACT—Looks at others when speaking or listening.	1	2	3

Comments:

SOCIAL COMMUNICATION SKILL	RATING		
	SELDOM	SOMETIMES	ALMOST ALWAYS
2. VOLUME—Uses a speaking volume appropriate for the situation. Comments:	1	2	3
3. TONE OF VOICE—Avoids using inappropriate voice tones (braggy, whiney, bossy, sarcastic). Comments:	1	2	3
4. FACIAL EXPRESSION—Avoids using inappropriate facial expressions (looking rude, pouty, stuck up). Comments:	1	2	3
5. POSTURE—Uses standing and sitting postures appropriate for the situation. Comments:	1	2	3
6. PERSONAL SPACE—Stands or sits a distance from others that is appropriate for the situation. Comments:	1	2	3
7. HYGIENE—Keeps body and clothes clean on a regular basis. Comments:	1	2	3

SOCIAL COMMUNICATION SKILL	RATING: SELDOM	SOMETIMES	ALMOST ALWAYS
8. BODY TALK—Uses body talk appropriate for the situation. (Body talk is a combination of skills 1–7.) Comments:	1	2	3
9. MANNERS—Uses manners which are appropriate for the situation (saying please, thank you, excuse me, and I'm sorry). Comments:	1	2	3
10. LISTENING BASICS—Uses body talk that says "I'm listening" and thinks about what is being said. Comments:	1	2	3
11. STAYING ON TOPIC/SWITCHING TOPICS—Sticks to the topic of a conversation or changes topics smoothly. Comments:	1	2	3
12. CONVERSATIONS—Starts conversations with a greeting, takes turns talking and listening, and ends with a farewell. Comments:	1	2	3
13. INTERRUPTING—Interrupts in an appropriate way and only when necessary. Comments:	1	2	3

SOCIAL COMMUNICATION SKILL	RATING: SELDOM	SOMETIMES	ALMOST ALWAYS
14. RIGHT TIME AND PLACE—Thinks about whether it is the appropriate time and place to do or say things. Comments:	1	2	3
15. BEING FORMAL OR CASUAL—Knows why and how to be more formal (proper and respectful) or more casual (relaxed, natural). Comments:	1	2	3

Student Social Skill Summary Form

STUDENT'S NAME:	Identified as a strength	Identified as problematic	Skill has been taught in class		
1. Eye Contact					
2. Volume					
3. Tone of Voice					
4. Facial Expression					
5. Posture					
6. Personal Space					
7. Hygiene					
8. Body Talk					
9. Manners					
10. Listening Basics					
11. Staying on Topic/Switching Topics					
12. Conversations					
13. Interrupting					
14. Right Time and Place					
15. Being Formal or Casual					

Class Summary Form

Mark social skills identified as strengths with a "+" and those identified as problematic with a "–".

SOCIAL SKILLS: / STUDENTS' NAMES										
1. Eye Contact										
2. Volume										
3. Tone of Voice										
4. Facial Expression										
5. Posture										
6. Personal Space										
7. Hygiene										
8. Body Talk										
9. Manners										
10. Listening Basics										
11. Staying on Topic/Switching Topics										
12. Conversations										
13. Interrupting										
14. Right Time and Place										
15. Being Formal or Casual										

Socialville Buildings

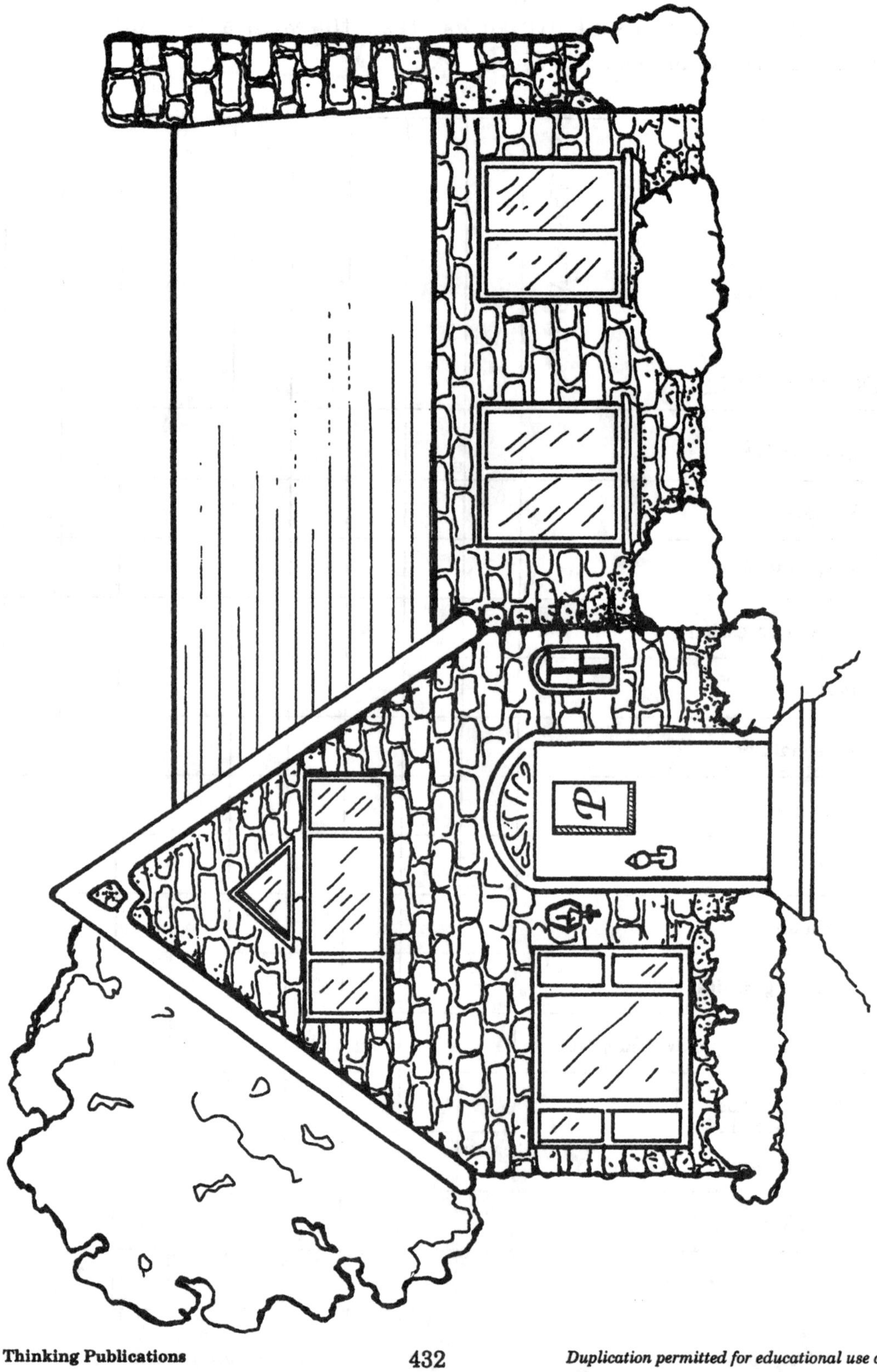

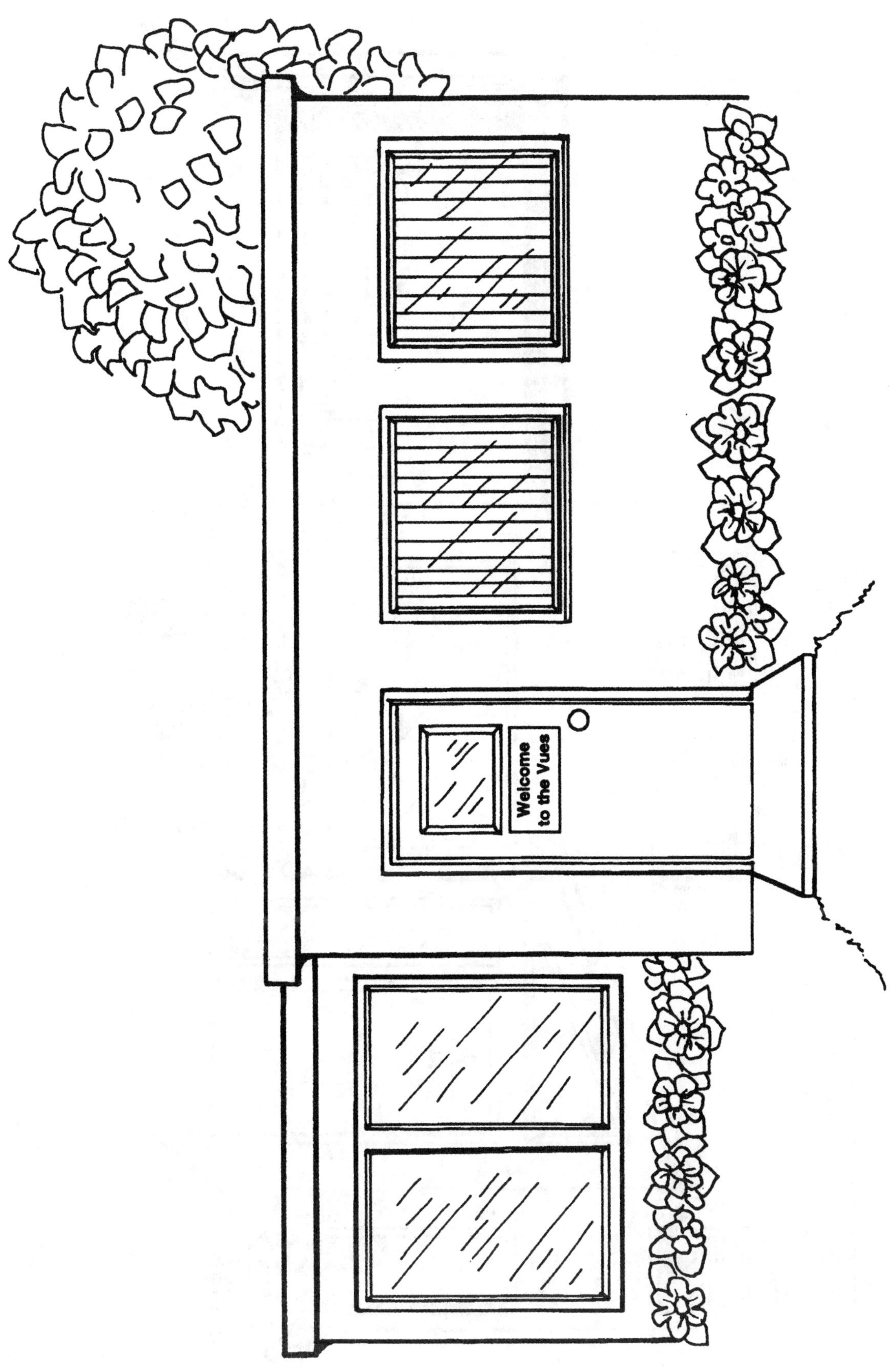
Welcome
to the Vues

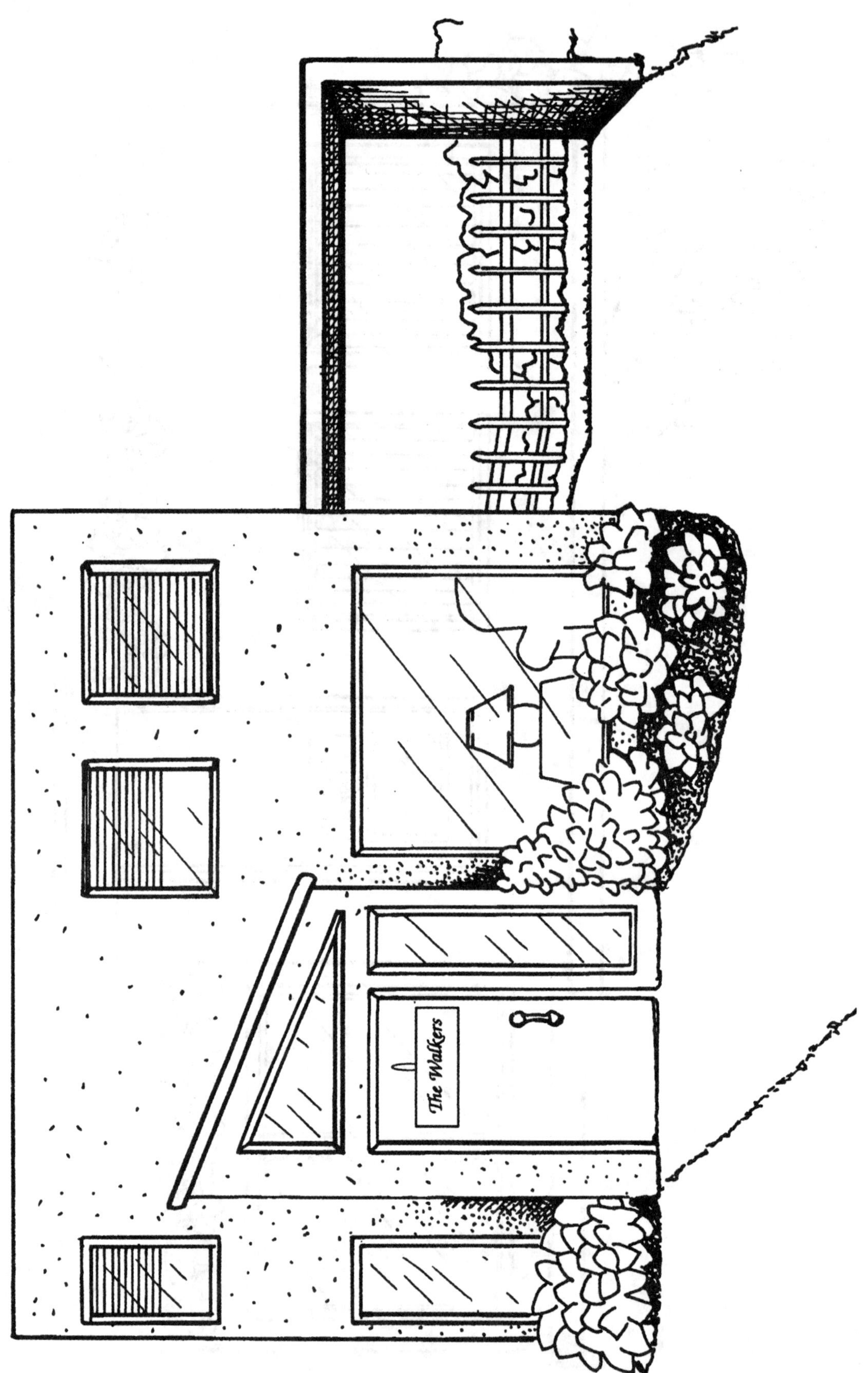
The Walkers

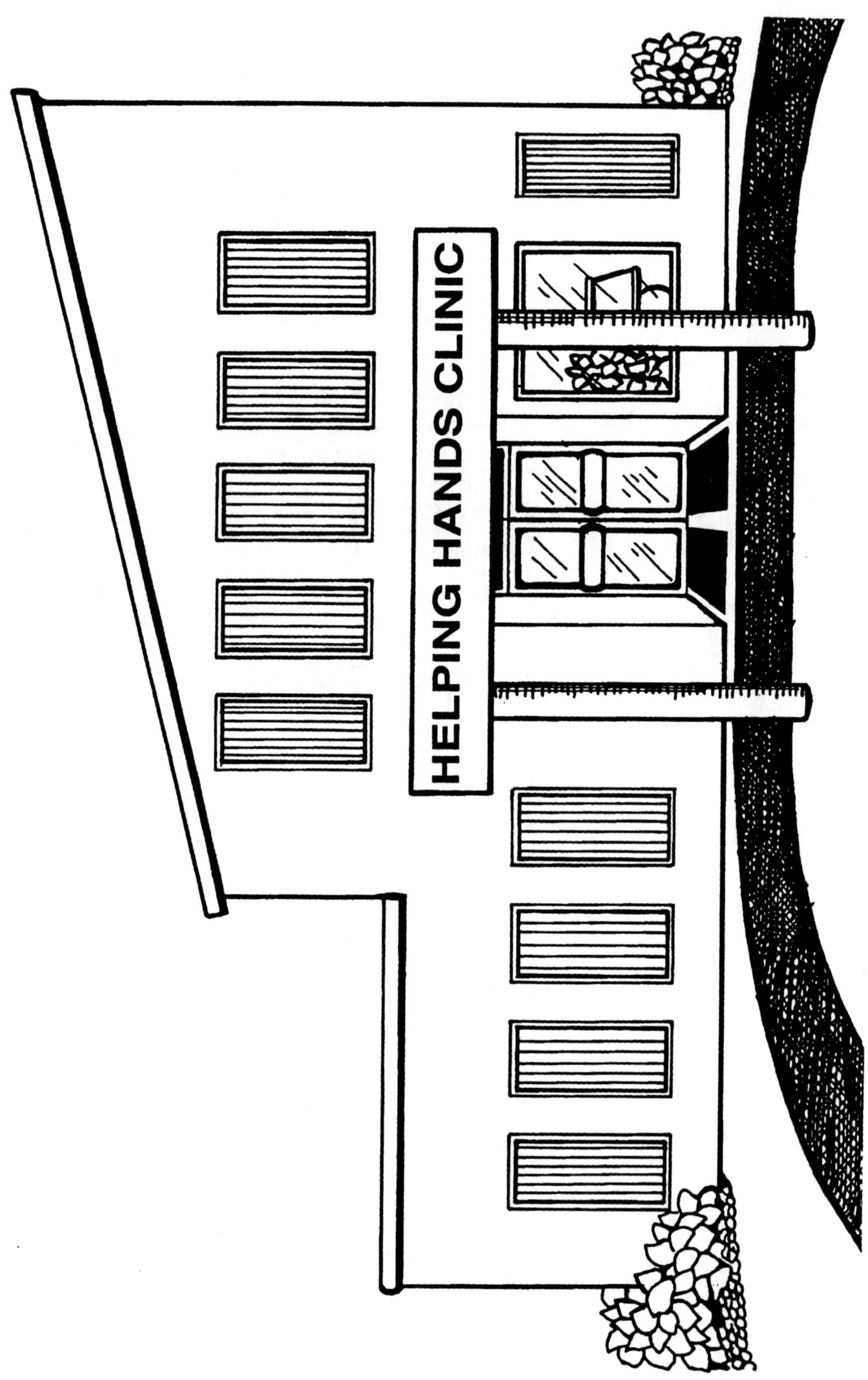
HELPING HANDS CLINIC

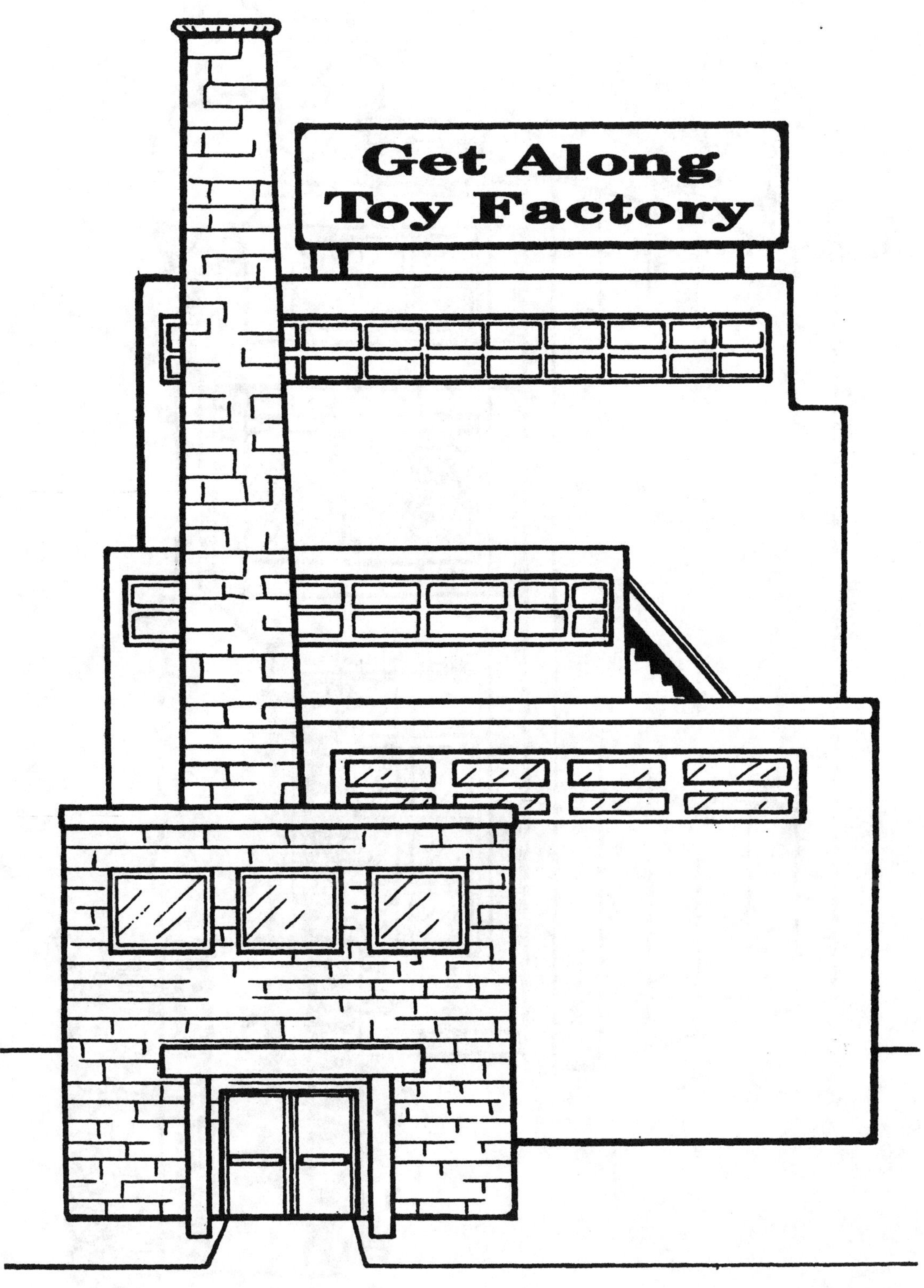
Get Along
Toy Factory

SOCIALVILLE
PARKS
DEPARTMENT
OPEN

Good Meals-Good Manners
Restaurant

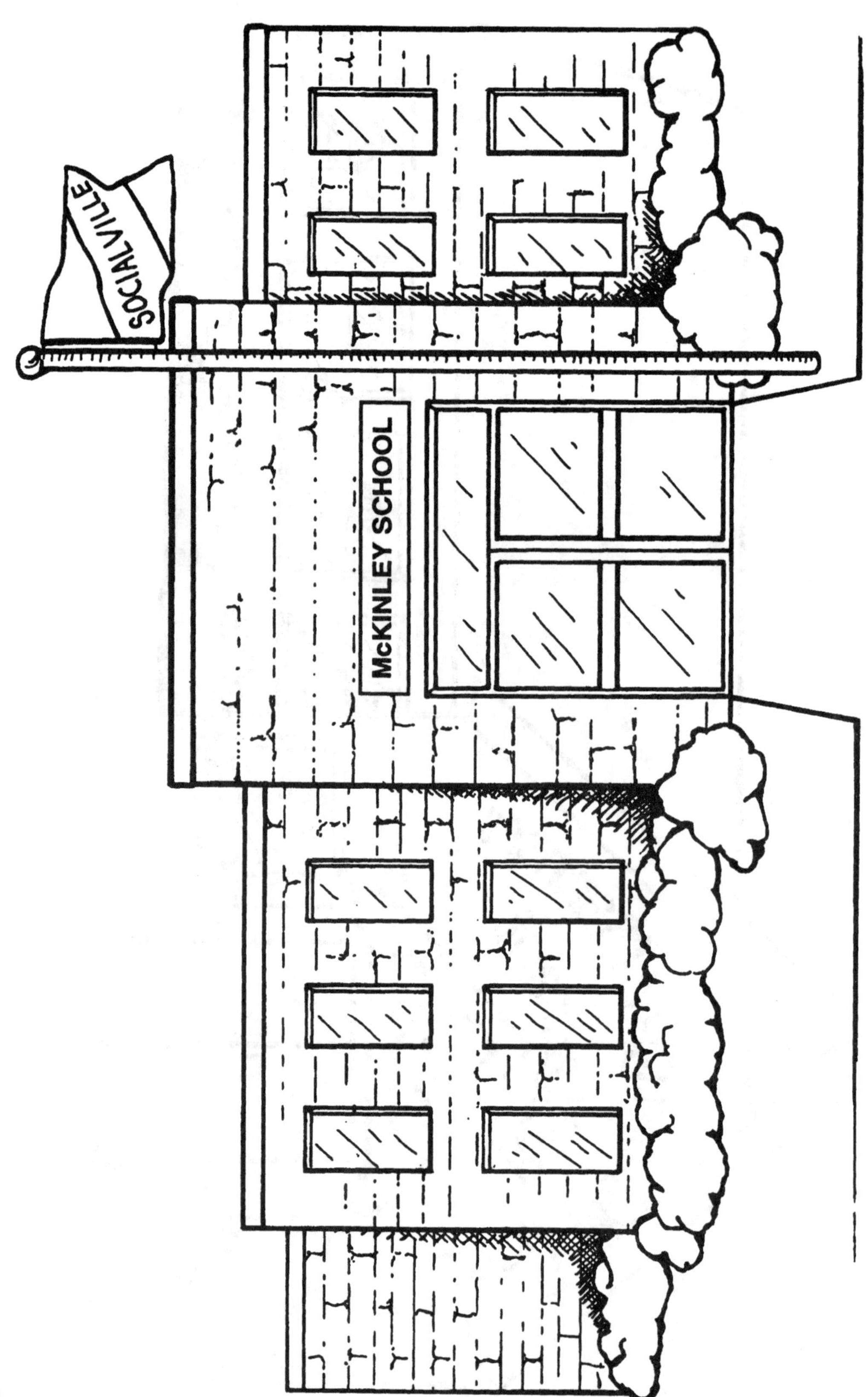
SOCIALVILLE
McKINLEY SCHOOL

Socialville Characters

JOLISA WALKER

LEE VUE

JESSE WALKER

CORIN WALKER

MIKA VUE

HO VUE

JOE JACKSON

MARY JACKSON

ANN OLSON

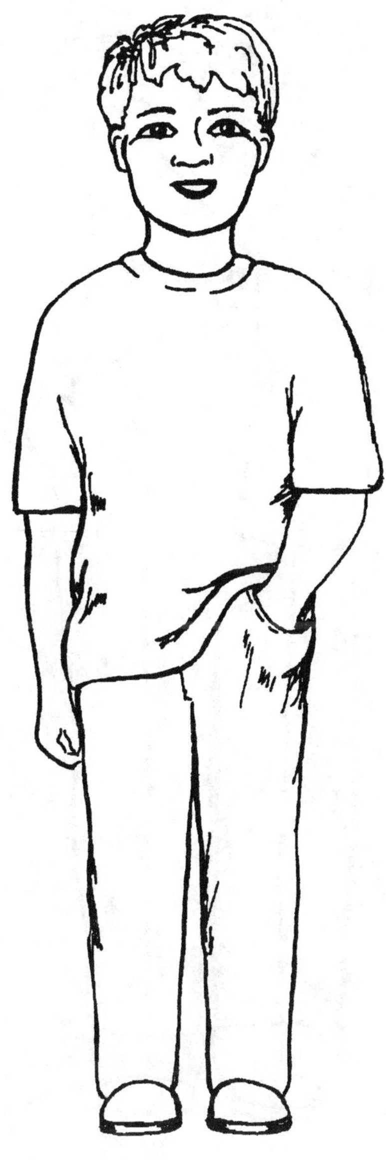

MIKE OLSON

RICARDO PARRA

DR. JUANITA PARRA

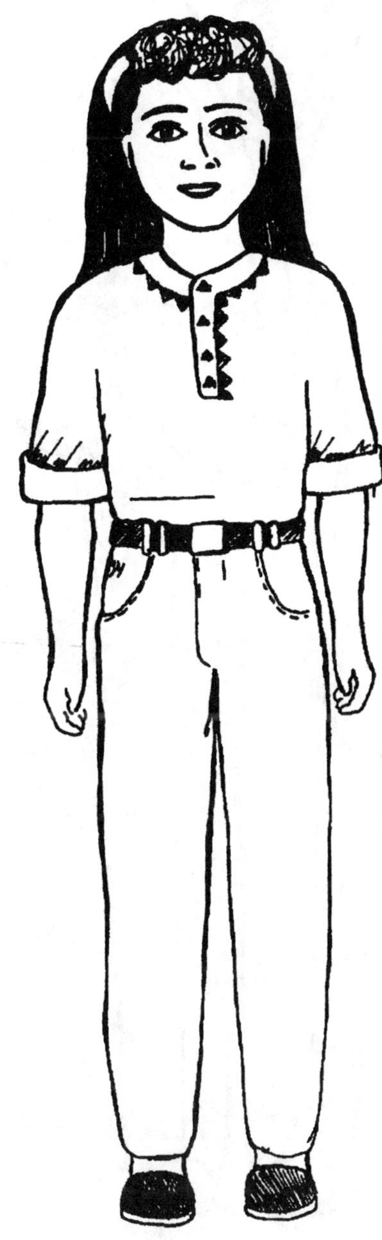

MARIA PARRA

VICTOR PARRA

MRS. CORA MARRERO

MR. MARCUS AARON

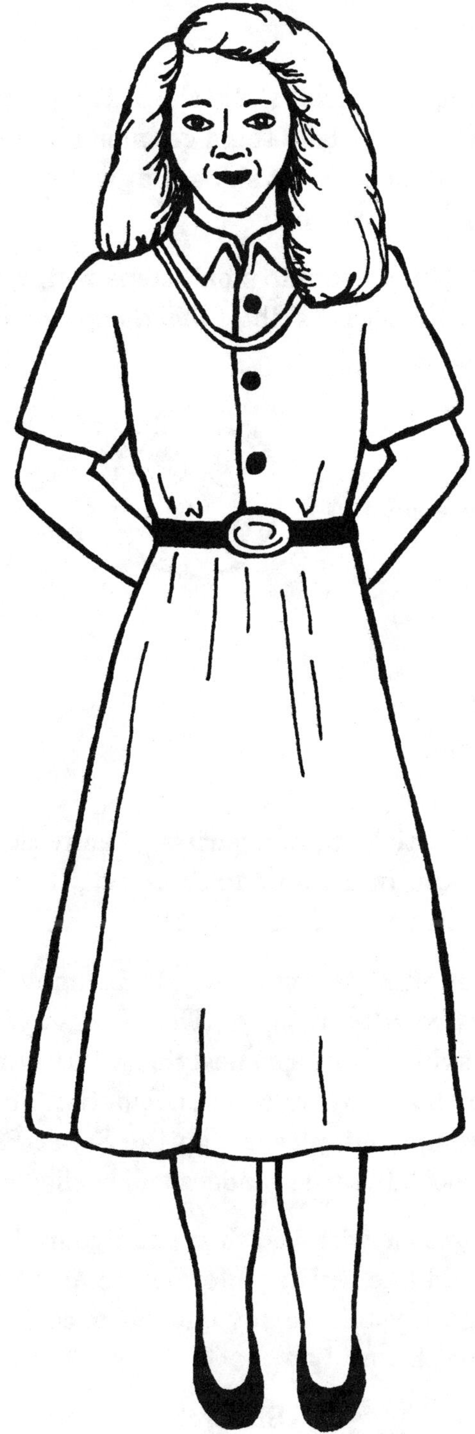

MS. PAULA HESS

Appendix G

Parent Letter

Dear

Your child will be participating in a social skills class. The purpose of the class is to teach children social skills which will help them get along better with others and to feel better about themselves. A list of social skills that will be taught during class is attached.

Each social skill taught is broken down into small steps with symbols to make them easier to learn. For example, the social skill of *facial expression* is divided into the following skill steps and symbols:

1. Ask myself: What is my face saying?

2. Stop: If my face can get me into trouble
   (rude, pouty, stuck-up)

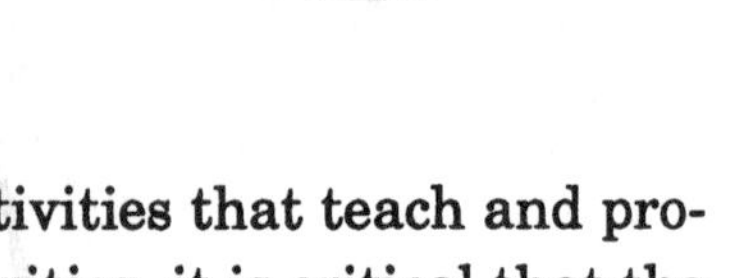

During class, your child will participate in a variety of activities that teach and provide practice for each social skill. In addition to these activities, it is critical that the skills be practiced in other settings including at home.

At the end of each social skill unit, your child will be bringing home a note called a *Home-A-Gram* and a *Super Social Star* badge. The *Home-A-Gram* will provide you with information about the skill. It will also describe an activity related to the skill for your child to complete at home with your participation and supervision. When the activity is successfully completed, please sign the *Super Social Star* badge and have your child return it to school. Returned badges will be displayed in the classroom.

I look forward to working together with you to expand your child's skills for getting along with others. If you would like further information about the class, please contact me any time. In addition, if you have any questions, concerns, or suggestions, I will be glad to discuss them with you.

Sincerely,

Self-Management Sheets

EDUCATOR DIRECTIONS: Fill in the name of a social skill and a description of the time during which it is to be evaluated (e.g., during science, during free time, during lunch) before making copies for student use.

DIRECTIONS: Rate yourself by circling either "great," "OK," or "needs improvement." Write your comments if you want. Ask your teacher to rate you too.

SOCIAL SKILL	MY RATING	THE TEACHER'S RATING
______	GREAT	GREAT
EVALUATED DURING:	OK	OK
______	NEEDS IMPROVEMENT	NEEDS IMPROVEMENT
______	Comments: ______ ______ ______ ______	Comments: ______ ______ ______ ______
		______ *Teacher's Signature*

EDUCATOR DIRECTIONS: Fill in the name of a social skill and a description of the time during which it is to be evaluated (e.g., during a meal, while playing with friends) before making copies for student use. Send the self-management sheet home with the student. Attach any necessary information for the students' parent(s) concerning use of the sheet.

DIRECTIONS: Rate yourself by circling either "great," "OK," or "needs improvement." Write your comments if you want. Ask a parent to rate you too.

SOCIAL SKILL	MY RATING	THE PARENT'S RATING
______________ **EVALUATED DURING:** ______________ ______________	**GREAT** **OK** **NEEDS IMPROVEMENT** Comments: ______________ ______________ ______________ ______________	**GREAT** **OK** **NEEDS IMPROVEMENT** Comments: ______________ ______________ ______________ ______________ ______________ *Parent's Signature*

EDUCATOR DIRECTIONS: Before making student copies of either self-management sheet below, fill in where you want them to be turned in (e.g., on your desk, in a box, in your hand). Write the name of a specific social skill in the talk bubble or let the students write the name of any social skill they want to tell you about.

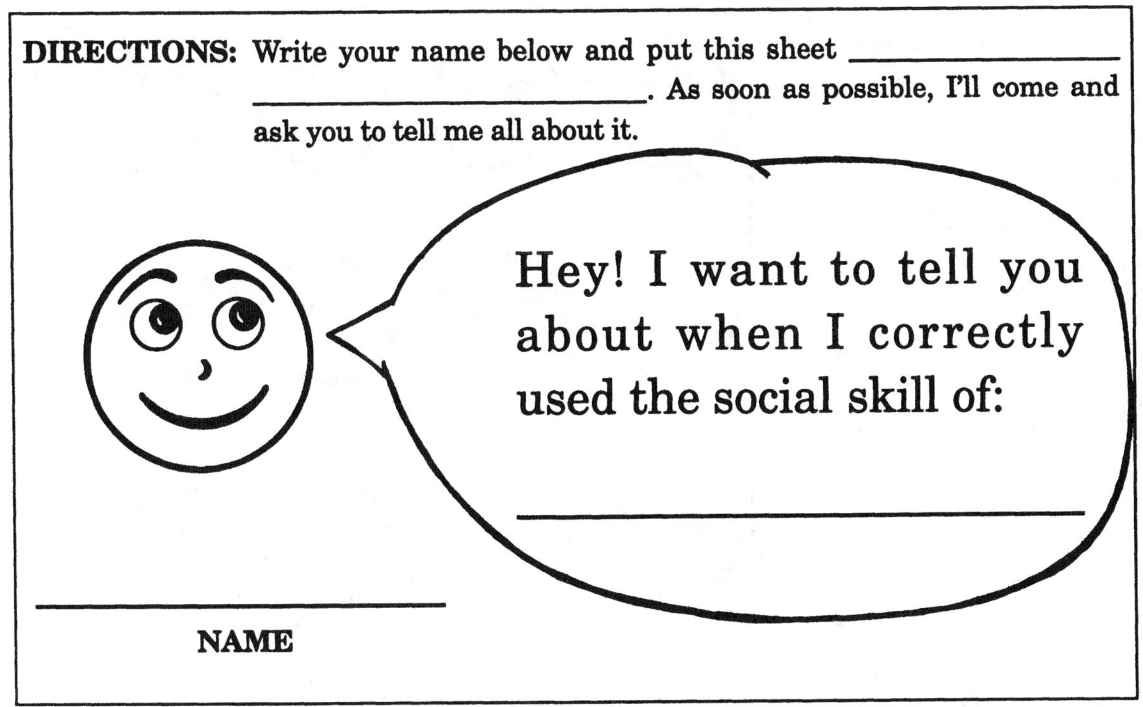

DIRECTIONS: Write your name below and put this sheet ______________________. As soon as possible, I'll come and ask you to tell me all about it.

Hey! I want to tell you about when I correctly used the social skill of:

____

____

NAME

DIRECTIONS: Write your name below and put this sheet ______________________. As soon as possible, I'll come and ask you to tell me all about it.

Just wait till you hear!
I did a great job with:

____

____

NAME

EDUCATOR DIRECTIONS: Fill in the name of a social skill and its skill step(s) on either self-management sheet below before making copies for student use.

DIRECTIONS: Draw a smile on one of the faces each time you use this social skill correctly. Then, IN YOUR MIND shout "Good Job!"

SOCIAL SKILL OF:

____

SKILL STEP(S):

____

____

____

____

NAME

DIRECTIONS: Mark a Social Star each time you use this social skill correctly. Then, picture yourself jumping up and down cheering for yourself.

SOCIAL SKILL OF:

____

SKILL STEP(S):

____

____

____

____

NAME

EDUCATOR DIRECTIONS: Before copying either self-management sheet below for student use, fill in the name of a social skill, or let students write the name of any social skill they have previously learned about.

DIRECTIONS: Fill in the blanks.

Great Job!

I did a great job using the social skill of:

____

When: ______________________________

Who with: ______________________________

I praised myself by: ______________________________

____

____

____

NAME

DIRECTIONS: Fill in the blanks.

I used the social skill of:

____

When: ______________________________

Who with: ______________________________

So? How did I do? ______________________________

____

____

Socialville

____

NAME

EDUCATOR DIRECTIONS: Fill in the name of a social skill and its skill step(s) on either self-management sheet below before making copies for student use.

DIRECTIONS: Each time you do a good job using this social skill, circle the next number below. (Start with 1.)

Social Skill: ______________________

Skill Step(s): ______________________

____

____

NAME

1 2 3 4 5 6 7 8 9 10 11 12

DIRECTIONS: Put a mark in the next space on the path each time you use this social skill correctly. (Start with space 1.)

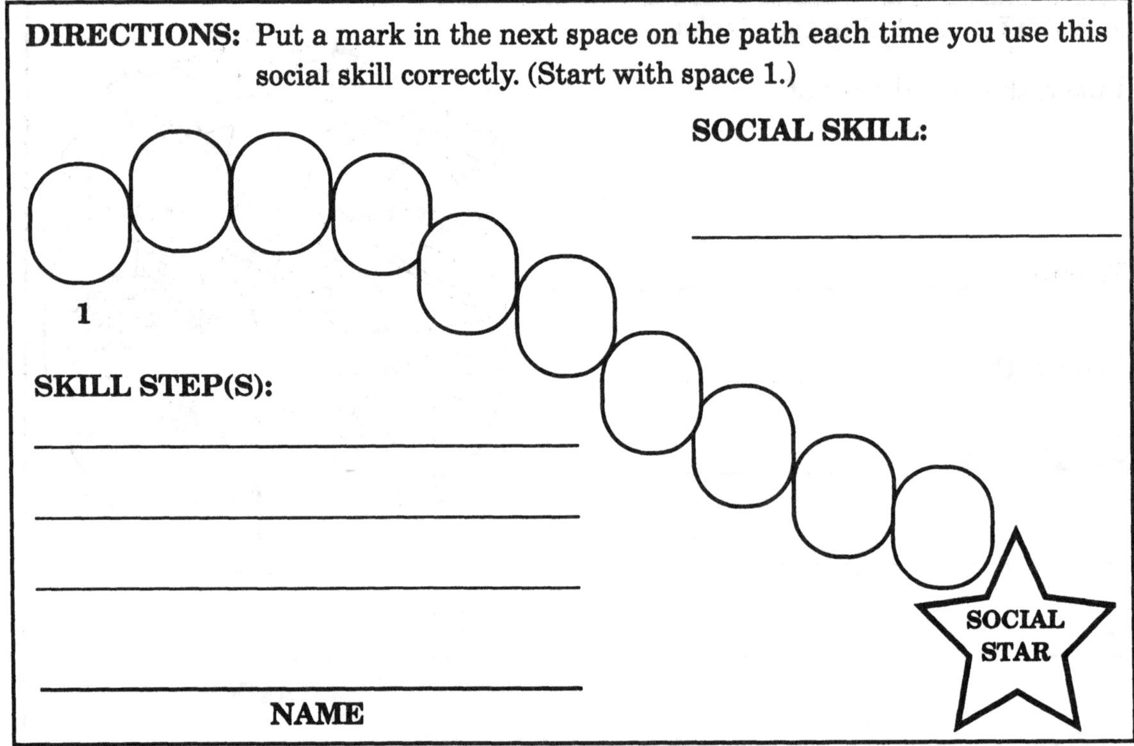

Checking Myself

Social Star

NAME: ______________________________

GOAL: During this class discussion, I will put an "X" in the box each time I:

____

____

I feel good about our class discussion because I:

____

____

Checking Myself

Social Star

NAME: ______________________________

GOAL: During this class discussion, I will put an "X" in the box each time I:

____

____

I feel good about our class discussion because I:

____

____

Social Gram

SOCIAL GRAM

______________________________,

you did a great job using the social skill of

____

when ______________________________

____

____

____

____
Signature

Great Coupon Caper

COUPON

NAME: ______________________

REASONS: ______________________

____

____

____
Signature

COUPON

NAME: ______________________

REASONS: ______________________

____

____

____
Signature

COUPON

NAME: ______________________

REASONS: ______________________

____

____

____
Signature

COUPON

NAME: ______________________

REASONS: ______________________

____

____

____
Signature

COUPON

NAME: ______________________

REASONS: ______________________

____

____

____
Signature

COUPON

NAME: ______________________

REASONS: ______________________

____

____

____
Signature

Blank T-Chart

Social Skill: ____________________

LOOKS LIKE...	SOUNDS LIKE...

Relaxation Scripts

RELAXATION SCRIPT FOR YOUNG CHILDREN

MATERIALS:

One sponge (or piece of a sponge) for each child

PLAN:

Pass out a sponge to each child. Say the following to students in a slow, calm manner.

1. Look at the sponge you have in your hands. Take the sponge and scrunch it up tight like mine. (Show the scrunched up sponge.)
2. Now, let go of your sponge very slowly. See how the sponge opens back up.
3. Try it again. Squeeze your sponge tightly. Now let go slowly.
4. Now I'd like to collect your sponges. (Collect sponges.)
5. Pretend that you are a sponge. Scrunch up your body tightly. Hold it.
6. Let your body out slowly just like when you let go of the sponge.
7. Your body should feel relaxed.
8. Try it again. Scrunch up your body. Take a deep breath.
9. Now, slowly let your body relax. Feel how nice your body feels.
10. Sometimes when you get angry, your body tightens up. You can act like a sponge and relax your body. This will help you stay in control.

A good resource for other relaxation activities is *Lazy Dogs and Sleeping Frogs* (1988) by Darrel Lang and Bill Stinson, Coulee Press, LaCrosse, WI.

PROGRESSIVE RELAXATION SCRIPT FOR OLDER CHILDREN

MATERIALS:

None

PLAN:

The following script should be read in a slow, calm manner:

1. We are going to learn a way to relax our bodies. When we keep our bodies relaxed, it is easier to have self-control.
2. Sit in your chair with your feet flat on the floor. Let your arms hang loosely at your sides.

3. You may close your eyes if you wish.
4. Take a slow, deep breath. Breathe in, two, three and out, two, three. In, two, three and out, two, three.
5. Keep breathing deeply and slowly.
6. Make your hands into tight fists. Keep making tight fists. (Pause for a few seconds.)
7. Now slowly open your hands again. You are teaching your muscles how to relax.
8. Now tighten your arms and your hands. Keep them tight. (Pause for a few seconds.)
9. Slowly relax your hands and then your arms.
10. Keep breathing deeply and slowly.
11. Now tighten your feet. Keep them tight. (Pause for a few seconds.)
12. Slowly relax your feet.
13. Now tighten your feet and your legs. Keep them tight. (Pause for a few seconds.)
14. Slowly relax your feet and legs.
15. Let's move up your body to your neck and face.
16. Scrunch up your face real tight. Keep it scrunched. (Pause for a few seconds.)
17. Let the muscles in your face slowly relax.
18. Keep breathing deeply and slowly.
19. Let your head slowly tilt forward so that your chin almost touches your chest.
20. Now slowly bring your head back up.
21. Let your head slowly tilt backward.
22. Slowly bring your head back up.
23. Tilt your head slowly from shoulder to shoulder. (Pause a few seconds.)
24. Take a slow, deep breath. Breath in, two, three, and out, two, three.
25. Just sit quietly for a few seconds. Think about how relaxed your body feels. (Pause for five to ten seconds.)
26. You can use this way of relaxing whenever you want. Remember, people who are more relaxed have better self-control.

Secret Formula Pages

★ ★ SECRET FORMULA ★ ★

STOP

I can stay calm by:

____

____

____

____

PLOT

My problem is: ______________________________

____

Choices:		Consequences:
1. ______________	→	______________
2. ______________	→	______________
3. ______________	→	______________

My choice: ______________________________

____

Social skills I need: ______________________________

____

GO

What I can say or do so I actually use my plan:

____

____

____

SO

How did my plan work?

____

____

____

____

★★★★ SECRET FORMULA ★★★★

STOP

I stayed calm by:

____

____

____

____

PLOT

My problem was: ______________________________

____

Choices:		Consequences:
1. ____________	→	____________
2. ____________	→	____________
3. ____________	→	____________

My choice was: ______________________________

____

Social skills I needed: ______________________________

____

GO

What I said or did so I actually used my plan:

____

____

____

SO

How did my plan work?

____

____

____

____

Thought Bubble

Pairing Activities

Pairing activities are fun activities for getting students into pairs. These activities increase the amount of socialization students do while learning new social skills. (Students cannot practice newly learned social skills if they are continually working by themselves.)

Each unit in *Social Star* includes several opportunities for students to work in pairs. Sometimes a specific pairing activity is suggested and other times the educator is asked to choose a pairing activity from the list that follows (or to develop a new one). Some of the pairing activities require prior preparation (e.g., copying, laminating, cutting). These materials are meant to be reused.

The pairing activities often require that students mingle and communicate with one another while forming pairs. Learning to work with several different people, despite personal preferences, is a critical skill. Before using pairing activities in the classroom, discuss with the students that the partner they work with may or may not be someone they were hoping for. Explain that they will be working with a variety of partners in class and that they need to cooperate and respect individual differences while working together. Students must learn to use body language that doesn't show disappointment. The educator may wish to demonstrate the body language (e.g., facial expression, voice tone, posture, proximity) students should use when they find their partners. It is helpful to demonstrate this in a humorous, exaggerated manner (e.g., use a huge smile, shake hands, say, "I'm so glad to be your partner").

SHOE MATCH

Have students remove one shoe and place it on a pile. The educator should hold up two shoes from the pile. The owners retrieve their shoes and become partners.

ANIMAL SOUNDS

Before this is used, duplicate two copies of the *Animal Cards* (see page 469). The educator should choose one pair of animal cards for every two students (e.g., two pigs, two cows). Distribute one animal card to each person. Students should walk around the room making the animal sounds on their card. When they find another student making the same animal sound, they become partners. For a variation, have students close their eyes during this activity.

LINE UP–FOLD UP

Students are asked to cooperatively form a line in a specific order (e.g., according to the months of their birthdays, the first letters of their first or last names, their heights). After telling students the chosen criteria for forming a line, the students should interact and line up with minimal educator assistance. As a variation, the students can be instructed not to talk and thus will have to find alternative methods of communicating with one another. After the students have formed a line, the line folds up and the two students at opposite ends become partners. The students who are second from each end become partners and so on towards the center of the line.

PICTURE PUZZLE

Before this activity is used, choose a variety of pictures. (These pictures can be drawn by students or cut from magazines.) Cut the pictures in half in "puzzle-piece" fashion. Choose one set of puzzle pieces for every two students. Give each student one puzzle piece. Students should find partners by locating other students whose puzzle pieces match theirs.

INSIDE-OUTSIDE CIRCLE

Ask half of the group to form a circle. Have the remaining students form an outside circle around the first circle. Have the students rotate in their circles in opposite directions until they are instructed to "stop." The inside circle should then face outward and the outside circle should face inward so that the students are looking at one another. The students are partners with the person each one is facing.

PICK-A-CARD ANY CARD

Write the name of each student on a separate card. Choose the top card, read the person's name, and ask that person to draw a card from the deck. The person named on the card chosen is the partner. Proceed in this manner until each student has a partner.

OPPOSITES MATCH

Before this activity is used, duplicate *Opposites Match—A* and *B* (see pages 470–471). Choose one pair of opposite cards for every two students (e.g., black/white, short/tall). Give one card to each student. Have each student find a partner by locating the person who has a card with a picture that is the opposite of the student's picture.

GO TOGETHER CARDS

Before this activity is used, duplicate *Go Together Cards—A* and *B* (see pages 472–473). Choose one pair of *Go Together Cards* for every two students (e.g., fishbowl/fish, beach/beach ball). Give one card to each student. Have students find their partner by locating the person who has a card that "goes together" with theirs. The educator may choose to make additional sets of matching cards related to concepts in the classroom. For example, matching states with state capitals, lowercase with uppercase letters, clock faces with numbered times, coins with numbered values, faces of famous men or women with descriptions of their accomplishments, song titles and composers.

NUMBERED STONES

Before this activity is used, gather one stone for each student. On each pair of rocks write the same number (e.g., two rocks would have the number one, two rocks would have the number two). Choose one pair of rocks for every two students and place the rocks in a bag. Ask each student to draw a rock from the bag. When all of the rocks are distributed, have the students find their partners by looking for the rock number that matches.

CARD MATCH

Using a deck of playing cards, choose one matching pair of cards for every two students (e.g., two fours, two kings). Give a card to each student. Have the students find their partners by locating the card number that matches.

ANIMAL CARDS

BEES

"Buzz-z-z-z"

BIRD

"Tweet-tweet"

CAT

"Meow"

COW

"Mooo"

DOG

"Woof-woof"

DONKEY

"Hee-haw"

DUCK

"Quack-quack"

FROG

"Ribbit"

HORSE

"Neigh"

LION

"Roar"

OWL

"Whoo"

PIG

"Oink"

SHEEP

"Baa"

SNAKE

"S-s-s-s"

ROOSTER

"Cock-a-doodle-do"

TURKEY

"Gobble-gobble"

OPPOSITES MATCH—A

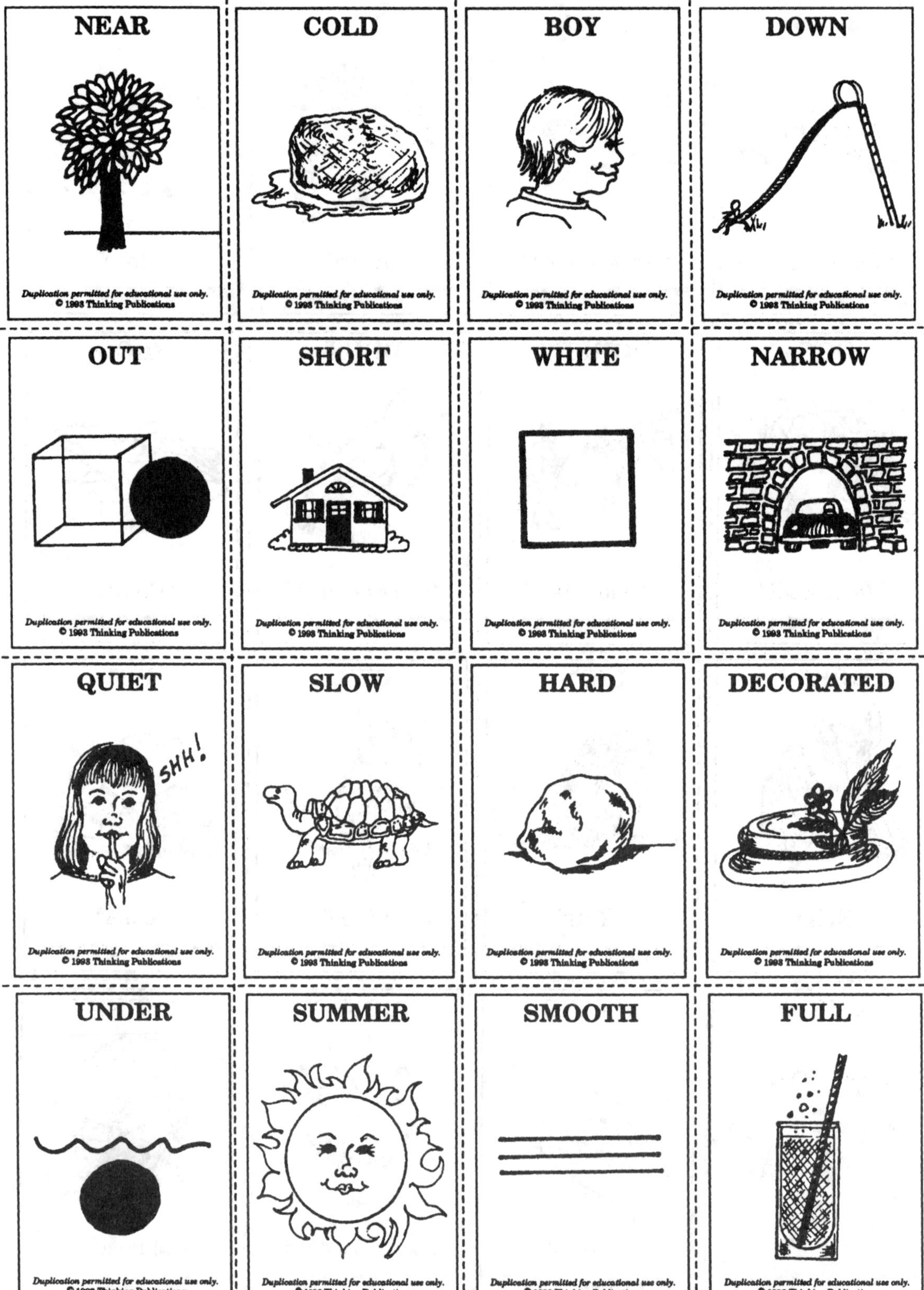

OPPOSITES MATCH—B

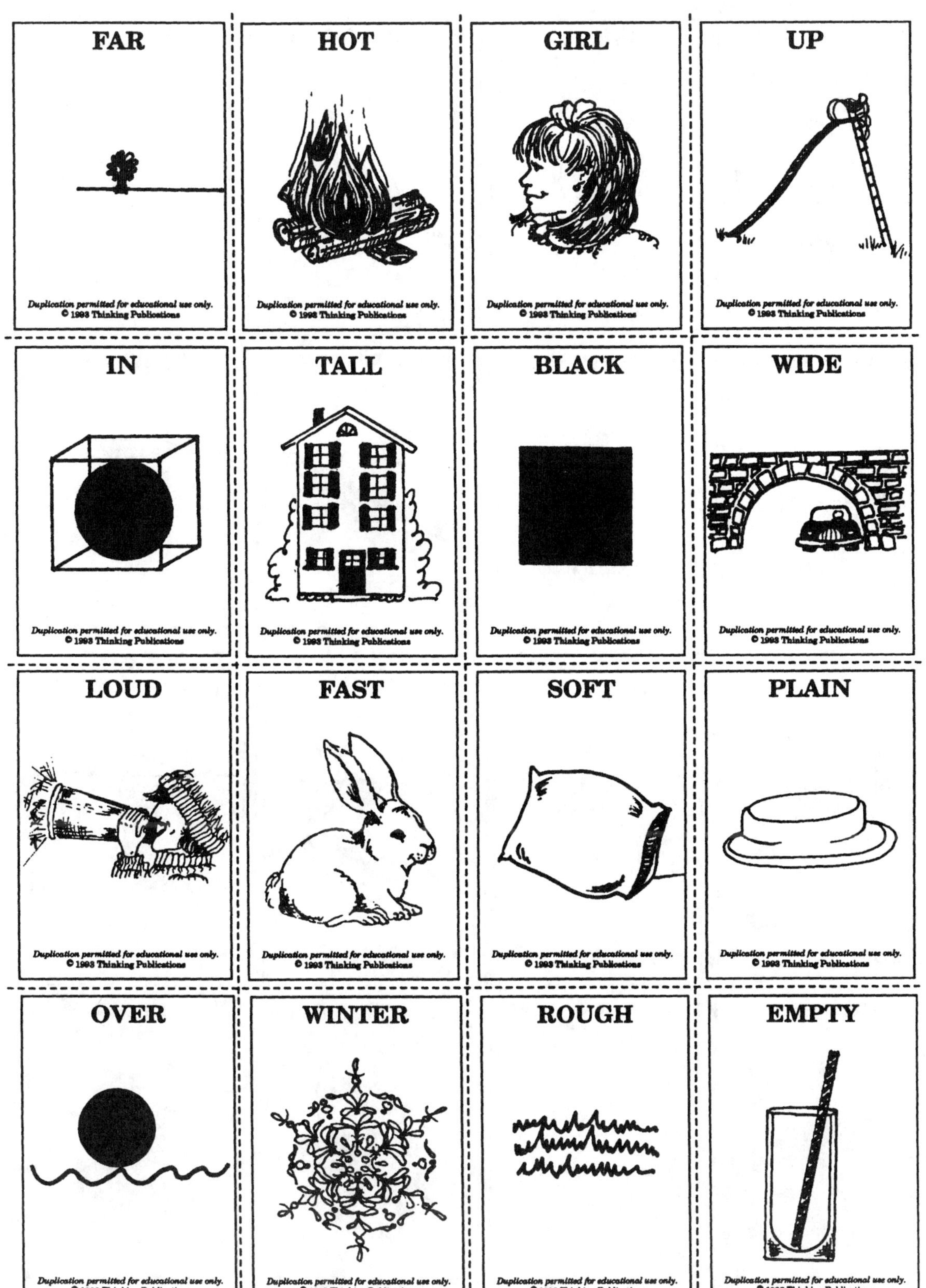

GO TOGETHER CARDS—A

GO TOGETHER CARDS—B

Appendix Q

Drill and Practice

Each *Social Star* unit contains at least two opportunities for students to work in pairs to tell each other the definition, skills step(s), and rationale for the social skill. As an option to provide more structure, to keep the activity moving in a timely fashion, and to make the activity more interesting and fun, students can be asked to assume new names during each drill and practice opportunity. The unit lesson plans provide the educator with the names of two notable people or story characters. After presenting students with those names, they are given an opportunity to use their social skills to decide who will take which name. Do not assign these names, but rather let the students decide. The names are also listed alphabetically below with a short comment about what each person or character is noted for. Most of the names are taken from *A First Dictionary of Cultural Literacy* (Hirsch, 1989), which includes information Americans should know. Dr. Hirsch defines the core knowledge that children need in order to understand American culture and to enhance their progress in school. The educator may wish to spend a short period of time giving information about the people or characters—not, however, to the extent that it would distract from the purpose of the activity (to drill and practice critical components of the social skill).

Aladdin—Character from *Arabian Nights* who rubbed a magic lamp, causing a genie to appear

Alcott, Louisa May—American author of the 1800s; wrote children's novels such as *Little Women* and *Little Men*

Ali Baba—Character from *Arabian Nights* who opened a cave by saying "Open, Sesame."

Alice in Wonderland—Character from Lewis Carroll's books *Alice's Adventures in Wonderland* and *Through the Looking-Glass*

Andersen, Hans Christian—Danish author of the 1800s; wrote *The Ugly Duckling, The Emperor's New Clothes,* and *The Princess and the Pea*

Antoinette, Marie—Queen of France; executed by revolutionaries

Armstrong, Neil—Astronaut; first person to walk on the moon

Bach, Johann Sebastian—German composer and organist

Barnum, P. T.—Showman of the 1800s; started the Barnum and Bailey Circus

Beethoven, Ludwig van—German composer; grew deaf midway through his career

Bell, Alexander Graham—Invented the telephone

Boone, Daniel—Pioneer who explored and settled Kentucky

Carver, George Washington—Improved farming methods in the south and discovered many uses for peanuts

Columbus, Christopher—Italian explorer who "discovered" America in 1492

Crockett, Davy—Frontier settler, politician, and folk hero of the early 1800s; known for his shooting abilities; died defending the Alamo

Curie, Marie (Madame)—Won Nobel prize; pioneered work with radioactivity

da Vinci, Leonardo—Italian artist who painted "The Last Supper" and the "Mona Lisa"

Disney, Walt—First to make full-length animated cartoons; created Mickey Mouse and Donald Duck (Disneyland, Walt Disney World, and Epcot are based on his ideas)

Douglass, Frederick—Abolitionist who escaped from slavery; wrote and spoke about slavery

Edison, Thomas—Invented the light bulb and phonograph

Finn, Huckleberry—Character from *The Adventures of Huckleberry Finn* written by Mark Twain; escaped from a cruel father and traveled down the Mississippi River

Frank, Anne—Dutch-Jewish girl who spent two years in hiding from Nazis; kept a diary

Franklin, Benjamin—A founding father of the U.S.; printer, author, scientist, and inventor (proved that lightning is electricity)

Geronimo—Apache chieftain; one of the last to fight against whites

Glenn, John—First American astronaut to orbit the earth

Grant, Ulysses S.—Union army general; later became U.S. president

Henry, John—Character in a popular folk song; strong black man with a hammer who tried to build more railroad track than a machine

Robin Hood—Legendary English outlaw who stole from the rich and gave to the poor

Captain Hook—Character from the story *Peter Pan*; an evil pirate whose hand was bitten off by a crocodile and was replaced by a hook

Jones, Casey—Character in a popular folk song; railroad engineer who died in a crash

Keller, Helen—American author; blind and deaf; learned sign language, overcame handicaps, graduated from college

Kennedy, John F.—36th U.S. president; first Catholic and youngest president; encouraged space program; assassinated

King, Martin Luther, Jr.—Clergyman who led the civil rights movement; promoted nonviolent means to overcome segregation and racial prejudice; assassinated

Lee, Robert E.—Confederate army general

Lincoln, Abraham—16th U.S. president (during the Civil War); abolished slavery

Magellan, Ferdinand—Portuguese explorer; first to sail around the world in the 1500s

Mozart, Wolfgang—Austrian musician; began composing at age five

Nightingale, Florence—Famous army nurse of 1800s

Odysseus—Character in Greek mythology who fought in the Trojan War in the *Odyssey*

Pandora—Character in Greek mythology who opened a box given to her by Zeus

Pasteur, Louis—French scientist who developed a vaccine to prevent rabies and proved that many diseases are caused by bacteria; the process of pasteurization is named after him

Picasso, Pablo—Famous Spanish contemporary painter

Pocahontas—Daughter of Indian chief; prevented her father from killing John Smith

Poseidon—Character in Greek mythology; god of the sea

Rembrandt—Famous Dutch painter

Revere, Paul—Revolutionary War patriot who took the midnight ride to warn colonists that the British were coming

Robinson, Jackie—First black man to play major league baseball

Ross, Betsy—Made the first American flag

Ruth, Babe—Baseball player for the New York Yankees; first great home run hitter

Salk, Jonas—Microbiologist who developed the first vaccine effective against polio

Sawyer, Tom—Character from *The Adventures of Tom Sawyer* written by Mark Twain; loved adventure (tricked friends into painting a fence)

Sitting Bull—Sioux chief who led warriors at the Battle of the Little Big Horn (Custer's Last Stand)

Smith, Captain John—English soldier; settled Jamestown, Virginia in the 1600s

Sullivan, Anne—Helen Keller's teacher

Tubman, Harriet—Slave who escaped and helped others escape through the underground railroad

Twain, Mark—Pen name of Samuel Langhorne Clemens, American author of the 1800s; wrote *The Adventures of Tom Sawyer* and *The Adventures of Huckleberry Finn*

Washington, George—First U.S. president; leader during the Revolutionary War

Washington, Martha—First "First Lady"

Whitney, Eli—Invented the cotton gin, which made it easier to get seeds out of cotton

Wright, Orville and Wilbur—Invented the airplane in the early 1900s

Zeus—Character in Greek mythology; ruler of the gods

Roadblock Sheet

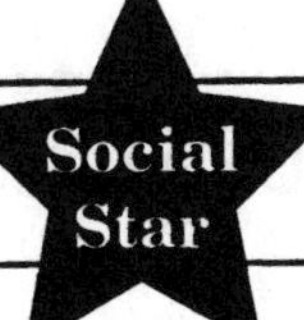

Social Star

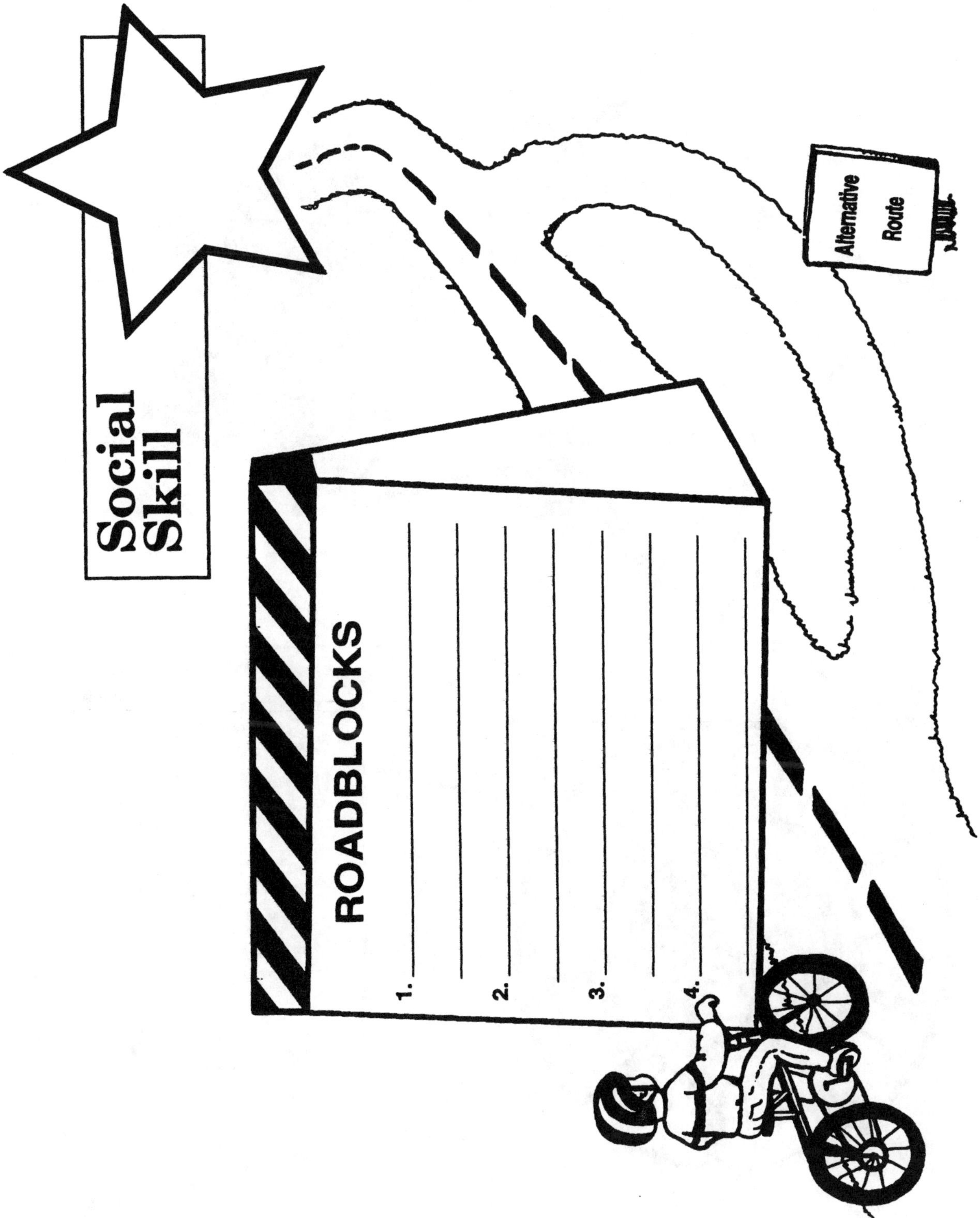
Social Skill
ROADBLOCKS
1.
2.
3.
4.
Alternative Route

Social Super Star Badges

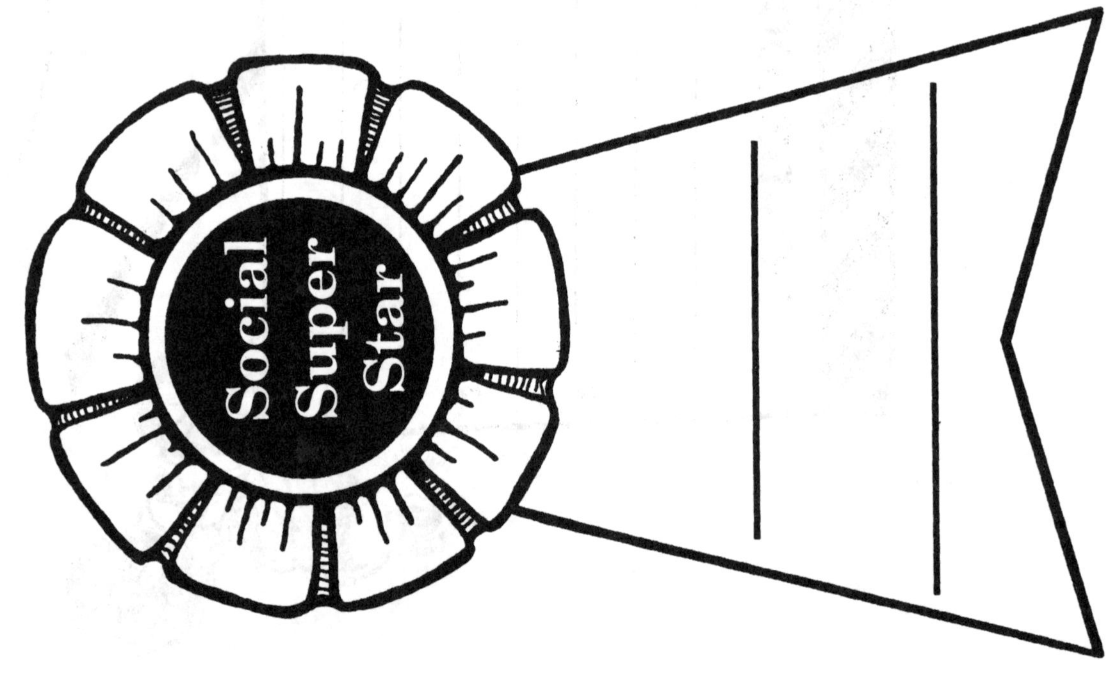

Social Super Star

Social
Super
Star

Thinking Skills Web

Dominoes

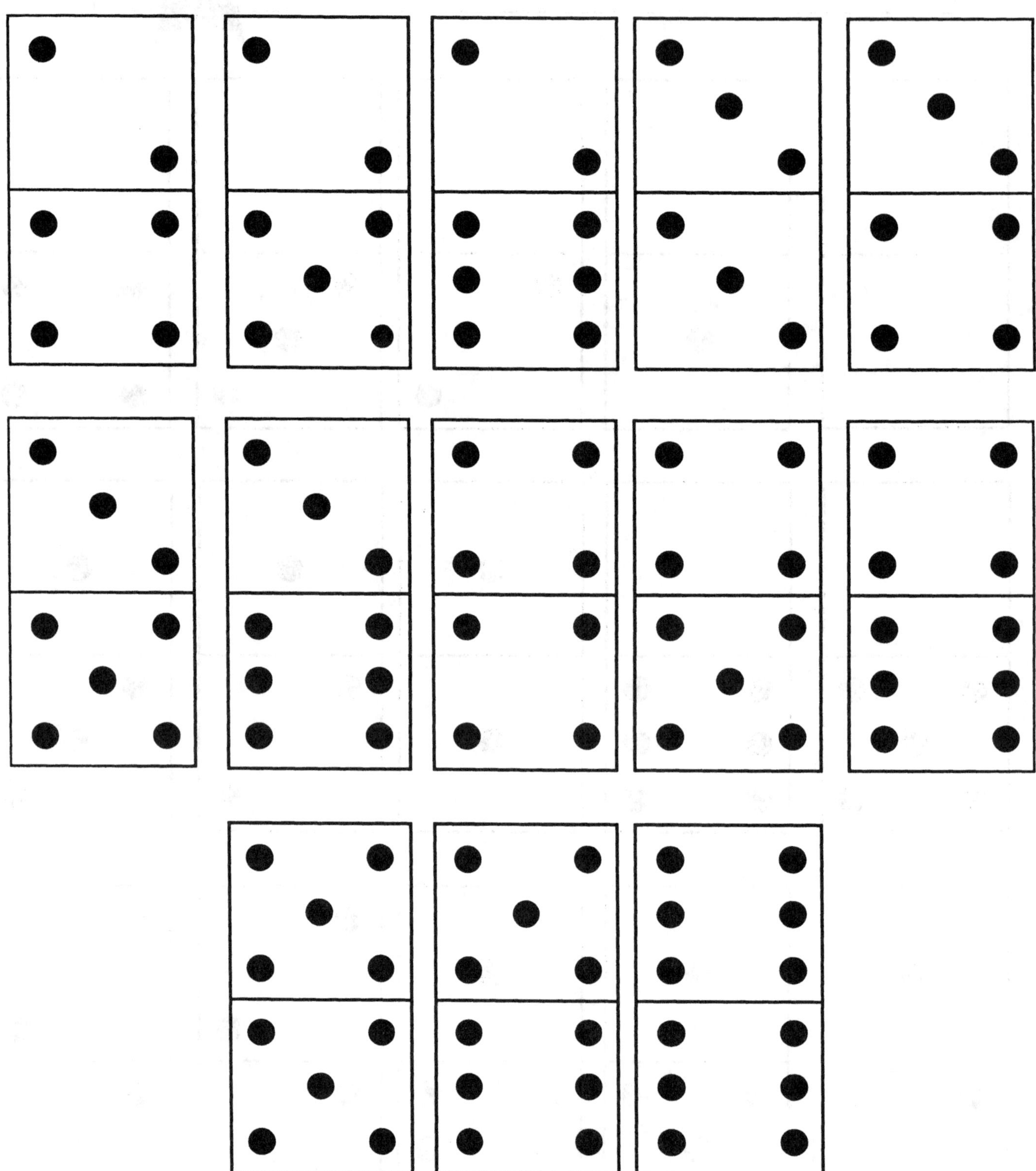

Appendix V

Mind Map

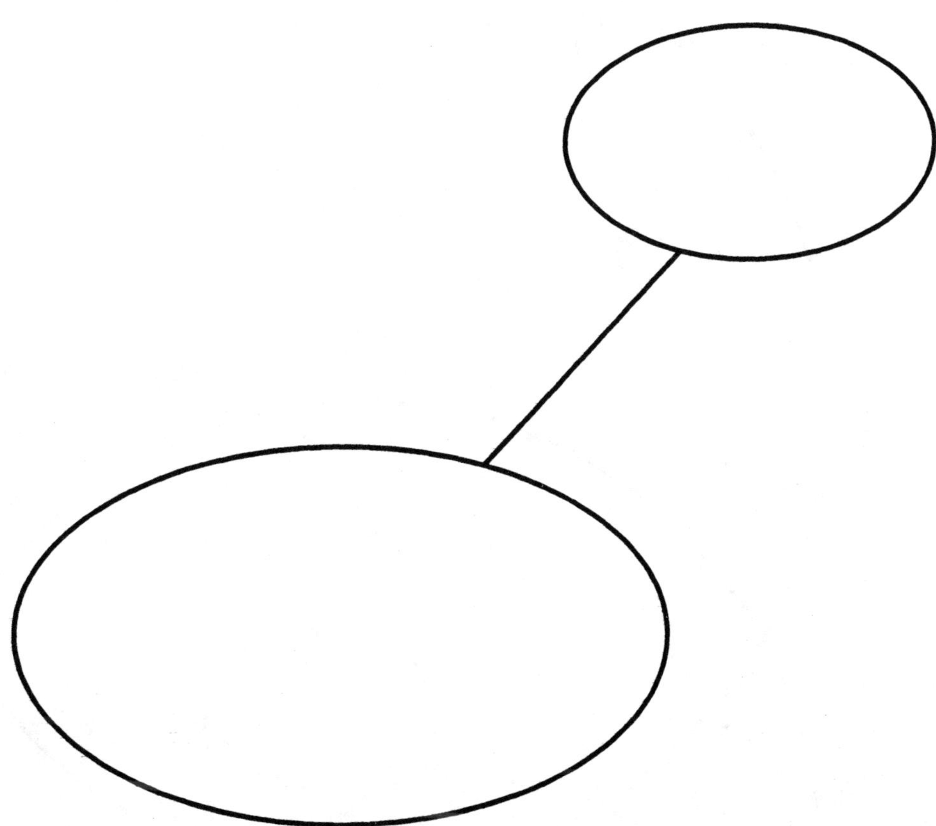

Venn Diagram

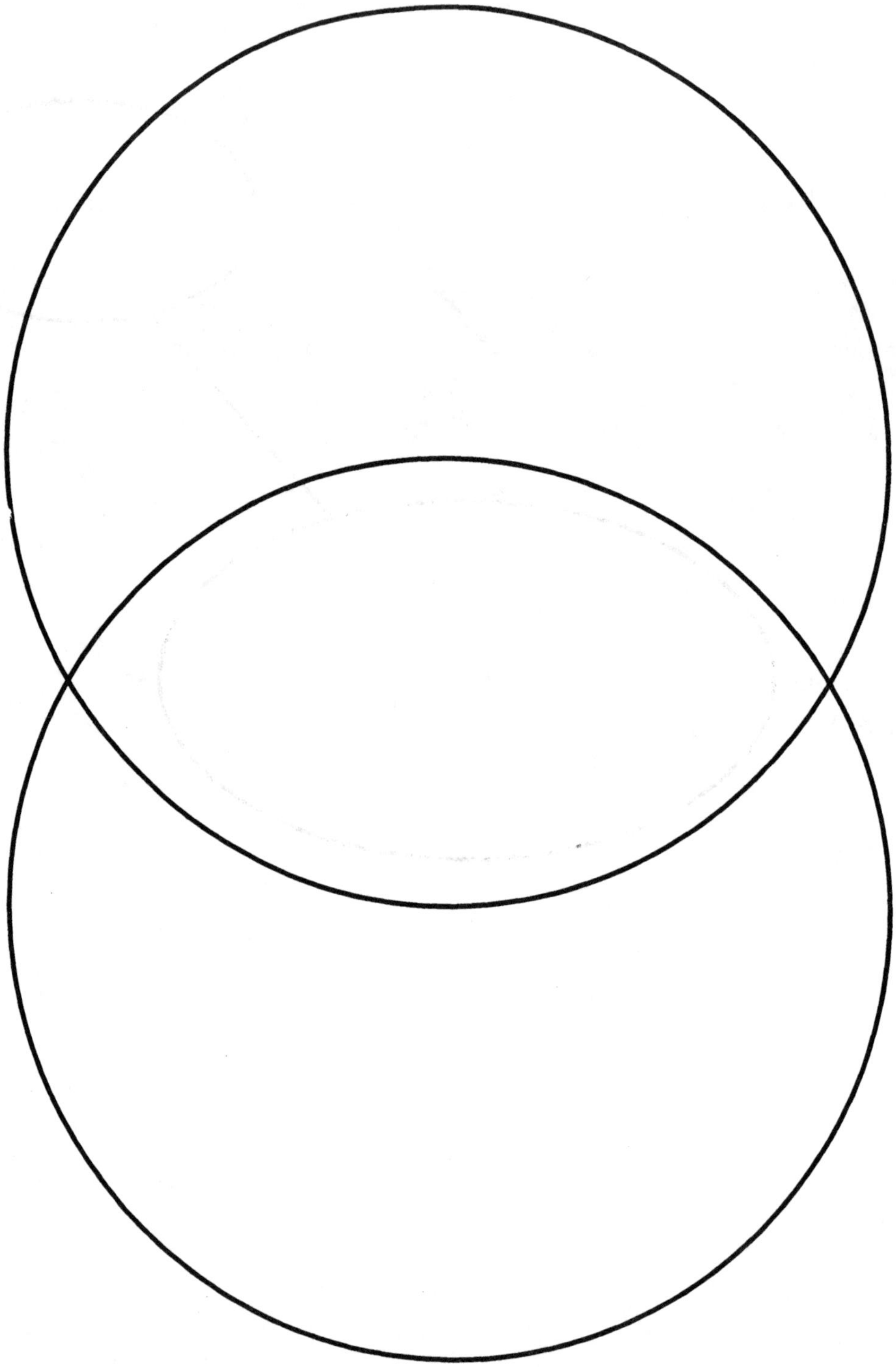